PROBLEMS AND ISSUES IN CURRENT ECONOMETRIC PRACTICE

Edited by

KARL BRUNNER

Professor of Economics
University of Rochester

COLLEGE OF ADMINISTRATIVE SCIENCE
THE OHIO STATE UNIVERSITY
COLUMBUS, OHIO
1972

College of Administrative Science Monograph No. AA-6

Cover Design by Diane Poulton

PREFACE

This volume is based on two Conferences held in 1967 and 1968 at The Ohio State University. The program posed some essentially logical issues in contemporary econometric practice. The development of large scale econometric models opened a new phase in our professional activities. Once our profession acquired the skill to construct, estimate and manipulate large scale econometric models the econometric apparatus appeared to evolve with a momentum of its own.

The emergence of the Brookings-SSRC econometric model shaped a peculiar language game into a standard routine of econometric practice. This game has developed its own characteristic rules governing the construction and appraisal of models and the use of data. Such rules remain frequently quite implicit. Still, the discussions surrounding the construction of models and the reasons adduced in justification of new constructions designed to replace the barely finished previous models, clearly manifest some major patterns deserving our attention.

The Conferences were organized in order to reexamine systematically the language game of econometric practice. In particular, one single fundamental question guided the unavoidable proliferation of somewhat technical detail: Does the language game actually pursued with admirable technical dexterity and ingenuity satisfy the requirements of a cognitive game? Two major criteria constrain such games. One pertains to the admissibility of classes of statements as empirical hypotheses or theories, and the other governs the relevance of test statements advanced with respect to some theory or hypothesis under examination. The admissibility criterion screens the beliefs submitted according to occurrence or non-occurrence of a positive empirical content. The test criterion on the other hand governs the suitable discrimination between relevant and irrelevant test statements. The logical analysis associated with the application of both criteria establishes that the formulae usually introduced at the beginning of an econometric enterprise are frequently without content. They require the full exploitation of a given sample for the necessary transformation into a theory or hypothesis with definite content. More disturbing is the recognition derived from a careful analysis of existing models that few satisfy the "admissibility requirement." This is not an "ontological necessity" of large scale econometric models. It simply reveals a fundamental misconception about the nature of our cognitive game by some econometric practitioners. This misconception is also manifested by the frequent use of forecasting statements as test statements bearing on a given theory or hypothesis. An analysis of the logical requirements of a relevant test statement reveals that forecasting statements violate crucial conditions imposed on an adequate test statement.

The first chapter contributed by Robert Basmann raises the fundamental question in most explicit form. It contends that econometric practice has evolved into a numerology analogous in some respects to astrology. Gary Fromm and Lawrence Klein defend in the second chapter the language game guiding most of the model constructions. A third chapter continues Basmann's searching reexamination. Basmann's chapters will probably appear strange or novel to many econometricians trained within the confines of the standard game. It should be noted however, that both chapters provide excellent examples of the semantic analysis (in the logician's sense) required for an adequate clarification and examination of the issues involved.

Wilford L'Esperance contributed in Chapter 4 a systematic survey of the issues pertaining to the choice between an interdependent and recursive system. An exchange of letters involving Herman Wold and Robert Strotz is added to this chapter. The chapter and the exchange of letters clarify some issues bearing on the choice between the two frameworks as suitable means to formulate empirical theories. Dale Jorgensen and Calvin Siebert presented a paper which belongs to an important and welcome trend. It develops some important steps required for a systematic assessment of alternative hypotheses. The chapter by Joseph Hanna approaches our major issue by an entirely different road in the context of a general examination of the cognitive content of econometric models. Jon Cunnyngham on the other hand attempts to systematize and synthesize the construction and predictive testing of econometric models. The last chapter, contributed by Jan Kmenta, summarizes the discussion at the Conference. The reader will possibly find this chapter particularly interesting. The issues and positions are clearly defined and the intellectual conflict sharply delineated.

This conflict does not question the potential relevance of econometric theory or the formulation of theories cast in the mold of an econometric model. But it should focus our attention on the requirements of a language game which contributes to the systematic growth of our cognition. Such attention seems most urgent in view of the proliferation of econometric models and conflicting claims concerning their relevance. Moreover, the urgency of a searching reexamination in our routinized practices is made quite apparent by a survey of the papers presented at the Conference on Forecasting, organized by the National Bureau of Economic Research in 1969. Such reexamination should exemplify in terms of specific investigations the nature of a cognitive language game expressed by *admissible* construction and *relevant* tests of hypotheses.

Karl Brunner

TABLE OF CONTENTS

PROBLEMS AND ISSUES IN
CURRENT ECONOMETRIC PRACTICE

1. THE BROOKINGS QUARTERLY ECONOMETRIC MODEL: SCIENCE OR NUMBER MYSTICISM?

R. L. Basmann*
Texas A & M University

In like manner, if I let myself believe anything on insufficient evidence, there may be no great harm done by the mere belief; it may be true after all, or I may never have occasion to exhibit it in outward acts. But I cannot help doing this great wrong towards man, that I make myself credulous. The danger to society is not merely that it should believe wrong things, though that is great enough; but that it should become credulous.

W. K. Clifford[1]

SECTION 1. INTRODUCTION

The Brookings Quarterly Econometric Model of the United States[2] can safely and justly be regarded as the exemplar of current research in econometrics. There is no clearer indication of the scope, purpose, philosophy, and method of current econometrics, and the aspirations of those who currently pursue econometrics, than that provided by Duesenberry and Klein in the introduction to the *Report*. That econometrics has become something other than the application of mathematics and mathematical statistics to quantitative problems posed by economic theories and economic

*I am especially indebted to Edward Ames for many hours of interesting conversation on the subject of this article. I am also indebted to Robert J. Rohr for assistance in counting equations, variables, coefficients and identities in the Brookings Model; neither of us has much confidence in the accuracy of our counts.

Blame for errors and omissions that may be detected in this article belongs to me alone.

facts emerges very clearly in the introductory remarks of the editors and in the purposive selection of empirical results finally reported in Chapter 18. The contribution under review here today will set the standard for, and exert a profound influence on, the development of econometrics and its teaching in our graduate schools for decades to come.

What is sought from me today is a critical evaluation of the Brookings Model and the *Report* from a philosophic point of view towards science, and towards quantitative economic science in particular, that by no means conforms to the philosophic and methodological outlook and practice of the econometricians who directed the construction of the Brookings Model. I propose to evaluate the Brookings Model and econometrics from the point of view of an ordinary economist who is at the same time literate in mathematics, statistics, and logic. It will become apparent as this evaluation unfolds that I am applying concepts of what constitutes progress in scientific economic knowledge that differ markedly from those concepts that underlie the philosophy and methodology put forward by Duesenberry and Klein in the *Report*.

There is some difficulty in determining from the *Report* exactly what is intended to be understood as *the* Brookings-SSRC econometric model. Chapter 18, which describes a system of economic equations, or econometric representation, is entitled "The Complete Model: A First Approximation." However, the authors leave us to speculate about what it is that the representation in Chapter 18 is an approximation of; presumably the actual Brookings-SSRC model is only a thought in the minds of the Brookings-SSRC econometricians, (say) a model containing 400 or more economic equations to be formulated, estimated, and published in the future. I am not going to try to guess what is on the minds of the Brookings-SSRC econometricians. For the present review, the Brookings Model is the system of equations put forward by Fromm and Klein in Chapter 18 of the *Report*.

There are listed 153 equations and 56 identities, together with symbols for 334 numerical time series allegedly representing quantities (*Report*, pp. 683-722). According to Fromm and Klein

> The exact number (of equations)[2] is not easy to state because there are many trivial and definitional equations that we refrain from eliminating by substitution, for matters of convenience. (*Report*, p. 722.)

We shall have occasion to return to this matter of the exact number of equations in the Brookings Model (Section 2). Four hundred and seventy-four structural coefficients have been estimated. The Brookings Model is indeed large. Anticipating, perhaps, some criticism on this score, Duesenberry and Klein write

> The Brookings-SSRC econometric model is very much larger than any other econometric model; it does have a more detailed sector breakdown. But we hope that we have not been victims of the fallacy that "bigger is better." . . . The relatively large size of the model reflects the purposes we have in mind and the methods used to develop the model. (*Report*, p. 6.)

Many of the equations and identities composing the Brookings Model are borrowed from simultaneous equations representations of 13 different economic sectors reported in Chapters 2-14. These sector models are the work of economists often referred to as "specialists" by Duesenberry and Klein (Chapter 1) and by Fromm and Klein (Chapter 18).[4] These sector models are not subsystems of the Brookings Model, however, for not all of the sector model equations reappear in the Brookings Model; many sector model equations reappear only in modified form and some of the numerical time series that allegedly represent economic quantities are differently defined in the sector models and the Brookings Model.[5] Consequently, the sector models represent economic hypotheses that are alternatives to the hypotheses represented by corresponding subsystems of the Brookings Model; in other words, subsystems of the Brookings Model can be tested against the corresponding sector models, at least in principle. However,

> The general outline of the model reflects a consensus on the part of the participants—a general agreement on the best set of working hypotheses about the nature of the economy. . . . there is a general agreement on the broad outline of the model. (*Report*, p. 3.)

In spite of that consensus it is difficult for the nonparticipant to see exactly what those hypotheses are, and whether the set of hypotheses is logically consistent. Fromm and Klein indicate that even the formulation of the Brookings Model is incomplete (or was incomplete at the time of publication of the *Report*):

> Having passed through an introduction outlining the philosophy of constructing this model [i.e., the Brookings Model], having studied the sectoral analyses of the various contributors, and having examined the composite equation system, it should be clear that the task of building a large-scale quarterly econometric model of the U. S. economy has only begun. Although the present model is significantly more advanced than its predecessors—in size, detail and finesse—some of its equation specifications need improvement, its internal compatibility between and within sectors is imperfect, and its statistical performance is unknown. (*Report*, pp. 727, 734.)

The issues I propose to raise concern the foundations of quantitative economics, of econometrics, and of the Brookings Model in particular. These issues are out of bounds for the mainstream econometrician—at least for the econometrician who is an adherent of the philosophy of econometrics put forward by Duesenberry and Klein, who express the hope

> that the Brookings-SSRC econometric model will represent a fairly widely accepted set of views as to the nature of the economy. If there is some degree of consensus on that point it may become worth while for a large number of workers to criticize and improve the model. In that way econometric model building can become a cumulative process. (*Report,* p. 9.)

Duesenberry and Klein view the current Brookings Model and its anticipated descendents as providing a frame of reference to which other econometricans or "specialists" can adapt their hypotheses about the structures of individual sectors of the economy (*Report,* pp. 8-9). Acting on the principle that one ought to keep one's belief under control, at least until such time that one can bring forward evidence (argument) of the appropriate kind and quality in support of the hypothesis in question, that credulousness is the cardinal sin of the scientist,[6] I have not allowed myself to participate in the consensus alluded to by Duesenberry and Klein. (This does not entail the proposition that I believe the Brookings Model is a false hypothesis.)[7] Hopefully Duesenberry and Klein do not mean that criticisms of the Brookings Model and suggestions for its improvement are not worthwhile if the one who raises them is not a participant in that consensus. For the questions I propose to ask are among those that one ought to try to answer before participating in that consensus of which Klein and Duesenberry write.

To begin with, I propose to evaluate the Brookings Model as a representation of a proffered quantitative explanatory economic hypothesis. Risking some oversimplification, we can say that the most important scientific question that can be asked about whatever hypothesis is represented by the system of equations that is the Brookings Model is the question concerning its adequacy as a proffered explanation of the objects and events of economic experience it is intended to account for. Before we can hope to answer that question we must determine just what the hypothesis expressed by the Brookings Model is. The size of the Brookings Model, the inability of its builders to say exactly how many structural equations it contains, its incompleteness and imperfect internal compatibility, and the general obscurity of the *Report* (Chapter 1 and Chapter 18) render empirical testing impossible at this time. In fact, the *Report* contains almost nothing of value for empirical testing. The Brookings Model is merely formulated and asserted to be consistent (*Report*, p. 722); in other words, there it is; take it or leave it. If we evaluate that part of the *Report* devoted to the Brookings Model itself as a report of a scientific investigation, then we must accord it failing marks. Until a considerable amount of information of the kind normally given in reports of scientific investigations is provided by the builders of the Brookings Model, we are compelled to begin our own evaluation from scratch.

The same cannot justly be said of the sector models. Some of the chapters on economic sectors contain a considerable amount of information that is valuable for purposes of scientific testing, and the temptation to concentrate this review on those representations has been strong. But Duesenberry and Klein assert of those sector models

> Probably any one of the studies could have been developed by another research worker; they are not unique contributions in this respect, but it is certain that no single individual or small team could have uncovered so many interesting and revealing relationships in a single model in a time span of three years. (*Report*, p. 22.)

Clearly the contribution for which the editors of the *Report* claim credit is the Brookings Model itself.

I have two chief criticisms to make:

(1) The structural economic hypothesis represented by the Brookings Model lacks sufficient "sharpness" of formulation to be empirically testable in practice;

(2) the quantitative foundations of the hypothesis represented by the Brookings Model are seriously defective.

Of course, each of the foregoing criticisms requires first to be clarified in respect of its meaning, and then supported by argument. The finer points of the concept of "sharpness of hypothesis" are especially elusive in all but the simplest cases. The *theory of quantity and magnitude*, which treats of quantitative foundations, is an intricate subject with which many econometricians seem to be unfamiliar. I shall do my best to clarify the foregoing ideas in a very few pages.

Section 2 is a brief exposition of the concept of explanatory economic hypothesis. The notion of proffered economic law is introduced, its connection with the concept of economic change relative to invariant economic structure, and its connection with pure economic theory indicated. Asymmetry of proffered laws in respect of the logical possibility of their verification and falsification, together with the concept of "degree of confirmation," is mentioned in order to clarify the general notion of "sharpness of hypothesis." (Additional clarification of the notion of "sharpness of hypothesis" is offered in connection with direct examination of the Brookings Model.)

Section 3 is an argument in support of the statement that the Brookings Model does not express an hypothesis that is sufficiently "sharp" to be empirically testable in practice.

Section 4 contains a brief exposition of the problem of quantitative foundations of supposedly quantitative economic hypotheses. This is accomplished with help of a few illustrations taken from the Brookings Model and one of the sector models. Argument in support of the criticism that the quantitative foundations of the Brookings Model are seriously defective is offered as the exposition proceeds.

Section 5 contains a few conclusions about quantitative economics and econometrics in general.

Intending this article for an audience primarily of younger economists and econometricians (more precisely, for graduate students), I have used citations rather freely in order to indicate where one can read up on the topics I touch on so very briefly here. Moreover, I give brief definitions of technical concepts where needed.

SECTION 2. THE CONCEPT OF EXPLANATORY ECONOMIC HYPOTHESIS

Throughout this and the succeeding sections the distinction between a *representation* and the *hypothesis* that is represented needs to be borne clearly in mind. An hypothesis is a *proposition*, which ascribes a definite property to some definite thing or things. Propositions are expressed by sentences (in some language or other). Two sentences that express the same proposition are said to be equivalent in meaning. A system of simultaneous economic equations like the Brookings Model represents, or expresses, some definite hypothesis which, in turn, ascribes a definite property to a system of objects of experience that we shall call the economy. In other words, a system of economic equations is a sentence (in mathematical language) that expresses a proposition. This distinction we find immediately useful to us in the present section, as well as in Section 3 and in Section 4.

Our immediate concern is with the logic of explanatory hypotheses. Of course, we cannot hope to do full justice to all of the important points, or to any of the finer points, of the subject. For more detailed accounts of the "logic of explanation" the audience is referred to the book by Nagel, 1961 (Chapters 2, 3) and to the article by Hempel and Oppenheim, 1948.

Every explanatory economic hypothesis—whether quantitative or nonquantitative—is a system of propositions arranged to compose the premises of a special type of logical argument form. That is to say, the propositions appearing in an explanatory economic hypothesis substantiate[8] another proposition not appearing in the explanatory hypothesis itself, and which is called the prediction-statement. In other words, the prediction-statement is the conclusion of an argument and follows from the premises which compose the explanatory economic hypothesis in the present case. At the risk of some misunderstanding due to oversimplification, we can say that the explanatory hypothesis is *intended* to explain the prediction-statement.[9]

The practical conduct of scientific inquiry, in particular the conduct of predictive testing of economic theories, is profoundly influenced by the logical character of the propositions that enter the explanatory hypothesis. In an explanatory economic hypothesis, at least one of the premises is a *proffered economic law*, the truth of which is always in question and is the object of predictive testing. Moreover, at least one of the premises is a factual, or *singular*, proposition.[10] The factual, or singular, statements that appear in an explanatory economic hypothesis are called its *statements of initial conditions*.

The proffered economic law appearing in the premises of an explanatory economic hypothesis has *universal conditional form* $(z)(Pz \supset Qz)$; read "For every z, if z has property P, then z has property Q." z is a variable that ranges over a set S of (systems of) objects of experience $\alpha, \beta, \gamma, \ldots$. Pz, Qz, and $Pz \supset Qz$ are called propositional functions; the set S is called the domain of Pz, Qz, and $Pz \supset Qz$. Pz is called the antecedent, and Qz is called the consequent of "$Pz \supset Qz$." $P\alpha$, $Q\alpha$, and $P\alpha \supset Q\alpha$ are the *values* of the functions Pz, Qz, and $Pz \supset Qz$ for α, respectively. $P\alpha$ is the proposition "α has property P" and $Q\alpha$ is the proposition "α has property Q." If the subset of all objects in S that have property P is infinite, then $(z)(Pz \supset Qz)$ is said to be *strictly universal*.[11] For instance, the rather iconoclastic proposition "For every z, if z is one of the fourteen leading scholars in economics, then z is not the author of *The Intellectual and the Market Place*" is universal in form, but it is not strictly universal, for the proposition can be expressed equivalently by the conjunction of a finite number (fourteen) of factual, or singular, statements. On the other hand, "For every z, if z is a fool, then z can find some y such that y is a fool, and y≠z, and y admires z" is a strictly universal statement because the defining characteristic "fool" does not imply that the set of all fools past, present, and future, is finite. Proffered economic laws are strictly universal conditional propositions.

The concept of proffered economic law is fundamental in economic science. Economists, as scientists, study changes in economic variables that range over sets of objects of economic experience. (Of course, the sets of real objects of experience with which economic science has to do are not fixed once for all.) We can speak (though imprecisely) of economic change being observable, albeit often only with help of very refined tools, which—it is important to recall—are not the tools of mathematical analysis. The concept of economic change involves, as essential to its meaning, the concept of *invariant structure of reality,* a fixed backdrop against which economic change can be observed to take place; all economic change is relative to this invariant economic structure. Proffered economic laws are hypotheses about relations among economic changes and, therefore, proffered economic laws are hypotheses about invariant economic structure as well. Consequently when we are presented with a sentence that (allegedly) represents a proffered law, we expect to find therein symbols for changing aspects of the economy and symbols for all of the invariant aspects relative to which those economic changes are presumed to take place. We shall return to this matter in Section 3.

Pure economic theories and simultaneous economic equation systems are not proffered economic laws. The nature of the connection between proffered economic laws and pure economic theories may be indicated briefly (and incompletely) as follows: The function of a pure economic theory is to describe the property Q, or, more precisely, to define the propositional function Qz that is the consequent of the proffered economic law $(z)(Pz \supset Qz)$. Regarding the pure economic theory as a deductive system in the sense of that term as employed in *Axiomatics*,[12] we can say that Qz is defined with help of any subset of statements belonging to the pure economic theory such that the remaining statements of the theory in question can be deduced therefrom as theorems.[13] In order to stress an important point (on which there is some confusion), we remark that the entire set of all statements belonging to the economic theory in question may be employed to define Q, although such a definition of Q would involve several redundancies.

Alternatively, we may regard Q as defined by the so-called assumptions of the economic theory in question, although to define Q by the so-called assumptions of a pure economic theory may be very inconvenient in practice. The confusion the foregoing remarks are intended to forestall is that which arises when it is supposed that the so-called assumptions of the pure economic theory in question are to be employed in defining the property P, or initial conditions.[14]

We have spoken so far of Q being described by a pure economic theory. Implicit in the foregoing remarks is the notion of Q being described by a system of simultaneous economic equations together with hypothetical restrictions placed on the parameters of the equation system. For the time being it is sufficient to notice that a system of simultaneous economic equations like the Brookings Model, together with hypothetical restrictions on its parameters, does no more than define the consequent Qz in a proffered economic law $(z)(Pz \supset Qz)$.

In other words, the formulation of a system of simultaneous economic equations and hypothetical restrictions on the parameters thereof is only a single step in the formulation of a proffered economic law.

The formulation of the initial conditions, or antecedent Pz, of a proffered economic law may be likened to the formulation of pure economic theories. *In all of the sciences the formulation of initial conditions P is intellectually the most taxing part of inquiry. It is the most frequently overlooked and, in mainstream econometrics, ubiquitously ignored;* in this connection see the book by Nagel, 1961, p. 32. Given a pure economic theory to define the consequent Qz, we have to formulate initial conditions P before we obtain a proffered law $(z)(Pz \supset Qz)$. Although the pure economic theory in question may *inspire* conjectures about appropriate initial conditions, it does not *entail* any specific initial conditions P. Thus much empirical research in economics is (or ought openly to be) directed towards the discovery of conditions under which pure economic theories are applicable. Admittedly, such is hard creative as well as critical work. (In this connection see the article by Basmann, 1965a, esp. pp. 160-161, pp. 173-175 on the role of the economic historian.) Nonetheless the specification of initial conditions P is a sine qua non of formulation of proffered economic laws, and the substantiation by scientific argument of the statement of initial conditions P is essential to predictive testing of proffered economic laws. It has been remarked already that an explanatory economic hypothesis is a system of propositions arranged to compose the premises of an argument form. Let us pause to examine this argument form to see just how the statement of initial conditions enters the argument.

The logical structure of the argument is as follows:

    (1) $\vdash: (z)(Pz \supset Qz) \supset (P\alpha \supset Q\alpha)$ [15]

    (2) $\vdash: (z)(Pz \supset Qz)$ (Proffered Law)

———————————

$\therefore$(3) $\vdash: P\alpha \supset Q\alpha$

    (4) $\vdash: P\alpha.$ (Initial Conditions)

———————————

$\therefore$(5) $\vdash: Q\alpha.$

From the assertion of the proffered law (2) we infer the assertion (3) of "$P\alpha \supset Q\alpha$" with help of the axiom, or rule, of universal instantiation (1).[16] The conclusion (5), or assertion of "$Q\alpha$," follows from (3) and the statement of initial conditions "$P\alpha$" by the rule of *modus ponens*.[17] Recall that the conclusion (5) is called the prediction-statement.

The logical conjunction of Pz and $\sim$Qz, i.e., the propositional function $Pz \cdot \sim Qz$, is called the "falsifier" of the proffered law $(z)(Pz \supset Qz)$. For if there exists at least one object α such that the singular proposition "$P\alpha \cdot \sim Q\alpha$" is true, then the proffered law $(z)(Pz \supset Qz)$ is false.

Supposing initial conditions P to have been formulated we find it an essential task in predictive testing of the proffered economic law $(z)(Pz \supset Qz)$ to substantiate "$P\alpha$." The lack of attention to the problem of initial conditions in econometrics is due in part to the widespread misconception of factual statements as being *perceived* facts (and partly due to prejudice that regards the process of substantiating factual statements as mere "fact grubbing.")

Although the statement of initial conditions $P\alpha$ is a factual, or singular, statement ($P\alpha$ is a fact only if it is a true statement) it is only in the rarest of circumstances that singular statements do not require substantiation by argument. Singular statements are of two kinds in this respect. There are *basic statements*, which do not require argument in their support; all other singular statements do. Following Bertrand Russell (1962, p. 15; also Chapter 10) let us say that basic statements are factual statements that, in connection with experiences, enjoy a high "degree of confirmation" independently of any argument in their support. The following illustration, inspired by a recent piece of methodological writing in econometrics (Strotz and Wold, 1960, p. 421), should suffice to contrast the notion of basic proposition with the notion of factual statements that require argument in their support.

Suppose we had before us a small aquarium and that each of

us is attentively watching the fish it contains. Suppose I cry out "Look! Some big black fish are now eating some little blue fish!" The proposition "Some big black fish are now eating some little blue fish" is a basic proposition. No one who understands the meaning of this proposition and whose attention is drawn quickly enough to the part of the aquarium I am looking at when exclaiming will require an argument in support of the assertion.

On the other hand, suppose that, in precisely the same circumstance, I exclaim "Look! The population of that species of black fish is causally dependent on the population of that other species of blue fish." Not only would you raise your eyebrows at this, but you would demand of me a clarification of concepts and special terms; a clear statement of premises, logical and nonlogical; and a sound argument leading to my assertion as the conclusion of that argument. The statement "The population of that species of fish is causally dependent on the population of that other species of fish" clearly is not a basic proposition in our sense.

Apart from the task of substantiating the statement of initial conditions $P\alpha$ and either $Q\alpha$ or $\sim Q\alpha$, the main conceptual problem with predictive testing of proffered economic laws resides in the interpretation to be afforded by favorable occurrences, i.e., $P\alpha \cdot Q\alpha$. Although a single instance, namely, $P\alpha \cdot \sim Q\alpha$, falsifies the proffered economic law $(z)(Pz \supset Qz)$ no finite set of favorable occurrences can verify $(z)(Pz \supset Qz)$, even in principle.[18] On the other hand, we conceive of favorable instances as tending to confirm the proffered economic law in question, as evidence tending to confer a "degree of confirmation" on $(z)(Pz \supset Qz)$. Moreover, we also conceive the notion of "degree of confirmation" afforded by a given set of favorable instances being dependent on the "sharpness" of the proffered law.

We will consider briefly the notion of "sharpness of hypothesis." A complete explication will not be attempted; moreover, I doubt that I could formulate a complete explication of the term even if unlimited time were available. Yet a few words on the subject may well clarify the criticism already levelled at the Brookings Model, a criticism that is made explicit in Section 3.

To begin with, we require only to compare hypotheses in respect of "sharpness." Moreover, we need not be able to order every pair of hypotheses in terms of the relation of "sharpness;" at least, we do not require to do so in the present discussion. Let q and r be hypotheses: we shall say that q is *sharper than* r only if q implies r. Furthermore, we shall say that q is sharper than r only if the hypothesis r has a determinate "degree of confirmation."

At this point we introduce some probability concepts.

By "probability" I mean any concrete realization of the so-called axioms of abstract probability, cf., for instance, Kolmogorov, 1951, pp. 1-2; Birnbaum, 1962, pp. 12-13. Following Carnap, 1950, Chapter II, esp. pp. 25-26, I mean by "probability$_1$" a concrete realization of the axioms of abstract probability that is a *logical relation* between an hypothesis *h*, or proposition, and evidence *e* (another proposition) that supports the hypothesis. I prefer to call this "probability$_1$" by "degree of confirmation of *h* by evidence *e*." "Probability$_1$" — as Carnap asserts and Jeffreys agrees — is formally similar to Jeffreys' theory of probability, the principles and axioms of which are to be found in *Theory of Probability*, 3rd Edition, 1961, Chapter 1; cf. Carnap, 1950, p. 24, p. 45; also Jeffreys, op. cit., p. 41. Jeffreys calls "probability$_1$" by "reasonable degree of belief."[19]

(In Section 3 we shall employ another realization of the axioms of probability, namely, "relative frequency." "Relative frequency$_1$" refers to supposedly finite populations of events.[20] "Relative frequency$_2$" refers to supposedly infinite populations of events and is, I suppose, to be regarded as an idealization of "relative frequency$_1$," akin to, if not identical with Fisher's concept.[21] "Relative frequency$_2$" appears only in the representation of hypotheses in this article. It is never used here in lieu of "probability$_1$" or with the intention of avoiding the use of "probability$_1$" where that concept is called for.[22])

Let *q* and *r* be hypotheses and let *p* be evidence relevant to *q* and *r*. Let $P(q/p)$ and $P(r/p)$ denote respectively the (determinate) degrees of confirmation of *q* by *p* and of *r* by *p*. If, and only if, *q* entails *r*, $P(r/p)$ is determinate, and $P(q/p) < P(r/p)$, then we say *q is sharper than r*.[23]

Now, given proposition *p*, which is understood to be empirical evidence, it is always possible to formulate the hypothesis *r* such that the degree of confirmation of *r* by *p* is indeterminate. A simple illustration that is readily generalized to apply to the Brookings Model is to be found in Jeffreys' book (Jeffreys, 1961, pp. 138-139). Let the representation be that of a simple normal population with mean μ and variance σ^2. If one chooses as *prior density function* (probability$_1$)[24] of σ a function proportional to σ^{-1} (as Jeffreys does);[25] and if *p* asserts a definite numerical value of a single observation on the population; then posterior density function (probability$_1$)[26] of μ is indeterminate; cf. Jeffreys, 1961, p. 139, equation (6). That one might have in the back of one's mind, so to speak, some additional hypothesis (say) '$\mu > 0$' not expressed in the representation does not alter the situation: such hypotheses receive no determinate degree of confirmation by a single observation.

Econometricians who reject the concept of probability$_1$ will be quick to point out that the use of Jeffreys' apparatus is not essential to the foregoing illustration; they will mention the fact that two unknown constants (μ, σ^2) cannot be uniquely estimated from a single observation. Their objection need not be debated here as the conclusion drawn is the same as ours, namely, that the foregoing hypothesis is not sufficiently "sharp" in relation to available empirical data. This criticism, applied to the Brookings Model in Section 3, should be equally intelligible to partisans of probability$_1$ and probability$_2$ (relative frequency in the long run); cf. Carnap, 1950, Chapter IV, esp. pp. 187-192.

The foregoing brief exposition of concepts is adequate for our present purposes. In particular, the account of "degree of confirmation" and "sharpness of hypothesis" is limited in scope by our actual needs in Section 3. (For references consult the bibliography in the book by Carnap, 1950 (Second Edition, 1962) pp. 583-604.)

SECTION 3. WHAT IS THE BROOKINGS HYPOTHESIS?

One of the major criticisms brought forward in Section 1 is that the hypothesis represented by the Brookings Model lacks sufficient "sharpness" of formulation to be empirically testable in practice. That criticism is clarified and supported in this section.

It must be borne in mind that the fundamental evidence for any criticism of the Brookings Model is the *Report* itself, which contains all the information that the builders of the Brookings Model chose to reveal to the public at large. The criticism is, of course, an inference from this documentary evidence, and the adequacy of the support I offer can be judged only in relation to relevant evidence that is made available in the *Report*.

Before attempting to clarify a few special rules of inference I have employed, I shall restate the criticism in a little more detail:

(1) As expressed by the list of equations in Chapter 18 of the *Report*, the Brookings Model does not represent the consequent Q of a proffered economic law that has a determinate degree of confirmation on the time-series data available.

(2) However, in the process of estimating the structural coefficients in the Brookings Model from the time-series

data available, Fromm and Klein have allowed the electronic computer to formulate a maintained structural economic hypothesis (restrictions on structural parameters) that has a determinate degree of confirmation on the data; *but the specific maintained structural economic hypotheses thus chosen by the electronic computer remain unknown to the builders of the Brookings Model.*

The process of formulating and testing a proffered economic law empirically can be analyzed into a sequence of major steps, the details of which are essential to record and report if that process is to be repeatable. This sequence of essential steps will be the touchstone. Where the *Report* omits to mention how any of the major steps in that sequence has been carried out and with what result, I have sought for relevant documentary clues. Acting on the assumption that none of the internal details of the Brookings Model is a State or commercial secret (e.g., the *Econometric Institute Model*)[27] I infer, in the absence of relevant clues, that such major steps have not been carried out or that the builders of the Brookings Model did not adequately record the details and have forgotten them.

In this connection, I hope there will be other independent critics who will subject the *Report* to further scrutiny and, perhaps, supply my own omissions and correct any mistaken inferences I may reach here.

The Brookings Model belongs to the class of linear representations denoted by the matrix equation

$$(3.1) \quad B^{*\prime}y'_{t\cdot} + B^{*}_{1}{}' y'_{t\text{-}1\cdot} + \ldots + B^{*}_{k}{}' y'_{t\text{-}r\cdot} + \Gamma^{*\prime} z'_{t\cdot} + u'_{t\cdot} = 0$$

where

$$y_{t\cdot} = \{y_{t,1}, \ldots, y_{t,G}\}$$

represents the vector *endogenous variable,*

$$z_{t\cdot} = \{z_{t,1}, \ldots, z_{t,K}\}$$

represents the vector *exogneous variable,* and

$$u_{t\cdot} = \{u_{t,1}, \ldots, u_{t,G}\}$$

represents the vector random disturbance. We assume that the exogenous vectors $t = 0, \pm 1, \pm 2, \ldots$ are uniformly bounded.[28] For convenience (and with no loss of generality that is essential to the present discussion) let us assume that the random vectors $u_{t\cdot}$ are independently and identically distributed for all t with probability density function

$$(3.2) \qquad f(u) = \frac{|\Omega^*|^{-1/2}}{(2\pi)^{\frac{G}{2}}} e^{-1/2u\Omega^{-1}u'}$$

$$-\infty < u < \infty,$$

where Ω^* is a symmetric positive definite real matrix. The probability density function (3.2) is to be understood solely as a *frequency function*. Our hypothesis ascribes to events a property of randomness, i.e., "relative frequency$_2$," and the probability density function (3.2) is its representation. Transparently, neither (3.2) nor the density function of any statistic derived from (3.2) expresses "probability$_1$," or "degree of confirmation."

The Brookings Model expresses no specific hypothesis about the distribution function of random disturbances in the structural equations. Presumably, however, that distribution function is supposed to satisfy all restrictions necessary for consistence of "limited information" and "two-stage least squares" estimators of structural coefficients (cf. *Report*, pp. 681-682; also p. 736).

The representation (3.1)-(3.2) defines the consequent property Q of a proffered economic law $(x)(Px \supset Qx)$. The components $y_{t,i}$ of $y_t.$, $z_{t,k}$ of $z_t.$ and $u_{t,i}$ of $u_t.$ are real numbers that are presumed to represent variable economic *magnitudes*. Let us pause to note that $y_{t,i}$, $z_{t,k}$, and $u_{t,i}$ are not themselves economic magnitudes, a point we shall clarify in Section 4. This distinction, introduced at the beginning of Section 2, is of fundamental importance to quantitative economic science; indeed, it is crucial to all quantitative science. The validity of econometric estimation and statistical tests of significance presupposes that the numerical $y_{t,i}$, $z_{t,k}$, and $u_{t,i}$ validly represent *magnitudes of quantities*. For the time being we shall continue as if that validity were taken for granted.

Changes in the vectors y_t, z_t, u_t (from period to period) are supposed to represent real economic changes. Samples (matrices) Y_α, Z_α of N observations of vectors y_t and z_t are associated with a definite instance α of x in $(x)(Px \supset Qx)$. We remark that the exogenous matrix Z_α expresses a part of the initial condition statement $P\alpha$. In this connection see the article by Basmann, 1965c, esp. pp. 389-390, 410-414. Both Y_α and Z_α are involved in the expression of the prediction-statement $Q\alpha$; cf. Basmann, 1965c, pp. 391-393, p. 415.

The elements of the real matrices $B^*, B^*_1, ..., B^*_r, \Gamma^*$, and Ω^* are structural economic constants, usually called structural parameters, e.g., price elasticities, income elasticities, marginal propensity to consume. The validity of the claim that $B^*, B^*_1, ..., B^*_r \Gamma^*$, and Ω^* can in principle represent the structure of economic events and objects of experience presupposes validity of the claim that the numerical values of $y_{t,i}$, $z_{t,k}$, and $u_{t,i}$ represent magnitudes of quantities.

It is just possible that the builders of the Brookings Model do not regard $B^*, B^*_1, ..., B^*_k, \Gamma^*$, and Ω^* as structural constants. The following remark about statistical estimates suggests that the Brookings Model, which belongs to the class of representations denoted by (3.1), may *not* be intended by the authors to represent or define the consequent property Q of a proffered economic law:

> The accuracy of parameter estimates is limited by the evolution of our economy. As technology, institutional arrangements, tastes and managerial techniques change, the relationships represented by our equations will inevitably shift. (*Report*, p. 14.)

I cannot determine whether there are supposed to be some invariant laws of evolution that underlie the hypothesis expressed by the Brookings Model. The second sentence is too imprecise to be of much help in this regard. Therefore I am going to assume that there is not supposed to be some set of invariant laws of evolution of technology, institutional arrangements, tastes and managerial techniques that inevitably cause the real relationships to shift and of which the builders of the Brookings Model nonetheless fail to provide a representation. Moreover, subsequent statements attributing properties to the statistical estimators used by Fromm and Klein presuppose the statement that $B^*, B^*_1, ..., B^*_r, \Gamma^*$, and Ω^* represent invariants; recall the earlier remark about consistence of "limited information" and "two-stage least squares" estimators.

The set B of all ordered $(r+3)$-tuples $(B, B_1, ..., B_r, \Gamma, \Omega)$ of structural matrices such that B is nonsingular and Ω is symmetric positive definite is called the *structural parameter space*. Any proper subset B_1 of B is said to be a structural economic hypothesis. More precisely, B_1 *represents* a structural economic hypothesis, which is

$$(B^*, B^*_1, ..., B^*_r . \Gamma^* . \Omega^*) \varepsilon B_1,$$

i.e., "the structural parameter $(B^*, B^*_1, ..., B^*_k, \Gamma^*, \Omega^*)$ belongs to the set B_1." Alternatively, B_1 is described with help of a set of *theoretical restrictions* on the structural constants, which are elements of B, Γ, and Ω.[29]

The first practical task is to formulate the maintained structural hypothesis such that a proffered economic law $(x)(Px \supset Qx)$, for which B describes the consequent property Q, has a determinate degree of confirmation on the available relevant empirical evidence.

If, and only if, the matrix B* is nonsingular,[30] then the representation (3.1) is logically equivalent to the representation

$$(3.3) \quad y'_{t+r} = (-B^{*\prime})^{-1}(B^*_1 y'_{t^1 r-1} + \ldots + B^*_r y'_t + \Gamma^{*\prime} z'_{t+r}) - (B^{*\prime})^{-1} u_{t+r},$$

which is commonly called the *reduced-form* of (3.1). In other words, (3.1) and (3.3) are equivalent sentences, i.e., sentences that express the same proposition about economic reality. Other representations equivalent to (3.1) are the system of ordinary nonhomogeneous linear difference equations derived from (3.1) or (3.3), and the *standardized semi-reduced forms* of (3.1); cf. Basmann, 1965c, esp. pp. 1087-1090. Statistical testing of structural economic hypotheses like B_1 is more conveniently carried out with help of the reduced-form. The maintained structural hypothesis B is mapped *into* the space of reduced-form parameters, the image of B being denoted by A; the structural economic hypothesis $B_1 \subset B$ is mapped *into* A, the image of B_1 being a proper subset A_1 of A. Thus A_1 expresses the same hypothesis as B_1. Any proper subset A'_1 of $A - A_1$ expresses a structural economic hypothesis that is alternative to A_1 hence to B_1; cf. Basmann, 1965b, pp. 1082-1089; also Basmann, 1965c, pp. 408-410.

Furthermore, if, and only if, the matrices $B^*, B^*_1, \ldots, B^*_r$ satisfy dynamical stability restrictions,[31] then the vector endogenous variable y'_t can be represented by

$$(3.4) \quad y'_t = \sum_{n=0}^{\infty} A^*_n{}' \Gamma^{*\prime} z'_{t-n} + \sum_{n=0}^{\infty} A^*_n{}' u'_{t-n}$$

where $\{A^*_n\}$ $n = 0,1,2,\ldots$ is a sequence of KxG matrices and the matrix series

$$(3.5) \quad \sum_{n=0}^{\infty} A^*_n{}'$$

is absolutely convergent.[32] The vector series on the right of equation (3.4) is called an entry or term of the *dynamical equilibrium path* of the vector endogenous variable. Notice that the matrices A^*_n $n = 0,1,2,\ldots$ are defined functions of the structural matrices $B^*, B^*_1, \ldots, B^*_r$.

The absolute convergence of the series (3.5), together with the uniform boundedness of the exogenous vector z_t, explains the observation that the endogenous variable y_t does not diverge to infinity. Consequently, in the formulation of economic representations it is highly desirable to restrict the maintained hypothesis B to a subset of $(r+3)$-tuples $(B, B_1, ..., B_r, \Gamma, \Omega)$ for which a dynamical equilibrium path exists, i.e., such that the series (3.5) is absolutely convergent.

For all practical purposes, a maintained hypothesis B that fails to restrict the structural matrices $B, B_1, ..., B_r$ to fulfil the conditions of dynamical stability can agree with any set of observations, although it is possible to explain the observed finite values of the endogenous variables by invoking very special *historical initial conditions* P that allegedly produce the required deviations from "dynamical equilibrium path." The formulation, either of hypothetical stability restrictions on the maintained structural economic hypothesis B, or of special historical initial conditions is an essential task in hypothesis formation; that it is not by any means an easy task to perform—requiring imagination in economic theorizing as well as skill in algebraic manipulations—does not refute the contention that it is essential.

Moreover, the cyclical behavior of the vector endogenous variable y_t over time is (hypothetically) determined in part by the random vector component

$$(3.6) \qquad \sum_{n=0}^{\infty} A^*_n u'_{t-n},$$

which is a definite *autoregressive process*[33] and in part by the sequence $\{z_{t-n}\}$ of vector exogenous variables.

Another one of the first tasks in the formulation of a representation like (3.1) is to verify, deductively, that the system of equations (3.1) is consistent under the maintained hypothesis B, for every vector exogenous variable z_t and every random vector u_t. That is to say, the system of propositions that describe B together with the representation (3.1) itself must be shown to be free of contradiction. To perform this essential task, the economist examines *each and every one* of the component equations in (3.1) as well as each and every one of the theoretical restrictions that describe the maintained hypothesis B, including every functional dependence, or identity, that endogenous and exogenous variables are specified to satisfy. If the economist has appropriate grounds for the assertion that the representation (3.1) is consistent, then, of course, he can state *exactly* how many equations (3.1) contains.

In this connection we recall the assertions by Fromm and Klein, namely, that the system of equations that is the Brookings Model is consistent, and that the exact number of equations in the Brookings Model is not easy to state; cf. *Report*, p. 722. I infer that Fromm and Klein have not actually carried out the process of checking the Brookings Model for consistency. However, Fromm and Klein also do not set forth the restrictions on structural matrices that define the maintained hypothesis *B* of the Brookings Model. Consequently, it is not possible for me (or them) to test deductively their claim that the Brookings Model is consistent, at least not with the paucity of information they provide in the *Report*.

Modern science, having adopted two-valued logic of propositions, has to regard as empirically false any hypothesis that is self-contradictory. Emerson's oft-quoted dictum is not applicable here (*Report*, p. 734).

Let us return to the matter of "sharpness" of hypotheses and the formulation of theoretical restrictions to describe the maintained hypothesis.

If the number N of successive observations of y_t and z_t is considerably greater than $Gr+K$, i.e., the total number of lagged endogenous and exogenous variables appearing in (3.1), then the pressure to reduce the number of functionally independent structural parameters in the maintained hypothesis *B* by hypothetical functional dependences—e.g.,

$$\beta_{12}+\beta_{13}+\beta_{14}=0,$$

may not be great. However, if N is not much greater than $Gr+K$, or if $N \leq Gr+K$, as is the case of the Brookings Model, then—for practical reasons in the first case, and for logical reasons in the second case—we are required to lay down a more stringent maintained hypothesis *B* to begin with. If $N \leq Gr+K$ we can adjust the system (3.1) to the sample of N observations perfectly in a nondenumerable infinity of ways; by "perfect" is meant that the matrix estimates $\hat{\Omega}=0$. In other words, there is no determinate degree of confirmation for *B*; recall the illustration in Section 2. This is purely arithmetical result sufficiently well-known that no one is likely to bring forward such a perfect fit or claim any significance for it. The practicable thing to do in case $N \leq Gr+K$ is to *openly* reduce the number of functionally independent structural parameters in the maintained structural economic hypothesis *B* by inventing hypothetical functional dependences among those structural parameters—in other words, do some economic theorizing. Of course, these new restrictions, which are to be part of the maintained hypothesis B, cannot be tested as long as there remains the paucity of observations which motivates such restriction of B in the first place. Here the aim is to provide ourselves with a class of alternative hypotheses we *can* test empirically. To put it another way, say that the aim is to begin with a maintained structural hypothesis B that has a determinate degree of confirmation on the empirical data available.

Pure economic theory may provide some hypothetical restrictions for this purpose. In this connection it is mentioned that the motive for using such hypothetical restrictions in describing B, or in describing a feasibly testable structural economic hypothesis $B_1 \subset B$, is not that such theoretical restriction of structural parameters "lends conviction to the chosen equation" (*Report*, p. 6) on which the restriction is imposed. *Conviction and consensus are beside the point.* Nor are such restrictions imposed by reason of any supposition that they are a priori true and, therefore, helpful by increasing efficiency of statistical estimation. The restrictions that define B_1 are, of course, the hypothetical restrictions we wish to test; cf. Basmann, 1965c, pp. 408-419.

(Notice, in passing, that the foregoing reduction of functionally independent structural[34] parameters does not necessarily result in the elimination of any endogenous or exogenous variables. That is to say, the mere size of the Brookings Model is not a fundamental issue here.)

For the case in which $N \leq Gr+K$ (which is the case for many reduced-form equations in the Brookings Model) there are *purely computational devices* for combining lagged endogenous variables and exogenous variables in such a way that a close fit (in terms of R^2) is obtained for the reduced-form equations (2.3) and hence for (2.1), without the embarassment of turning up a perfect fit. For instance, consider the reduced-form (3.3) and let

$$(3.7) \qquad y_{t+r,i} = \sum_{h=1}^{G} \alpha^{(1)}{}_{ih} y_{t+r-1,h} + \sum_{h=1}^{G} \alpha^{(2)}{}_{ih} y_{t+r-2,h} +$$

$$\dots + \sum_{h=1}^{G} \alpha^{(r)}{}_{ih} y_{t,h} + \sum_{k=1}^{K} \bar{\alpha}_{ik} z_{t+r,k} + \eta_{t+r,i}$$

be the ith component equation of (3.3) where

$$(3.8\text{a-c}) \quad \begin{cases} \alpha^{(m)}{}_{ih} = -\sum_{j=1}^{G} \beta^{ij} \beta^{(m)}{}_{jh}, \quad m = 1, 2, \ldots, r \\[2ex] \overline{\alpha}_{ik} = -\sum_{j=1}^{G} \beta^{ij} \gamma_{jk}, \\[2ex] \eta_{t,i} = -\sum_{j=1}^{G} \beta^{ij} u_{t,j}; \end{cases}$$

β^{ij} is the typical element of $(B')^{-1}$, and $\beta^{(m)}{}_{jh}$ is the typical element of B_m. (Asterisks are omitted from matrices to avoid cluttering.) If, in applying the computations of least squares to equation (3.7) we ignore at least $(Gr + K - N - 1)$ of the predetermined variables then we avoid the embarrassment of a spuriously perfect fit. The set of predetermined variables to be ignored may be chosen in a definite number of ways.

The choice of predetermined variables to be excluded from the ith reduced-form equation can be programmed so that it can be accomplished by the electronic computer as a constrained maximum problem, e.g., to determine the set of excluded predetermined variables such that the sample multiple correlation coefficient R^2_i is a maximum subject to constraints on the total number of predetermined variables remaining in the ith equation. Moreover, the exclusions for the whole set of G reduced-form equations (3.3) can be made mutually dependent so that each of the $Gr + K$ predetermined variables appears in at least one reduced-form equation. The immediate idea to be grasped is that the foregoing procedure is equivalent to that of specifying functional dependences among the structural parameters. For if we ignore (say) $\alpha^{(m)}{}_{ih}$ and $\overline{\alpha}_{ik}$ where $i, h, m,$ and k are specified, this is equivalent to imposing the restrictions

$$(3.9\text{a-b}) \quad \begin{aligned} \alpha^{(m)}{}_{ih} &= 0, \\[1ex] \overline{\alpha}_{ik} &= 0, \end{aligned}$$

i.e.,

$$(3.10\text{a-b}) \quad \sum_{j=1}^{G} \beta^{ij} \beta^{(m)}{}_{jh} = 0$$

$$\sum_{j=1}^{G} \beta^{1j} \gamma_{jk} = 0$$

respectively.

Let us consider another popular procedure, namely *principal components*, cf. Tintner, 1952, pp. 102-114. Let X be the sample matrix of predetermined variables in (3.7). X has N rows and $Gr+K$ columns, hence the real matrix $X'X$ is symmetric and has $Gr+K$ rows. A purely arithmetical feature of $X'X$ is that it has at most N positive characteristic roots [35] $\lambda_1, ..., \lambda_N$ and $Gr+K-N$ characteristic roots equal to zero, i.e., $\lambda_{N+1}=0, ..., \lambda_{Gr+K}=0$. Let Λ be the diagonal matrix of characteristic roots and let V be the orthogonal matrix such that

$$(3.11) \qquad V'(X'X)V = \Lambda. \text{[36]}$$

Let $\overline{X}$ be defined by the transformation

$$(3.12) \qquad X = \overline{X}V'.$$

Now

$$(3.13) \qquad \overline{X}'\overline{X} = \Lambda.$$

Since $\lambda_{n+1}=0, ..., \lambda_{Gr+K}=0$ and the elements of the matrix $\overline{X}$ are real numbers, the last $Gr+K-N$ columns of X contain zeroes only.[37] Letting the column vector $\alpha_{.i}$ denote the reduced-form coefficients in (3.7), the column vector $y_{.i}$ the N observations on $y_{t.i}$, and the column vector $\eta_{.i}$ corresponding N random disturbances, we write (3.7) in terms of samples as

$$(3.14) \qquad y_{.i} = x\alpha_{.i} + \eta_{.i}.$$

With help of (3.12) we write (3.14) as

$$(3.15) \qquad y_{.i} = \overline{X}(V'\alpha_{.i}) + \eta_{.i}.$$

Application of the method of least squares yields statistical estimates of exactly N linear functions of $Gr+K$ unknown reduced-form coefficients, namely,

$$(3.16) \qquad v'_{.m}\alpha_{.i} \qquad m=1,2, ..., N$$

where $v_{.m}$ is the characteristic vector corresponding to λ_m.

From here one proceeds to ignore some of the transformed predetermined variables $\overline{x}_{.m}$, $m=1,2, ..., N$, (say) those that correspond to the smaller positive characteristic roots of $X'X$. This procedure is equivalent to that of imposing hypothetical restrictions of the form

$$(3.17) \qquad v'_{.m}\alpha_{.1} = 0,$$

which, in turn, is equivalent to the imposition of hypothetical restrictions on the structural parameters. Moreover, since the vector $v_{.m}$ in the restriction (3.17) is a function of sample observations (predetermined variables) and $\alpha_{.1}$ is a constant, the foregoing procedure may be interpreted as implicitly introducing additional definitional identities or structural relations, which, however, vary from sample to sample.[38]

Even more sophisticated versions of the foregoing computational procedures have been employed in the process of estimating the reduced-forms and, hence, the structural equations of the Brookings Model. For an excellent technical description see the paper by Franklin Fisher (*Report*, Chapter 15). Procedures similar to, or identical with, those described by Fisher have been employed by Fromm and Klein in Chapter 18; however, the latter give no indication of what instrumental variables (*Report*, p. 622) were actually used by them. That is to say, when the reader is confronted by the numerical values of structural coefficient estimators, the reader cannot determine from the *Report* how those statistics have been computed from the sample. Put another way: Each of the estimators is a definite function of *sample observations on the endogenous and exogenous variables*. Knowledge of the exact forms of such functions is essential to the appraisal of the numerical values of estimators and test statistics. There is nothing in the *Report* to indicate that Fromm and Klein know specifically what instrumental variables have been used, (cf. *Report*, p. 736).

The electronic computer, not the Brookings econometricians, has determined the maintained hypothesis B expressed by the Brookings Model. That is to say, the electronic computer has imposed some hypothetical restrictions on structural economic parameters. Of course those hypothetical structural restrictions imposed by the computer can feasibly be retrieved from storage (at least such retrieval could have been planned for). However, I have found no indication in the *Report* that a description of the maintained structural hypothesis B has been thus retrieved. Even if the maintained structural hypothesis B expressed by the Brookings Model is known to the Brookings econometricians, they have not bothered to reveal it in the *Report*.

There is no indication that the Brookings econometricians

have given adequate attention to the pre-estimation analysis of structural dynamical stability. It may be that post-estimation analysis involving numerical computation of the roots of the implicit auxiliary polynomial and numerical simulation of the dynamical equilibrium paths of the endogenous variables will reveal that the structural estimates $\hat{B}, \hat{B}_1, ..., \hat{B}_r$ for the Brookings Model (*Report*, Chapter 18) do, indeed, satisfy the dynamical stability conditions. But the sampling properties of those estimators depend on the fulfilment of the stability conditions by the structural constants B^*, $B^*_1, ..., B^*_r$.[39]

Finally, structural coefficient estimates of $B^*, B^*_1, ..., B^*_r, \Gamma^*$ have been calculated either by the method of limited information or by the method of two-stage least squares. Limited information estimates were preferred except where those estimates became explosive, i.e., had relatively large estimates of sampling error associated with them (*Report*, p. 682n; see also p. 606). It cannot be determined from the *Report* whether any given equation in the Brookings Model has been estimated by the one method or the other. Application of these methods has been made with help of techniques of instrumental variables but, as already mentioned, the specific instruments used for each equation have not been revealed.

Statistical estimates of structural disturbance variances and covariances, i.e., of Ω^* are not revealed in the *Report*, Chapter 18. It is apparent, however, that estimates of variances were calculated, since each of the estimated equations (*Report*, p. 684 ff.) is accompanied by numbers—in parentheses beneath coefficient estimates—that seem to be estimates of standard deviations.

Statistical estimates (unconstrained except by B) of the reduced-form (3.3) of the Brookings Model are not revealed in the *Report* (Chapter 18). These estimates contain statistical information that is discarded in the process of estimating structural constants, i.e., statistical information relevant to the disconfirmation of any hypothetical identifying restrictions that are not employed in the maintained structural hypothesis B. Such identifying restrictions help to define a structural hypothesis B_1 that is testable against a class of alternative hypotheses belonging to $B-B_1$; cf. Basmann, 1965b, esp. pp. 1087-1089; also Basmann, 1965c, esp. pp. 404-408.

It would be of considerable practical value to have available the statistical estimate $\hat{\Sigma}$ (unconstrained except by B) of the variance covariance matrix Σ^* of the reduced-form disturbances, (3.3).

In view of the fact that the total number $Gr + K$ of predetermined variables exceeds the sample size N and the computational procedures employed to get around that difficulty, it would be helpful to compare the estimates $\sqrt{\hat{\sigma}_{ii}}$ with the residual computational round-off error. Such a comparison underlies an evaluation of the significance of structural estimates and their estimated standard deviations, which Fromm and Klein do report in Chapter 18. Alternatively, a comparison of the latter estimates with residual round-off error in their computation would be helpful. In other words, there is no evidence in the *Report* that tends to refute the claim (if it be raised) that the close fit is spurious in spite of the efforts that have been made to get around the "degrees of freedom" problem.

The inadequacy of the *Report* (Chapter 18), the failure of the Brookings econometricians to formulate an explicit structural economic hypothesis—in other words, to theorize—that has a determinate degree of confirmation on the empirical data currently available, to formulate initial conditions, all derive from the peculiarities of the "philosophy of econometrics" put forward by Duesenberry and Klein (*Report*, Chapter 1). About that philosophy I shall say more in Section 5.

SECTION 4. WHAT IS THE BROOKINGS MODEL AN HYPOTHESIS ABOUT?

The Brookings Model belongs to the class of simultaneous equations representations typified by equation (3.1). In that representation there occur symbols for the purely arithmetic operations of addition (subtraction) and multiplication (division) on real numbers. The components of the endogenous and exogenous vectors are supposed to *represent* magnitudes of economic quantities. The numerical estimates of structural coefficients in the Brookings Model (Chapter 18) are supposed to represent some invariant aspects of economic reality. In calculating those estimates the Brookings econometricians have employed the purely arithmetic operations of addition (subtraction) and multiplication (division) of numerical time series. In performing such operations and claiming that their results stand for some unique aspects of economic reality, the Brookings econometricians tacitly assume some proffered empirical laws, which are the foundations of *quantitative economics;* those proffered laws, the confirmation of which is an essential task of quantitative economics, are taken for granted by the Brookings econometricians.[40]

The claim that the numerical coefficients (statistical estimates) appearing in the structural equations of the Brookings Model represent propositions about the structure of economic events and objects of experience rests on the logically prior assertion that the numerical time series from which the numerical coefficients are calculated represent *quantities*.[41] That assertion ought not to be taken for granted, however, and need not be taken for granted; for the assertion that those numerical time series do represent quantities can—and must—be supported by appropriate empirical evidence.

From old Pythagoras and his followers this demand for evidence would elicit only a fish-eyed stare. For the Pythagoreans, ancient and modern, have viewed numbers as the real constituents of all things—as the very essence of events and objects of experience. (See Barnes, 1937, pp. 125-126; Taton, 1963, esp. p. 187; Sarton, 1927, Vol. 1, p. 73; and Sarton, 1952, pp. 203 ff., esp. p. 216.) To demand justification for representing the events and objects of economic experience by numbers is, to the Pythagoreans and many modern econometricians, mere captiousness. But for several centuries now modern science has been outgrowing number mysticism; the demand for, and the constructive response to the demand for, justification of mathematical representation of hypotheses about events and objects of experience has become the hallmark of quantitative science, and the touchstone for distinguishing between quantitative science and numerology.

The *Report* gives no indication that the econometricians who formulated the Brookings Model have given due attention to the foregoing matter. It has merely been taken for granted that the numerical time series from which the statistical estimates of parameters have been computed represent quantities. The following quotation from Duesenberry and Klein is especially revealing:

> The questions economists ask are questions about quantities—prices, outputs, incomes—and the relations among them. So-called "literary" economics does not use mathematics or statistics. *It is nonetheless an analysis of relationships among variables which are, in principle, capable of numerical measurement or ordering.* (*Report*, p. 4.)[42]

Duesenberry and Klein are here casting dust in the reader's eyes while dodging the fundamental question, namely, that concerning the adequacy of the quantitative foundations of the Brookings Model and the statistical estimates of its equations.

It is simply not the case that literary economics is an analysis of relationships among variables that are capable of numerical measurement or ordering. There are excellent reasons for economic scientists eschewing the use of mathematical representations of economic events and objects of experience; in particular, there are excellent reasons for not employing the addition and multiplication operations involved in the calculation of sample means, sample variances and covariances, correlation coefficients, regression coefficients, and estimates of "structural parameters." In the face of inadequate quantitative foundations, a very proper concern can lead an economic scientist to express facts and hypotheses in a nonquantitative language in order that he deceive neither himself nor others.

Frank Knight is supposed to have said that in the face of defective quantitative foundations many social scientists cling to the methodological slogan, "If you cannot measure, measure anyhow." (See Kuhn, 1961, p. 164n.) Duesenberry and Klein offer just one more confirming instance of Knight's generalization, as the foregoing quotation reveals.

Economists ask questions about a wide variety of variable properties of economic events and objects of experience. A few (probably very few) of those variable properties are actually *quantities*.[43] (I shall offer more precise and workable definitions of *variable property* and *quantity* later on in this section.) There might be some context in which it is meaningful and decisive (of some issue or other) to say that a variable property is, *in principle*, capable of numerical measurement or ordering; in the present context it is not. A variable property either is *orderable* or it is not; if it is not orderable, then it is not *orderable in principle*. What is of importance in quantitative economics is the evidence that supports the assertion that some specified variable property or other is *orderable*. An *orderable* variable property either is a *quantity*, or it is not; if it is not a quantity, then it is not *capable of numerical measurement in principle*. The significant question in the present context is whether evidence, of the appropriate kind, has been brought forward to support the assertion that each of the alleged variable properties represented by numerical time series in the Brookings Model is a quantity. For the Brookings econometricians treat each of their time series as if it represented a quantity.

For sake of discussion, let us grant that each of the numerical time series appearing in the Brookings Model represents some definite variable property. Moreover, let us also grant that each of the numerical time series appearing in the Brookings Model accurately represents a definite variable property that is *orderable*. We are taking much for granted here, of course, but only for sake of the present discussion. I do not claim that there are good empirical grounds for the assertion that all (or any) of the numerical time series that appear in the Brookings Model actually do represent variable properties, not to mention orderable variable properties.

In elementary statistics courses we learn that it is fruitless to attempt to test or estimate a hypothetical relation between a pair of variable properties X and Y by means of ordinary correlation coefficients and regression statistics when at least one of those variable properties is only orderable.[44] For instance, let X be "inclination to buy cars" and let Y be "demand for automobiles." George Katona and Eva Mueller have constructed a numerical index of "inclination to buy cars" (Katona and Mueller, 1957, Chapter 4; see esp. p. 59), which appears in one of the Brookings Model equations, namely,[45]

$$(4.1) \qquad C^{54}_{DA} = -21.19 + 0.0501\, Y^{54}_{D} - 8.333 \left[\frac{P_{CDA}}{P_C} \right]$$
$$\qquad\qquad (12.9)\ \ (0.0053) \qquad (11.7)$$
$$\qquad\qquad + 0.2950\ [ATT]_{-1};$$
$$\qquad\qquad (0.0411)$$

which is equation (18.3) in the *Report*, p. 684. (ATT is the Katona-Mueller *index* of "inclination to buy cars." Katona and Mueller acknowledge that there are no good grounds for regarding "inclination to buy cars" as a *quantity* (Katona and Mueller, 1957; see esp. pp. 6-11) although this acknowledgment is fragmentary and obscure.[46] In the Brookings Model, however, and in the consumption sector model by Suits and Sparks (*Report*, Chapter 7), "inclination to buy cars" is treated as a *quantity*, and Suits and Sparks make statistical inferences that are justifiable only by the kind of empirical evidence that would support the assertion that "inclination to buy cars" *is* a quantity, either fundamental or derived. From the numerical time series, Suits and Sparks estimate the structural demand function for automobiles from numerical time series by the method of least squares as follows:[47]

$$(4.2) \qquad C^{54}_{DA} = 0.0790\ (Y^{54}_{D} - V^{54} + V^{54}_{INSGF}) - 0.5124\ (CARS)_{-1}$$
$$\qquad\qquad 9).275) \qquad\qquad\qquad (0.092)$$
$$\qquad\qquad + 0.2329\ (ATT)_{-1} - 19.6860 \qquad \overline{R}^2 = 0.686$$
$$\qquad\qquad (0.646)$$

(*Report*, p. 208, equation 7.1). The numbers shown in parentheses below coefficients are partial correlation coefficients. Suits and Sparks assert

The most powerful factor in the equation is consumer attitudes (partial $R^2 = 0.646$), indicating that much of the observed behavior in the automobile market is traced to consumer psychology rather than endogenous economic factors. On the other hand, it is clear that consumer attitudes are themselves, to some extent, determined by economic events. (*Report*, p. 211.)

Neither of the foregoing statments is clear at all—even in meaning—unless every one of the time series in the foregoing equation, C^{54}_{DA}, Y^{54}_{D}, ..., ATT, is presumed to represent a *quantity*, not merely orderable variable properties.[48] If "inclination to buy cars" is only an *orderable* property, then an infinite set of different least-squares estimates of the equation in question are—so to speak—in equally good agreement with the real events the time series used by Suits and Sparks are supposed to represent. For the numerical time series ATT used by Suits and Sparks can be replaced by any other numerical time series that can be obtained from the index ATT by any *order-preserving transformation* (cf. Stevens, 1946, p. 143); and each of these new indexes represents "inclination to buy cars" equally as well as does the index ATT. To each index of "inclination to buy cars" there corresponds a definite least-squares regression line, multiple correlation R^2, and partial R^2 for "inclination to buy automobiles." Partial R^2, which is 0.646 for the index ATT employed by Suits and Sparks, varies from index to index; for one choice of index partial R^2 might (say) $= 0.10$; for another choice, partial R^2 might (say) $= 0.90$.[49]

A simple numerical illustration will help to make the foregoing point clear. Consider a set S of objects each of which has two definite properties X and Y. (S is not proved to be finite.) For the time being, suppose that Y is a quantity. However, suppose that X is a variable property that is only *orderable*. Let y and x denote measurements of Y and X respectively. Now let us suppose that someone regards as a meaningful hypothesis (about the objects of experience belonging to S) that properties X and Y are connected by a real empirical relation that can be *represented* by the equation

$$(4.3) \qquad y = hx + k + u$$

where h,k are definite structural constants with real values and u is a random real variable with zero expectation.

One now draws a finite *sample* of objects of experience (say) α, β, γ and measures Y and X in order to obtain numerical series for application of the method of least squares to (4.3). Using one scale of measurement for X, one obtains (say)

$$\text{(4.4)} \quad \begin{cases} x_\alpha = 14, & y_\alpha = 200 \\ x_\beta = 1, & y_\beta = 100 \\ x_\gamma = 15, & y_\gamma = 300. \end{cases}$$

Direct application of the method of least squares to the foregoing time-series (4.4) yields[50]

$$\text{(4.5a-b)} \quad y = 11.48x + 85.2 + \hat{u} \qquad R^2 = 0.81$$
$$\phantom{\text{(4.5a-b)} \quad y =} (3.24) \quad (38.5)$$

$$\text{Var } (u) = 1280.8.$$

However, since the property X is only orderable, the following set of measurements on α, β, γ describes that sample equally well as the set of measurements (4.4):

$$\text{(4.6)} \quad \begin{cases} x_\alpha' = 5 & y_\alpha = 200 \\ x_\beta' = 3 & y_\beta = 100 \\ x_\gamma' = 7 & y_\gamma = 300. \end{cases}$$

The time series x' in (4.6) is obtained from the time series x in (4.4) by an order-preserving transformation. Application of the method of least squares to the numerical time series (4.6) yields

$$\text{(4.7a-b)} \quad y = 50x' - 50 + \hat{u} \qquad R^2 = 1.0$$
$$\phantom{\text{(4.7a-b)} \quad y =} (0) \quad (0)$$

$$\text{Var } (u) = 0.$$

Let us report (tongue in cheek, of course) that there is a large un-explained residual in our estimate (4.5a-b) of the relation (4.3) and suggest that this residual is due to some unknown factor (property?) on which the property Y depends in part. We might also attribute the large residual in (4.5a-b) to sampling error in the estimate—after all a sample of size three is a small sample indeed. On the other hand, had we started out measuring X on the second scale, our result (4.7a-b) would lead us to much different conclusions.

Of course, the numerical differences between the least-squares estimates (4.5a-b) and (4.7a-b) are without any significance for the objects of experience $\alpha, \beta, \gamma, \ldots$ belonging to S. In particular, the numerical value of the correlation coefficient is without significance for objects of experience. To put the matter in more fundamental terms, there is no relation between properties Y and X in objects of experience $\alpha,\beta,\gamma,\delta, \ldots$ with which the representation (4.3) can agree or disagree—there is simply no relevant connection between the equation (4.3) and the empirical facts (α,β,γ) at all.[51]

To save equation (4.1) and equation (4.2) from the criticism just levelled at (4.5a-b) and (4.7a-b) Suits and Sparks, as well as Fromm and Klein, need to support the pretermitted assumption that the index ATT measures a quantity, i.e., that "inclination to buy cars" is not merely an orderable property on the set of all groups of consumers; and what they are required to show in respect of ATT holds equally for the rest of the time series appearing in those equations. In singling out the index ATT I do not mean to draw an invidious comparison between that time series and any of the remaining 333 series that appear in the Brookings Model.[52] I do not assert that any of the remaining time series represents a quantity; I do not deny it, either; and this simply is because I cannot find evidence of the kind that tends to support or refute such assertions. Tradition and lore of econometrics are not relevant evidence.

To justify the claim that the Brookings Model can *in principle* represent an hypothesis about economic events and objects of economic experience requires that every one of the time series that appear in its equations represent a *quantity*—that is to say, the contention that those time series represent *quantities* requires relevant empirical support. I have already cast doubt on the fulfilment of this condition in respect of the Katona-Mueller index (ATT) of "inclination to buy cars," which appears in equation (18.3) of the Brookings Model (*Report*, p. 684). Having done so, I ought to sketch how one is to go about supporting the statement that some specified variable property is a *quantity*, for it is clear that I regard that task as fundamental to quantitative economics.

Clearly we need more precise definitions of variable property and of quantity than those which have sufficed in our discussion so far.

The concept of variable property involves the following notions:

(1) An infinite set S of objects of experience, $\alpha,\beta,\gamma, \ldots$;
(2) A repeatable empirical operation O_1 on any ordered pair of objects α,β belonging to S, for which exactly one of the three outcomes (relations between α and β) holds

$$\alpha \sim \beta$$
$$\alpha > \beta,$$
$$\beta > \alpha;$$

(3) The empirical relation $\sim$ determined in (2) is an equivalence relation, viz., for all distinct α,β,γ in S, the following conditions hold:

(a) $\alpha \sim \alpha$,
(b) if $\alpha \sim \beta$, then $\beta \sim \alpha$,
(c) if $\alpha \sim \beta$ and $\beta \sim \gamma$, then $\alpha \sim \gamma$.

(In general it is impossible in principle to confirm the statement (a) empirically. However, statements (b) and (c) can be confirmed empirically for distinct objects, i.e., $\alpha \neq \beta$, $\alpha \neq \gamma$, $\beta \neq \gamma$. The statement (a) is introduced to complete the definition of $\sim$ as an equivalence relation.)

(4) The *partition* Q of S under the equivalence relation $\sim$, viz.,

$$Q = \{a,b,c, \dots \}$$

where $a,b,c, \dots$ are nonempty subsets of S such that every object in S belongs to exactly one of the subsets a,b,c; and if α and β are any two objects belonging to a given subset a, then

$$\alpha \sim \beta.$$

The sets a,b,c are said to be *equivalence classes* under the partition of S by the relation $\sim$.

Given a set S of objects of experience α,β,γ and an empirical operation that defines an empirical equivalence relation $\sim$ on S, we say that the ordered triple (S,O_1,Q) is a variable property of the objects $\alpha,\beta,\gamma, \dots$ belonging to S. Moreover, the *value of the property* for any object α belonging to S *is* the equivalence class a to which α belongs.

Two or more distinct empirical operations on S may define an equal number of distinct variable economic properties, the values of which may be related in some definite ways. Even if those variable properties are not quantities or even orderable properties, the relations among their values (equivalence classes) may be worthy of scientific study. Of course, a mode of representation of hypotheses has to be employed that is appropriate to the circumstance that the variable properties in question are not quantities or even orderable properties.

A variable property $Q(S,O_1,Q)$ is said to be an *orderable* or *topological* property only if the following statement holds for all distinct objects α,β,γ belonging to S:

(5) If $\alpha > \beta$ and $\beta > \gamma$, then $\alpha > \gamma$.

In other words, the empirical operation O_1 determines a *weak ordering* on the set S of objects of experience.

Of course, we cannot *verify* empirically that a specified operation O_1 defines a weak ordering on S since S is not provably finite (from its defining characteristic). In principle, at least, we can falsify the statement that a specified operation O_1 defines a weak ordering on the given set, although the procedure is beset by practical difficulties, e.g., the practical inability of O_1 to discriminate among $\alpha \sim \beta$, $\alpha > \beta$, and $\beta > \gamma$ for some pairs of objects α, β.

Furthermore the *existential statement* "There is some operation O_1 such that O_1 defines an empirical weak-ordering on the given set S" cannot be falsified, as the set of all possible operations that may be tried out is not provably finite.

For $\alpha \varepsilon a$ and $\beta \varepsilon b$ write

    (i)   a > b if $\alpha > \beta$
    (ii)   b > a if $\beta > \alpha$
    (iii)   a = b if $\alpha \sim \beta$.

It can be proved that Q is linearly ordered, viz., for all values (equivalence classes) a,b,c of Q exactly one of (i), (ii), and (iii) holds, and the statement

    (6) If a > b and b > c, than a > c, holds.

For instance, the concept of *utility* as employed in ordinary theories of consumer demand is that of a variable property that is only orderable. The objects of experience are budgets, the operation that defines > and $\sim$ is choice between pairs of budgets; the equivalence classes *a,b,c,* ... are indifference "curves."[53]

A *quantity* is an ordered quadruple (S,O_1,O_2,Q) with the following properties:

    (1) The operation O_1 defines a weak ordering on S; viz., (S,O_1,Q) is an orderable variable property;

    (2) O_2 is an empirically realizable operation for *combining* any two objects α, β belonging to S such that the combination of α and β, denoted by $\alpha \oplus \beta$, belongs to S. (Let $\alpha \varepsilon a$, $\beta \varepsilon b$. Then a $\oplus$ b denotes the equivalence class to which the combination $\alpha \oplus \beta$ belongs.)

    (3) Together the operations O_1 and O_2 satisfy the following *axioms of quantity and magnitude*:

        I. For every pair of a,b belonging to Q, exactly one of the following holds:

a > b,
b > a,
a = b, (*a* and *b* are identical).

II. If α belongs to Q, then there is a class *b* in Q such that
a > b.

III. There is an operation $\oplus$ on objects of experience
such that to every pair *a,b* in Q there corresponds a
uniquely determined class a $\oplus$ b in Q.

IV. For every pair of *a,b* in Q

$$(a \oplus b) > a$$

and

$$(a \oplus b) > b.$$

V. If b > a, then there is a class *x* in Q such that

$$a \oplus x = b$$

and a class *y* in Q such that

$$y \oplus a = b.$$

VI. For all classes a,b,c

$$(a \oplus b) \oplus c = a \oplus (b \oplus c).[54]$$

VII. For every pair *a,b* in Q such that b > a there is a
whole number *n* such that

$$na > b.[55]$$

The foregoing conditions are due to the mathematician O. Hölder
(1901, pp. 5-7) and are called *axioms of quantity*. The system of
Axioms I-VII can be formulated equivalently in different ways,
of course, and Hölder offers several equivalent formulations in his
essay.[56] In this connection see especially the article by Suppes, 1951,
and the article by Menger, 1959.

For sake of brevity we shall have to omit all but the most important details. Another equivalent formulation, involving 12 axioms, has been put forward by Ernest Nagel in his well-known essay
on measurement (Nagel, 1930).[57]

Of course, for the quantitative economist the foregoing conditions are not to be regarded as axioms in the ancient sense of the
word; *they are not self-evident propositions about empirical opera-*

tions on objects of experience. Nor are they to be regarded as postulates, but as expressions of hypotheses to be tested and supported empirically. Indeed, the statements I-VII are empirical hypotheses implicitly represented by every economic simultaneous equations representation like the Brookings model, and they are its most fundamental empirical hypotheses. Quantities are empirical realizations of the foregoing axiom system.

The assertion that a specified pair of operations O_1 and O_2 on a given set S define an empirical quantity is here regarded as a proffered law, strictly universal in form (recall Section 2). As such the assertion is conceptually open to strict falsification, but not open to strict verification. (In this connection see the concluding remarks by Suppes, 1951, p. 172.) The formulation and testing of such proffered laws of quantity belongs to, and is essential to, the trade of the quantitative economist and econometrician.

If a variable property (S,O_1,O_2,Q) satisfies conditions I-VII, then the equivalence classes a,b,c belonging to Q are said to be *magnitudes of the quantity* (S,O_1O_2,Q). An isomorphism f between the set Q of magnitudes and a set R of positive real numbers under the empirical operation "$\oplus$" (on Q) and the purely arithmetic operation "$+$" on R can be set up: To each magnitude a ε Q, there corresponds exactly one real number $f(a)$ ε R; to each real number t ε R there corresponds exactly one magnitude $f^{-1}(t)$ ε Q. For every a,b ε Q the magnitude a $\oplus$ b ε Q and we have

$$f(a \oplus b) = f(a) + f(b)$$

Moreover, for every a,b such that b > a, we have

$$f(b) > f(a),$$

and to the real number

$$f(b) - f(a)$$

there corresponds exactly one magnitude c ε Q such that

$$a \oplus c = b.$$

Finally, there is no magnitude that corresponds to the real number O, and O is not contained in R.

Multiplication $\odot$ of magnitudes is defined in terms of the empirical operation "$\oplus$", cf. Hölder, 1901, pp. 32-37. The rule of correspondence f, already mentioned, is an isomorphism between Q and the set R of positive real numbers under $\odot$ on Q and the purely arithmetic operation of multiplication on R. Thus, for every $a, b \; \varepsilon \; Q$, $a \odot b \; \varepsilon \; Q$, and

$$f(a \odot b) = f(a) f(b).$$

For every $a, b \; \varepsilon \; Q$ there is exactly one magnitude $c \; \varepsilon \; Q$ such that $a \odot c = b$; moreover,

$$f(c) = \frac{f(b)}{f(a)}.$$

Isomorphisms typified by f, set up for each quantity that is represented by an endogenous or exogenous variable in the system of simultaneous economic equations (3.1), establish the connection between that system of equations and economic reality.

In order to indicate (but briefly) how the foregoing isomorphism f confers empirical significance on the kind of sample statistics employed in estimation and testing of simultaneous equations systems, we consider the sample arithmetic mean of n observations $r_1, r_2, ..., r_n$, i.e.,

$$\bar{r} = \frac{r_1 + r_2 + ... + r_n}{n}.$$

If $r_1, r_2, ..., r_n$ represent magnitudes $a_1, a_2, ..., a_n$ of a quantity (S, O_1, O_2, Q)—let

$$r_i = f(a_i)$$

where f is the isomorphism just mentioned—then there corresponds under f a definite magnitude $\bar{a}$ to $\bar{r}$, i.e.,

$$\bar{a} = f^{-1}(\bar{r})$$

such that

$$n\bar{a} = a_1 \oplus a_2 \oplus ... \oplus a_n.$$

That is to say, there corresponds to the arithmetic mean $\bar{r}$ exactly one class $\bar{a}$ of objects of experience, this class being defined in terms of $a_1, a_2, ..., a_n$ with help of the operation "$\oplus$." The operation "$\oplus$" is essential to the empirical interpretation of $\bar{r}$. For additional details consult the paper by Stevens, 1946.

Magnitudes of quantities may be *oriented*, thus leading to the introduction of *scales of measurement* containing negative real numbers as well as the real number zero. I mention this only to forestall possible confusion. For details see the paper by Menger, 1959, esp. pp. 105-107.

Our discussion so far has been about fundamental quantities only. *Derived quantities* are defined with help of empirical relations involving two or more fundamental quantities and an orderable variable property (which, in the process of definition, is replaced by the derived quantity). The classic example is the quantity called "density" in elementary physics: cf. Nagel, 1930, pp. 136-137, and Pap, 1962, pp. 131-132. Although almost all economic quantities are likely to be derived quantities, we need go no further than to mention that derived quantities satisfy the same conditions as fundamental quantities, and the problem of empirical justification is equally important for them. For additional discussion see Nagel, 1930, pp. 135-140; Pap, pp. 131-135; Bergmann and Spence, 1944, pp. 108-112.

In view of the mode of representation adopted, and the computations of numerical estimates employed by the Brookings econometricians, the answer to our question, "what is the Brookings Model an hypothesis about?" turns out to be, "what economic *quantities* are represented by the 334 numerical time series?"

Suppose we encounter the claim that the components of a specified time series in the Brookings Model represent magnitudes of an economic quantity. With no loss of generality that is essential here, let us suppose that this putative quantity is supposed to be a *fundamental quantity*. To justify this claim, the econometrician who makes it must reveal (at least)

(1) the appropriate set S of objects of experience α, β, γ, ...;

(2) the specific operations O_1 and O_2 that define the weak ordering $(>, \sim)$ and addition $\oplus$ an S;

(3) a nonempty subset S_1 of S, i.e., a sample of objects α, β, γ, ... belonging to S such that the axioms I-VII are in good agreement with the results of an actual performance of O_1 and O_2 on S_1.[58]

If discussion of the claim is not to be endless and fruitless the econometrician who makes it must not be allowed to retreat to security behind a nonfalsifiable existence statement. The existential statement, "There is some S, some pair of operations O_1, O_2 on S, such that (S, O_1, O_2, Q) is a quantity, and such that magnitudes of (S, O_1, O_2, Q) are represented by the time series in question" is not evidence in support of the kind of claim we are now considering, nor does it support the practice of treating such time series as representing magnitudes of quantities. The chief defect of such a methodology is transparent enough, but the strength of the temptation to employ such methodology should never be underestimated.[59]

At the beginning of this section I said that the *Report* gives no indication that the econometricians who formulated the Brookings Model have given due attention to the problem of its quantitative foundations. By this I mean that, in formulating their project, they failed to allocate any resources for the critical examination of quantitative foundations of their hypothesis. To be sure, they have mentioned "measurement error" and other inaccuracies in the numerical time series; but measurement error in a series of numerical data is a conceptual problem that is logically posterior to the problem of quantitative foundations; a series of numbers that do not represent magnitudes of a quantity or rankings of an orderable property do not contain measurement error in the sense of that term as it is employed in the *Report*. However, that some, or all, of the numerical series employed in estimating the parameters of the Brookings Model fail to represent magnitudes of any quantities has been ignored.

If it be supposed that economic science, rather unlike physical science, deals with fundamental quantities only, then that supposition might be adduced in support of a division of labor between econometricians, who would specialize in formulating simultaneous equations systems and quantitative experts who would discover and measure economic quantities. However, on the basis of experience in the physical sciences, it is more probable that most, if not all, economic quantities that ever will be discovered will be *derived quantities*, that is, quantities defined with help of relations among measurements of other quantities, ultimately in terms of relations among measurements of fundamental quantities. In such circumstances, the division of labor between econometricians and quantitative experts would have little to recommend it. Of course, many quantitative economists will have to concentrate on discovery and measurement of economic quantities, if macroeconometrics is ever to receive an adequate quantitative foundation.

In pursuit of realism, mainstream econometricians will continue to increase the dimensions of representations primarily in terms of the numbers of economic variables, endogenous and exogenous, those representations contain. Existing numerical time series (which probably do not represent quantities) are disaggregated and the components thereof are treated as representing measurements of *quantities*, and those putative quantities are named. But new economic quantities are not thereby discovered or invented, and the process of disaggregation is not measurement.

In this connection the following is significant: Duesenberry and Klein assert

> In the present state of knowledge it is inevitable that forecasts, however made, will be subject to error. (*Report*, p. 13.)

No economist is likely to expect any method of forecasting to be free of error, now or ever. Curiously enough, however, the foregoing is one assertion Duesenberry and Klein do try to support by argument; ten different sources of forecasting error are mentioned, with all of which most economists are already very familiar. Yet Duesenberry and Klein fail to mention the most fundamental and transparent explanation for the failure of econometric models like the Brookings Model to make accurate forecasts over an extended period, namely, *the absence of well-confirmed quantitative foundations for such* quantitative *representations*. To compute a forecast of the endogenous variables appearing in the Brookings Model you must add and multiply numbers that purportedly represent the magnitudes of economic quantities; and the forecasts you compute in this fashion purportedly represent magnitudes of quantities. If you are without good evidence of the kind that supports the assertion that the numbers you use and the numbers you calculate to represent magnitudes, then you are in possession of no grounds for supposing you can use such a model to forecast at all. The catalog of well-known sources of forecasting error and the conspicuous omission of the problem of quantitative foundations can be explained by the assumption that Duesenberry and Klein are not writing for professional economists and econometricians at all, but for industrial clients and governmental economic policy-makers. (Much space in the Duesenberry-Klein article is given over to description of policy applications; almost none to purely scientific applications.) Presumably, Duesenberry and Klein view policy-makers as prone to judge every econometric model too harshly in respect of the inaccuracy of its forecasts; and, at the same time, Duesenberry and Klein view the policy-makers as indifferent to the problem of quantitative foundations.

SECTION 5. STONING THE PROPHETS?

Upon reading through the *Report* for the first time I concluded that it would be inappropriate to evaluate the Brookings Model primarily as a contribution to economic science. (Recall my comments about the sector models in Section 1, however.) The philosophy of econometrics put forward by Duesenberry and Klein

(Chapter 1) reveals a preoccupation with industrial and governmental policy applications and the anxious concern for gaining consensus that almost always accompanies that preoccupation. Interest shown in scientific questions is peripheral. The main methodological tenet is:

> We must view the economy as a system of quantitative relationships. Those relationships may be more or less persistent in time, but they may be disturbed in a variety of ways. Yet, however that may be, it is important to find out as much as we can about the quantitative characteristics of the economic system. (*Report*, p. 4.)

Yet the consequences of this tenet are promptly and completely ignored, as has been mentioned in Section 4.

The *Report* indicates on the part of the Brookings econometricians a lack of interest in knowing and revealing exactly what maintained structural economic hypothesis has been produced for them by the electronic computer.

The *Report* indicates that exploration of background and initial conditions for application of the economic hypothesis represented by the Brookings Model has not been undertaken.

On the evidence of the *Report* it is probable that the goal of the Brookings research project is to mould national economic policy, the Brookings-SSRC Model—to which the Brookings Model (Chapter 18) is a first approximation—being but a means to that end. (I have not seen the original project proposals that were submitted to the foundations that so generously support the Brookings project; it is possible that the goals are made explicit in those proposals.) If the purpose of the Brookings Model and its projected descendents is that they be used primarily to gain consensus on national economic policies, then it would be unfair to the Brookings econometricians and the foundations who support the project, to economic policy-makers and their immediate economic advisers, and to the public, for one to evaluate the Brookings Model solely as a contribution to economic science.

Consequently, in this article I have concentrated on the two major scientific questions that responsible policy-makers—policy-makers who adhere to Clifford's ethic—as well as scientists must always ask about econometric representations like the Brookings Model: How secure are its quantitative foundations? What is the hypothesis expressed by the representation and is it better supported by the available evidence than any other alternative? Of course responsible policy-makers ask such questions as these with a laconicism that is rare in most scientists and seemingly cryptic to those unfamiliar with that style; but responsible policy-makers ask such questions; *for the logical and empirical foundations of economic policy making and pure economic science are identical.*

To some readers my criticisms will seem too harsh; to a few it may even seem that I have been stoning the prophets.[60] For all that, it should not be overlooked that it was always open to the authors of the *Report* to disclose fully the hypotheses and methods, including shortcuts, that have been employed in the construction of the Brookings Model.

NOTES

[1]Quoted by J. Bronowski, 1956, p. 84.

[2]Duesenberry, J. S., G. Fromm, L. R. Klein, and E. Kuh, *The Brookings Quarterly Econometric Model of the United States,* Chicago: Rand McNally and Company, 1965.

In subsequent citations this document will be referred to as the *Report.*

"Brookings Model" refers to the system of structural equations and identities described in the *Report,* Chapter 18.

[3]Parentheses inserted by R. L. Basmann.

The exact number of independent equations in a system of equations ought to be easy to state by anyone who knows that that system of equations is consistent. (Consult any textbook of elementary algebra.) This quotation, which is immediately preceded by the assertion that the system of equations that composes the Brookings Model is consistent, is one of the least perspicuous passages in the *Report.*

Having tried several times to obtain an accurate count of the equations, identities, structural coefficients, and numerical time series in the Brookings Model (*Report,* Chapter 18), I can understand the difficulty faced by the authors. All the same, the obligation to provide an accurate count lies with them.

[4]The specialists and their contributions are:

Jorgenson, Dale W., "Anticipations and Investment Behavior," (Chapter II).

Eisner, Robert, "Realization of Investment Anticipations," (Chapter II).

Darling, Paul G., and Michael C. Lovell, "Factors Influencing Investment in Inventories," (Chapter II).

Dutta, Manoranjan, "Business Anticipatory Demand: An Analysis of Business Orders, 1948-1962," (Chapter II).

Maisel, Sherman J., "Nonbusiness Construction," (Chapter III).

Suits, Daniel B., and Gordon R. Sparks, "Consumption Regressions with Quarterly Data," (Chapter III).

Kuh, Edwin, "Income Distribution and Employment Over the Business Cycle," (Chapter IV).

Schultze, Charles L., and Joseph L. Tryon, "Prices and Wages," (Chapter IV).

Lebergott, Stanley, "The Labor Force and Marriages as Endogenous Factors," (Chapter IV).

Rhomberg, Rudolf R., and Lorette Boissonneault, "The Foreign Sector," (Chapter V).

Fox, Karl A., "A Submodel of the Agricultural Sector," (Chapter V).

De Leeuw, Frank, "A Model of Financial Behavior," (Chapter VI).

Ando, Albert, E. Cary Brown, and Earl W. Adams, Jr., "Government Revenues and Expenditures," (Chapter VI).

[5]For example, Maisel (*Report,* Chapter 6) puts forward the hypothesis—which is employed as an empirical definition—that the number of housing units completed in a given quarter HU_{FIN} is equal to the sum of the number of single-family private housing units started HU^S_{STS} two quarters back and the number of multifamily private housing units started HU^M_{STS} four quarters back, viz.,

$$HU_{FIN} = [HU^S_{STS}]_{-2} + [HU^M_{STS}]_{-4},$$

equation (6.11a), *Report,* p. 181. On the other hand, in the Brookings Model,

$$HU_{FIN} = [HU_{STS}]_{-2} = [HU^S_{STS} + HU^M_{STS}],$$

equation (18.7), *Report*, p. 686.

[6]Recall the remarks of Clifford at the head of this article.

[7]Let p be a proposition and let $\sim$ p be the negation of p.

From the proposition

$$\sim (\text{R.L.B. believes p})$$

one cannot infer

$$\text{R.L.B. believes } \sim \text{p.}$$

Propositions such as "L.R.K. believes p" and "R.L.B. believes $\sim$ p" may be interesting pieces of biographical information or gossip, but they are not part of economic science. Similarly "a blue-ribbon committee of econometricians believe p" is not part of any *scientific* argument in support of proposition "p."

Because of the paucity of scientific argument in support of the hypothesis that is represented by the Brookings Model, the remarks by Duesenberry and Klein about consensus take on a significance (as clues to methodology) those remarks would not otherwise have.

[8]A logical argument is a sequence of propositions in which at least one of the propositions is put forward to substantiate another. The premises are *intended* to substantiate the conclusion, or proposition that is said to follow from those premises. The intention is not always realized, of course. However, we need not consider explanatory hypotheses that are defective in this sense.

[9]In the present drastically simplified account the prediction-statement turns out to be equivalent to the statement that Hempel and Oppenheim (1948, p. 321) call the *explanandum* or sentence that describes the phenomenon to be explained.

However, by "prediction-statement" I mean any statement validly inferred from an explanatory hypothesis and such that it can be disconfirmed by the statement that describes the phenomenon to be explained by the explanandum. Thus, prediction-statements may be probability statements (relative frequency) about events, which may be disconfirmed by statistical tests of significance.

[10]A singular proposition asserts that a specified object or event occurred at a given place and time. Faris, 1964, p. 16, distinguishes between quantified and unquantified singular statements, and his definition is more precise than ours. However, ours will do for the present discussion.

By "fact" we mean "true singular statement." Thus not all factual statements are facts.

[11]More precisely, the universal proposition (z) (Pz $\supset$ Qz) is said to be strictly universal if the proposition "the set of all objects that have property P is finite" is not provable from the statement of the defining characteristic, namely, P.

A set S is said to be *infinite* if it contains a proper subset S' such that a one-to-one correspondence can be set up between S and S'. Sets that are not infinite are said to be *finite*. Easy cases are "the null set O is finite" and "the set containing a single element is finite"; neither of the foregoing sets contains a proper subset. In this connection see the remarks of Hempel and Oppenheim, 1948, pp. 339-340. See also Popper, 1959, pp. 62-64.

[12]See the book by Blanché, 1962, Chapter 2, especially pp. 25-27. See also Cohen and Nagel, 1934 (reprinted in Feigl and Brodbeck, 1953, pp. 129-147; see especially pp. 139-140 on equivalent deductive systems).

[13]For instance, consider the following special theory of consumer demand due to Ragnar Frisch, 1954. The demand schedules for n commodities $\{1, 2, ..., n\}$ are expressed by

$$x_i = \frac{\beta_i}{p_i} \left[M - \sum_{k=1}^{n} \gamma_k p_k \right] + \gamma_i$$

$$i = 1, 2, ..., n$$

where $\gamma_k > 0$ for every $k = 1, 2, ..., n$; $\beta_i > 0$ for every i, and

$$\sum_{i=1}^{n} \beta_i = 1.$$

The demand functions are defined for all commodity prices and income M such that

$$\left\{ \begin{array}{l} p_k > 0 \\[2mm] M - \sum_{k=1}^{n} \gamma_k p_k > 0. \end{array} \right.$$

All of the remaining statements of the theory of consumer demand are derivable from the foregoing, i.e., the theorems about substitution terms s_{ij} (Hicks, 1946, p. 314)—here

$$s_{ij} = \frac{\beta_i \beta_j}{p_i p_j} \left[M - \sum_{k=1}^{n} \gamma_k p_k \right]$$

for $i \neq j$;

$$s_{ii} = \frac{(\beta_i - 1)\beta_i}{p_i^2} \left[M - \sum_{k=1}^{n} \gamma_k p_k \right] -$$

and the assumptions about the *utility function*, viz.,

$$u(x_1, \ldots, x_n) = \prod_{i=1}^{n} (x_i - \gamma_i)^{\beta_i}$$

on the preference field $x_i > \gamma_i$, $i = 1, 2, \ldots, n$, and

$$\sum_{i=1}^{n} \beta_i = 1.$$

That is to say, the foregoing statement about demand functions is equivalent to the special theory itself.

[14]If we use the so-called assumptions of the economic theory in question to define P, then the proffered law reduces to $(z)(Qz \supset Qz)$ or $(z)(Pz \supset Pz)$, which are trivial.

[15]The prefix |-: indicates that the proposition following it is asserted.

[16]See Quine, 1962, p. 88, *103; see also Faris, 1964, p. 58, rule (14); and Halberstadt, 1960, pp. 172-174.

[17]See Faris, 1964, p. 56, rule (2); and Halberstadt, 1960, pp. 15-19.

[18]This is the problem of asymmetry of proffered laws in respect of verification and falsification. For a detailed account see the book by Popper, 1959, Chapter III.

[19]In granting a place under the sun (and an important one) to "probability₁" I do not wish to be understood as agreeing with some claims recently put forward by Bayesian econometricians regarding the alleged superiority of Bayesian techniques to sampling theory techniques of inference. In particular, I do not agree with several claims in this regard put forward by Zellner in his unpublished paper "Bayesian Inference and Simultaneous Equations Models" (Zellner, 1965) in which the claim rests on the supposition that the so-called classical statistician would fail to employ the *exact* finite sample distributions of his estimators, although in the case treated by Zellner those *exact* distributions are readily derived and, indeed, already known before he conducted his Monte Carlo experiment; for details see the paper by Rohr, 1966. No trained statistician would construct classical confidence intervals as Zellner does. Sympathetic with the scientific objectives of research undertaken by Zellner and others, still I cannot approve of such devices for gaining consensus as were used by Zellner. (In this connection see the remarks of Roberts, 1966, p. 26, at top of left column.)

[20]In this connection, however, recall the difficulty of proving that a set is *finite* from its defining characteristic; cf. note 11. The principles laid down by Jeffreys rule out definition of "probability" in terms of infinite sets of possible observations; cf. Jeffreys, 1961, p. 11, rule (3).

[21]See Jeffreys, 1961, pp. 373 ff. for a discussion of this notion.

[22]However, see Jeffreys, 1961, p. 34, p. 368, and p. 401.

[23]From Jeffreys' axioms we can deduce

$$P(q/p) \leq P(r/p)$$

with help of the logical theorem

$$\vdash: q \supset r: \supset: qVr.\sim q. \equiv .r,$$

cf. Jeffreys, 1961, p. 22.

[24]See Jeffreys, 1961, p. 28.

[25]Of course, a different form of prior density function might have been chosen, thus affecting the result in this illustration.

[26]See Jeffreys, 1961, p. 28.

[27]See the article by H. Wold, 1960, esp. p. 4, p. 9, and p. 23. Wold reports "promising forecast performance from a recently constructed PCC-(pure causal chain) system with 85 relations" owned by the Econometric Institute, Inc., of New York, a commercial firm selling economic forecasts for profit. Wold, as consultant to Econometric Institute, Inc., was in a position to give a brief and informative account of the forecasting performance of this model (without details, of course) to a small group of economists at General Electric (TEMPO) composed of H. Asher, E. J. Mosbaek, Arnold Zellner, and myself in June, 1960. See also the article by Basmann, 1965b, pp. 1090-1091.

Because of the very great practical interest that would attach to a forecasting comparison between the Brookings Model and the Econometric Institute Model mentioned by Wold, I hope the latter model will soon cease to be a commercial secret, as the Econometric Institute, Inc., now seems to be defunct.

[28]I.e., there is a positive real number M such that

$$|z_{t,k}| < M$$

for every $k=1,2, ..., K$ and every t.

[29]See Birnbaum, 1962, Chapter 17, esp. pp. 289-291. Also see the following articles: Basmann, 1965b, esp. pp. 1082-1083; Basmann, 1965c, pp. 394-399.

[30]I.e., $|B^*| \neq 0$, where $|B^*|$ is the determinant of matrix B^*.

[31]The *explicit dynamical form* of the representation (3.1) is a system of G ordinary linear difference equations with constant coefficients (Allen, 1956, pp. 192-194)

$$y_{t+q,1} - p_1 y_{t+q-1,1} + p_2 y_{t+q-2,1} - ... (-)^q p_q y_t$$

$$= q_1(\{z_{t+q-n}\}) + h_1(\{\eta_{t+n-n}\})$$

for $i=1,2, ..., G$, where $\{z_{t+q-n}\}$ denotes the sequence of all past exogenous vectors and $\{\eta_{t+q-n}\}$ denotes the sequence of all past vectors of random disturbances. g_1 and h_1 are linear functionals of the respective sequences. The constants $p_1, ..., p_q$ are common to all G equations and are functions of the structural constants $B^*, B^*_1, ..., B^*_r$; the constants appearing in g_1 and h_1 are functions of $B^*, B^*_1, ..., B^*_r$, and Γ^*.

The **explicit dynamical form** of (3.1) is equivalent to (3.1), i.e., **expresses the same** hypothesis about economic structure.

The explicit dynamical form, hence also (3.1) expresses the hypothesis that the economic system is structurally dynamically stable if, and only if, from the maintained structural hypothesis the following can be deduced: *For every root* λ_j, $j=1,2, ..., q$, *of the auxiliary polynomial*

$$\lambda^q - p_1 \lambda^{q-1} + p_2 \lambda^{q-2} - ... (-)^q p_q = 0,$$

the modulus is less than unity, i.e., $|\lambda_j| < 1$, $j=1,2, ... , q$. Necessary and sufficient conditions (on the constants $p_1, ..., p_q$) have been discussed extensively by mathematicians and mathematical economists, e.g., Samuelson, 1948, pp. 429-439.

[32]I.e., $\sum\limits_{n=0}^{\infty} A^*_n{}'$ is a real matrix each element of which is an absolutely convergent real series.

[33]See Wold, 1953, esp. pp. 162-164. We illustrate the role of the stability restrictions on B by the following example: Consider a simple case in which A_n and u_{t-n} are real:

$$w_t = \sum\limits_{n=0}^{\infty} A_n u_{t-n}$$

satisfies an ordinary linear difference equation (say)

$$w_{t+3} - p_1 w_{t+2} + p_2 w_{t+1} - p_3 w_t = 0,$$

where p_1, p_2, p_3 are real valued function of structural constants. The sequence $\{A_n\}$ satisfies

$$A_{n+3} - p_1 A_{n+2} + p_2 A_{n+1} - p_3 A_n = 0$$

for $n = 0, 1, 2, \ldots$, with

$$A_0 = 1, \quad A_1 = p_1, \quad A_2 = p_1^2 - p_2.$$

Hence the A_n are functions of structural parameters. Formally, the variance of the random disturbance in the dynamical equilibrium path of w_t is

$$E(w_t^2) = \sigma^2 \sum_{n=0}^{\infty} A_n^2$$

$$= \frac{\sigma^2 (1 + p_2 - p_1 p_3 - p_3^2)}{[(1+p_2)^2 - (p_1 + p_3)^2](1 - p_2 + p_1 p_3 - p_3^2)},$$

if $\{u_t\}$ is a purely random process, (Wold, 1953, p. 159), i.e., if $E(u_t u_{t \pm \theta}) = 0$ for all $t, \theta, \theta \neq 0$. σ^2 is the variance of u_t. The foregoing formula is valid only if the series

$$\sum_{n=0}^{\infty} A_n$$

is absolutely convergent, i.e., only if the structural constants satisfy dynamic stability conditions, which are

$$1 - p_1 + p_2 - p_3 > 0$$

$$1 + p_1 + p_2 + p_3 > 0$$

$$3 - p_1 - p_2 + 3p_3 > 0$$

$$3 + p_1 - p_2 - 3p_3 > 0$$

$$1 - p_2 + p_1 p_3 - p_3^2 > 0$$

can be deduced from hypothetical restrictions on structural parameters; cf. Samuelson, 1948, pp. 432-433. Serial covariances can be worked out with help of the foregoing expression by the procedure indicated by Wold, 1953, p. 163, equations (13a-b).

This example illustrates the kind of purely deductive analysis that occurs in connection with simultaneous equations representations of structural economic hypotheses.

[34]"Considering all the lagged (endogenous) variables we would have had more predetermined variables to use for each first-stage regression than there were degrees of freedom available." (*Report*, p. 736.)

[35]Cf. Aitken, 1949, p. 73, p. 89.

[36]Cf. Aitken, 1949, pp. 140-141, Ex. 32.

[37]Let $\lambda_m = 0$, $m = N+1, \ldots, Gr+K$, and let $\bar{x}_{\cdot m}$ correspond to λ_m. Since $\bar{x}_{\cdot m}$ is real and

$$\bar{x}'_{\cdot m} \bar{x}_{\cdot m} = \lambda_m = 0,$$

$$\bar{x}_{\cdot m} = 0 \text{ for } m = N+1, \ldots, Gr+K.$$

[38]λ_m and hence $v_{\cdot m}$ are random variables and differ from sample to sample.

[39]In some simple cases it has been shown that consistence of least-squares estimators of constant coefficients in ordinary linear difference equations is achieved even if the equation is dynamically unstable.

Such cases do not include the present, namely, the Brookings Model. If the *Brookings* econometricians wish to include in their maintained hypothesis B the possibility that the underlying structure is dynamically unstable, then they are required to show that consistence of two-stage least squares and limited information estimators is possible for the Brookings Model, since they do claim those estimators to be consistent.

[40]Those proffered laws are models of the *axioms of quantity and magnitude* (listed in this section). To be sure, those axioms are often assumed implicitly in the work by *mathematical*

economists, but solely as *axioms* in the modern sense of the word (cf. Blanché, 1962, esp. pp. 9-11), not as self-evident empirical truths. For the quantitative economist, and for the econometrician as well, the discovery of concrete realizations of the axioms of quantity is a sine qua non of their disciplines.

[41]In this article three different kinds of variable properties are distinguished:
(1) classificatory;
(2) orderable;
(3) quantities.

Many social scientists object to this nomenclature as too narrow, and seek to establish a usage in which orderable variable properties (2) are called "quantities" and the numbers used to represent them "measurements"; cf. Stevens, 1946, pp. 141-142. In principle there is no objection that can be raised to this broader usage as long as the logical and empirical distinction between concepts (2) and (3) is remembered in practice. As it is precisely that distinction that is at issue here, I am employing the narrower terminology.

[42]Italics are mine, R. L. B.

[43]Even in the physical sciences only a very few properties are *fundamental quantities*, e.g., weight, length, but not time. In addition to fundamental quantities there is a modest number of *derived quantities*, which are defined by empirical relations between fundamental quantities. (See Nagel, 1930, p. 128, pp. 135-140; Pap, 1962, pp. 1313-135.)

[44]See the book by Snedecor, 1946, pp. 164-167; see also the book by Walker and Lev, 1953, pp. 278-287.

[45]The symbols denote numerical time series as follows:

C^{54}_{DA}:   personal consumption expenditures for new and net used automobiles and parts, billions of constant 1954 dollars.

Y^{54}_D: personal disposable income, billions of constant 1954 dollars.

P_{CDA}:   implicit price deflator for personal consumption expenditures on new and net used automobiles and parts, 1954 = 1.00.

P_C: implicit price deflator for personal consumption expenditures, 1954 = 1.00.

ATT: index of consumer attitudes and inclinations to buy, 1954 = 100.

See *Report*, pp. 683-685.

Presumably the numbers shown in parentheses directly below coefficient estimates are estimates of sampling standard deviations of estimates.

[46]In the future someone might discover a way of defining "inclination to buy cars" so that this new property is a quantity.

[47]The symbols V^{54} and $^{54}INS_{GF}$ denote numerical time series as follows:

V^{54}:   transfer payments to persons, billions of 1954 dollars.

$V^{54}INS_{GF}$:   servicemen's insurance dividend component of transfer payments to persons, billions of 1954 dollars.

CARS: end-of-quarter stock of new cars and new car equivalents of used cars, millions.

See *Report*, pp. 209-210.

[48]Apparently one of the (psychologically) most difficult things to understand is that it is possible, even in principle, for national income statistics like the time series denoted by Y^{54}_D (personal disposable income in billions of 1954 dollars) to fail to represent a *quantity*. It is probably the case that the time series (say) Y^{54}_D has become conflated in thought with the supposed *quantity* "personal disposable income" it is supposed to represent.

[49]If C^{54}_{DA} does not represent a quantity but only an orderable property, then by changing the time series C^{54}_{DA} with help of an order-preserving transformation we can at will make the partial R^2 take on any arbitrary value in the interval (0,1).

[50]The estimate Var (u) = 1280.8 has not been corrected for loss of degrees of freedom. Numbers in parenthese are estimates of standard deviations of coefficient estimates.

[51]Edward Greenberg, in his comment on the first draft of this article, supplies an omission of mine. "Dummy variables" may validly be used to represent temporary changes in parameters. As dummy variables do not represent variable properties, my remarks about orderability do not apply to them.

[52]My attention has been attracted to presence of the time-series ATT (inclination to buy) in the Brookings Model largely because in one of my own articles there appears a time series purporting to represent a *quantity* called "private investor confidence" (Basmann, 1965c, p. 396, pp. 413-414). Since I offered there no empirical support for the assertion that private investor confidence is a *quantity*, I am—perhaps—vulnerable to a riposte of the *tu quoque* form, which, however, would not tend to secure the quantitative foundations of the Brookings Model at all. Still I hope some econometrician will deliver the *tu quoque* retort as it provides an opportunity to debate important differences between the "philosophy of econometrics" as expressed by Duesenberry and Klein, on the one hand, and the more modern philosophy of

economic science to which I adhere. (In this connection see the article, Basmann, 1965c, esp. p. 414.)

I take the liberty of mentioning that even if the supposed quantity "private investor confidence" is eliminated from the representation in my article the quantitative foundations remain defective, as the status of gross national product, gross investment, and "quantity of money" as *quantities* remains unsupported and doubtful (Basmann, 1965c, pp. 411-412).

[53]For example, see Hicks, 1946, Chapter 1. Some experimental evidence has tended to disconfirm the hypothesis that *utility*—as defined by the simple operation of choice—is an *orderable property;* e.g., see the articles by May, 1954; Luce, 1956; Georgescu-Roegen, 1958.

It is appropriate to recall that von Neumann and Morgenstern (1953, Chapter 3; see esp. pp. 23-27) point out the possibility of discovering natural operations in addition to the operation of choice which, together with the latter, might determine "utility" as a *derived quantity.* This proposed operation involves the combination of two utilities with two given alternatives probabilities (it being taken for granted that an operation defining probability as a *quantity* is available). Of course, von Neumann and Morgenstern do not claim that their axioms of quantitative utility (von Neumann and Morgenstern, 1953, pp. 26-27) have been confirmed by empirical observation.

[54]The empirical operation $\bigoplus$, when found, defines—for fundamental quantities—the relations $\alpha > \beta$ and $\alpha \sim \beta$ directly.

For example, where weight is the variable property in question, the relations $\alpha \sim \beta$ and $\alpha > \beta$ are defined with help of a pendulum balance and its pointer; the operation $\bigoplus$ is the process of placing two objects in the same pan of the balance, viz., $\alpha \bigoplus \beta$ is an object formed by objects α and β placed on the same pan of the balance. An excellent account is found in the book by Campbell, 1957, pp. 279 ff.

[55]The product of a natural number n and a magnitude a (a is not a number) is defined by the equations

$$\left\{ \begin{array}{l} 1a = a, \\ (n+1)a = na \bigoplus a; \end{array} \right.$$

cf. Hölder, 1901, p. 8.

[56]In fact, *Axiom VII* above is deduced as a theorem in Hölder's first formulation (Hölder, 1901, p. 7 and pp. 10-13).

Every quantity is orderable. Let Q be a quantity and let a,b,c, ... be magnitudes of Q; if a > b and b > c, than a > c. Assume a > b and b > c. There is a magnitude x such that

$$b \bigoplus x = a$$

and there is a magnitude y such that

$$c \bigoplus y = b;$$

by *Axiom V.* By making substitutions, we obtain

$$(c \bigoplus y) \bigoplus x = a;$$

then

$$c \bigoplus (y \bigoplus x) = a,$$

by *Axiom VI,* Hence a > c by *Axiom IV.*

[57]Nagel's formulation of axioms is easier than Hölder's to test empirically. The first six axioms involve identity and ordering relations only; for instance, the theorem proved in Note 56, namely, "if a > b and b > c, than a > c" is one of Nagel's axioms. The remaining six axioms involve the operation $\bigoplus$. Some theorems that are derivable from Hölder's axioms appear as axioms in Nagel's formulation, e.g., the commutative law

$$b \bigoplus a = a \bigoplus b.$$

[58]The number of objects contained by the sample S_1 must be sufficiently large that the set of axioms I-VII, taken as an hypothesis, has a determinate degree of confirmation. Recall Section 2.

[59]In this connection see the essay "On What There Is" by Quine, 1963, pp. 1-19.

[60]Some excellent advice for prophets and intellectual leaders is found in Liddell Hart, 1954, p. 19.

REFERENCES

1. Aitken, A. C. *Determinants and Matrices.* Edinburgh: Oliver and Boyd, 1949.
2. Allen, R. G. D. *Mathematical Analysis.* New York: St. Martin's Press, 1956.
3. Barnes, H. E. *An Intellectual and Cultural History of the Western World.* 3rd Revised Edition, Vol. 1. New York: Dover Publications, Inc., 1965.
4. Basmann, R. L. "The Role of the Economic Historian in the Predictive Testing of Proffered 'Economic Laws,' " *Explorations in Entrepreneurial History, Second Series,* Vol. 2, 159-186, 1965a.
5. "A Note on the Statistical Testability of 'Explicit Causal Chains' Against the Class of 'Interdependent' Models," *Journal of the American Statistical Association,* Vol. 60, 1080-1093, 1965b.
6. "On the Application of the Identifiability Test Statistic in Predictive Testing of Explanatory Economic Models," *Indian Economic Journal,* Vol. XIII, 387-423, 1965c.
7. Bergmann, G. and K. W. Spence. "The Logic of Psychophysical Measurement." Reprinted in Feigl and Brodbeck, 1953, 103-119.
8. Birnbaum, Z. W. *An Introduction to Probability and Mathematical Statistics.* New York: Harper and Brothers, 1962.
9. Blanché, R. *Axiomatics.* New York: Dover Publications, 1962. Translated by G. B. Keene.
10. Bronowski, J. *Science and Human Values.* New York: Harper and Brothers, 1959.
11. Campbell, N. R. *Foundations of Science.* New York: Dover Publications, 1957.
12. Carnap, R. *Logical Foundations of Probability.* Chicago: University of Chicago Press. (Second Edition, 1962).
13. Churchman, C. W. and P. Ratoash, editors. *Measurement: Definitions and Theories.* New York: John Wiley and Sons, Inc., 1959.
14. Cohen, M. R. and E. Nagel, "The Nature of a Logical or Mathematical System." Reprinted in Feigl and Brodbeck, 1953, 129-147.
15. Danto, A. and S. Morgenbesser. *Philosophy of Science.* New York: Meridian Books, Inc., 1960.
16. Faris, J. A. *Quantification Theory.* New York: Dover Publications, Inc., 1964.
17. Feigl, H. and M. Brodbeck. *Readings in the Philosophy of Science.* New York: Appleton-Century-Crofts, Inc., 1953.
18. Frisch, R. "Linear Expenditure Functions," *Econometrica,* Vol. 22, pp. 505-510.
19. Georgescu-Roegen, N. "Threshold in Choice and the Theory of Demand," *Econometrica,* 26 (1958), 157-168.
20. Halberstadt, W. *An Introduction to Modern Logic.* New York: Harper and Brothers, 1960.
21. Hempel, C. G. and P. Oppenheim, "The Logic of Explanation." Reprinted in Feigl and Brodbeck, 1953, 319-352.
22. Hicks, J. R. *Value and Capital,* 2nd Edition, Oxford: Oxford University Press, 1946.
23. Hölder, O. "Die Axiome der Quantität und die Lehre vom Mass," *Leipzig: Berichte, Königl. Sachsischen Gesellschaft,* Bd. 53, 1901, 1-64.
24. Jeffreys, H. *Theory of Probability,* 3rd Ed., Oxford: Oxford University Press, 1961.
25. Katona, George and Eva Mueller. *Consumer Expectations 1953-1956,* Ann Arbor: Survey Research Center, Institute for Social Research, University of Michigan, 1957.
26. Kolmogorov, A. N. *Foundations of Probability,* New York: Chelsea Publishing Co., 1951.
27. Kuhn, T. "The Function of Measurement in Modern Physical Science," *Isis,* 52 (1961), 161-193.
28. Liddell Hart, B. H. *Strategy,* Revised Edition, New York: Frederick A. Praeger, 1954.
29. Luce, R D. "Semi-orders and a Theory of Utility Discrimination," *Econometrica,* 24 (1956), 178-191.
30. May, K. O. "Intransitivity, Utility and the Aggregation of Preference Patterns," *Econometrica,* 22 (1954), 1-13.
31. Menger, K. "Mensuration and other Mathematical Connections of Observable Material," in Churchman and West, Chapter 5, 1959.
32. Nagel, E. "Measurement." Reprinted in Danto and Morgenbesser, 1960, 121-140.
33. ————. *The Structure of Science.* New York: Harcourt, Brace and World, Inc., 1961.
34. Pap, A. *An Introduction to the Philosophy of Science.* New York: The Free Press of Glencoe, 1962.
35. Popper, K. R. *The Logic of Scientific Discovery.* New York: Basic Books, Inc., 1959.
36. Quine, W. V. O. *Mathematical Logic.* New York: Harper and Row, 1962.
37. ————. *From a Logical Point of View.* Second Edition, New York: Harper and Row, 1963.

38. Rohr, R. J. "Bayesian *vs* Classical Inference: A Comment on a Monte Carlo Experiment," *Institute for Research in the Behavioral, Economic and Management Sciences.* Unpublished manuscript.
39. Roberts, H. V. "Statistical Dogma: One Response to a Challenge," *American Statistician,* Vol. 20, No. 4 (1966), 25-27.
40. Russell, B. *An Inquiry into Meaning and Truth.* Baltimore: Penguin Books, 1962.
41. Samuelson, Paul A. *Foundation of Economic Analysis.* Cambridge: Harvard University Press, 1948.
42. Sarton, G. *Introduction to the History of Science.* Vol. 1, Washington: Carnegie Institution of Washington, 1927.
43. —————. *A History of Science, Ancient Science Through the Golden Age of Greece.* Cambridge: Harvard University Press, 1952.
44. Snedecor, G. W. *Statistical Methods,* 4th Edition. Ames: Iowa State College Press, 1946.
45. Stevens, S. S. "On the Theory of Scales of Measurement." Reprinted in Danto and Morgenbesser, 1960, 141-149.
46. Strotz, R. H. and H. O. A. Wold. "Recursive *vs* Nonrecursive Systems: An Attempt at Synthesis," *Econometrica,* 28 (1960), 417-427.
47. Suppes, P. "A Set of Independent Axioms for Extensive Quantities," *Portugaliae Mathematica,* 10 (1951), 163-172.
48. Taton, R. *Ancient and Medieval Science.* New York: Basic Books, Inc., 1963.
49. Tintner, Gerhard. *Econometrics.* New York: John Wiley and Sons, 1952.
50. Von Neumann, John and Oskar Morgenstern. *Theory of Games and Economic Behavior,* Princeton: Princeton University Press, 1953.
51. Walker, H. M. and J. Lev. *Statistical Inference.* New York: Holt, Rinehart and Winston, 1953.
52. Wold, H. *Demand Analysis.* New York: John Wiley and Sons, 1953.
53. Wold, H. O. A. "Construction Principles of Simultaneous Equations Models in Econometrics," *L'Institut International de Statistique,* 32 Session, Tokyo, 1960.
54. Zellner, A. "Bayesian Inference and Simultaneous Equations Models," (multilithed) University of Chicago, Chicago, Illinois, 1965.

THE BROOKINGS ECONOMETRIC MODEL:
A RATIONAL PERSPECTIVE*

Gary Fromm
Brookings Institution

Lawrence R. Klein
University of Pennsylvania

That as renowned a scholar as Robert Basmann should review the first volume on the Brookings model and consider it the
exemplar of research in econometrics is gratifying.[1] Further, to feel
that the volume will set the standard for and exert a profound influence on the development of econometrics and its teaching in
graduate schools for decades to come is high praise indeed.

However, having expressed these laudatory sentiments in his
opening paragraph, Basmann goes on to launch an extremely critical attack on econometrics in general, and on the Brookings model
in particular. But, then, that isn't too surprising. Basmann states
early in the game that he is not an econometrician; after reading
his paper we are sure of it. Unfortunately, Basmann's critique is
centered entirely on Volume I as though it could be isolated from
the rest of an ongoing project. Associated working papers, research
studies, manuscripts for Volume II, and similar materials are readily available to him and other interested scholars. The content of
these other materials is pertinent to much of his criticism.

Aside from some specific points which largely stem from an
incomplete reading and a misinterpretation and overemphasis of

*This paper, essentially in its present form, was first presented as a reply to Mr. Bas-
mann at the 1966 meetings of the Southern Economic Association. Basmann revised his SEA
paper for the May 1967 Ohio State conference on econometrics. Following the conference, Basmann revised his paper again; we did not.

certain statements in the volume, his critique is addressed mainly to the philosophy of statistical inference and its usefulness in ascertaining structural or behavioral relationships. As such, this is a criticism of all metrics (especially those of the nonphysical sciences), and not solely of the Brookings model. But, let us leave that aside for the moment and cover the specifics.

First, the minor point (which, to Basmann, seemingly, is a major issue) of the model as a consensus. To cast this in perspective, a brief history of the project may be fruitful. The model is a direct outgrowth of a 1959 SSRC conference on stability and instability in the U.S. enonomy. At that conference, held in Ann Arbor, several papers (at least one of which is now regarded as a classic) were presented. After hearing the papers, and after several days of discussion, the conferees decided that really very little was known about the structure of the economy, its responsiveness to shocks, its inherent stability, its reaction to government policy changes, and many other questions relating to the functioning of the economy as a system. It was, of course, recognized that a host of classical, neoclassical, and Keynesian theoretical structures of parts of entire systems were available. But many contained unrealistic assumptions and most had never been empirically verified.

In fact, the empirical work that had been done, including that presented at the conference, left much to be desired. There were problems of misspecification, of inappropriate estimation techniques, of unreasonable complete system response, and other faults. Generally, the profession could tell its students, or others whom it advised in government or business, less than desired in a quantitative way (excepting an input-output table or concentration ratios) about the structure of the economy or its potential conditional reaction to any exogenous or endogenous shift.[2] In response to this situation, the conferees recommended that the SSRC sponsor a significant effort to help fill the void. Furthermore, it was suggested that in order to compress the time required to obtain the results, in order to make them more accurate than would otherwise be true, and in order to make them more meaningful and useful to the profession as a whole, that a large number of experts, specialists, and leading econometricians participate in the venture.

Now as to consensus, the aim was not to force a compromise agreement on a specific model structure and parameters on the participants or on the profession. The aim was, and is, to achieve general acceptance of a framework for a model system as a whole and of some of its major parts, without necessarily having agreement on the details among all economists.[3] We do not believe that having built an initial model by the efforts of many leading experts implies such acceptance. The participants did spend many weeks together discussing the outlines of a model and the hypotheses underlying much of its structure, resolving a large number of issues. What agreement has been reached has merely been in those terms. However, acceptance of a model by them, or by any of us, must await explorations of its completed system properties, evaluations of sector specifications, and many other tests.

Moreover, this involves an evolutionary process and not the examination of a particular version. To quote Chapter 18:[4]

> It is evident that we do not view the present model as a finished product. Truly, although significant advances have been achieved, we have only completed the preliminary phases of constructing a large-scale quarterly model of the economy that accurately reflects its true structure and is useful for forecasting purposes, for the evaluation of government policy alternatives, and for the examination of cycle and growth theories. Our continuing efforts are dedicated toward achieving that goal.

All members of the profession are invited to participate in that effort.

Which brings us to the second point. Basmann, throughout his paper, refers to the Brookings Model and equates this to Chapter 18, which is entitled "The Complete Model: A First Approximation." To begin with, as should already be clear, there is no *the* Brookings model. The model is an evolving composite. Chapter 18 contains a set of consistent (statistical) estimates of the individual sector results given in earlier chapters by specialists. In a *few* cases, specifications were altered slightly in order to achieve compatibility in the definition of variables or to increase the endogeneity of the system. Also, where variables "did not appear to give sensible statistical results" they were deleted; sometimes others were substituted. Now we could have presented all the estimates and we could have added 50 pages (to the 767 that most will already find too long) of elaborate explanations of the changes and their justification. Perhaps we should have done so. But, the important thing to us was not the exact specifications or the parameter values, but the spirit of what was to be accomplishd.[5] It was anticipated (cf. p. vii) that before the model could be solved as a complete system that, due to data incompatibilities, many of the equations would have to be reestimated; in the process, some specifications were likely to change because of the superior explanatory power of alternative versions.

As to the precise number of equations in the model, another point which concerns Basmann, the reason why no exact count can be given stems from two sources. First, in almost any system of equations of moderate size, it is possible to include or exclude convenient definitional identities. For example, either GNP can be entered as an explicit variable or it can appear implicitly as the sum of expenditure or income components. Of course, in the reduced form of the system it(or another component) would be eliminated. But, secondly, even in the reduced form the size of the system is not fixed as long as there are alternative versions of different order of segments of the system. For example, either business investment can be explained directly or it can be explained via the route of realizations on investment anticipations. In fact, this modular feature is one of the unique aspects of the Brookings model. For several sectors, either very elaborate, extensive versions or alternative condensed versions can be used in the complete system. For example, there is a 6–equation financial sector and one of 30 equations. Both yield the outputs required by the nonfinancial part of the model (interest rates and demand and time deposits). However, the more detailed version determines these by explicitly considering reactions internal to the financial sector, while the condensed version does so implicitly. Finally, in the realm of the size of the system, it is always possible to delete endogenous relationships and treat the variables exogenously. Where such variables only weakly interact with other parts of the model, little impact will be felt either in the selection of predetermined variables or the magnitude of parameter estimates. Net interest income in manufacturing may be taken as an example. Furthermore, variables that are poorly explained in individual chapters and are expressed as simple trends or pure autoregressions could just as well be reclassified as exogenous.

On another specific point, the question of initial conditions, it should be noted that the model contains many variables that reflect disequilibrium situations, both as regards artificial constraints (such as on supply) and stochastic perturbations. Furthermore, it has also been estimated over several alternative periods and covariance tests performed to determine whether parameters changed significantly where the sample space was shifted.[6]

As to Basmann's discussion of specification, estimation, and degrees of freedom in making statistical inferences about the Brookings model, it should be noted that his critique is formulated in the context of a linear model—one that is linear both in parameters and variables. While it is true that each equation considered in isolation can, with approximate transformations, be expressed linearly in parameters and variables, the complete system is far from linear. We have no explicit reduced form equations (in closed mathematical form) and must resort to nonlinear numerical methods for analysis of the system. This is an important characteristic and makes it awkward or infeasible to do some of the things that Basmann desires.

Although the system is not linear in the variables, we have used linear estimation methods in applying single-equation techniques such as LIML or TSLS because it is well-known that consistency properties are preserved for incomplete systems. We follow, in this respect, the arguments of Chernoff and Rubin on estimation under generalized conditions.[7]

First let us consider the question of degrees of freedom in the estimation of Basmann's equation (3.1), acting as though our system is completely linear.

$$\sum_{i=0}^{r} B_i Y_{t-i} + \Gamma Z_t = U_t$$

We shall assume that the errors are normally distributed with zero means and covariance matrix Ω. B_0 is square and nonsingular $(G \times G)$; Y_{t-i} has G elements for each time period; Γ is rectangular $(G \times K)$; and Z_t has K elements for each time period. Let N represent the number of data (time) points. Depending on the method of estimation used, there are various critical values of N in order to have adequate degrees of freedom. For FIML or other full-information estimates that treat all equations simultaneously in estimation, we must have $N \geqslant G$. This is so, since the estimates of Ω will be determined from the sample covariance matrix of residuals.

$$\text{est. } \Omega = \left\| \sum_{t=1}^{N} \hat{U}_{it} \hat{U}_{jt} \right\|,$$

where $\hat{U}_{it}$ is the residual estimated from the i-th equation in the system, and if $N < G$, $|\text{est. } \Omega| = 0$.

In the usual algorithms, for computing FIML estimates, we proceed iteratively from one successive approximation to another. At the p-th stage of the iterative process,

$$\left\| \sum_{t-1}^{N} \hat{U}_{it}^{(p)} \hat{U}_{jt}^{(p)} \right\|,$$

must be inverted and this matrix is singular if $N < G$.

This problem was faced in connection with A. L. Nagar's stochastic simulation of the Brookings model, when we desired to draw random numbers with a given value of Ω based on sample estimates.[8] The block treatment of the model used by Nagar for simulation corresponds closely to the block treatment that would have to be used for estimation if FIML methods were to be applied. We have refrained from using such methods in estimating the Brookings model for this reason and because such estimates are highly sensitive to specification errors. However, we have estimated small models with as many as 15 simultaneous equations by FIML methods, and if we could use F. Fisher's approach of block recursive structuring of the whole system, we could use FIML methods for each of several small blocks, containing no more than 20 equations in each block.

Consider next the inequality

$$GN \leqslant G^2(r+1) + GK - R$$

The quantity $G^2(r+1) + GK$ gives the number of parameters of predetermined variables in the entire system. We subtract R where R is the number of parameter restrictions imposed including normalization rules. The right hand side, therefore, shows the number of parameters to be estimated from the sample. If this number exceeds GN, we can fix

$$G^2(r+1) + GK - R - GN$$

parameters at arbitrary values and solve for the remaining GN from the GN equations

$$\sum_{i=0}^{r} B_i Y_{1-i} + \Gamma Z_1 = 0$$

$$\sum_{i=0}^{r} B_i Y_{2-i} + \Gamma Z_2 = 0$$

$$\sum_{i=0}^{r} B_i Y_{N-i} + TZ_N = 0.$$

This gives an infinite set of parameter estimates (since some are chosen arbitrarily) that produce zero residuals for all equations at all data points. Thus, est. $\Omega = 0$.

Basmann uses this well-known argument with the inequality, $N \leqslant Gr + K$. In this situation, we could choose *reduced form* parameters so as to make *reduced form* residuals all zero. He claims that this would make est. $\Omega = 0$. But this is not necessarily true because Ω is the covariance matrix of disturbances in the *structural* equations, and may be estimated by a variety of methods other than transformation of the reduced form covariance matrix.

In the case of the Brookings model, we are confronted with the inequality, $N < G$. There are fewer data points than equations. This does not mean that we cannot estimate the whole system, but it does mean that we cannot apply FIML methods in their most general form. The second inequality does not prevail; i.e., there are not more parameters to be estimated than GN. *We cannot form a "perfect fit" of the whole model*, by simple or obvious methods, to the 70-odd quarterly observations of the postwar period.

Finally, let us consider Basmann's inequality, $N \leqslant Gr + K$. Presumably, what he has in mind in his discussion of this inequality is that the *unrestricted reduced forms* of the system cannot be estimated (except with zero residuals) unless the number of data points exceeds the number of predetermined variables. In the Brookings model, there is an excess of predetermined variables over the number of time points in the sample. We recognized this from the beginning and took explicit steps to get round this difficulty.

We considered two initial approaches for meeting this difficulty.[9] On the one hand we could choose instrumental variables on the basis of the block recursive structure of the system, according to the rules suggested by F. Fisher in his chapter.[10] We did this, and stated quite explicitly which instruments were chosen in each case.[11] It is difficult to grasp the significance of Basmann's complaint in this connection. The Fisher approach is one among many that rest on the ideas of treatment of incomplete systems.

On the other hand, we could choose instrumental variables by some more mechanical data reduction method such as principal components. We considered this approach at the time we were making estimates but did not have our computer programs sufficiently well developed to accommodate it efficiently. We now have excellent programs for TSLS and LIML estimation based on principal components of predetermined variables and will use them in the present phase of reestimation of the whole model. These programs have already been employed to good advantage with systems that are somewhat smaller than the Brookings model.

Either method—the Fisher method or the use of principal components of predetermined variables—is basically one of data reduction. They prescribe that if $N < Gr + K$, choose some subsets or groupings of the predetermined variables into instruments, I, such that $N > I$.

We think that the alternative suggestions of Basmann are peculiar. He would use a parameter reduction instead of a data reduction method. He suggests if $N < Gr + K$, "*inventing* hypothetical functional dependences" (i.e., restrictions) among the parameters

(p. 21). Surely, restrictions should be based on a priori economic knowledge and not upon the relationship between N and the number of predetermined variables. Because they influence the interpretation of results and the stability of the system, restrictions are not to be taken lightly. The number of restrictions should not be expanded or contracted, depending on the sample of data at hand. Economic theory, knowledge of institutions, and similar bodies of information unrelated to sample observation should form the basis of parameter restrictions. The principles of a priori specification that give us identification (or lack of it) should remain invariant under changes in sample size.

Basmann implies that the greater the number of complex dependencies in a model, the more realistic and valid are its estimates and its explanation of structure (of the phenomena it supposedly represents). This need not be true. Certainly if restrictions apply in the real world but are largely conjectural (invented) in the formulation of a model, then the model should first be estimated in unrestricted form and the results contrasted to the theoretical a priori restrictions. If the results satisfy the restrictions, a case might be made for their existence. If they do not and yet applying the restrictions yields statistically significant results, then an explanation must be given as to why the unrestricted results are not identical. Just as bigger is not necessarily better in a model, neither do more restrictions necessarily imply greater validity.

Basmann also remarks (p. 22) that $N \leqslant Gr + K$ for "many" reduced-form equations in the Brookings model. Since $Gr + K$ is a value that refers to the whole system of equations, we find it puzzling that he says the inequality holds for *many* reduced-form equations of the Brookings model and not for all. If Basmann is using the block recursive structure and reducing the number of predetermined variables to instruments, as we, in part, did, then we have adequate degrees of freedom for all equations in the sense that no reduced-form expression contains more instruments than data points. This part of Basmann's exposition is quite unclear as is the remark (p. 26) that statistical estimates of the reduced forms of the Brookings model are not revealed. Although we have been discussing the problem of degrees of freedom from the viewpoint of linear systems, the Brookings model is obviously not linear. We have used the Chernoff-Rubin suggestions for this kind of system to obtain some reduced-form expressions that are useful in estimation, but these reduced forms are not the ones that would be obtained by solving the *estimated* system for values of Y_t given values for Y_{t-i} and Z_t.

We have obtained such solutions in many cases and presented them in a number of research papers before meetings of the Econometric Society and similar bodies. These will be published in due course but involved many months of work to prepare after the first volume on the model was completed. Linear approximations, at a particular point in the space of Y_{t-i} and Z_t, can be obtained for the whole system and statistical estimates of the reduced-form equations can be calculated. But, because of the nonlinear nature of the system, these would change from point to point and seem to be less useful than the wide variety of numerical solutions that we have obtained by nonlinear methods and presented to a wide audience. In A. L. Nagar's paper, there is a complete solution over the sample period for endogenous variables from both stochastic and nonstochastic versions of the estimated model. All these calculations involve substantial effort. As the years go by, we shall present more and more of them, hopefully meeting some of Basmann's requirements as we progress.

Now let us consider the general issue raised by Basmann. Are the time-series observations on the variables in the model orderable, are they quantities? Certainly, except in a very restricted sense, the observed numbers are quantities. For example, personal consumption expenditures involve an exchange of money for goods (we are sure even Basmann can count the dollars in his monthly paycheck and the slices of bread he buys and eats). Literary economics hypothesizes that there is a utility associated with the possession of money (which is a proxy for command over resources) and the consumption of goods. Moreover, it says that the consumer selects states in this utility space so as to maximize his welfare, i.e., utility. Supposedly, the states are at least orderable (the concept of ordinal utility) if not measureable (cardinal utility). But, since utility is not directly observable, this is conjecture. What can be observed are market transactions of goods and money. If there is a strong functional dependency between utility and these transactions, and if utility is orderable or quantifiable, then it should be possible to relate the consumption of goods to the expenditure of income or assets. But, suppose that either of these two assumptions (functional dependency and orderability or quantifiability) does not hold. Then, it would be surprising to find a relationship that fits with any degree of precision.

Obviously, especially where variables are only orderable (as Basmann's recitation of well-known principles illustrates), care must be taken not to be misled by high degrees of goodness of fit.[12] The ultimate, underlying structure of the observed phenomena may still be well hidden, if not falsified. However, if one has begun with a reasoned a priori theory of the phenomena to be explained, then it is not untoward to presume that some structural knowledge might have been furthered, if not acquired.

It is unnecessary here to argue about the nature of science and the discovery of truth. We need merely observe that knowledge is cumulative and that tests of the theories of the present are the steppingstones to the progress of the future.

If we pursued Basmann's thesis to its ultimate conclusion, inductive science must perish. Nothing can be quantified absolutely (except by God), for everything is relative. For example, given Einstein's theory of relativity, even a perfect balance could not find two Basmann-equivalent weights.

The economic analysis, stabilization, and growth problems of our day may not be solved by the Brookings model. But neither are they served by Basmann's nihilistic call to return to the fundamentals. We are well acquainted with the principles of quantitative logic, yet thank Basmann for his pedantic restatement. Our only lament is that he did not concentrate his considerable talents on more vital econometric and statistical problems. We need methods of selecting from among alternative specifications, methods for resolving multi-collinearity difficulties, complete system nonlinear estimation techniques, better measures of seasonal variation, and many other items to improve the state of economic science. It seems to us that it is Basmann who would be the prophet, not we. If so, then more constructive leadership and contributions are needed than his present critique.

NOTES

[1] J. S. Duesenberry, G. Fromm, L. R. Klein, and E. Kuh (eds.), *The Brookings Quarterly Econometric Model of the U.S.,* (Chicago and Amsterdam: Rand-McNally—North Holland, 1965).

[2] Nor, incidentally, has that been remedied to any appreciable degree, even today. For example, while there are a few estimates, further econometric study of the stimulative impact of the 1964 personal income tax reduction needs to be done.

[3] As should be clear from several statements in the first volume, the specialists worked on their sectors in relative isolation, giving rise to disagreements on quite a few specifications (cf. pp. 681 and 734).

[4] *Op. cit.,* p. 736.

[5] This does not mean that we believe the specifications should not be subjected to intensive scrutiny and criticism. This has been done elsewhere, G. Fromm and Paul Taubman, *Policy Simulations with an Econometric Model,* Brookings Institution, (Washington, 1968). That volume also contains a listing of a condensed version of the complete, compatible model and results and simulations of complete system solutions.

[6] *Ibid.,* p. 16.

[7]H. Chernoff and H. Rubin, "Asymptotic Properties of Limited-Information Estimates Under Generalized Conditions," *Studies in Econometric Method,* ed. by Wm. Hood and T. Koopmans (N. Y.: John Wiley and Sons, 1952).

[8]A. L. Nagar, "Stochastic Simulation of the Brookings Econometric Model," in J. S. Duesenberry, G. Fromm, L. R. Klein and E. Kuh (eds.), *The Brookings Model: Some Further Results* (Chicago and Amsterdam: Rand-McNally—North Holland, 1970).

[9]Another approach, which is only feasible after an estimate of the structural parameters of the model have been obtained, is to use the values of endogenous variables generated from stochastically shocked solutions of the system as additional data observations.

[10]"Dynamic Structure and Estimation in Economy-Wide Econometric Models," in *The Brookings Quarterly Econometric Model of the United States, op. cit.,* pp. 589-636.

[11]*Ibid.,* pp. 736-38.

[12]As an aside, we might report that the attitudes variable was dropped from the autos consumption function more than two years ago. Nevertheless, judging from present events (1966-67), it may still be of value for forecasting purposes.

ARGUMENT AND EVIDENCE IN THE BROOKINGS—S.S.R.C. PHILOSOPHY OF ECONOMETRICS

R. L. Basmann*
Texas A & M University

1. INTRODUCTION

Gary Fromm and Lawrence Klein have circulated their note, "The Brookings Econometric Model: A Rational Perspective," which they intend as a reply to my review, *The Brookings Quarterly Econometric Model of the U.S.: Science or Number Mysticism?*[1] The Fromm-Klein reply affords me an opportunity to clarify further, with help of specific examples, the more important of the criticisms I levelled at the philosophy of econometrics that underlay the formulation of the Brookings—S.S.R.C. Model project. That philosophy will affect both the counsel that the Brookings—S.S.R.C. Model econometricians will offer to policymakers and the concrete interpretations that policymakers can make of that counsel. The recommendations put forward by economists and econometricians are by no means uniquely or even narrowly determined by the empirical evidence and scientific economic hypotheses that are available, but also by the philosophic attitudes of the economists and econometricians towards the conduct of scientific investigation in economics. Ultimately, those attitudes will profoundly influence what the consulting econometrician predicts will

*For helpful comments and criticisms I am indebted to Edward Ames, Karl Brunner, Robert Rohr, and Gregory Schoepfle. Responsibility for the views expressed in this essay belongs solely to me.

be the change (say) in the actual operations of members of the
Internal Revenue Service in response to specified legislation, and
what definite effect this change in operation will have on the actions
of men, women, and children in sheltering, clothing, feeding themselves and enjoying their leisure time.

Although it was apparent that the Brookings—S.S.R.C. econometricians are preoccupied with economic forecasting uses of
their models, I undertook to evaluate the Brookings—S.S.R.C.
Model in Chapter 18 of the book by Duesenberry, et al. (1965) as
an intended contribution to economic science. The chief reason
for doing so is as follows: Experience seems to have taught the
Brookings—S.S.R.C. econometricians the unwisdom of promising
better forecasting results than those offered by their competitors
who employ much less costly computational techniques. According to Duesenberry and Klein,

(1.1)   But the case for the usefulness of econometric models in forecasting
does not rest entirely, or perhaps even mainly, on the record of past
success. Naive forecast methods are, almost by definition, difficult
to improve. Econometric models can be improved. (Duesenberry,
et al., 1965, p. 14.)

Another Brookings—S.S.R.C. econometrician, Edwin Kuh, in his
article "Is a New Age Dawning?" writes

(1.2)   While it is still too early to reach secure judgments, it appears reasonable to suppose that macroeconomic forecasters using present
aggregate techniques will do at least as well and in some instances
better than forecasts based on large detailed models. Their present
mixed bag of tricks seems to work quite effectively: . . . (Kuh, 1965,
p. 363.)

George A. W. Boehm, writing about econometric forecasting models
in THINK (International Business Machines Corporation), makes
the same point (Boehm, 1967, p. 8). I cannot claim to know in precisely what sense the so-called naive forecast methods are "almost
by definition" difficult to improve, or whether (in the same or some
other sense) econometric models are not equally difficult to improve;
however, I am willing to assert that the Brookings—S.S.R.C.
econometricians intend their claims on behalf of the forecasting
ability of their models to apply to future performance rather than
present. As they view the matter, the public relevance of their
promises of future performance rests on the alleged *scientific* character of their econometric research:

(1.3)   Economics is a mathematical science. (L. R. Klein, quoted by
Boehm, 1967, p. 8.)

The electronic computer is one of the foundations of economic science:

(1.4) The final ingredient in this list of the main foundations of large-scale quantitative economics has been the computer. It takes less time to whip off a multiple regression, together with an awesome battery of test statistics than it does to read this paragraph. (Kuh, 1965, p. 363.)

Finally, for policymakers and members of the lay public, there is the assurance of the ingenuity of econometricians in relating economic "variables" and of their "shrewd economic judgment to select the right equations, i.e., to pick variables and relationships that are important and ignore those that really don't matter very much." (Boehm, 1967, p. 10.)

The alleged scientific character of the Brookings—S.S.R.C. research project is the general issue under consideration in "Science or Number Mysticism?" and in the present essay. More precisely our general question refers to the claim expressed by (1.3). In what sense is it the case that econometrics, as pursued by the Brookings—S.S.R.C. econometricians, is a mathematical science? When a physicist asserts

(1.5) Classical mechanics is a mathematical science

he makes reference to a set of definite empirically confirmed isomorphisms between systems of mathematical symbols, on the one hand, and a definite class of sets of physical objects, on the other. The sentence (1.5) is not a slogan or directive principle enjoining the physicist— in advance of fundamental empirical investigation— to formulate classical mechanics as a system of equations built up of analytic functions. Are we to understand (1.3), as applied to the Brookings—S.S.R.C. research, in the same way as we understand (1.5)? In "Science or Number Mysticism?" I indicated that the answer is "No" and awaited the reply by Fromm and Klein.

Of the Duesenberry-Klein introduction to the *Report*, I have written, "There is no clearer indication of the scope, purpose, philosophy, and method of current econometrics, and the aspirations of those who currently pursue econometrics . . ." I said that the Brookings volume would set the standard for, and profoundly influence, the development of econometrics and its teaching in graduate schools for decades to come. This statement is a falsifiable prediction, derived—with help of some tacit (but readily supplied) generalizations about the behavior of human beings—from the fact that government agencies, large corporations, and foundations have made very generous grants in support of econometric work, of which the Brookings—S.S.R.C. Model is typical. I did not say, and nothing I did in fact say, implies that the standard would be high or that the influence of the Brookings—S.S.R.C. project on the teaching of econometrics would be beneficial. (I regret that Fromm and Klein inferred from my prediction that I was praising their work; cf. Fromm and Klein, 1972, p. 52). In that earlier review[2] I promised to evaluate the Brookings—S.S.R.C. project with help of concepts that differ markedly from those concepts that underlie the philosophy and methodology put forward by Duesenberry and Klein in the *Report* (cf. Basmann, 1972, p. 34). The discussion heard at the *Ohio State University Conference on the Current State of Econometrics*[3] tends to confirm the view I expressed, namely, that there are fundamental differences of opinion between the Brookings—S.S.R.C. econometricians and some other quantitative economists in respect of how empirical data are to be used, how the results of empirical econometric studies are to be interpreted, reported, and evaluated for the lay people, i.e., for economic policymakers in government and private commerce, and for individual citizens. More precisely, *those differences of opinion are differences of attitude towards asserted economic propositions, and the extent to which economists and econometricians are obligated to provide evidence for the propositions they assert in their roles as economists and econometricians.* The central issue — which the Fromm-Klein reply to "Science or Number Mysticism?" is very helpful in bringing into the open—is whether the econometrician's own attitude of belief, or conviction, towards the economic propositions he asserts is to be treated as valid support for those propositions.

The chief criticisms I put forward, first in the 1966 meetings of the Southern Economic Association, and subsequently at the *Ohio State University Conference on the Current State of Econometrics*, were

(1) The structural economic hypothesis represented by the Brookings—S.S.R.C. Model lacks sufficient "sharpness" of formulation to be empirically testable in practice.

(2) The quantitative foundations of the economic hypothesis represented by the Brookings—S.S.R.C. Model are seriously defective. More precisely, the Brookings—S.S.R.C. Model presupposes a large number of independent proffered laws of quantity and magnitude that have not been tested empirically; in spite of this lack of confirmation,

it has been taken for granted by the Brookings—S.S.R.C. econometricians that each of the many numerical time series from which parameter estimates have been computed represent quantities. In formulating their project the Brookings—S.S.R.C. econometricians failed to allocate any resources for the critical examination of quantitative foundations of their hypothesis.

Of the two chief criticisms I levelled at the Brookings—S.S.R.C. Model, the second, which refers to its quantitative foundations, is the more fundamental and important to economic science and economic policymaking. Moreover, the second criticism has turned out to be the more controversial, and the response of the Brookings—S.S.R.C. econometricians, and other econometricians, to that criticism is the more interesting. Klein and Fromm regard my second criticism as *nihilistic* (Fromm and Klein, 1972, p. 61), i.e., as denying all existence or, perhaps, as totally rejecting the consensus of my fellow economists. In "Science or Number Mysticism?" I wrote:

(1.6)   The formulation and testing of such proffered laws of quantity belong to, and are essential to, the trade of the quantitative economist and econometrician. (Basmann, 1972, p. 37.)

In their reply, Fromm and Klein asserted:

(1.7)   If we pursued Basmann's thesis to its ultimate conclusion, inductive science must perish. (Fromm and Klein, 1972, p. 61.)

Now the empirical testing of the proffered laws of quantity and magnitude presupposed by a given quantitative economic hypothesis is "inductive" in one important sense of that word, at least; yet, according to Fromm and Klein, if economists make thorough inductive investigations of proffered economic quantities, then "inductive science" must perish.

An equally interesting, even if apparently less extreme, attitude towards *theory of quantity and magnitude* and its applications in economics is the claim that that theory and its applications are metaphysical. This point of view was expressed by several econometricians attending the *O.S.U. Conference*. Some caution is required in dealing with this claim. Like "nihilistic," the adjective "metaphysical" is often employed as a snarl word in common speech, and if the econometricians who call *theory of quantity and magnitude* metaphysical intend merely to snarl at that theory and its application, then—I admit—their reaction is quite uninteresting and totally irrelevant to economic science and philosophy. On the other hand, it is possible that those econometricians intend to convey some significant information about the *theory of quantity and magnitude* and its applications, namely, that the theory and its applications are metaphysical in the technical sense. Fromm and Klein do try to refute the criticism (2), however; they do try to reassure their readers that the numerical time series appearing in the Brookings— S.S.R.C. Model are indeed "quantities" in some relevant sense (excluding as irrelevant the meaning of "quantity" as used in the theory of quantity and magnitude).

The criticism (1), namely, that the structural economic hypothesis represented by the Brookings—S.S.R.C. Model lacks sufficient "sharpness" of formulation to be empirically testable in practice, and the refutation attempted by Fromm and Klein are not of immediate practical concern; they become so only when the criticism (2) is adequately refuted, i.e., when the defectiveness of quantitative foundations is repaired. Furthermore, Fromm and Klein have attached to the statements that compose my criticism (1) some subjective meanings, which are not the objective, or *semantic*, meanings of those statements. As a consequence, Fromm and Klein have misrepresented the criticism (1), in all its essential aspects. (In this introduction, I assert the foregoing two sentences without offering evidence in their support for the time being. However, the relevant evidence is mentioned in Section 4.) Moreover, Fromm and Klein misrepresent my *mention* of alternative methods for circumventing the so-called degrees of freedom problem as a *recommendation* (cf. Basmann, 1972, pp. 22-25; also Fromm and Klein, 1972, pp. 58-59). Fromm and Klein—without explicitly saying so and without offering the requisite mathematical deductions— deny the mathematical theorem I mentioned in "Science or Number Mysticism?" (Basmann, 1972, pp. 24-25), namely, that their procedures for circumventing the so-called degrees of freedom problem are equivalent to the specification of additional definitional identities or structural relations, which, however, vary from sample to sample.[4]

Furthermore, Fromm and Klein do not understand why a system of structural relations[5]

$$(1.8) \quad \begin{cases} f_1(y_1, \cdots, y_G; x_1, \cdots, x_K, u_1) = 0, \\ \quad \cdot \qquad\qquad\qquad\qquad\qquad \cdot \\ \quad \cdot \qquad\qquad\qquad\qquad\qquad \cdot \\ \quad \cdot \qquad\qquad\qquad\qquad\qquad \cdot \\ f_G(y_1, \cdots, y_G; x_1, \cdots, x_K, u_G) = 0 \end{cases}$$

has to be checked for consistency and the existence of a unique *reduced form*[6]

$$(1.9) \quad \begin{cases} y_1 = \phi_1(x_1, \cdots, x_K, u_1, \cdots, u_G) \\ \quad \cdot \qquad\qquad\qquad \cdot \\ \quad \cdot \qquad\qquad\qquad \cdot \\ \quad \cdot \qquad\qquad\qquad \cdot \\ y_G = \phi_G(x_1, \cdots, x_K, u_1, \cdots, u_G) \end{cases}$$

before that system can be claimed to represent an empirically significant hypothesis about economic things and events, or the philosophy of econometrics to which they adhere admits logically contradictory statements as empirically significant. From their statement that they found the exact number of equations (say) G_1 in the system of equations in Chapter 18 (Duesenberry et al., 1965) hard to state,[7] I deduced that Fromm and Klein did not in fact check that system for consistency (Basmann, 1972, p. 21). To refute this criticism Fromm and Klein merely gave additional reasons for their assertion that the exact number of equations is hard to state—I had not disputed the implication of their original assertion, namely, that they did not know how many equations there were in the Brookings—S.S.R.C. Model—and they gave no reasons whatsoever for their having asserted that that system of equations had been put together in a consistent way (cf. Duesenberry, et al., 1965, p. 722; also Fromm and Klein, 1972, pp. 54-55).[8]

In addition to the reasons given by Fromm and Klein for finding the exact number of independent equations in the given system of Chapter 18 hard to state, they mention that that system of equations is not *the* Brookings—S.S.R.C. Model:

> (1.10)   Basmann, throughout his paper, refers to the Brookings Model and equates this to Chapter 18, which is entitled 'The Complete Model: A First Approximation.' To begin with, as should already be clear, there is no *the* Brookings model. The model is an evolving composite. (Fromm and Klein, 1972, p. 54.)

In other words, by Brookings Model Fromm and Klein intend to denote a *class* of models including that presented in Chapter 18 (Duesenberry et al., 1965) and all its descendents yet unborn. Therefore (it would be possible for Fromm and Klein to argue) any critical statement that happens to be true of a given member of that *class*, e.g., the model in Chapter 18, may continue indefinitely to be regarded as false when applied to the class, i.e., untrue of "*the* Brookings Model."

Fromm and Klein tell us that the important thing to *them* was not the exact specifications or parameter values (of a given model in the evolving composite), "but the spirit of what was to be accomplished." (Fromm and Klein, 1972, p. 54.) Apparently, Fromm and Klein wish to persuade the rest of us to evaluate the Brookings

—S.S.R.C. project not in terms of its specific accomplishments, but in terms of the aspirations of those who conduct it—that we should not be so critical of a single version since an alternative (better?) version is always forthcoming. In this connection notice that one of the reasons Fromm and Klein mentioned for finding it hard to state the exact number of equations in Chapter 18 to be checked for consistency is that alternative versions, viz., different systems of equations, will contain different numbers of equations.

It is apparent that my remarks on these technical aspects of econometric statistics in Section 3 of "Science or Number Mysticism?" were too highly compressed and that a separate article dealing solely with those technical problems, and in considerable detail, is called for.[9] However, as the response of Fromm and Klein to my criticism in respect of their assertion that the Brookings—S.S.R.C. Model has been put together in a consistent way suggests, the misinterpretations of my technical remarks have their source in the philosophy of econometrics to which the Brookings—S.S.R.C. econometricians adhere.

The following remark, quoted from "Is a New Age Dawning?" serves well to introduce the specific issue on which the present essay concentrates attention:

(1.11)   Econometrics presently stands at the intersection of theory and experience, as a much more sharply defined apparatus for developing and testing relationships than previously existed, or been part of accepted practice. (Kuh, 1965, p. 363.)

As in the case of "Science or Number Mysticism?", the question dealt with in the present article is about the so-called intersection of numerically expressed theory and experience. However, the central focus is on the character of this "experience" of which Kuh writes. We shall ask *what* is experienced, by *whom*, and by what *methods*. Fortunately, the reply by Fromm and Klein does give a rather clear indication.

In this rejoinder to the Fromm-Klein reply, I propose to draw the reader's attention to a few fundamental and closely related features of the Brookings—S.S.R.C. philosophy of econometrics, namely, its *theory of definition* (of abstract entities such as numbers, magnitudes of quantities, etc.) and its *theory of meaning* (of propositions). More precisely, I call attention to evidence (in the Fromm-Klein reply) that supports the hypothesis that adherents to the Brookings—S.S.R.C. philosophy of econometrics, while borrowing the logical constants[10] of mathematics, do not define those logical constants by *constructions*, as is done in pure and applied mathematics;[11] and I call attention to evidence that supports the hypothesis that adherents of the Brookings—S.S.R.C. philosophy of econometrics, while speaking and writing of empirical evidence, do not mean by "empirical evidence" the basic statements of intersubjective experience articulated by logical argument.[12]

Specifically, I propose to examine two of the Fromm-Klein arguments in considerable detail:

> I. The Fromm-Klein refutation of my assertion that the quantitative foundations of the Brookings—S.S.R.C. Model are defective. (Fromm and Klein, 1972, pp. 60-61.)
> II. The Fromm-Klein argument that some statements of mine about the formulation of "sharp" economic hypotheses for empirical test *imply* that
>
> > the greater the number of complex dependencies in a model, the more realistic and valid are its estimates and its explanations of structure (of the phenomena it supposedly respresents). (Fromm and Klein, 1972, p. 59.)

The Fromm-Klein refutation (I) rejects applied theory of quantity and magnitude as metaphysical[13] and therewith the method of definition of abstract entities by constructions (the method of mathematics), which is the salient feature of theory of quantity and magnitude. On the other hand, in arguing that the "observed numbers" in the time series appearing in the Brookings—S.S.R.C. Model are "quantities," Fromm and Klein make very clear just what kind of circumstance they regard as empirical evidence in support of

> the observed numbers are quantities.

That Fromm and Klein reject the process of defining abstract entities by constructions (as in mathematics and quantitative science) is brought into the open by the analysis of their refutation (II).

Such an investigation as the present one can throw much light on the Brookings—S.S.R.C. philosophy of econometrics, and on widely shared philosophical and methodological commitments of mainstream econometricians: To begin with, Fromm and Klein set themselves the task of refuting the criticisms put forward in "Science or Number Mysticism?". Fromm and Klein did not find those criticisms obscurely expressed, nor did they find the arguments difficult to follow. If they intended to refute the foregoing criticisms, then they tried to use arguments that are widely accepted as valid by econometricians. Klein, the older of the two, has been a leading member of the econometrics profession for about twenty years, a fact which supports the hypothesis that he is a shrewd judge of the types of argumentation that are acceptable to econometricians in general. Under pressure of criticism they regard as "an extremely critical attack on econometrics" (cf. Fromm and Klein, 1972, p. 52), the intellectual leaders of the econometrics profession might feel called upon to exert their abilities to the utmost, restrained only by the limitations imposed by their "philosophy," in setting the matter straight. All of this tends to support the statement that the semantic precision and logical validity of argumentation exhibited in the Fromm-Klein reply do not fall below current minimum standards for econometrics. There is nothing that more effectively indicates the nature of the fundamental presuppositions of a philosophy than the form and quality of the arguments its adherents actually use in refuting criticisms levelled at it and its applications, except a competent explication of that philosophy by its adherents themselves.

After some preliminary remarks in Section 2 we shall examine the refutation (I) in Section 3. In Section 4 we shall examine the argument (II). Some conclusions about the Brookings—S.S.R.C. philosophy of econometrics and the practical signficance of that philosophy are mentioned in Section 5.

2. CONCEPTS AND METHODS OF ANALYSIS

In "Science or Number Mysticism?" I tried to alert my readers to the fact that I was evaluating the Brookings—S.S.R.C. Model, its formulation and foundations, against standards quite different from those that serve the Brookings—S.S.R.C. econometricians. I also made it plain that those standards are not original with me. In their reply Fromm and Klein indicate that they are aware that the difference of standards exists, as the following quotation indicates:

(2.1)   However, having expressed these laudatory sentiments in his opening paragraph, Basmann goes on to launch an extremely critical attack on econometrics in general,[14] and on the Brookings model in particular. But, then, that isn't too surprising. Basmann states early in the game that he is not an econometrician; after reading his paper we are sure of it. (Fromm and Klein, 1972, p. 52.)[15]

That is to say (as I foretold in "Science or Number Mysticism?"), Fromm and Klein found me questioning some fundamental presuppositions and directive principles the adherence to which they regard as the touchstone for distinguishing econometricians from

other economists who employ mathematics and mathematical statistics (as well as the system of logic presupposed by mathematics)
in their research. That Fromm and Klein are aware that the difference of standards exists does not entail that they understand what
constitutes that difference. After all, Fromm and Klein, using
some tacit premises of psychology, inferred—somehow—from "the
Brookings—S.S.R.C. contribution will set the standard for, and
exert a profound influence on, the development of econometrics and
its teaching in our graduate schools for decades to come" that that
statement was "high praise indeed." (Fromm and Klein, 1972, p.
52.) That the foregoing inference is incorrect alerts us to the possibility that Fromm and Klein have inferred several more incorrect
statements about the difference of standards of scientific practice
that is in question. Indeed, it is possible (I say very probable, but
my readers are to judge for themselves) that Fromm and Klein
have drawn many incorrect inferences from statements expressed
in "Science or Number Mysticism?" and thus have failed to understand my criticisms adequately. Apparently, feeling sure that "Basmann is not an econometrician," Fromm and Klein have taken that
statement as a relevant and complete explanation of my having
criticized various features of the Brookings—S.S.R.C. Model.

Accordingly, before undertaking analysis of the refutations offered by Fromm and Klein in their reply, I propose to augment my
earlier remarks in "Science or Number Mysticism?" concerning
the foundations of my criticisms of the Brookings—S.S.R.C. Model
by some remarks that should be helpful to the reader in following
the analysis in subsequent sections of this rejoinder, and which
may forestall mistaken inferences in respect of the precise nature
of my criticisms of the Brookings—S.S.R.C. Model. I shall keep
these remarks brief.

In Section 5 I shall put forward an hypothesis about the philosophy of econometrics adhered to by the Brookings—S.S.R.C.
econometricians. This hypothesis ascribes some definite semantical
and logical concepts to that philosophy of econometrics. The hypothesis is intended ultimately to account for the technical practices
of the Brookings—S.S.R.C. econometricians in their formulation
and empirical testing of econometric models. For the time being,
however, we shall be concerned with the matter of accounting for
the assertions that Brookings—S.S.R.C. econometricians have
made about their philosophy and methods and about alternative
philosophies of quantitative science.

The chief sources of basic evidence used in this rejoinder are the
following documents:

Duesenberry, J. S., et al. (eds), *The Brookings Quarterly Econometric Model of the United States*, Chicago, 1965.

Basmann, R. L., "The Brookings Quarterly Econometric Model: Science or Number Mysticism?" Problems and Issues in Current Econometric Practice, 1972.

Fromm, Gary and Lawrence R. Klein, "The Brookings Econometric Model: A Rational Perspective," Problems and Issues in Current Econometric Practice, 1972.

In addition to the foregoing sources of evidence some additional sources will have to be mentioned explicitly, especially in Section 4, since Fromm and Klein have attributed to me several assertions that did not appear in "Science or Number Mysticism?"

The following remarks will assist the reader in understanding my analysis of the Fromm-Klein reply, "A Rational Perspective":

(1) It is assumed (tentatively) that the sole purpose of the Fromm-Klein reply is to refute, by "logical" argument adducing factual evidence as basic premises, some (at least) of the statements expressed in "Science or Number Mysticism?"

(2) I have made no attempt to partition the sentences of "A Rational Perspective" into nonintersecting subsets of statements for which Fromm and Klein are individually responsible. The question regarding which of the authors of that joint reply is responsible for which statements—a question brought up by Klein at the *O.S.U. Conference*[16] —is (I admit) relevant to a broader discussion of the influence of cultural traditions and social practices on the current "philosophy" of mainstream econometrics, but that question is beyond the scope of the present discussion and I must refuse to deal with it for the time being.[17]

The basic evidence is a collection of words and sentences *used* by the authors of the foregoing documents. Words and sentences that are only *mentioned*, however, are not considered basic evidence.[18] However, wherever Fromm and Klein use a sentence of the form

(2.2)   We are sure that A

in which "A" denotes a declarative sentence, it will be inferred that Fromm and Klein intend to use, or assert, the proposition expressed by the sentence "A."[19]

By the way, I take all such propositions as (2.2) which refer to the emotional state of the writer(s) denoted by the pronoun, as strongly confirmed. Notice, however, that it is (2.2) rather than "A" that is taken as strongly confirmed.

I shall make no attempt to define "word," "symbol," "sentence," "statement," or "proposition" in a formal way. If a given word denotes, in a given use, an object, then the word is said to be *concrete*, e.g., "paycheck" is a concrete word. If a given word denotes an entity such as a set or class, or relation, the word is said to be *abstract*, e.g., "number," as used in theory of arithmetic, is abstract. Sentences, which are strings of words (symbols) put together in accordance with a system of formation rules, are said to express statements, or propositions. A sentence that contains the logical words, or *connectives*,[20] "not," "and," "or," "if . . . , then . . .," "if, and only if" is said to express a compound, or *molecular* statement. A sentence that does not contain connectives is said to express a simple, or *atomic*, statement.

The *semantic meaning* of a given atomic sentence is the class of intersubjectively experienceable circumstances that make the statement expressed by that sentence *true*. For instance, the circumstances that made Klein write the sentence,

"Nothing can be quantified absolutely (except by God) for everything is relative"

true is not difficult to describe and specify, and needs no special comment.[21] It is not usually easy to specify the circumstances that make a given sentence true. However, the important idea to be grasped is that it is possible to specify what objective circumstances make a given atomic sentence true, and thus to formulate a concept of meaning that is independent of the emotions the speakers, writers, and listeners attach to the sentences they use, hear, or read.

Please notice that I do not attribute the foregoing concept of semantic meaning to the Brookings—S.S.R.C. philosophy of econometrics.

Meanings of molecular sentences are determined by the meanings of the atomic sentences that are their constituents and the rules governing the use of the logical connectives. In this paper the logical words "not," "and," "or," "if . . . , then . . . ," and ". . . if, and only if, . . ." are always to be understood as having the meanings of the connectives $\sim$, &, $\supset$, $\vee$ and $\equiv$ respectively in the *truth-functional calculus of propositions*. The rules governing the use of the connectives are summarized in the following *truth-value assignment table*.[22]

A	B	A & B	A ∨ B	A ⊃ B	A ≡ B	~ B
t	t	t	t	t	t	f
t	f	f	t	f	f	t
f	t	f	t	t	f	
f	f	f	f	t	t	

It will be recalled that sentences such as

$$A \supset (B \supset A)$$

$$\sim A \supset (A \supset B)$$

which receive truth-value t, i.e., "true," under the foregoing rules no matter how truth-values are assigned to the constituents "A" and "B," are said to be *tautologies*. Sentences such as

$$(\sim A) \, \& \sim (A \supset B)$$

$$A \, \& \, (\sim A)$$

which receive truth-value f, i.e., "false," under the foregoing rules no matter how truth-values are assigned to "A" and "B," are said to be *contradictions*. When an economic hypothesis has a large number of constituent hypotheses, e.g., the Brookings—S.S.R.C. Model, some special effort has to be taken to demonstrate that the economic hypothesis is not a contradiction, i.e., not logically false. Recall the discussion of consistency of the Brookings—S.S.R.C. Model in Section 1. Sentences that are neither tautologies nor contradictions are said to be *contingent sentences*.

In expository, or propositional, English the verb "imply" always takes one or more statements as its subject and one statement as its direct object: Only statements, or the sentences that express them *imply;* only a statement, or sentence that expresses a statement is *implied.* A statement "A" is said to *imply* a statement "B" if, and only if, from "A" we can reach "B" through a finite sequence of deductions in accordance with the *rules of propositional logic*, i.e., the deductive rules governing introduction of connectives (including double negation ∼∼), repetition, and substitution of formulas on successive lines of deductive arguments (cf. Anderson and Johnstone, 1962, Chapter 2).[23]

The rules of deduction most frequently used in this paper are the rule of *modus ponens*

if A, then B

A

∴ B

and the rule of *modus tollens*

$$\text{If A, then B}$$
$$\text{not B}$$
$$\therefore \text{not A.}$$

The difference between the system of standards I used in evaluating the Brookings—S.S.R.C. Model and the system of standards the Brookings—S.S.R.C. econometricians employed in formulating and "testing" that model are rooted in the differences between respective concepts of semantic meaning (of statements) and of the role of deductive argument in economic science.

Proffered economic laws, or hypotheses, are supposed to be systems of mutually consistent statements, which, although they contain abstract terms, are connected with, and thus testable by, experiences that can be described by statements that describe objects and events, and relations among them.

Now my criticism of the Brookings—S.S.R.C. Model in respect of its quantitative foundations had to do with the inadequate attention the Brookings—S.S.R.C. econometricians paid to the matter of developing the explicit connection between the time series, on one hand, and atomic statements about economic objects and events, on the other. To fix ideas, let us consider a simple illustration of the kind of question that arises in connection with the interpretation of an economic time series. Imagine an economic policymaker, who, on being told by an economic advisor that the total production of mineral fuels in the United States during 1939 was approximately the same as during 1936, and that the total production of mineral fuels in the United States during 1951 was approximately twice the total production for 1931, refuses to accept as evidence the numerical time-series data exhibited. Suppose that policymaker (to test the competence of his advisor, perhaps) suggests that the discussion begin with a consideration of piles of coal extracted from the mines, barrels of crude oil and tanks of natural gas pumped from the wells during the years in question, terms of which—unlike the abstract term "total mineral fuel production"—the policymaker claims to have sound intuitive notions.

What this policymaker demands is a concrete interpretation, or constructive definition, of the abstract term "total production of mineral fuels." Transparently, the following answer cannot meet that demand: "For 1936, total production of mineral fuels = 21,679 trillion B.T.U.; for 1939, total production = 21,753 trillion B.T.U. You see, those numbers differ by less than one-half of one percent;

they are approximately equal. Etc." The policymaker might reply, "You are only talking about number symbols. Talk about fuels." However, in this case the economist, with help of a few well-confirmed scientific laws, can give a satisfactory clarification—a clarification that can be as complete as the policymaker will allow time for—without help of any highly abstract terms the policymaker does not understand, because the scientific homework (thermodynamics) already has been done adequately.

A pure economic theory is an uninterpreted *axiomatic system* composed of primitive terms, definitions, undemonstrated propositions, explicit definitions (of additional terms), and demonstrated propositions, which are called *theorems* (with respect to the undemonstrated propositions). Every axiomatic theory presupposes a system of predicate logic, which provides connectives, quantifiers,[24] and propositional rules, or deduction schemata, e.g., the rule of *modus tollens*. The presupposition of a system of logic is essential; the strictly economic propositions cannot be combined to form new propositions without help of connectives and quantifiers, nor can new propositions be demonstrated without help of deduction schemata. (For a very readable account of axiomatics the reader should consult the book by Blanché, 1962; also Suppes, 1957, Chapter 12, esp. pp. 246-249.)

It is important to notice that, in addition to presupposing the system of predicate logic, axiomatic theories—including pure economic theories—generally presuppose one or more other theories. Let T be a theory and let a theory T_1 be presupposed by T. Some of the terms peculiar to T are defined with help of primitive terms and operations of the theory T_1, and some theorems of T are proved with help of undemonstrated propositions and theorems of T_1. For example, pure geometry presupposes the theory of natural numbers; recall that the natural number denoted by the symbol "3" is employed in the definition of "triangle." It is a fact that expositors of theories often fail to mention explicitly the theories that are presupposed by the axiomatic systems they put forward; but that fact does not entail that such *prior* theories are not presupposed.

Consider the problem of giving a concrete interpretation to a theory T that presupposes another theory T_1, where T_1 is not the presupposed system of logic, but is another scientific theory. Some of the terms of the theory T, which we have to interpret, are explicitly defined by terms appearing in theory T_1. In order to provide a concrete interpretation of theory T, we must provide a concrete interpretation of the prior theory T_1. For example, suppose that T is geometry and T_1 is Peano's theory of natural numbers, which is presupposed by geometry. Suppose we wish to give a concrete interpretation of "triangle"; transparently, we cannot do so without first giving a concrete interpretation to the natural number that is denoted by the number 3. The concept of finite *cardinal number* and the operations of addition and multiplication of cardinal numbers afford the requisite concrete interpretation of T_1, Peano's theory of natural numbers, (cf. Russell, 1919, Chapter II). The class of all sets whose numbers can be put into one-to-one correspondence with the members of the set that contains my left eye, my right eye, my nose, and nothing else, *is* the cardinal number 3. That class serves as the concrete interpretation of the natural number that is denoted by the numeral 3.

A theory is quantitative if, and only if, it presupposes the *theory of quantity*, a brief exposition of which is given in Section 3. The economic hypothesis that is represented by the Brookings— S.S.R.C. Model presupposes that theory of quantity. Consequently, the undefined primitive terms and operations that are mentioned in the theory of quantity presupposed by the Brookings hypothesis require definite concrete interpretations by classes of objects and events of economic experience. More details will be given in the course of the discussion in Section 3.

3. THEORY OF QUANTITY: SCIENCE OR METAPHYSICS?

The assertion

(3.1) If we pursued Basmann's thesis to its ultimate conclusion, inductive science must perish. (Fromm and Klein, 1972, p. 61.)

has already been mentioned. An essential premise of the argument by means of which the Brookings—S.S.R.C. econometricians reach the foregoing conclusion is that the theory of quantity is a *metaphysical theory* in the technical sense, viz., the propositions of the theory of quantity are claimed to be knowledge of something that is in principle beyond experience. Fromm and Klein, who tell us that they are well-acquainted with the theory of quantity, interpret the propositions of that theory as metaphysical in the technical sense when they assert

(3.2) Nothing can be quantified absolutely (except by God), for everything is relative. (Fromm and Klein, 1972, p. 61.)

Another Brookings—S.S.R.C. econometrician who commented on "Science or Number Mysticism?" at the *O.S.U. Conference* expressed the view that the criticism respecting quantitative foundations of the Brookings—S.S.R.C. Model and the whole discussion of economic quantity and magnitude are metaphysical. I suppose that he meant to assert that the propositions of the theory of quantity are assertions about something that is in principle beyond all experience.

Before we attempt to trace the foregoing attitude to its source in the philosophy of econometrics adhered to by the Brookings—S.S.R.C. econometricians, let us reconsider the axiomatic theory of quantity and its antecedents in experience. Let us first consider the experience that foreshadows the development of the axiomatic theory.

The physical property called *weight* affords one of several ancient natural *models* for the concept of quantity. The physical property called *length* is another. We shall employ *weight* as our model in the present discussion. Human beings began acquiring experience with the behavior of pendulum balances a great many centuries ago, before 2500 B.C., at least (cf. Skinner, 1954, esp. pp. 779-780). The practice of representing what we now call a *magnitude of weight* by a number is very ancient, and the discovery of the strict analogy between the combination of two objects (on a given pan of a pendulum balance) and the arithmetic sum of their weight numbers must have followed closely the beginning of frequent exchanges of gold and other precious metals and preceded the introduction of coinage (cf. Seltman, 1955, Chapter 1; also Burns, 1927, Chapter 1). A standard weight, a stone object with the form of a duck and inscribed with the words "ten manahs" has been found at ancient Nineveh, and dates from about 2500 B.C. (Seltman, 1955, p. 8); the inscription on a clay tablet found at Knossos has been read "60 ox-hide ingots (on being weighed in the balance) equal $52\frac{1}{2}$ talents" (Seltman, 1955, p. 10). The experiences of many thousands of human beings of the behavior of pendulum balances, and of the analogy between physical addition of objects and arithmetical addition, provide data sufficient for the construction of an axiomatic *theory of quantity*.

As mentioned in "Science or Number Mysticism?" there are many versions of the theory of quantity extant.[25] The following axiomatic system differs in form from, but is equivalent to, the system sketched in "Science or Number Mysticism?"

The primitive notions are as follows:

(1) A set S, the elements α, β, γ, . . . of which are called objects of experience.

(2) An operation O_1, on ordered pairs of objects α, β belonging to S, the possible outcomes of which are denoted by $\alpha > \beta$, $\beta > \alpha$, and $\alpha \sim \beta$. (The theory of sets, relations, and mappings is presupposed.)

(3) An operation O_2 for combining the objects in any ordered pair α, β of objects in S. The combination of α and β by O_2 is denoted by $\alpha \oplus \beta$.

(4) *Definition of nα.* The product of any nonzero natural number n and any object α in S is defined by

$$1\alpha = \alpha$$
$$(n+1)\alpha = n\alpha \oplus \alpha \text{ for every n.}$$

(The axiomatic *theory of natural numbers* is presupposed. Here we employ Peano's induction postulate.)

The undemonstrated statements of the theory are:

   I. *For every α, β in S, exactly one of the following holds*
       (a) $\alpha > \beta$
       (b) $\beta > \alpha$
       (c) $\alpha > \beta$.

  II. *For all distinct α, β, γ in S, if $\alpha > \beta$ and $\beta > \gamma$, then $\alpha > \gamma$.*

 III. *For every $\alpha \ \varepsilon$ S there is $\alpha' \ \varepsilon$ S such that $\alpha \neq \alpha'$ and $\alpha \sim \alpha'$.*

 IV. *For all α, β in S, if $\alpha \sim \beta$ then $\beta \sim \alpha$.*

  V. *For all α, β, γ in S, if $\alpha > \beta$ and $\beta \sim \gamma$, then $\alpha > \gamma$.*

 VI. *For every $\alpha \ \varepsilon$ S there is $\beta \ \varepsilon$ S such that $\alpha > \beta$.*

VII. *For all α, β in S there is γ in S such that $(\alpha \oplus \beta) \sim \gamma$.*

VIII. *For every α, β, α' in S if $\alpha \sim \alpha'$ then $(\alpha \oplus \beta) > \alpha'$.*

 IX. *For every α, β, α', β' in S, if $\alpha \sim \alpha'$ and $\beta \sim \beta'$, then $(\alpha \oplus \beta) \sim (\alpha' \oplus \beta')$.*

  X. *For every α, β in S $(\alpha \oplus \beta) \sim (\beta \oplus \alpha)$.*

 XI. *For every α, β, γ in S $(\alpha \oplus \beta) \oplus \gamma \sim \alpha \oplus (\beta \oplus \gamma)$.*

XII. *For every α, β in S if $\beta > \alpha$, then there is a natural number n such that $n\alpha > \beta$.*

It will suffice to mention only a couple of theorems that may be deduced from the foregoing undemonstrated statements with help of the presupposed system of logic and theory of sets and relations. The theorems to be mentioned enable us to describe the concepts of quantity and magnitude of a quantity succinctly.

THEOREM 1. The relation $\sim$ defined by O_1 is an equivalence relation on S viz., for all distinct α, β, γ in S:

(i) $\alpha \sim \alpha$.
(ii) If $\alpha \sim \beta$, then $\beta \sim \alpha$.
(iii) If $\alpha \sim \beta$ and $\beta \sim \gamma$, then $\alpha \sim \gamma$.

Statement (ii) appears among the undemonstrated statements as
IV. Statement (i) and statement (iii) are demonstrated, with help
of the logically prior *Rule of Negation Introduction* of propositional logic, by means of reduction ad absurdum proofs (cf. Anderson and Johnstone, 1962, p. 33). The undemonstrated propositions used in the proofs are I, III, IV, and V.

THEOREM 2. *The relation $\sim$ defined by O_1 determines a
unique partition Q of S, i.e.,*

$$Q = \{,a,b,c, ...\}$$

where a, b, c, ... *are nonempty subsets of* S *such that every object
in* S *belongs to exactly one of the subsets, and if α and α' are any
two objects belonging to a given subset* a, *then $\alpha \sim \alpha'$.*

(The foregoing theorem is proved in theory of sets and relations, which is presupposed by the present theory of quantity.)

The subsets a, b, c, ... mentioned in the foregoing theorem are
said to be equivalence classes under the partition Q by the relation $\sim$.

We are now in a position to define the concept of quantity concisely: A *quantity* is an ordered quadruple (S, O_1, O_2, Q) where S
is a set of objects of experience α, β, γ, ..., O_1 and O_2 are operations
defining ($>$, $\sim$) and $\oplus$ respectively such that the undemonstrated
statements I-XII hold. The equivalence classes a, b, c, ... belonging to the partition Q of S under the relation $\sim$ defined by O_1
are said to be *magnitudes* of the quantity (S, O_1, O_2, Q).

We mention the following definitions, with help of statements
that appear in the axiomatic theory described in "Science or Number Mysticism?" (Basmann, 1972, Sec. 4) can be deduced as theorems:

DEFINITION 1. Let α, β be any objects in S, and let a, b
be classes (magnitudes) in Q such that $\alpha \varepsilon a$, $\beta \varepsilon b$; then

(i)   a>b if $\alpha > \beta$;
(ii) b>a if $\beta > \alpha$;
(iii) a=b if $\alpha \sim \beta$.

DEFINITION 2. Let $\alpha \varepsilon$ a, $\beta \varepsilon$ b be as in **DEFINITION 1**.
The magnitudes (class belonging to Q) that contains ($\alpha \oplus \beta$) is
denoted by (a $\oplus$ b).

Notice that the symbol $>$ in (a>b) and the symbol $>$ in

$(\alpha > \beta)$ are determined by the meaning of $>$ in $(\alpha > \beta)$, but the meanings are not identical. Similarly, the symbol $\oplus$ in (a $\oplus$ b) and the symbol $\oplus$ in $(\alpha \oplus \beta)$ denote two distinct operations. The practice of using a single symbol to denote two or more distinct but structurally similar operations in theory of quantity is foreshadowed by the practice of using the one symbol + to denote four distinct operations, as in the *theory of arithmetic*. We shall refer to the existence of these distinctions later on in connection with some details of the Brookings—S.S.R.C. philosophy of quantity and number.

The remaining theorems of quantity and magnitude, including those theorems that justify the representation of magnitudes (classes of objects) a, b, c by real numbers r_a, r_b, r_c, ..., and, especially, the representation of (a $\oplus$ b) by $(r_a + r_b)$, presuppose the *theory of arithmetic* (cf. Hölder, 1901, pp. 19-28).

Like any uninterpreted axiomatic theory, the foregoing theory of quantity asserts no propositions about experience as long as its primitive concepts S, O_1, and O_2 remain uninterpreted. Moreover, like any other uninterpreted axiomatic system, the uninterpreted theory of quantity asserts no propositions about something that is beyond experience. Uninterpreted axiomatic theories are not metaphysical—at least not in the useful technical sense of that word.

Whenever the primitive concepts of an axiomatic theory are given concrete interpretation so that the statements thereof assert propositions about classes of real objects, then it is possible to test those propositions against experience, at least, in principle. Normally a theory thus concretely interpreted is regarded as scientific, not as metaphysical. In the case of the theory of quantity, several such concrete interpretations have been made. Moreover, the search for new concrete interpretations of any axiomatic theory, which is the attempt to find domains of experience to which the statements of that theory are applicable, is widely regarded by scientists as a scientific activity, not as a form of metaphysical speculation.

It is probable that the roots of the view that holds the theory of quantity to be metaphysical are to be found in the fact that under any concrete interpretation we give to the primitive terms and operations of that theory, the undemonstrated statements *I - XII* fail to agree exactly with our descriptions of objects and events, which we might suppose to be accurate. For example, having noted the position of the pointer of a pendulum balance at rest, with pans empty, we place the object α on the left pan and the object β on the right pan, and then allow the arms of the balance to swing freely.

Often we are unable to determine whether the oscillating pointer returns to the initial position of rest exactly, and we remain uncertain as to which of the following statements best agrees with the observation: (1) $\alpha > \beta$, (2) $\beta > \alpha$ or (3) $\alpha \sim \beta$, viz., we cannot be sure whether the objects α and β have the same magnitude of weight. The pendulum balance that we happen to be using appears to fail to partition the set S of all objects into a set of magnitudes a, b, c, ... because it appears to fail to describe precisely the observed instance (α, β).

Neither the goldsmiths and jewelers of antiquity, nor the physicists and instrumentmakers of today, have abandoned the concept of weight (as a quantity) in the circumstances just described.[26] They have not done so, because the concept of "imperfection" in the actual pendulum balance, far from being merely verbal, has several important concrete realizations. N. R. Campbell discusses some of them in his account of measurement (cf. Campbell, 1957, pp. 279 ff).[27] Definite *initial conditions* (learned from experience)[28] are essential for accurate discrimination of magnitudes of weight. However, it is precisely the circumstance just described, namely, in which the pendulum balance in actual use seemingly fails to discriminate between the objects α and β in respect of magnitude of weight, that Fromm and Klein (probably) were referring to when they wrote:

(3.3) For example, even a perfect balance could not find two . . . -equivalent weights. (Fromm and Klein, 1972, p. 61.)[29]

That there is supposed to be a connection between the foregoing assertion and the set of mutually supporting views of Fromm and Klein regarding the metaphysical status of theory of quantity and the dangers its application presents to inductive science can be made clear by examination of the context.

> If we pursued Basmann's thesis to its ultimate conclusion, inductive science must perish. Nothing can be quantified absolutely (except by God), for everything is relative. For example, even a perfect balance could not find two . . . equivalent weights. (Fromm and Klein, 1972, p. 61.)

It might appear to the reader that one of the directive principles of the Brookings—S.S.R.C. philosophy of econometrics is the proposition that every concretely interpreted theory that fails to agree perfectly with statements describing relevant experiences, is to be regarded as metaphysical. That supposition is not without its merits, for, conjoined with the statement that the statements of theory of quantity do not agree perfectly with statements describing relevant experiences, the supposed directive principle yields the statement that theory of quantity is metaphysical. However, it is more probable that the Brookings—S.S.R.C. econometricians do not regard the foregoing principle as applicable to all theories, but applicable according to the dictates of expediency.

To the adherents of the Brookings—S.S.R.C. philosophy of econometrics my assertion that the Brookings hypothesis presupposes the theory of quantity seems absurd and hence of no significance for the practical conduct of econometric research. One prominent econometrician present at the *O.S.U. Conference* (but who has not been associated with the Brookings—S.S.R.C. project) expressed the opinion that, instead of concrete interpretations of the theory of quantity, what is really needed is a large collection of "good" and "reliable" numerical economic time series. This point of view, just as that attributed to the Brookings—S.S.R.C. econometricians, denies to theory of quantity its essential role, namely, to provide a consistent system of statements that defines the logical form of the connections that must exist between numerical time series, on the one hand, and objects and economic events of experience on the other, if those numerical time series, and the statistics that are computed from them, are to convey any empirical information that is "good" and "reliable" and of importance to economic science.

The foregoing attitude towards theory of quantity derives from a presupposition that confuses *theory of arithmetic* with *theory of quantity* but which does not identify the one theory with the other completely. Thus it appears (to those who make the presupposition) that the act of introducing arithmetical symbols, e.g., +, into the *representation* of an economic hypothesis, with help of objectifications of common speech, alone suffices to render that hypothesis quantitative and connected in a significant way with objects and events of economic experience. The presupposition is readily traced in the exposition of the Brookings—S.S.R.C. philosophy of econometrics presented by Duesenberry and Klein (Duesenberry, et al., Chapter 1). However, the presupposition is brought closer to the surface by Fromm and Klein in their reply to my criticism respecting quantitative foundations of the Brookings—S.S.R.C. hypothesis.

In their reply to "Science or Number Mysticism?" Fromm and Klein devote a single short paragraph to the criticism I levelled at the Brookings—S.S.R.C. Model in respect of its quantitative foundations. Only two of the sentences in that paragraph reveal very much about the Brookings—S.S.R.C. philosophy of econometrics.[30]

Fromm and Klein wrote:

(3.4) Now let us consider the general issue raised by Basmann. Are the time-series observations on the variables in the model orderable, are they quantities? Certainly, except in a very restricted sense, the observed numbers are quantities. (Fromm and Klein, 1972, p. 60.)

Our primary task is to determine how the term "quantity" functions in the Brookings—S.S.R.C. philosophy of econometrics. That numbers can be observed, and that numbers *are* quantities (or, perhaps, Fromm and Klein mean *magnitudes* of quantities) are supposed to be intuitively obvious to the reader. However, we notice that "quantity," which does not have a concrete referent (object) in ordinary discourse, is not defined anywhere in the Fromm-Klein article. That fact suggests that we ought to avoid jumping to the conclusion that the function of the word "quantity" in the Brookings—S.S.R.C. philosophy of econometrics is to express a meaning in the strict semantic sense. Consider

(3.5) For example, personal consumption expenditures involve the exchange of money for goods (we are sure even Basmann can count the dollars in his monthly paycheck and the slices of bread he buys and eats). (Fromm and Klein, 1972, p. 60.)

Our immediate task is to try to understand the statements expressed in the foregoing quotations. To begin with, we notice that certain terms have concrete referents, e.g., "slices of bread," "count," "exchange." We have no difficulty predicting the appearance of our paychecks if we fold, spindle, or multilate them. The act of *observing* something—to see, touch, smell, taste, or hear— is concrete in our intuition. On the other hand, "number," "observed number," "quantity," etc., are abstract terms. We shall need to know what is meant by saying that a number is *observed*, and that *observed numbers are quantities*.

Let us turn to the theory of arithmetic for some of the definitions we require.

By "number" is meant any of the following: (a) natural number, (b) rational positive number, (c) rational number, (d) real number, (e) complex number. These are all purely mathematical entities. By "numeral" is meant any symbol that is used to denote a number, e.g., the combinations of Greek letters inscribed on Athenian coins to indicate denomination or months of issue (cf. Neugebauer, 1957, esp. pp. 9-17). It will be helpful to recall that "natural number" is an undefined primitive mentioned in *Peano's* system of *postulates*, the other primitives being "0" and "successor." Recall, too, that these primitives are open to an infinity of different interpretations, any of which satisfies the *postulates* (Russell, 1919, Chapter I; Blanché, 1962, esp. pp. 31-33.) The operations of addition and multiplication of natural numbers are primitive definitions. The relation denoted by ">" on the set of all natural numbers is defined with help of the operation of addition.

The *rational positive numbers* are defined constructively in terms of ordered pairs of natural numbers and the operation of multiplication of natural numbers. As each rational positive number is a definite class of ordered pairs of natural numbers, no rational positive number is identical with any natural number. The operations of addition and multiplication of rational positive numbers and the relation of order on the set of all rational positive numbers are defined constructively in terms of the operations of addition and multiplication, and the ordering relation for the natural numbers (cf. Thielman, 1953, pp. 5-8). Addition of rational positive numbers is not the same operation as addition of natural numbers, even if the same symbol, namely +, is used to denote either of those operations.

The system of natural numbers is said to be *constructively extended* to the system of rational positive numbers. The system of rational positive numbers is, in a similar way, constructively extended to the *system of rational numbers* (cf. Thielman, 1953, pp. 8-9). Since each rational number is a definite class of ordered pairs of rational positive numbers, no rational number is identical with any rational positive number; moreover, no rational number is a natural number, etc. Finally the system of rational numbers is constructively extended to the *system of real numbers* by the introduction of *Dedekind cuts* (cf. Thielman, 1953, pp. 9-15). A Dedekind cut, or real number, is a special kind of partition of the set of all rational numbers. The partitions are of two distinct kinds, (a) *irrational* and (b) *rational*. Since each real number is a definite partition of the set of all rational numbers, no real number is a rational number

In Section 2 it was mentioned that the concept of finite *cardinal number* affords a concrete interpretation of natural number. Cardinal number is a property of all sets of objects of experience. Two sets, A and B, are said to have the same *cardinal number* if, and only if, a one-to-one correspondence can be set up between those sets such that to each element of A there corresponds exactly one element of B and to each element of B there corresponds exectly one element of A. A *cardinal number* is the class of all sets that can be put into one-to-one correspondence with a specified set; e.g., the *cardinal number 5* is the *class* of all sets that can be put into one-to-one correspondence with the set containing nothing else but the fingers now on my right hand. The set containing nothing else but the fingers now on my left hand is a member of the *class* that is the *cardinal number 5*. The *class* of all sets that can be put into one-to-one correspondence with the set that contains nothing else but my nose is the *cardinal number 1*. We need not recite the details of the procedures by means of which the primitive terms "0" and "successor" are interpreted concretely; nor do we require (for present purposes) to explain the operational definitions of addition and multiplication of cardinal numbers (Thielman, 1953, p. 39). What is important here is that this concrete interpretation of "natural number," "0," and "successor" gives us "the right allowance of fingers and eyes and noses." (Russell, 1919, p. 9.)

By "counting" is meant a definite process; to *count* a finite collection, or set, is to assign each member of the collection a term in the sequence of natural numbers, i.e., to arrange the members of that collection in an ordered succession until the collection is exhausted (cf. Dantzig, 1954, pp. 8-9). All of us have performed the operation of counting collections of objects on many different occasions. For instance, we may count the slices of bread we eat at a given meal.

Modern theory of arithmetic does not provide us with all of the definitions we require in order to understand the meaning of the foregoing quoted statements of Fromm and Klein. Theory of arithmetic does not tell us what is meant by saying that a number is "observed." Common sense tells us that we cannot observe any of the numbers that are defined in theory of arithmetic. No one can observe the *cardinal number 5;* no one observes the *class* of all sets that can be put into one-to-one correspondence with the set that contains nothing else but the fingers on my right hand. One can observe only the objects, (say) the fingers on my left hand, that are elements of a set that is a member of the class that is cardinal number 5. (There is, of course, a sense in which "observed number" is a meaningful slang term among scientists consciously making application of theory of quantity. However, we are trying here to follow Fromm and Klein in doing without theory of quantity.) Moreover, the term "quantity" is not defined in theory of arithmetic. As neither Duesenberry and Klein (Duesenberry et al., 1965, Chapter 1) nor Fromm and Klein have bothered to define the terms "observed number" and "quantity," we shall have to find appropriate interpretations for ourselves. In seeking those interpretations we can avail ourselves of the findings of semantical studies of language.

Noticing that "count," which appears in the quotation (3.5), has two different meanings in that sentence, and cannot in both uses be taken to mean what "count" means in theory of arithmetic, or even in the language of common discourse, we are led to a probable interpretation of "observed number." Apparently, Fromm and Klein intended the statement

(3.6)   . . . we are sure that even Basmann can count the dollars in his monthly paycheck,

to lend support to the statement expressed by

(3.7)   the observed numbers in the time series that appear in the Brookings —S.S.R.C. Model are quantities.

For the time being we shall consider only the following part of the sentence (3.6):

(3.8)   Basmann can count the dollars in his monthly paycheck.

To begin with, we notice that in asserting (3.6) Fromm and Klein are telling us about their own emotional states, namely, that they believe the proposition expressed by (3.8). Furthermore, the word "even," which Fromm and Klein use in (3.6) serves a definite purpose, namely, to suggest some other statements that Fromm and Klein prefer to leave implicit. Although we shall return to a more detailed consideration of the Fromm-Klein assertion of (3.6) and indicate how the usage of "we are sure that" and "even" in that statement is related to the Brookings—S.S.R.C. philosophy of econometrics, we shall first consider the possibility that Fromm and Klein intended to adduce (3.8) in support of the conclusion they seek to establish, namely, the statement expressed by (3.7).

Let us try to determine the meaning of the statement expressed by (3.8). In the amended sentence (3.8) "Basmann" and "monthly paycheck" have definite objects as referents; "dollars" and "count" do not. If we conceive of "dollars" as definite objects, like slices of bread, and if we interpret "count" in accordance with its definition in theory of arithmetic, or in common speech, the resulting image is ludicrous: there is simply no "collection of dollars in the paycheck" that could be counted. It is probable that Fromm and Klein interpret "dollars" as the abstract unit of "money," which they only allege a "quantity;" by "dollars in paycheck" Fromm and Klein probably mean a specific *numeral* printed on the slip of paper that is the paycheck, and they assert that Basmann can *read* (not count) that numeral. Our adopting this concrete interpretation of the proposition expressed by "Basmann can count the dollars in his monthly paycheck" has the merit of being in good agreement with experience, and also that in adopting it we do not interpret Fromm and Klein as talking nonsense about experience. Thus interpreted, however, the foregoing statement fails to support either the assertion that "money is a quantity" or the assertion that each of the numerical time series in the Brookings—S.S.R.C. Model is a quantity.

I can read my present Selective Service Number as well as my old army serial number; moreover, I can add those numbers, or multiply them; but it does not follow from this that my Selective Service Number and my army serial number are quantities.

Since Fromm and Klein assert

(3.9)   We are well acquainted with the principles of quantitative logic,[31] yet thank Basmann for his pedantic restatement. (Fromm and Klein, 1972, p. 61.)

I shall assume, without detailed argument, that Fromm and Klein realize that the statement expressed by (3.8) does not provide any support for the assertion of the proposition expressed by (3.7); hence, I conclude that Fromm and Klein did not intend to adduce (3.8) in support of (3.7). These assumptions, however, leave us to consider that

   (a) Fromm and Klein adduce (3.6) in support of the conclusion they wish to establish, namely, (3.7);

or

   (b) Fromm and Klein introduce the sentence (3.6) to carry out the nonexpository function of causing their readers to doubt their critic's intelligence or competence. (The use of the word "even" suggests this possibility.)[32]

Notice that both (a) and (b) may be the case. If (a) is not the case, and (b) is the case, then (3.6) is nothing more than an expression of annoyance. Let us assume that (a) is the case.

Let us interpret "observed number," as Fromm and Klein use that term, as "numeral" or "recorded numeral." This affords a definite concrete interpretation of "observed number." Our next step is to find an interpretation of

(3.10)   Certainly, except in a very restricted sense, the observed numbers are quantities. (Fromm and Klein, 1972, p. 60.)

The foregoing sentence requires pruning; the adverb "certainly," which does the question-begging, must be dropped for the time being. Notice that the sentence (3.10) has the same structure as

(3.6): "certainly" performs the same function as "we are sure that," namely, to call attention to the fact that its authors, Fromm and Klein, experience the emotion of belief in the statement expressed by

(3.11)   the observed numbers are quantities.

Although Fromm and Klein intended to adduce the statement expressed by (3.10) in support of (3.7), we shall postpone discussion of how the fact that Fromm and Klein *believe* (3.11) is supposed to support (3.7). Our first task is to determine the semantic meaning of (3.11).

We have to interpret the term "very restricted sense" for ourselves. The following interpretation is meaningful, and is consistent with the tenor of the entire Fromm-Klein argument: The "observed numbers" viz., *numerals*, in the time series of the Brookings—S.S.R.C. Model are neither "quantities" nor "magnitudes" solely in the *very restricted sense* those terms have in the theory of quantity.

The foregoing interpretative statement is true. The terms "quantity" and "magnitude of quantity" are, indeed, restricted in meaning by the definitions and statements of the theory of quantity; moreover those terms are further restricted by the concrete interpretations that are assigned to them in each empirical application of the theory of quantity. It is a normal function of the definitions and statements of any axiomatic theory to specialize the meanings of the terms it contains.

Furthermore, within the context of theory of quantity and its concrete applications no quantity or magnitude of a quantity is a *number*. (It has already been mentioned that the theory of quantity presupposes theory of arithmetic, thus taking over, without alteration, the several concepts of "number" implicitly and explicitly defined in theory of arithmetic. Concrete interpretations of theory of quantity presuppose finite cardinal number, a concrete interpretation of "natural number".) Consequently, (for example) the physical quantities *weight* and *length* are not numbers; nor are their magnitudes numbers. The class of all physical objects each of which on one pan of a pendulum balance will balance my watch on the other pan is not a number; that class (magnitude of weight) is not a natural number or cardinal number; that class of physical objects that is called the weight of my watch, is not any Dedekind cut in the set of all rational numbers, which, in turn, are classes of ordered pairs of rational positive numbers, etc. The class of all physical objects that is the magnitude of weight of my watch is not a numeral; that class of physical objects is not even the numeral that designates it.

So much for that "very restricted sense" in which the "observed numbers" i.e., numerals, in the time series that appear in the Brookings—S.S.R.C. Model are not quantities or magnitudes of quantities. In what sense are the "observed numbers" in those time series quantities? Neither Duesenberry and Klein in their account of the guiding principles of the Brookings—S.S.R.C. philosophy of econometrics (Duesenberry et al., 1965, Chapter 1), nor Fromm and Klein in their reply to "Science or Number Mysticism?" (Fromm and Klein, 1967, pp. 60-61), have taken the trouble to afford the scientific reader, or the reader whose interests are technological, any enlightenment on that score. The tenor of their remarks is towards the conclusion that the meaning and truth of (3.11), "the observed numbers are quantities," are self-evident to all sound minds; after all, most of us, in everyday discourse, use "number" as a synonym for "numeral," and in common speech we all employ "quantity" and "magnitude" as almost, but not completely, synonymous with "number." What Fromm and Klein tell us in the passage just quoted is that "number" and "quantity" are synonymous in everyday usage of words. The "observed numbers" in the numerical time series of the Brookings—S.S.R.C. Model are supposed to be quantities because in ordinary discourse, people very frequently employ the word "quantity" to denote "number" or "numeral."

Today, however, synonyms are widely recognized to be unserviceable as definitions of abstract terms. Constructive implementation of the directive principle that exhorts us to define the abstract terms of scientific theories explicitly by concrete terms is the hallmark of modern empirical science. We seek to define "money" or "amount of money" with help of the referents of the concrete terms "coin," "Federal Reserve Note," "check," and "exchange." The theory of quantity sketched in this section is designed to assist the practical execution of the foregoing policy. A little reflection ought to bring with it recognition of the fact that defining of abstract terms with help of equally abstract terms does not provide any information that is of significance for science or its technological applications. By rejecting theory of quantity (because of its alleged metaphysical status) the Brookings—S.S.R.C. econometricians leave the representation of the Brookings—S.S.R.C. hypothesis disconnected from any definite classes of objects and events of economic experience that might otherwise compose its domain of application. The system of approximately 150 structural equations that is called the first approximation (Duesenberry et al., 1965, Chapter 18), with its letter symbols replaced by number symbols, or numerals, is merely one of those arithmetic illustrations of the type that are found in textbooks of elementary economics, although, unlike the latter, the Brookings—S.S.R.C. Model is not useful for pedagogy because of its Brobdingnagian dimensions.

That the foregoing characterization of the Brookings — S.S.R.C. Model is rejected by the Brookings—S.S.R.C. econometricians goes without saying. They can point out that the numerical coefficients in the first approximation to the Brookings—S.S.R.C. Model, and the numerals that appear in the time series from which those coefficients have been computed, are not completely dissociated from economic experience, not in thought, at least. "Quantity," after all, is not strictly synonymous with "observed number," or "numeral" in common speech, and it seems as if "the observed numbers are quantities" actually does yield significant information about the numerical time series in the Brookings —S.S.R.C. Model, and about the relations of those numerals to economic experiences. "Number" and "quantity," like all nouns, or *names*, seem to express existences of things. ("If you can name it, it must exist.") Nouns have the power of producing in us the feeling of having got hold of something substantial; this rhetorical power is not confined to nouns with concrete referents, e.g., "coal," "crude oil," "natural gas," "coin," "Federal Reserve Note," etc., but is shared by abstract nouns such as "inflation," "supply," "demand," "marginal propensity to consume," etc. "GNP—1962, in 1954 dollars" seems to be evidence of something almost palpable, and "GNP—1962, 475,000,000,000 (1954 dollars) is approximately twice as great as GNP—1941, 238,000,000,000 (1954 dollars)" seems to convey significant information about that something. Nouns differ in respect of their power to produce the sensation of substance; "quantity" seems more substantial than "number," or "numeral." To assert that "475,000,000,000 (1954 dollars)" is a quantity seems to endow "475,000,000,000 (1954 dollars)" with substance.

In the role of evoking the image of substance we find the function of the word "quantity" in the Brookings—S.S.R.C. philosophy of econometrics. Consider the following: (1) The noun "quantity" does not have a concrete referent in common speech. (2) If the explicit definition of "quantity" in theory of quantity is appealed to, then the key statement of the Fromm-Klein argument, namely, "the observed numbers are quantities," is false. (3) If Fromm and Klein had intended the word "quantity" to convey a definite *semantic meaning*, then they would have introduced a constructive definition, as in theory of quantity and magnitude. (4) The noun "quantity," which Fromm and Klein predicate of the "observed numbers" in the time series of the Brookings—S.S.R.C. Model, attaches to those numerals a penumbra of objectifications that seems to be something the model expresses an hypothesis about.

Now we are in a position to consider what "evidence" Fromm and Klein suppose the statement expressed by (3.10) to contain, and how that "evidence" supports (3.7), namely, the statement that the observed numbers in the time series that appear in the Brookings—S.S.R.C. Model are quantities.

Fromm and Klein give us just one indication of the nature of the "evidence" they intend to adduce in support of

the observed numbers are quantities.

That indication is the adverb "certainly," in (3.10), which serves to draw attention to their own attitudes towards the foregoing statement. It has already been mentioned that, as used by Fromm and Klein, the adverb "certainly" directs attention to the fact it asserts, namely, that they believe, with an intensity that amounts to certainty, that the "observed numbers" in the time series used in the Brookings—S.S.R.C. Model are "quantities." In other words, the circumstances that Fromm and Klein accept as confirming the statement expressed by (3.7) are the emotions of belief experienced by them and—perhaps—by other econometricians associated with the Brookings—S.S.R.C. project, as indicated by consensus. They do not mention any other kind of evidence, e.g., objective empirical evidence, for (3.7). If they had presented the kind of objective evidence called for by theory of quantity and magnitude, then that presentation of evidence might have afforded an effective refutation of my criticism, namely, that the quantitative foundations of the Brookings—S.S.R.C. Model are seriously defective. They do not possess such objective evidence or they consider such evidence to be much less cogent than the "evidence" they do offer, namely, their own emotions of belief.

The foregoing analysis of the Fromm-Klein reply suggests the hypothesis that the Brookings—S.S.R.C. econometricians adhere to the *objectification theory of semantic meaning.* This theory, which takes objectifications of the mental images of abstract words like "quantity" and "number" for the semantic meanings of such terms, will be discussed in more detail in Section 5, where I shall elaborate on the hypothesis that the objectification theory of meaning is an essential part of the philosophy of mainstream econometrics.

4. THE BROOKINGS — S.S.R.C. CONCEPTION OF ARGUMENT

When we examine the patterns and content of the arguments by means of which Fromm and Klein try to refute criticisms I levelled at the formulation and mathematical elucidation of the Brookings—S.S.R.C. Model we find additional evidence that tends to support the hypothesis mentioned at the end of the preceding section. Rhetorical analysis[33] of the Fromm-Klein reply suggests the hypothesis that the purpose of that reply was not expository, that Fromm and Klein intended to create a mood that would lead their readers to dismiss my criticisms of the Brookings—S.S.R.C. Model without giving those criticisms a second thought. Let us assume the negation of that hypothesis, viz., let us assume that Fromm and Klein intended "A Rational Perspective" to be strictly expository, and sought to communicate with their readers in propositional English. This hypothesis has some definite consequences which we can check against the patterns of the arguments that are offered by Fromm and Klein. Let us examine one of their more prominent arguments; Fromm and Klein assert:

(4.1)   Basmann implies that the greater the number of complex dependencies in a model, the more realistic and valid are its estimates and its explanation of structure (of the phenomena it supposedly represents). (Fromm and Klein, 1972, p. 59.)

Let us modify the foregoing sentence as follows:

(4.2)   Basmann has asserted the propositions A, B, C, etc., *and* from A, B, C, etc., the following proposition (call it D)
          the greater the number of complex dependencies in a model, the more realistic and valid are its estimates and its explanation of structure (of the phenomena it represents)
          can be deduced.

Justification for the modification (4.2) of the sentence (4.1) is as follows: The verb "imply" in propositional, or expository, English, calls for the name of a definite declarative sentence as its subject (recall Section 2). The sentence "Basmann implies D" is not meaningful in propositional English; accordingly I take it for granted that Fromm and Klein did not intend their sentence (4.1) to be taken literally, but as a sort of slang form of expression for the modified sentence (4.2).

Fromm and Klein assert the proposition expressed by (4.2). There are two questions to be answered:

(1) How (and how well) do Fromm and Klein support their assertion of (4.2)?

(2) Which specific statements actually expressed in "Science or Number Mysticism?", or elsewhere, do (4.2) and/or D tend to refute, and how do (4.2) and D tend to refute the given statements?

Notice that the proposition expressed by (4.2) is a conjunction, the constituent propositions of which are

(4.3a)   Basmann has asserted the propositions A, B, C, etc.
(4.3b)   D is deducible from A, B, C, etc.

To begin with let us try to determine what conclusion Fromm and Klein are trying to establish. In "A Rational Perspective" the sentence

(4.4)   This is not necessarily true. (Fromm and Klein, 1972, p. 59.)

immediately follows the sentence (4.1). We continue to interpret (4.1) by (4.2). Now we have to decide whether "this" denotes (4.2) or D. We apply the rules of *modal logic* here (cf. Anderson and Johnstone, 1962, pp. 129-136.) "(4.2) is not necessarily true" means that (4.2) is not a *tautology*, i.e., it is not of necessity the case that Basmann asserted propositions A, B, C, etc. and that from A, B, C, etc., D is deducible. Clearly "(4.2) is not necessarily true" gives us no help. Let us suppose that "this" in (4.4) denotes D. "D is not necessarily true" means that D is not a tautology. For Fromm and Klein to tell their readers that D is not a tautology would be relevant to the discussion of my remarks only if I had asserted that D was a tautology.[34] Before we consider what evidence Fromm and Klein might have for my having asserted that D is a tautology, let us consider what evidence they might adduce in support of (4.2).

If Fromm and Klein specify definite sentences A, B, C, etc., then (4.3a) is a contingent, or empirical proposition; the empirical statement expressed by (4.3a) is true if it is the case that I have at some times and some places asserted the definite sentences A, B, C, etc., attributed to me by Fromm and Klein; otherwise, the statement expressed by (4.3a) is false. Moreover, if (4.3a) is true, then Fromm and Klein should have little difficulty in confirming that proposition. Confirmation of (4.3a) would be especially easy for Fromm and Klein if the definite sentences A, B, C, etc., happen to be asserted in one of my published articles. On the other hand, if the definite sentences A, B, C, etc., were not asserted in writing, but orally, then Fromm and Klein would experience a little more difficulty in confirming (4.3a), but not much. In showing how Fromm and Klein actually do deal with the rather easy problem of confirming (4.3a), we can throw considerable light on those directive principles of the Brookings—S.S.R.C. philosophy of econometrics which govern its adherents' use of empirical evidence.

Now consider (4.3b). The sentences A, B, C, etc., are supposed to be those specified by Fromm and Klein in (4.3a); recall that D is that clause of (4.2) that follows the word "implies." The sentence (4.3b) refers implicitly to a set of *propositional rules*, or *rules of deduction*, and expresses the statement that, in accordance with those propositional rules, the definite sentence D—introduced by Fromm and Klein—is deducible from the definite sentences A, B, C, etc., allegedly asserted by me at some times and places. More precisely, (4.3b) expresses the statement that, by virtue of

(1) the specific molecular forms of A, B, C, etc., and D in the logical connectives and the binding of variables to quantifiers,

and

(2) the mention in at least one of A, B, C, etc., of each the predicates "realistic" and "valid"—which are, as Fromm and Klein use them, *dyadic relations*[35]—and the ascription by at least one of A, B, C, etc., of "realistic" and "valid" to "parameter estimates" and "explanations of structure,"

the sentence D is deducible from A, B, C, etc., in accordance with the tacit propositional rules. To justify or support their assertion of the proposition expressed by (4.2), Fromm and Klein must indicate specifically what rules of deduction govern the derivation of D from the definite sentences A, B, C, etc., and they must demonstrate that they have applied those rules correctly.

Now let us examine how Fromm and Klein justify their assertion of the statement (4.2). They do not indicate the specific propositions A, B, C . . . from which the proposition D allegedly can be deduced, nor do they indicate what deduction rules are to be applied in the argument leading from A, B, C . . . as premises, to D as conclusion. In the face of this failure to be specific about A, B, C and the requisite deduction rules, there is little their readers can do to determine for themselves how well-supported is the assertion (4.2). The most one can say is that, unless they are using some esoteric language system, at least one of the unspecified propositions A, B, C, etc., must contain "estimate" and "explanation of structure" as individual variables[36] and "realistic" and "valid" as definite two-term relations. The reader of the Fromm-Klein reply might be led to suppose that specific sentences A, B, C, etc., of the required type actually appear somewhere in "Science or Number Mysticism?", or perhaps, elsewhere in one or more of my published articles; and, furthermore, that A, B, C, are so well-known that Fromm and Klein are (somehow) justified in not quoting those alleged statements or indicating exactly where they are to be found. If they had considered it to be important that their readers be able to examine the basic evidence that allegedly supports (4.2), then they would have indicated where that basic evidence can be found. However, since they do not indicate which definite propositions A, B, C, etc., their readers are to believe that I have asserted, or where those propositions are to be found in my publications, they do not consider it important that their readers be able to examine the alleged evidence for themselves. Before asking (in Section 5) how the foregoing attitude towards sharing basic empirical evidence with their readers may be justified in the philosophy of econometrics to which Fromm and Klein adhere, I shall indicate where some statements relevant to the Fromm-Klein assertion (4.2) can be found, and—in general—what my views in respect of their proposition D actually are. In "Science or Number Mysticism?" the relevant statements about hypothetical restrictions on structural parameters are to be found in Section 3 (pp. 18-20). Previous relevant statements of mine are found in several articles (cf. Basmann, 1963, esp. pp. 943-945; 1965a, esp. pp 1082-1084; 1965b, esp. pp. 387-388, pp. 391-393; also 1966, passim). All of my published articles in econometric statistics stress the distinction between (1) testing hypothetical functional dependences on structural parameters with help of sample statistics *unconstrained* by those functional dependences and (2) the imposition of hypothetical functional dependences on structural estimates. In this connection see my criticisms of the practice of suppressing publication of unconstrained test statistics (Basmann, 1963, p. 945). In respect of the publication of statistics for testing hypothetical functional dependences, I have written:

> Preoccupied with *estimation* of structural economic parameters rather than with the *testing* of theoretical economic premises about parameters, most econometricians have made no use of the identifiability test statistics. Nonetheless, the testing of theoretical premises about an economic parameter is logically prior to its estimation. This is particularly so in case theoretical restrictions, supposedly constraining true parameters, have been imposed on their statistical estimates and this imposition of restrictions is claimed to be effective in enhancing efficiency of estimation. (Basmann, 1965b, pp. 387-388; also Basmann, 1960, p. 658.)

I have been critical of suppression of publication of identifiability test statistics, a suppression which has been habitual with Klein and many other econometricians.

I have stressed that explicit functional dependences among the structural parameters of a representation express economic *hypotheses;* that the formulation and deductive checking of *hypothetical* restrictions for logical consistency are to be regarded as pure economic theorizing. Statements of functional dependences and inequalities are not put forward as knowledge claims, whether empirical or a priori; not, at least, by anyone who reflects on the matter. Such hypotheses can be tested empirically.

My suggestions in respect of formulating and testing hypothetical functional dependences and inequalities are the following:

(1) Formulate as many hypothetical functional dependences and linear equalities as you may find interesting; then formulate a few more. Thus construct a structural economic hypothesis B_1. This construction includes proving the consistency of the set of all structural equations, identities among variables, functional dependences among parameters, and linear equalities. (cf. Basmann, 1972, pp. 19-20.)

(2) Formulate a set of statistics for testing the functional dependences and inequalities that express the structural hypothesis B_1. Transparently, you do not impose on this set of statistics the very restrictions you propose to test. Use knowledge of distributions of test statistics to "sharpen" the hypotheses put forward in part (1).

(3) If you have available a sufficiently large sample to compute the foregoing test statistics uniquely, and this without imposing additional restrictions on (say) parameter estimates, perform the test and provide a complete report of its outcome, i.e., one that is uncensored by your own interpretation of that outcome.

The foregoing procedures are concisely illustrated in a recent article (Basmann, 1965b).

If one follows the foregoing recommendations, one produces a structural economic hypothesis that is—potentially, at least—capable of being integrated into a broader unified economic theory; and one displays all of the empirical evidence that might tend to disconfirm one or more of hypothetical functional dependences and inequalities in a convenient form for subsequent use, especially by others.

(1)-(3) above summarize and probably exhaust the recommendations that can be gleaned from my publications and lectures with ordinary rules of inference. The *aim* served by these recommendations is the development of a unified general economic theory that is well-supported by empirical evidence. One of the more immediate *objectives* of formulating and testing the hypothetical functional dependences and other parameter restrictions is to provide the general economic theorists with a collection of empirically well-supported hypotheses that assert rather precise claims about real economic structure. Another immediate practical objective of testing hypothetical parameter restrictions is that of eliminating (tentatively) many less promising hypotheses, thus assisting general theorists in reducing the number of alternative hypotheses they have to consider. The reasons for being candid with the theorists do not require special comment.

I have never offered the foregoing recommendations as a guarantee of success in economic research. Methodological recommendations are not propositions that belong to the subject matter of economics; nor are they mathematical propositions about distributions of econometric estimators and test statistics. Given an economic hypothesis H_0, an alternative hypothesis $H\text{-}H_0$, the exact finite sample distribution function of a statistic $\hat{\theta}$ for testing H_0 against $H\text{-}H_0$, and a specified level of significance, we can determine the range of observations that are in agreement with H_0 at that level of significance. The narrower is the range of observations that agree with H_0, the "sharper" H_0 is said to be.[37] In many cases, the greater the number of restrictions—functional dependences and inequalities—the "sharper" is H_0, the economic hypothesis in question. It is probable that Fromm and Klein claim to have deduced their sentence D about functional dependences "realistic" and "valid" estimates and "explanations of structure" from my remarks about "sharpness" of economic hypotheses in "Science or Number Mysticism?". However, I, for one, do not know what specific dyadic relations Fromm and Klein intend to denote by "realistic" or "valid," nor do I know how to deduce their sentence D from my statements about "sharpness" of economic hypotheses. Now "realistic" and "valid" are not predicates I apply to parameter estimates. On the other hand, "realistic" and "valid" (as applied to statistical estimates) are terms that belong to, and occur frequently in, the language employed by the econometricians. Klein—by precept, at least—suggests that if such functional dependences are regarded by the econometrician as a priori knowledge or a priori information, then those functional dependences may be imposed on parameter estimates, and their statistical test may safely be dispensed with.

Furthermore, Fromm and Klein offer the following methodological advice:

> Economic theory, knowledge of institutions, and similar bodies of information unrelated to sample observation should form the basis of parameter restrictions. (Fromm and Klein, 1972, p. 59.)

Propositions A, B, C, etc., containing two-place predicates "realistic" and "valid" and ascribing such predicates to parameter estimates and so-called explanations of structure cannot be found in "Science or Number Mysticism?" or in any other paper written by me. Accordingly, evidence of the appropriate kind disconfirms the sentence (4.3a) and, since (4.3a) is a constituent of the sentence (4.2), which is a logical conjunction, evidence that disconfirms (4.3a) disconfirms (4.2).

If Fromm and Klein had specified the definite sentences A, B, C, etc., and indicated definite rules of deduction, then we could determine whether or not their sentence D can be deduced from A, B, C, etc. (For this demonstration it is not required that A, B, C, etc., express propositions actually asserted by me.) Fromm and Klein did not bother to specify the deduction rules, hence we cannot determine whether D follows from some sentences A, B, C, etc.

Although it is an easy task to examine the basic empirical evidence that is relevant to the truth of the sentence (4.3a), apparently Fromm and Klein did not do so; at least they did not indicate what the evidence is supposed to be. *We should not jump to the conclusion that their handling of the empirical data was incompetent without first considering* (as we shall do in Section 5) *whether the philosophy of econometrics to which they adhere places any great value on confirming empirical premises objectively.* In this connection recall that the evidence they offered for their assertion that the numerical time series in the Brookings—S.S.R.C. Model are quantities was *introspective,* not empirical and objective.

In one sense the failure of Fromm and Klein to indicate the specific sentences A, B, C, etc., and provide their readers with evidence that confirms the proposition that I asserted those specific sentences, affords stronger support—stronger than their failure to cite objective evidence for (3.7)—to the hypothesis that Fromm and Klein do not consider the matter of confirming empirical premises by objective evidence to be important. The very great technical difficulties involved in confirming the statement that the so-called observed numbers in the time series that appear in the Brookings—S.S.R.C. Model are quantities might have been cited as a partial excuse for not having laid down more secure quantitative foundations (Fromm and Klein make no reference to those technical difficulties, however). Such an excuse would not be acceptable in respect of the failure of Fromm and Klein to indicate the specific sentences A, B, C, etc., they have in mind and the evidence supporting the statement that I have asserted A, B, C, etc.

To assert, or even to prove, that D is not a tautology, does not tend to refute my criticism, namely, that the Brookings—S.S.R.C. Model lacks sufficient "sharpness" to be empirically testable in practice. If D is a tautology, then D contains no information; to assert that D is not a tautology is tantamount to asserting that D contains information (presumably about statistical estimates and "explanations of structures"). However, Fromm and Klein nowhere indicate the meaning of D.

Evaluated as an attempt to communicate in propositional English, the Fromm-Klein refutation of my criticism in respect of the "sharpness" of the Brookings—S.S.R.C. hypothesis has to be assigned failing marks.

The Fromm-Klein reply is an incompetently written piece of intended propositional English *or* the Fromm-Klein reply is intended to serve a nonexpository function, e.g., to serve as a message of reassurance to econometricians. (The connective "or" is not exclusive; recall Section 2.) Let us assume that the Fromm-Klein reply is intended to be an expository composition but is unskillfully done. From this assumption we can deduce that Fromm and Klein, in their work on econometric models, have had little opportunity to practice in writing and speaking, reading and listening to, propositional English. From this statement we can deduce in turn that adherents of the Brookings—S.S.R.C. philosophy of econometrics do not put much stress on logical argument and objective empirical support of contingent premises.

Now let us assume that the Fromm-Klein reply is intended to serve a non-expository function. Introducing (4.1) and proceeding to assert about (4.1), or D, that it is not necessarily true, viz., that (4.1) or D are not tautologies, Fromm and Klein found occasion to use several logical words, e.g., "imply," "necessary," "valid," etc., which tend to give their remarks the flavor of logical argument. Readers of "A Rational Prespective" may thus be led to believe that Fromm and Klein have refuted some statements or other without, however, inquiring precisely which statements have been refuted, and exactly how Fromm and Klein have done this. The function served by their reply is to reassure the readers of "A Rational Perspective" in the face of my criticisms of the Brookings —S.S.R.C. Model, and the means to that end are the logical and psychological fallacies. The assumption that the Fromm-Klein reply is intended to serve a nonexpository function leads to the same conclusion as the previous assumption, namely, that adherents of the Brookings—S.S.R.C. philosophy of econometrics do not put much stress on logical argument and objective empirical support of contingent premises.

That the adherents of the Brookings—S.S.R.C. philosophy of econometrics do not put much emphasis on logical argument and the citation of objective empirical support for premises (where such support is called for) is a statement that calls for explanation. The explanation proffered has also to account for the salient fact mentioned in connection with the Fromm-Klein assertion

> Certainly, the observed numbers are quantities. (Fromm and Klein, 1972, p. 60.)

in Section 3, namely, that the only indication of the kind of empirical evidence Fromm and Klein consider relevant is the word "certainly," which points to their own belief that "the observed numbers are quantities."

5. CONCLUSION

A person is said to *objectify* an abstract word or other symbol if he presents that word to himself as denoting an object—as a thing that can be touched, tasted, smelled, heard, or seen. The mental image that is formed by a person who objectifies a given abstract word is said to be an *objectification* of that word. The *objectification doctrine of meaning* treats such mental images of given words, phrases, and sentences, as *semantic* meanings. Adherents of the *objectification doctrine*, who take their own objectifications of abstract terms like "number" and "quantity" as the proper meanings of those terms, tacitly assume that everyone else, or at least everyone who is intelligent and whose mind is sound, forms very nearly the same objectifications and takes objectifications for meanings.[38]

To the adherent of the objectification doctrine of meaning, the meaning and truth of a given atomic sentence, e.g.,

(5.1)   ... the observed numbers are quantities. (Fromm and Klein, 1972, p. 60.)

depend in part on his mental images of the abstract terms and logical words that sentence contains. The foregoing sentence, for example, is considered true by adherents of the objectification doctrine if each adherent forms a mental image of "quantity" that is the same mental image he forms of "observed number." For example, if Fromm forms identical mental images of "observed number" and "quantity," and Klein forms identical mental images of "observed number" and "quantity," then Fromm and Klein participate in a *consensus* in respect of "the observed numbers are quantities." (It does not follow, however, that Fromm's mental images are similar to Klein's.) According to the objectification doctrine the circumstance that makes a statement true—e.g., makes the statement expressed by (5.1) true—is the consensus of all persons of sound mind and intelligence that the statement in question is true.

Now it is not the case that adherents of the objectification doctrine assume that everyone of sound mind and intelligence *immediately* forms the correct mental image, or proper meaning, of an abstract term upon first encountering it; one must learn how to form the correct image. For instance, not being an econometrician, one might fail to form the proper mental image of "realistic estimate," or of "one estimate being more realistic than another estimate" and, hence, not grasp the proper meaning of "realistic" as that term is applied to statistical estimates or "explanations of structure" by econometricians.[39] Thus, the meanings and truth of atomic statements are not considered as purely egocentric by all adherents of the objectification doctrine of semantic meaning. *Introspection* is the process whereby an individual adherent of the objectification doctrine determines for himself the meaning and truth of a given atomic statement. On the other hand, for the individual, the test of his grasp of the proper meaning and truth of a given atomic statement is the breadth of the consensus among other individuals in respect of the truth or falsity of that given statement.

In this connection notice that it is by no means the case that scientists who reject the view that mental images excited by symbols (words and sentences) are the semantic meanings of those symbols deny that such images and objectifications are helpful in the speculative formulation of scientific hypotheses, and in pedagogy. What they do deny is that the feeling of conviction (no matter who, or how many, happen to experience that emotion) associated with images and objectifications excited by symbols and strings of symbols is appropriate evidence in support of scientific propositions.

Notice, also, that the objectification doctrine of meaning of atomic statements is compatible with any of the presently known systems of propositional logic. Let A and B be any atomic statements whose meanings and truth-values adherents of the objectification doctrine determine by the processes of *introspection* and *consensus*. It is open to adherents of the objectification doctrine of meaning to determine truth-values of the molecular statements $\sim A$, $A \& B$, $A \lor B$, $A \supset B$, and $A \equiv B$ in accordance with the system of truth-value assignment tables for the logical connectives (recall Section 2). Strict adherence to the deduction rules of logic is a course of action open to the adherent of the objectification doctrine of meaning. However, many persons who adhere to the objectification doctrine of meaning also adhere to the doctrine that holds logic and its rules of deduction to be a system of proffered laws of thinking, i.e., a branch of empirical psychology; many adherents of the objectification doctrine consider the rules of deduction as hypotheses that are testable against the propositions established by introspection and consensus, as rules that are to be discarded if they disagree with statements regarded as verified or confirmed by introspection and consensus.

Sentence-by-sentence examination of the methodological article by Duesenberry and Klein (Duesenberry et al., 1965, Chapter 1) and the reply to "Science or Number Mysticism?" by Fromm and Klein (1972), leads me to put forward the hypothesis that the *objectification doctrine of meaning* is an integral part of the philosophy of econometrics that underlies the formulation of, and technical work on, the Brookings—S.S.R.C. Model. Although this hypothesis is somewhat less adequate as a proffered explanation of the seriously defective arguments used by Fromm and Klein in their reply, it does have the merit of being capable of accounting for the fact that, where empirical support is called for, Fromm and Klein explicitly call attention to their own emotional states, i.e., their own *beliefs* in the proposition that is in question, and offer their readers nothing else. Fromm and Klein have objectified the constructive defining of "magnitude of a quantity," e.g., of cardinal numbers and weights as a creative act of God, an act of "quantifying absolutely" (Fromm and Klein, 1972, p. 61). Verbal description of the concept of constructive definition of "magnitude" and "quantity" is objectified by Fromm and Klein as an attempt by the scientist to "quantify absolutely" an unspecified act of creation they assert only God can perform. Fromm and Klein have misunderstood each of the criticisms I raised in "Science or Number Mysticism?"; their misunderstanding of constructive definition is profound. For instance, in "Science or Number Mysticism?" I gave a short illustration of the *irrelevance* of regression estimates and the *ordinary* correlation coefficient R^2 when at least one of the numerical series represents the ranking of a property so defined by construction that it is only orderable (Basmann, 1967a, Section 4).[40] The two artificial series are perfectly correlated by rank, viz., the statistic appropriate for properties that are only orderable, *Spearman's rank correlation coefficient* (Snedecor, 1946, pp. 164-165), is equal to +1.0 for every *order-preserving transformation* of the series that represents the orderable property. I showed that the *ordinary correlation cofficient* R is not invariant against such order-preserving transformations, giving values of R for two cases, namely, R=1.0 and R=0.9 (R^2=0.81), and hence that R is technically inappropriate. Let us examine the comment Fromm and Klein made on my illustration, since that comment shows that their philosophy of econometrics is not without its impact on their technical work in econometric statistics:

(5.2)   Obviously, especially where variables are only orderable (as Basmann's recitation of well-known principles illustrates) care must be taken not to be misled by high degrees of fit. (Fromm and Klein, 1972, p. 60.)

Fromm and Klein miss the point. There is exactly one circumstance in which the ordinary correlation coefficient R does *not* misrepresent the empirical circumstance described by the numerical series and that is the circumstance in which R is as large as it can possibly be, namely, when R=1 and the "fit" of the regression is perfect. Fromm and Klein would be misled by R=0.9, or some smaller value of R that can be obtained by introducing another order-preserving transformation of the basic numerical series. The "well-known principles" they supposed me to have recited in "Science or Number Mysticism?" are their own objectifications of what I actually did write. For them, that a variable property is only orderable is not determined by any constructive definition, nor does the selection of a statistic for measuring the association (similarity of order) of the given orderable property with another property depend on any constructive definition of that property. They do not explain *how* they come to know that a given numerical series represents a property that is only orderable. According to my hypothesis, however, they would answer

(5.3)   Certainly, the observed numbers are only orderable magnitudes.

More precisely, according to my hypothesis, what determines for Fromm and Klein that the "observed numbers" are only orderable is the image or objectification excited by the word that names the allegedly existing property. (The numbers themselves are not only orderable but also additive.) The quotation (5.2) also suggests the hypothesis that, for the Brookings—S.S.R.C. econometricians, images of names of orderable properties seem to merge into images of additive properties, or quantities, so that orderable properties may be imagined to approximate quantities in some subjective sense, thus making valid the numerical representation of orderable properties as if they were quantities, provided that in doing so one takes account of the "approximation" and takes "care not to be misled by high degrees of fit."

Fromm and Klein have taken issue with me over the importance of the role of *consensus* in the Brookings—S.S.R.C. philosophy of econometrics (Fromm and Klein, 1972, p. 53). They assert that the question of consensus is a minor one. However, the frequency with which "band wagon" words and phrases occur in the writings of the Brookings—S.S.R.C. econometricians has to be explained. Ordinarily, a disputant, whose use of such band wagon terms has been detected and criticized already, avoids using more band wagon and question-begging terms, especially if he is trying to refute his opponent's suggestion that band wagon terms are essential to his previous argument. Let us consider what Fromm and Klein have to say:

(5.4) The model is a direct outgrowth of a 1959 S.S.R.C. conference on stability and instability in the U.S. economy. At that conference, held in Ann Arbor, several papers (at least one of which is now regarded as a classic) were presented. (Fromm and Klein, 1972, p. 53.)

Let us consider the function of the sentence appearing in parenthesis. Fromm and Klein intend their readers to understand that at least one paper (and, perhaps, all of the papers) is now regarded as a classic, i.e., that its excellence is avowed, that its excellence is a matter of consensus. Getting the reader to believe that the excellence of one of the conference papers that preceded the construction of the Brookings—S.S.R.C. Model is a matter of consensus does not tend to support the Fromm-Klein contention that consensus is a minor matter in the Brookings—S.S.R.C. philosophy of econometrics. Furthermore, the precise paper that allegedly is now conceded to be a classic is not identified for the reader of the Fromm-Klein reply; this suggests that Fromm and Klein do not consider it important for their readers to be able to form a judgement for themselves in respect of the quality of that paper. (In this connection recall the suppressed propositions A, B, C, etc., discussed in Section 4.) The hypothesis that Fromm and Klein are preoccupied with getting consensus accounts for their having asserted the band wagon sentence in their argument. Fromm and Klein do tell us that they did not seek full consensus on all details of the initial Brookings Model, etc.

(5.5)   The aim was, and is, to achieve general acceptance of a framework for a model system as a whole and some of its major parts, without necessarily having agreement on the details among all economists. (Fromm and Klein, 1972, p. 53.)

The objectification doctrine of meaning readily allows for its adherents disagreeing on details. None of the remarks of Fromm and Klein tends to disconfirm my hypothesis. As I do not argue this point here, my readers should consult the Fromm-Klein reply for the evidence.

The chief practical issue raised in "Science or Number Mysticism?" has to do with the allocation of resources among the several research activities involved in the formulation and empirical testing of quantitative economic hypotheses. To allocate some part of the available resources to the formulation and testing of the proffered laws of quantity that are presupposed in the formulation of simultaneous equation system that represents some economic hypothesis is by no means tantamount to allocating all available resources to that activity alone. Among economists who agree with the view I expressed in "Science or Number Mysticism?" (see quotation (1.6) in this paper) some considerable disagreement can arise in respect of alternative allocations. To defend a given allocation against the criticism that too small a fraction of resources has been devoted to the securing of quantitative foundations, a quantitative economist need not employ the arguments that have been introduced by the Brookings—S.S.R.C. econometricians; to counter the criticism that too little effort has been expended on testing of presupposed laws of quantity, one need not go to the extreme of claiming that the concepts of quantity and magnitude are (say) metaphysical, etc. That Fromm and Klein, and other econometricians as well, have gone to that extreme makes improbable the hypothesis that they are merely defending an allocation that they have made on practical grounds alone. It is more probable that they view the issue as fundamental and imagine the application of the theory of quantity, with its emphasis on constructive definitions of abstract economic quantities, to be a threat to the conception they have formed of the empirical basis of econometrics. The hypothesis that the Brookings—S.S.R.C. econometricians adhere to the objectification doctrine of meaning accounts (in part) for the following assertion by Fromm and Klein:

(5.6)   If we pursued Basmann's thesis to its ultimate conclusion, inductive science must perish. (Fromm and Klein, 1972, p. 61.)

It is probable that if economists adopt constructive definitions of abstract economic entities, building up concepts of quantity and magnitude as classes of objects of experience, and classes of classes of such objects, then introspection and consensus as methods of discovering the meanings and determining the truth of economic propositions that involve abstract terms like "number" and "economic magnitude" would cease to be so widely employed by econometricians as those methods are at present. According to the hypothesis introduced in this section, by "inductive science" Fromm and Klein mean the processes of introspection and consensus. If my thesis were pursued to its ultimate conclusion, then reliance on introspection and consensus as methods of acquiring economic knowledge might well perish.

A little speculation may be permitted here. At the present time the real-valued function of one or more real variables, and systems of equations in such functions, have become hypostatized as the leading paradigms of structural economic relation in econometrics. Whether or not the attempt to force economic hypotheses to fit those paradigms has inhibited the economist's ability to represent, in a fruitful scientific way, the (apparently) rather complicated events of real economic affairs cannot be determined without considerable economic research that deals with such events more or less directly, as research that is aimed at providing constructive definitions of fundamental and derived economic entities must do. The class of well-established economic quantities may well turn out to be small in number, and the class of abstract economic entities that are more complex than quantities may turn out to be relatively very much larger in number. Such a state of affairs would indicate that the attempt to deal with the complexity of economic structure by formulating grand systems of simultaneous equations in real-valued functions of real variables and the accompanying proliferation of numerical time series that allegedly are "quantities" are ineffective and wasteful. In such circumstances few economists would be impressed by the electronic computer's ability to whip off a multiple regression, together with an awesome battery of test statistics, in a few seconds, but would require of the electronic computer that it be able to perform more sophisticated and scientifically more useful operations.

The foregoing remarks are speculative, but they are not farfetched. It is not very improbable that an economic science, based on constructive definitions of its abstract economic entities, could relegate the Walrasian image of economic structure to a minor role; perhaps this outcome is what Fromm and Klein are referring to when they write of inductive science perishing.

Fromm and Klein, in their reply "A Rational Perspective," have failed to meet any of the criticisms put forward in "Science or Number Mysticism?" Nonetheless, they must be given credit for doing about as well in that respect as adherence to the objectification doctrine of economic meaning permits.

NOTES

[1]Review of Duesenberry, J. S., G. Fromm, L. R. Klein, and E. Kuh (eds.), *The Brookings Quarterly Econometric Model of the U.S.*, Chicago, Rand McNally, 1965.

[2]Review presented at meetings of the Southern Economic Association, Atlanta, November 10, 1966. Discussants were Charles Ferguson, Gary Fromm, and Edward Greenberg.

[3]Columbus, Ohio, May 18-19, 1967.

[4]I intend to deal with this technical question in another paper. See *Note 9*.

[5]In "Science or Number Mysticism?" (Section 3) the illustration I employ is a system of equations linear in the structural coefficients. The remarks I made there apply to nonlinear systems of structural relations as well as to systems linear in structural coefficients.

[6]Suppose that (1.8) is linear in the coefficients and in the variables $y_1, ..., y_G, x_1, ..., x_K, u_1, ..., u_G$; i.e.,

(i) $$B'y' + \Gamma'x' + u' = 0$$

where y is a row-vector of G components, x a row-vector of K components, u a row-vector of G (random) components, and let the random vector u have probability density (frequency) function $g(u)$. To demonstrate that (i) is *consistent* one applies elementary row and column operations to the system (i) to deduce

(ii) $$\text{rank } [B' : \Gamma'x' + u'] = \text{rank } B'$$

with probability=1 for all vectors x in the domain of x. The common rank of the matrices shown in (ii) is the number of independent equations in the system (i). The rank of $[B':\Gamma'x'+u']$, with probability=1, and rank of B' depend on the hypothetical parameter restrictions on B', Γ', the restrictions on the parameters of the density function $g(u)$, and the domain of x.

If equation (ii) does not hold, then the system (i), under the hypothetical parameter restrictions, is *inconsistent*. In such a case, the structural hypothesis is a *logical contradiction*.

To check (1.8) for uniqueness of the reduced form (1.9) one determines whether—under the parameter restrictions put forward for the system (1.8)—the conditions of the *implicit function theorem* are met (cf. Spivak, 1965, pp. 40-42; Basmann, 1965b, p. 402).

[7]Referring to the system of equations in Chapter 18 Fromm and Klein assert:

The system of equations, when put together in a consistent way as we have done here, comes to more than 150 equations. The exact number is hard to state because there are many trivial and definitional identities that we refrain from eliminating by substitution, for matters of convenience. (Duesenberry, et al., 1965, p. 722).

Notice that the elimination of definitional identities is accomplished by elementary column operations on the matrices $[B':\Gamma'x'+u']$ and B' (mentioned in *Note 6*) and is involved in the process of determining the consistency of the system (i) and the existence of a unique reduced form. In other words, according to Fromm and Klein,

(a) operations required in checking consistency of the system in Chapter 18 have not been carried out;

and

(b) the Brookings—S.S.R.C. econometricians have put that system together in a consistent way.

According to Fromm and Klein some of the identities they refrained from eliminating are "trivial." On the other hand, in mathematics, at least, no identity (equation) in a system of equations is trivial, especially where the matter at issue is the consistency of the system of equations in which that identity appears. This usage of "trivial" by Fromm and Klein as an alleged technical term of mathematics throws some light on the question asked in Section 1, namely, in what sense is it the case that econometrics, as pursued by the Brookings—S.S.R.C. econometricians, is a mathematical science? Recall (1.3). The Brookings—S.S.R.C. econometricians are introducing some esoteric modifications of fundamental mathematics itself.

[8]Fromm and Klein put forward several "arguments" in order to refute my criticism. They give two reasons why the exact number of equations in the system of equations in Chapter 18 is hard to state:

> First, in almost any system of equations of moderate size, it is possible to include or exclude convenient definitional identities (Fromm and Klein, 1972, p. 55.)

In other words, given any system of equations some of which are definitional identities, the mathematical operations by means of which that system is checked for consistency can be performed; recall *Notes 5, 6, 7.*

> But, secondly, even in the reduced-form the size of the system is not fixed as long as there are alternative versions of different order of segments of the system. ... Finally, in the realm of the size of the system, it is always possible to delete endogenous relationships and treat the variables exogenously. (Fromm and Klein, 1972, p. 55.)

Let us paraphrase the foregoing quotation: Let

(i)
$$B'y' + \Gamma'x' + u' = 0$$

denote the system of equations in Chapter 18 with (say) G endogenous variables and K predetermined variables. Let

(ii)
$$\bar{B}'\bar{y}' + \bar{\Gamma}'\bar{x}' + \bar{u}' = 0$$

denote any other system of equations, (say) an alternative version of the Brookings—S.S.R.C. Model. Let (ii) contain $\bar{G}$ endogenous variables and $\bar{K}$ predetermined variables. Fromm and Klein tell us that, in general,

$$\bar{G} \neq G$$
$$\bar{K} \neq K$$
$$\text{rank } \bar{B}' \neq \text{rank } B'$$
$$\text{rank } [\bar{B}' : \bar{\Gamma}'\bar{x}' + \bar{u}'] \neq \text{rank } [B' : \Gamma'x' + u']$$

In other words, different econometric models have different numbers of equations and different numbers of independent equations, etc. It is hard to state the exact number of independent equations in the specific system of equations shown in Chapter 18 because some different version would have a different number of independent equations; cf. quotation (1.10).

Neither of the foregoing "refutations" touches my criticism.

The second kind of argument used by Fromm and Klein is solely rhetorical. They stress that the question about the consistency of the system of equations in Chapter 18 is "another point which concerns Basmann" (Fromm and Klein, 1972, p. 54). As the reader of "Science or Number Mysticism?" is already aware, the avoidance of logical contradictions in economic hypotheses, the checking of structural hypotheses for consistency does concern me, and the matter of the precise number of equations is bound to that question. However, in the light of the *objectification theory of meaning,* to which Fromm and Klein adhere (see Section 5) the stress they put on this point is not gratuitous, but essential, from their point of view; see the quotation (2.1) in Section 2. The Brookings—S.S.R.C. econometricians feel certain that the system of equations in Chapter 18 is free of logical contradiction, and (to them) their feelings of certainty are adequate support for their assertion that the system has been put together in a consistent way. Such considerations throw some additional light on the intended meaning of

Economics is a mathematical science;

recall quotation (1.3).

In this connection it would be equally illuminating were Fromm and Klein to excuse their use of the term "consistent," which they applied to the system of equations in Chapter 18, by saying that they did not mean by that term what it always means in mathematics when applied to systems of equations.

[9]Such a technical article would constitute an attempt to establish communication with the Brookings—S.S.R.C. econometricians chiefly. To make that attempt now would be premature in view of the existing linguistic obstacles.

[10]E.g., cardinal number, real number, $+$, $\times$, $>$, etc.

[11]Consult any text on the foundations of arithmetic, for instance. Some constructive definitions of entities encountered in pure mathematics will be mentioned in Section 2 and

Section 3.   The employment of constructive definitions of concepts of fundamental quantity and magnitudes of quantities is (according to the point of view to which I adhere) a sine qua non of quantitative science generally, and quantitative economics in particular.

[12]Some clarification of the concept of empirical evidence is provided in *Note 15* and *Note 21*.

[13]By "metaphysical statement" is meant any statement about some entity or other that is beyond any experience, direct or indirect. There are entities, like cardinal numbers and magnitudes of other kinds of fundamental quantities, that cannot be experienced directly, yet which are not metaphysical, simply because such entities are constructively defined in terms of objects that can be directly experienced by everyone, and defined in such a way that statements about those entities can be tested by operations on the objects out of which they are composed.

The negation of any metaphysical statement is a metaphysical statement.

[14]Not so.   There are many econometric studies that do not share the defects I ascribe to the Brookings—S.S.R.C. Model.   Many others do, however, and it is probable that Fromm and Klein are tacitly using the argument—well-known to students of rhetoric—that if a given practice is widely followed, then something good can be said for it; more precisely, "A defect widely shared is no defect at all."   Adherents of the *objectification doctrine of meaning* are inclined to regard such an argument as especially cogent, consensus being regarded as a method of confirmation of propositions. See Section 5.

[15]I hope readers will not accuse me of false modesty for my saying I am not an econometrician.   The remark to which Fromm and Klein refer was deleted from the second draft of "Science or Number Mysticism?" (which was circulated to the participants in the *O.S.U. Conference*).   Its purpose was to emphasize the point mentioned in the first sentence of the present section.   Fromm and Klein have construed the remark quite another way; for econometricians who are adherents of the *objectification doctrine of meaning* the proposition expressed by the last sentence of this quotation, namely, that Fromm and Klein are sure that the present critic is not an econometrician, is crucial, as it limits the domain of economists required for an effective consensus; see Section 5.   Recall *Note 8*, penultimate paragraph.

[16]In his oral presentation of "A Rational Perspective" at the *O.S.U. Conference,* Klein denied that he wrote the sentence (3.2) quoted in Section 3, viz.,

Nothing can be quantified absolutely (except by God) for everything is relative.

(see Fromm and Klein, 1972, p. 61).   Klein asserted that Fromm wrote the sentence (3.2). The sentence (3.2) expresses a key proposition of the Fromm-Klein argument; see Section 3, esp. *Note 29*.   For the present, I remark only that, on the hypothesis I shall put forward in Section 5, namely, that the *objectification doctrine of meaning* is an essential part of the Brookings—S.S.R.C. philosophy of econometrics; Klein's rejection of responsibility for the sentence (3.2) is not to be regarded as a breach of the ethics of joint authorship.   On that hypothesis, Klein (probably) intended to make clear that he and Fromm were not in consensus in respect of (3.2) and, accordingly, that the statement expressed by (3.2) was to be regarded as less well-established than some other statements in their joint paper on which Fromm and Klein are in consensus.

[17]There are few clues to specific authorship of individual sentences and paragraphs in "A Rational Perspective."

[18]Many textbooks of logic contain an explanation of "use" and "mention."   The following illustrations may assist the reader:

(a) Fromm wrote, "Nothing can be quantified absolutely (except by God) for everything is relative."
(b) "Fromm" is a German adjective employed as a surname

"Fromm" is said to be *used* in (a) as the name of an author of "A Rational Perspective."   The word "Fromm" is said to be *mentioned* in (b); the sentence (b) expresses a proposition about the word "Fromm," not about the man Fromm.

[19]Other forms are

(a) "Certainly, A"
(b) "It is self-evident that A"
(c) "Obviously, A"
(d) "Everybody knows that A"

I take each of (a)-(d) as tantamount to the assertion of "A" on the part of anyone writing or speaking those sentences. See Section 3 and Section 5.

[20]Other logical words introduce conclusions of arguments, e.g., "therefore," "it must be," "consequently," "hence," etc., or indicate premises of arguments, e.g., "for," "since."

[21]Let the sentence be made more precise as follows:

(a) Between 3:40 and 3:41 p.m., E.S.T., October 19, 1966, Klein wrote legibly, "Nothing can be quantified absolutely (except by God) for everything is relative."

(Notice that I am mentioning, but not asserting, (a).)   The meaning of (a), the circumstance that makes (a) true, is of such nature that, if that circumstance occurred, any reader of this paper could, by being in close proximity to Klein at the time stated in (a), experience that circumstance; and such that all readers would experience that circumstance by the same kind of perceptual process.

Now contrast (a) with

(b) Nothing can be quantified absolutely (except by God) for everything is relative. (Fromm and Klein, 1972, p. 61.

The sentence (b) has a different *kind* of meaning from that of (a) and, if the "meaning of (b)" is experienced, then that "meaning" is experienced in a different way. I hope that I do not offend any reader's religious sensibilities by saying that, to begin with, we cannot experience "God quantifying (something) absolutely" in the same way that we can experience "Klein writing a sentence legibly." If there is a circumstance that makes (b) true, then that circumstance is a personal emotional experience of one who asserts (b).

Later on (Section 3, esp. *Note 29*) we shall consider precisely how Fromm and Klein make use of the sentence (b) in their attempted refutation of my criticism of the quantitative foundations of the Brookings—S.S.R.C. Model. The appearance of (b), and its logical function, in the Fromm-Klein reply, "A Rational Perspective," affords the opportunity of drawing the sharpest possible distinction between the kind of statement—represented by (a)—that is regarded as basic empirical evidence in scientific argument, and the kind of statement—represented in its most extreme form by (b)—that is not so regarded.

²²For details see the book by Carnap, 1958, pp. 1-32.

²³In Section 4, where I analyze the Fromm-Klein argument (II), the system of *modal logic* is required. More specifically, the modal concept of *strict implication* is required for interpreting some of the assertions put forward by Fromm and Klein. The following examples will serve to make clear the notion of strict, or necessary implication. Consider the tautology

$$A \supset (B \supset A)$$

Since (according to the rules of truth-functional calculus) the statement $B \supset A$ must be assigned truth-value t if A is assigned truth-value t, we say that

$$A \text{ strictly implies } (B \supset A).$$

For additional details consult the book by Anderson and Johnstone, 1962, pp. 129-136. For another application in economics, see the recent article by Brunner (1967, pp. 174-179).

²⁴Recall "Science or Number Mysticism?", Section 2. The term "quantify" as applied to statement functions in predicate logic (cf. Anderson and Johnstone, 1962, Chapter 5) bears an entirely different meaning from that of the same word as it is sometimes used in connection with applications of the theory of quantity and magnitude. By the way, it is not to be regarded as entirely clear what Fromm and Klein refer to by "principles of quantitative logic" in the following quotation:

We are well acquainted with the principles of quantitative logic, yet thank Basmann for his pedantic restatement. (Fromm and Klein, 1972, p. 61).

It is possible that Fromm and Klein intended to inform their readers that they are well acquainted with the logic of universal and existential statements and are referring to my brief and highly informal discussion of such statements in Section 2 of "Science or Number Mysticism?". However, I have interpreted the foregoing remark as intended by Fromm and Klein to emphasize that the Brookings—S.S.R.C. econometricians are well acquainted with the theory of quantity and magnitude and its applications; see Section 3, quotation (3.9).

²⁵The axioms are those of Nagel (1930, pp. 123-124). See also Hölder (1901) and Suppes (1951).

It was mentioned in "Science or Number Mysticism?" that there are several different formulations of theory of quantity. Not all formulations are equivalent, but the differences are differences of detail, and their existence does not affect the validity of the criticism I levelled at the Brookings—S.S.R.C. project.

For a comprehensive bibliography, consult the book by Ellis (1966).

²⁶The present theory of quantity was unknown to the ancients.

²⁷Cf. Campbell (1957, p. 28). "Or a discrepancy might appear if the nature of the bodies weighed was unsuitable, even if the balance was perfect when other bodies were used. Suppose one body was a magnet and the other a piece of soft iron; ... if the magnet were balanced against a nonmagnetic body and we placed in each pan a piece of soft iron of equal weight, the balance would be disturbed." In other words, *under the foregoing empirical conditions* the statement IX, viz., "for every $\alpha \sim \alpha'$, $\beta \sim \beta'$, then $(\alpha \oplus \beta) \sim (\alpha' \oplus \beta')$" does not hold. The effect is attributed to Earth's magnetic field.

²⁸The concept of "perfect balance" may have no actual physical model, viz., it may be the case that no actual pendulum balance ever constructed, in the past, present, or future is a

perfect balance. The scientific usefulness of the concept of perfect balance, however, does not depend on its physical realization. The concept, which is that of a balance that can discriminate among

$$\alpha > \beta$$
$$\beta > \alpha$$
$$\alpha \sim \beta$$

for all pairs (α, β) of physical objects under appropriate initial or external conditions, is involved in the syntactical meaning of "imperfection" of actual balances. The concept of perfect balance is commercially as well as scientifically important, viz., it is important for instrument makers and vendors, as well as for physicists, who may be faced by the failure of a given balance to discriminate magnitudes of weights, to decide between potential causes: is the failure due to an imperfection in the construction, or is it due to a careless arrangement of initial conditions that causes even a perfect balance to fail to discriminate? (Recall *Note 27*).

[29]Two remarks about the proposition asserted in the quotation (3.3) are in order here: The remarks are about (a) the deletion of the proper name "Basmann" from the neologism "Basmann-equivalent weight," which appears in the text of the Fromm-Klein reply: and (b) some details of the logical relation between the propositions expressed by (3.3) and (3.2). Let us consider (b) first.

As is indicated in the text Fromm and Klein intend (3.2) to support (3.3), which, in turn, is intended to support (3.1). Let us first consider the logical problem of verifying (3.3). What is the meaning of (3.3)? (Recall *Note 28*). Fromm and Klein assert that a perfect balance (defined as a pendulum balance which, under appropriate initial conditions, can discriminate between the magnitudes of weight of any two physical objects α and β) cannot discriminate between the magnitudes of weight of any two physical objects α and β even under appropriate conditions. Notice that Fromm and Klein do not mention that they intend "perfect balance" in (3.3) to mean something different from its common denotation, which is mentioned in *Note 28*. In order to avoid interpreting the quotation (3.3) as expressing the proposition

(i) A perfect balance is not a perfect balance,

I shall interpret (3.3) as the negation of an existential statement, viz., as

(ii) It is not the case "There is at least one actual pendulum balance that is a perfect balance."

The proposition "There is at least one actual pendulum balance that is a perfect balance" is strictly existential, i.e., its domain cannot be proved to be a finite set of individuals. No statement that asserts that every pendulum balance belonging to a finite sample of balances examined so far has been found to be imperfect can falsify the proposition, i.e., verify (ii). In this connection recall "Science or Number Mysticism?" Section 4, pp. 39-40. To get over this difficulty, which the strict nonverifiability of (ii) presents, Fromm and Klein tacitly appeal to a modal category, i.e., "impossibility." The function of the theological sentence (3.2) is to entail (3.3), i.e., the impossibility of a perfect balance.

How (3.3) might support (3.1) is not indicated explicitly by Fromm and Klein. The fact that so far no actual pendulum balance has been found to be perfect has not prevented physical scientists from making explicit use of the concept of weight and laying sound foundations under the quantitative branches of their science. Similarly, my criticisms of the Brookings —S.S.R.C. Model do not rest in any way on the presupposition that there are perfect instruments of measurement, or perfect technical methods of discriminating between magnitudes of economic quantities. The use of the neologism "Basmann-equivalent weight," coined by Fromm and Klein, gives some indication of how they intend (3.3) to support (3.1). My sole remark about weight and pendulum balances in "Science or Number Mysticism?" appears in note 54 (p. 49) and refers the reader to the book by N. R. Campbell, 1957, pp. 279 ff. Readers of "A Rational Perspective," aware that the notion of weight is so very ancient, would not expect the neologism "Basmann-equivalent weight" to be introduced except to denote some idiosyncratic concept of mine that differs markedly from the concept actually used in the physical sciences. The function of the neologism "Basmann-equivalent weight" is to persuade the readers of the Fromm-Klein reply to believe that it is the case that the concept of quantity sketched in "Science or Number Mysticism?" is idiosyncratic. More precisely, the reader of "A Rational Perspective" is supposed to believe that "the ultimate conclusion" of my thesis is that unless proffered economic quantities are *proved* to be quantities all numerical econometric work should cease (however, see "Science or Number Mysticism?", p. 36, pp. 39-40).

In (3.2) the logical word "for" expresses some alleged logical relation between the strictly universal statement

(iii) everything is relative

and the theological statement expressed by

(iv) Nothing can be quantified absolutely (except by God).

Recall *Note 20*. Normally the logical word "for" indicates the relation of *implication*, ⊃, sometimes *strict implication*. Fromm and Klein have not indicated the meanings of either of the foregoing sentences; in particular the scope, or domain of individuals, of the universal sentence "everything is relative" has not been specified. The sentence (iii) is open to many different interpretations, a few of which I have considered but do not regard as warranting any mention here. That Fromm and Klein provide no explicit interpretation of (iii) may be explained by the hypothesis that they regard the meaning of (iii) as transparent and its truth a matter of consensus among the readers for whom they wrote "A Rational Perspective."

[30]Fromm and Klein tell us

Literary economics hypothesizes that there is a utility associated with the possession of money (which is a proxy for command over resources and the consumption of goods). (Fromm and Klein, 1972, p. 60.)

Econometricians also construct numerical time series C_1, C_2, ..., C_n, Y_1, Y_2, ..., Y_n, supposedly measuring "consumption of goods" and "expenditure of income and assets" (whose status as *quantities* Fromm and Klein set out to show). According to Fromm and Klein, if it is supposed that it is not the case that

(i) there is a strong functional dependency between the hypothetical utility and "transactions of goods and money";

and

(ii) the hypothetical utility is at least orderable,

then it would be surprising (to Fromm and Klein) to find a relationship between C_t and Y_t, $t=1, 2, \ldots, n$ that "fits" with any degree of precision (Fromm and Klein, 1972, p. 60).

I assume that Fromm and Klein do not mean that they would be surprised to find that

(iii) $C_t = a_0 + b_1 Y_t + b_2 Y_t^2 + \ldots + b_{n-1} Y_t^{n-1}$

$t=1, 2, \ldots, n$

fits the numerical data (Y_t, C_t) $t=1, 2, \ldots, n$ with a high degree of precision. (Having determined the n unknown structural coefficients from the first n observation, Fromm and Klein might be surprised to find the next m (Y_t, C_t) $t=n+1, n+2, \ldots, n+m$ fit (iii) perfectly, in part because the Brookings — S.S.R.C. econometricians are inclined to expect structural parameters like a_0, b_1, ..., b_{n-1} to undergo change (Duesenberry, et al., 1965, p. 6.) I interpret the Fromm-Klein remarks as follows: If the numerical time series C_t Y_t, $t=1, 2, \ldots, n$ *do* represent magnitudes of quantities, and if (C_t, Y_t) $t=1, 2, \ldots, n$, fit

(iv) $\phi(C_t, Y_t) = 0$

with a high degree of precision, where the function (iv) is validly deduced from a specified utility function and one or more specific constraints on the maximization process (of choice), then the hypothesis that there is such utility as represented by the specified utility function in question, is in good agreement with the conjunction of the data, the constraints, and the general hypothesis of maximizing behavior. Nonetheless, neither the good fit of the numerical series to the functional dependence (iv) alone, nor in conjunction with the statement that Fromm and Klein would be made to experience the emotion of surprise by that good fit if the utility hypothesis were not true, tends in any way to support what Fromm and Klein set out to establish (but assumed in the process of their argument) namely, that the numerical time series in the Brookings — S.S.R.C. Model represent quantities.

[31]Recall *Note 24*. I take it for granted that "principles of quantitative logic" refers to the theory of quantity and magnitude.

[32]That is to say, the function of the word "even" in (3.6) is to suggest that, in view of my criticisms of the quantitative foundations of the Brookings — S.S.R.C. Model, there is good reason to doubt my ability to read the numeral that expresses my salary on my monthly paycheck. Here Fromm and Klein are trying to reassure their readers that, my criticisms being so outlandish as to warrant this doubt, those criticisms need not be taken seriously, i.e., need not be refuted by argument. Recall *Notes 15, 16* and *29*.

[33]I.e., analysis of words, phrases, and sentences in order to discover how they may affect the reader's understanding — whether the function (of a given word or sentence) is expository or nonexpository in its context. Recall the discussion of "metaphysical" in Section 1, also the discussion of "even" in (3.6) in *Note 32*.

[34]I am using the word "tautology" in its broader sense to include reference to quantified propositions that are logically true.

Notice that (4.2) is the conjunction of (4.3a) and (4.3b). The conjunction of any two or more statements, at least one of which is contingent, is a contingent statement. The statement (4.3a) is contingent — it is not necessarily the case that Basmann has asserted propositions A, B, C, etc., hence (4.2) is a contingent statement.

The sentence D — I had never read or heard this sentence before seeing it in the Fromm-Klein reply — is too vaguely formed to warrant much analysis, and I shall simply take it for granted that D is not a tautology, if that is what Fromm and Klein intended to assert about D.

If Fromm and Klein intended (4.4) only to inform the readers that the sentence D does not excite the feeling of "necessity" in Fromm and Klein, viz., that reading or hearing D does not cause either Fromm or Klein to feel an irresistable impulse to assert D, it remains for Fromm and Klein to show their readers how this emotional state, which is a matter of consensus between Fromm and Klein, bears on the questions actually raised in "Science or Number Mysticism?". Under this interpretation (4.4) merely expresses an emotional state of Fromm and Klein towards a proposition (probably original with them) the semantic meaning of which Fromm and Klein have not made clear.

[35]Let R and V be predicate constants "realistic" and "valid," respectively. Let x, y, z be individual variables over the specified domains (containing definite estimates and explanations of structure) of R and V. The propositional functions Rxy and Vxy are to be read

x is more realistic than y,
x is more valid than y,

respectively. Presumably — Fromm and Klein do not say — the relations denoted here by R and V are linear order relations or weak ordering relations.

[36]More precisely, at least one of A, B, C, etc., must be a quantified proposition the scope of which contains Rxy as a constituent; and at least one of A, B, C, etc., must be a quantified proposition the scope of which contains Vxy as a constituent. Moreover, the domain of the variables x, y must contain specific estimates and specific "explanations of structure." That is to say, since D contains Rxy and Vxy, those propositional functions must appear in at least one of the premises from which D is deducible, as Fromm and Klein assert.

[37]A simple example helps to elucidate the notion of sharpness. Suppose that $(x_1, x_2, ..., x_n)$ is any sample drawn from the parent population

$$f(x; \theta, 1) = (2\eta)^{-1/2} e^{-1/2(x-\theta)^2} \qquad -\infty < x < \infty$$

and let H be the maintained hypothesis

$$H: \; -\infty < \theta < \infty \; ,$$

let H_0 be the hypothesis

$$H_0: \; 2 < \theta < 4 \; ,$$

and let H'_0 be the hypothesis

$$H'_0: \; 2.5 < \theta < 3.5 \; .$$

Let α be the common level of signficance for the tests of H_0 against H-H_0 and H'_0 against H-H'_0. The corresponding acceptance regions of R_0 and R'_0 are intervals centered at $\theta = 3$. The length of R'_0 is less than the length of R_0 and the hypothesis H'_0 is said to be *sharper* than H_0.

Notice that the variance of the maximum likelihood estimator $\bar{x}$

$$\bar{x} = \frac{1}{n}(x_1 + x_2 + ... + x_n)$$

is the same for both hypotheses H_0 and H'_0. In more complicated cases the concentration of the joint distribution of parameter estimators differs from hypothesis to hypothesis and, consequently, affects the relative sharpness of alternative hypotheses.

The chief point to be grasped is that no conception of "realistic" or "valid" is applied to the estimator $\bar{x}$ in elucidating the notion of the relative sharpness of H_0 and H'_0.

[38]To forestall a probable misinterpretation, I emphasize that "mental image" and "objectification" are not here intended to denote *hallucinations*, which are sensory perceptions, without corresponding sensory stimuli, due to malfunctioning of the human brain. Readers who can appreciate poetry and its imagery should have little difficulty with the concept of "mental image." Our ability to form mental images of words and sentences is often helpful in acquiring a grasp of a scientific theory; for example, recall the image of the physical atom as a miniature planetary system.

Semanticists would have good reasons for criticizing the hypothesis introduced in this Section, namely, that the Brookings — S.S.R.C. econometricians adhere to a *doctrine* of meaning. After all, "doctrine" suggests a more or less well-formulated system of concepts and rules of interpretation, and there is little evidence to support the assertion (if it were to be made) that the Brookings — S.S.R.C. econometricians have given much attention to the semantic problems encountered in the application of mathematics to the domain of economic experience. Confusion of *intensional meanings*, or private mental images of symbols, with their public, *extensional meanings*, i.e., with objects, classes of objects denoted by symbols, is very common; likewise, the supposition that every symbol has — in addition to its *intensional meaning* — an *extensional meaning* is widespread. The difference between intensional meaning and extensional meaning — fundamental in science — is not widely appreciated among people who seek to mould public policy with the help of "social science." It is probable that the Brookings — S.S.R.C. econometricians have no definite semantic theory, or system of semantic concepts and formation rules.

[39]Consequently, it is frequently the case that noneconometricians call for publication of the statistical estimates that are considered to be "not realistic" and "not valid" by econometricians. In this connection consult the discussion in "A Rational Perspective" (Fromm and Klein, 1972, p. 54).

[40]Refer to Section 3, axioms I-VI. An ordered triple (S, O_1, Q) where the operation O_1 defines $(>, \sim)$ such that axioms I-VI hold, is said to be an *orderable variable property*. Real numbers are employed to "measure" or *rank* the classes belonging to Q (recall DEFINI-TION 1) as follows: For every a, b ε Q, real numbers r_a, r_b are assigned to a and b in accordance with the rules

  (i) $r_a > r_b$ if $a > b$;
  (ii) $r_b > r_a$ if $b > a$;
  (iii) $r_a = r_b$ if $a = b$.

The ordering of the real numbers in the scale of measurement here has a definite extensional interpretation in terms of the operation O_1 on ordered pairs of entities belonging to S. Every order-preserving transformation $f(r)$, i.e., such that

$$f(r_a) > f(r_b) \quad \text{if } r_a > r_b$$
$$f(r_b) > f(r_a) \quad \text{if } r_b > r_a$$
$$f(r_a) = f(r_b) \quad \text{if } r_a = r_b,$$

has the same interpretation in terms of O_1 on S.

On the other hand, there being no specified operation O_2, the arithmetic operation $r_a + r_b$ has no interpretation, or extensional meaning.

REFERENCES

1. Anderson, J. M. and H. W. Johnstone, Jr. *Natural Deduction.* Belmont, California: Wadsworth Publishing Company, Inc., 1962.

2. Basmann, R. L. "On Finite Sample Distributions of Generalized Classical Linear Identifiability Test Statistics," *Journal of the American Statistical Association,* 55 (1960), 650-659.

3. Basmann, R. L. "Remarks Concerning the Application of Exact Finite Sample Distribution Functions of GCL Estimators in Econometric Statistical Inference," *Journal of the American Statistical Association,* 58 (1963), 943-976.

4. Basmann, R. L. "A Note on the Statistical Testability of 'Explicit Causal Chains' Against the Class of 'Interdependent' Models," *Journal of the American Statistical Association,* 60 (1965a), 1080-1093.

5. Basmann, R. L. "On the Application of the Identifiability Test Statistic in Predictive Testing of Explanatory Economic Models," *Econometric Annual of Indian Economic Journal,* XIII (1965b), 387-423.

6. Basmann, R. L. "On the Application of the Identifiability Test Statistic in Predictive Testing of Explanatory Economic Models—Part II," *Econometric Annual of the Indian Economic Journal,* XIV (1966), 233-252.

7. Basmann, R. L. "The Brookings Quarterly Econometric Model: Science or Number Mysticism?", in Karl Brunner (ed.), *Problems and Issues in Current Econometric Practice.* Columbus, Ohio: College of Administrative Science, The Ohio State University, 1972.

8. Blanché, R. *Axiomatics.* New York: Dover Publications, Inc., 1962. (Translated by G. B. Keene.)

9. Boehme, G. A. W. "How They Predict the Economic Future," *THINK,* (July-August 1967), 7-11. (Published by International Business Machine Corporation, Armonk, New York 10504.)

10. Brunner, K. "A Case Study on the Importance of Appropriate Rules for the Competitive Market in Ideas and Beliefs," *Schweizerische Zeitschrift für Volkswirtschaft und Statistik,* 103 (1967), 173-190.

11. Burns, A. R. *Money and Monetary Policy in Early Times.* New York: Reprints of Economic Classics, 1965.

12. Carnap, R. *Introduction to Symbolic Logic and its Applications.* New York: Dover Publications, Inc., 1958.

13. Campbell, N. R. *Foundations of Science.* New York: Dover Publications, Inc., 1957.
14. Dantzig, T. *Number: The Language of Science,* 4th Ed. New York: Macmillan, 1954.
15. Duesenberry, J. S., G. Fromm, L. R. Klein, and E. Kuh (eds.), (1965), *The Brookings Quarterly Model of the United States.* Chicago: Rand McNally Company, 1965.
16. Ellis, B. *Basic Concepts of Measurement.* Cambridge: Cambridge University Press, 1966.
17. Fromm, G. and L. R. Klein, "The Brookings Econometric Model: A Rational Perspective," in Karl Brunner (ed.), *Problems and Issues in Current Econometric Practice.* Columbus, Ohio: College of Administrative Science, The Ohio State University, 1972.
18. Hölder, O. "Die Axiome der Quantität und die Lehre vom Mass," *Leipzig: Berichte, Königl. Sachsischen Gesellschaft,* 1901.
19. Kuh, E. "Econometric Models: Is a New Age Dawning?", *American Economic Review,* 55 (1965), 362-369.
20. Nagel, E. "Measurement," 1930, reprinted in Danto, A., and S. Morgenbesser, *Philosophy of Science.* New York: Meridian Books, Inc., 1960, 121-140.
21. Neugebauer, O. *The Exact Sciences in Antiquity.* Providence: Brown University Press, 1957.
22. Russell, B. *Introduction to Mathematical Philosophy,* London: Allen and Unwin, Ltd., 1919.
23. Seltman, C. *Greek Coins,* 2nd Ed. London: Methuen, 1955.
24. Skinner, F. G. "Measures and Weights," in Singer, Charles, et al., (eds.), *A History of Technology,* Vol. I. New York: Oxford University Press, 774-784.
25. Snedecor, G. W. *Statistical Methods,* 4th Ed. Ames: Iowa State College Press, 1946.
26. Spivak, M. *Calculus on Manifolds.* New York: W. A. Benjamin, Inc., 1965.
27. Suppes, P. "A Set of Independent Axioms for Extensive Quantities," *Portugaliae Mathematica,* 10 (1951), pp. 163-172.
28. Suppes, P. *Introduction to Logic,* Princeton: D. Van Nastrand Company, Inc., 1957.
29. Thielman, H. P. *Theory of Functions of Real Variables,* New York: Prentice-Hall, Inc., 1953.

INTERDEPENDENCE VS. RECURSIVENESS: A REVIEW OF THE DEBATE AND NOTIONS OF CAUSALITY IN ECONOMICS

W. L. L'Esperance*
The Ohio State University

1. INTRODUCTION

Since the early 1950s, much discussion and many articles have concentrated on two approaches for building econometric models. Each approach—one referred to as a recursive system, the other an interdependent system—has its practitioners and advocates.

The debate about the two approaches has been peculiarly one-sided. While most builders of econometric models use an interdependent system, and have, as a result, accumulated much empirical evidence, virtually all of the debate has consisted of criticisms of interdependent systems by proponents of recursiveness who bring to battle an imposing array of conceptual and theoretical arguments, but very little empirical evidence. In making claims for the legitimacy of recursive systems they have sparked a number of rebuttals by only a few economists who, maintaining a neutral stance rather than making an a priori selection of either system for model building, have argued that such claims are unjustified.

The primary purpose of this paper is to review the arguments for both the acceptance and the denial of each system as a paradigm of the economic world. A secondary purpose is to deny the alleged

*I am particularly grateful for the comments and criticisms of H. O. A. Wold, R. H. Strotz, R. L. Basmann, none of whom is responsible for any errors of interpretation that may remain to haunt me. I am indebted to Jon Cunnyngham for his comments.

superiority of recursive over interdependent systems and to expose the narrow definition of causality used by proponents of recursive systems. No brief for the superiority of either system is presented. The author, writing from the viewpoint of an empirical economist, grapples with some notions of causality and the meaning of observational equivalence in economics as they apply to econometric model building. He leaves to others the difficult and vexatious question of the estimation aspects of the debate (single versus simultaneous equation estimation), of which much has been written. For a recent review, see Fisher [11, p. 599].

We shall begin by defining both a recursive and an interdependent system, and then discuss the issues of the controversy. It is perhaps too easy to polarize the views of advocates of either system; nevertheless, some dichotomy of views is worth discussing as it sharpens the issues of the debate. Next, there is an extended discussion of operational notions of causality in economics and the meaning of observational equivalence, two central issues in the controversy.

2. RECURSIVE AND INTERDEPENDENT SYSTEMS

In an earlier review of the debate on simultaneous versus single equation[1] estimation, Wold, the leading proponent of recursive systems, stated that the "traditional methods of regression analysis are essentially sound, and that much of the confusion about the controversial issues can be removed simply by bringing out more explicitly the basic logical principles behind the regression methods" [39, p. 29]. This can easily be seen, Wold noted, by reviewing the main purposes of regression analysis. They are (a) "to estimate or *predict* one variable, given one or more other variables, and (b) to obtain a *causal explanation* of one variable as a function of one or more other variables" [39, p. 30]. The crux of the debate is still on how one goes about obtaining a causal explanation and the extent to which one is restricted to regression analysis in finding such an explanation. Or, to what extent can one find a causal explanation without recourse to regression analysis?

If we single out one variable as causally dependent on another variable, as we do in a strictly experimental sense (e.g., yield per acre and the amount of fertilizer), there should be no confusion about the direction of causation; hence, ordinary least squares can be used. But suppose the two variables are not easily distinguishable in regard to "cause" and "effect." More specifically, suppose the direction of causation changes. Or even more problematical, suppose an investigator cannot establish the direction of causation and decides that the two variables are mutually dependent, what notion of causality is then applicable?

Before we attempt to answer this question, let us compare and contrast recursive and interdependent systems. Interdependent systems are often expressed as

$$(1) \quad By + \Gamma z = u$$

where y is the vector of G endogenous variables; z, the vector of K predetermined variables; u, the vector of G random disturbances; and the B matrix of the coefficients of the y's in (1) can be written as

$$(2) \quad \begin{bmatrix} \beta_{11} & \cdots & \cdots & \cdots & \beta_{1G} \\ & \cdot & & & \cdot \\ & \cdot & & & \cdot \\ & \cdot & & & \cdot \\ \beta_{G1} & \cdots & \cdots & \cdots & \beta_{GG} \end{bmatrix}$$

If B is a triangular matrix,

$$(3) \quad \begin{bmatrix} \beta_{11} & \cdots & \cdots & \cdots & \beta_{1G} \\ & \cdot & & & \cdot \\ & & \cdot & & \cdot \\ 0 & & \cdot & & \cdot \\ & & & \cdot & \cdot \\ & & & & \cdot & \beta_{GG} \end{bmatrix}$$

and if the exact part of the system has the following recursive character,

$$(4) \quad \begin{aligned} \beta_{11}y_1 + \beta_{12}y_2 + \ldots + \beta_{1g}y_g + \beta_{1,g+1}y_{g+1} + \ldots + \beta_{1G}y_G + \sum_K \gamma_{1K}z_K &= u_1 \\ \beta_{22}y_2 + \ldots + \beta_{2g}y_g + \beta_{2,g+1}y_{g+1} + \ldots + \beta_{2G}y_G + \sum_K \gamma_{2K}z_K &= u_2 \\ \ldots \qquad\qquad\qquad\qquad\qquad\qquad & \\ \beta_{gg}y_g + \beta_{g,g+1}y_{g+1} + \ldots + \beta_{gG}y_G + \sum_K \gamma_{gK}z_K &= u_g \\ \qquad\qquad\qquad\qquad\qquad & \\ \beta_{GG}y_G + \sum_K \gamma_{GK}z_K &= u_G \end{aligned}$$

then the system is called recursive[2] or a causal chain.

In each equation the y variable with the unit coefficient is regarded as the dependent variable and the other y variables and the z's are taken as causal variables. The sequence of events in the above recursive system is one-way-directed, upward through (4) beginning with the last equation.

A recursive system [38, pp. 83-84] can be illustrated by the following example: Suppose there is an endogenous economic variable (the price of coffee beans, for instance) that is affected by only one exogenous variable, Brazilian weather. There is a second endogenous variable, the price of a cup of coffee, that is affected by another exogenous variable, the tax on coffee beans, and the previous endogenous variable. Finally, there is a third dependent variable, the number of hours spent by employees for coffee breaks, that depends on the previous dependent variable, and a third exogenous variable, the amount of incoming gossip. This recursive system is as follows:

$$\begin{bmatrix} \beta_{11} & \beta_{12} & 0 \\ 0 & \beta_{22} & \beta_{23} \\ 0 & 0 & \beta_{33} \end{bmatrix} \begin{bmatrix} y_1 \\ y_2 \\ y_3 \end{bmatrix} + \begin{bmatrix} \gamma_{11} & 0 & 0 \\ 0 & \gamma_{22} & 0 \\ 0 & 0 & \gamma_{33} \end{bmatrix} \begin{bmatrix} z_1 \\ z_2 \\ z_3 \end{bmatrix} = \begin{bmatrix} u_1 \\ u_2 \\ u_3 \end{bmatrix}$$

where y_1 = number of hours spent by employees for coffee breaks

y_2 = price of a cup of coffee

y_3 = price of coffee beans

z_1 = the amount of incoming gossip

z_2 = tax on coffee beans

z_3 = Brazilian weather

The chain of events begins with the explanation of y_3 and progresses in one direction to the explanation of y_1.

Wold [41, p. 359] points out that systems (2) and (4) differ in three respects:

a. System (2) may involve two or more current endogenous variables in all the equations in the system, whereas this is not the case with (4).

b. The residual u_g of the g'th relation in (4) is uncorrelated with the endogenous variables, y_{g+1}, y_{g+2}, ..., y_G. In (2), however, these endogenous variables may be correlated with u_g.[3] Finally,

c. The residuals u_i and u_j that enter in the same period may be intercorrelated in (2) but not in (4).

Wold also distinguishes the two systems in terms of the uses to which they are put:

a. In both systems behavioral relationships are basic material in the construction of the model. With causal chains the behavioral relationship can be "interpreted in terms of conditional expectations and exploited for predictive and causal inference" [41, p. 367]. This can be done by predicting a current endogenous variable, say y_g, using the relationship for y_g that is specified by the model. On the other hand the procedure dealing with an interdependent system is not as straightforward because it involves finding the reduced form.

b. The second use concerns substitutive elimination of endogenous variables. In the causal chain system substitutive elimination for a given endogenous variable results in a difference equation of the form

$$(5) \quad y_t + \lambda y_{t-1} + \ldots + \lambda_h\, y_{t-h} = L$$

where L is a linear expression in residuals and exogenous variables, all with or without lags. In the interdependent system the reduced form must be deduced in order to find the comparable relationship.

The notion of causation embodied in recursive systems, according to Wold, has a rather exact meaning in the sense that "cause and effect" occur in a laboratory where controlled experiments involving stimulus-response relationships can be performed. In this way the effect of one variable on another can be measured, *ceteris paribus*. Recursive systems attempt to achieve causation in this sense.

Recursive systems are completely dynamic, whereas interdependent systems are not. The latter, according to Wold, are static-dynamic hybrids involving equilibrium relations, identities, and other static trimmings. It should be pointed out, however, according to Bentzel and Hansen, recursive systems can have static equilibrium constraints [6, p. 161].

Wold claims that "causal chains have the advantage of providing the formal framework for a stimulus-response interpretation of the behavior relations that constitute the system. At bottom, this is the key argument for putting the behavior relations to direct operative use in this approach. In interdependent systems the behavior relations do not lend themselves to the same direct stimulus-response interpretation, and in accordance herewith, the operative use of the model is based on the reduced form" [43, p. 449].

Explicit causal chains, characterized as completely dynamic and recursive, are distinguished from implicit causal chains that are nonrecursive and not entirely dynamic. The causal interpretation of explicit causal chains is clearly defined according to the Strotz-Wold notion of causality [35, pp. 420-421]. The notion of causality associated with recursive systems is called *explicit causality* [35, p. 422]. Causal interpretation of nonrecursive systems depends on the form of the nonrecursive system. Builders of interdependent systems, a type of nonrecursive system, employ a notion of causality (labeled *vector causality* by Strotz and Wold) that goes beyond the stimulus-response interpretation of causality found in explicit causal chains. Other types of nonrecursive systems, classified as implicit causal chains (bicausal chains and causal circles) are distinguished from interdependent systems. Because implicit causal chains are not completely dynamic they afford an accommodation with interdependent systems in which the advantages of recursiveness and nonrecursiveness are combined. The crucial difference between interdependent systems and implicit causal chains is "that the behavioral relations of implicit causal chains are specified as conditional expectations subject to disturbance, thus providing a formal framework for predictive and causal inference directly from the behavioral relations" [41, p. 369].

A causal circle can be represented by the following system:

(6a) $\quad p(t) = \alpha_1 + \beta_1 q(t) + \gamma_1 z_1(t) + u_1(t)$

(6b) $\quad q(t) = \alpha_2 + \beta_2 p(t) + \gamma_2 z_2(t) + u_2(t)$

where $z_1(t)$ and $z_2(t)$ are exogenous, $p(t)$ and $q(t)$ are endogenous, and $u_1(t)$ and $u_2(t)$ are the random disturbances. The notion of causality contained in a stimulus-response relationship does not apply here because $q(t)$ and $p(t)$ are mutually dependent. An equilibrium constraint must be imposed on (6) to explain this mutual dependence. The explanation, however, is not a causal one. The explanation lies in predicting "something about equilibrium values under *control*" [35, p. 424]. To make predictions about $p(t)$ (or $q(t)$) one must control $q(t)$ (or $p(t)$), which means invalidating equation (6b) (or 6a).

The other type of implicit causal chain, a bicausal chain, has the following form:

(7a) $\quad q(t) = \alpha_1 + \beta_1 p(t) + \gamma_1 z_1(t) + u_1(t)$

(7b) $\quad q(t) = \alpha_2 + \beta_2 p(t) + \gamma_2 z_2(t) + u_2(t)$

where $p(t)$ and $q(t)$ are endogenous, $z_1(t)$ and $z_2(t)$ are exogenous, and $u_1(t)$ and $u_2(t)$ are the random disturbances. Like the above causal circle, the laboratory notion of causality does not apply. Again, an equilibrium constraint must be imposed on (7) so that $q_d(t)$, quantity demanded, is equal to $q_s(t)$, the quantity supplied. The explanation of the equilibrium values lies in predicting them, given either the values of $p(t)$ and the exogenous values or a distributed lag explaining $p(t)$ and values of the exogenous variables.

In summary, Strotz and Wold have constructed an impressive taxonomy in which interdependent systems are to be distinguished from causal chains. The latter are subdivided into two classes: (1) explicit or pure causal chains—recursive—and (2) implicit causal chains—nonrecursive. Causal chains and interdependent systems ". . . emphasize different aspects of the model of construction. Causal chains focus on behavior relations as a tool for predictive inference, interdependent systems on prediction from one period to the next" [41, p. 410].

Recursive systems are alleged to be inherently superior to interdependent systems for representing the real economic world. In fact, Wold claims that such systems represent a more fundamental approach to model building than do interdependent systems because they purport to explain in a "strictly causal sense of stimulus response relationship . . . whereas . . . interdependent systems aim at explanations in the sense of predictability . . . and that . . . the two notions (predictability and causality) are distinct" [42, p. 5].

Also, Wold, critical of interdependent systems because they are a motley assortment of identities, equilibrium conditions, and so forth, states that ". . . in the evolution from static to dynamic models pure causal chain systems are the end station . . . from this point of view interdependent systems are a retrogression, for static elements are allowed in the model construction" [44, p. 12].[4]

Most economists have reacted to these conclusions in a rather defensive way. Empirical barriers, such as limited data, unobservable phenomena, and aggregation difficulties are given as reasons for reverting to an interdependent system. These may very well be cogent reasons for using an interdependent system, but they do not necessarily mean that interdependent systems are inherently inferior to recursive systems.

In an earlier review of interdependent and recursive systems Bentzel and Hansen [6] recognized that a strong theoretical case can be made for a causal chain model because of the recognition of distinct time intervals between acts of decision making. Also, in the real world, they point out, econometricians are faced with estimation problems involving aggregation across time[5] and elimination of variables so that interdependency becomes necessary.

Bentzel and Hansen conclude that "*a priori* reasoning does not lead to priority for any one of these types of models. Whether a model should be made recursive or interdependent must be decided from case to case, dependent on the economic problem to be illuminated and due regard being taken to the nature of the statistical material at hand" [6, p. 154].

The difficulty of estimating a recursive system as an economy-wide model is also discussed by Fisher [11, pp. 592-597].

In all of these discussions a recursive system as a valid conceptualization of the economic world is compromised by real world problems. In fact, if the investigator specifies a recursive system, but fits instead an interdependent system because of the above real world problems, he introduces a specification error in his system.[6]

But suppose the investigator has an interdependent model in mind, but because of data limitations fits a recursive system. Under what circumstances is a specification error introduced? An example of this apparently perverse case is given by Anderson and L'Esperance [1].

In a recent article, Basmann denies the dictum of Bentzel and Hansen that observations should decide whether a model is to be recursive or interdependent. He claims that whether one system "is a more accurate representation of economic reality than the other cannot even in principle be *settled by appeal* to observations" [5, p. 1080].

The arguments for both systems revolve around several meanings of causality used in economics, and they must be reviewed in the light of Basmann's proof [5] of the observational equivalence of explicit causal chains and interdependent systems. This point is particularly relevant to a case study of the watermelon market made by L'Esperance [20] involving a comparison between an interdependent and a recursive specification (explicit causal chain) of the market for watermelons. The set of endogenous and exogenous variables was the same for both systems. The forecasting efficiency of the systems was the basis of the comparison. The experimental results showed that the interdependent system was a better predictor of the levels and the changes of direction of the endogenous variables than the explicit causal chain.

This test was disputed by Stojkovic [33] who contended that it is not meaningful to compare the two systems because they explain different phenomena. In addition he points out that there are other criteria for testing the validity of the systems beside forecasting efficiency. In the reply by L'Esperance [21] it is argued that the phenomenon is what it is—namely, a market for a particular commodity whose behavior is measured by a set of variables common to both systems, and the purpose at hand is to explain the phenomenon by an econometric model. Furthermore, it is emphasized that the arguments for an interdependent specification of the watermelon market are more relevant than the ones for a recursive system.

More important than these debating points is the relevance of Basmann's proof as it applies to this case study. What he is saying in effect is that both systems contain one and the same statistical hypothesis, and that observations cannot distinguish between either system. The fact that one system is a better predictor than the other is due, not to one being an interdependent system and the other, a recursive system, but to the better "agreement" of the statistical hypothesis contained in the interdependent system with the observations. We shall return to a discussion of observational equivalence in the last part of the paper.

3. SEMANTIC ISSUES

Causality in Economics

> All philosophers, of every school, imagine that causation is one of the fundamental axioms of science, yet, oddly enough, in advanced science, such as gravitational astronomy, the word "cause" never occurs. ... *The* law of causality, I believe, like much that passes among philosophers, is a relic of a bygone age, surviving like the monarchy, only because it is erroneously supposed to do no harm [28, p. 387].

If economists believed in causality as a general law, then the future of economic events would be unambiguously "determined" by *its* past and present. However, if the future is determined, it can only be determined by law. It must then introduce the idea of an omniscient intelligence [13, p. 263].

While economists are hardly interested in *the* law of causality, they are becoming more aware of operational notions of causality in formulating and testing economic theories. Whether any particular notion of causality in economics is better than another remains an open question. The history of economics is rife with controversy[7] about the meaning of such words as "value," "welfare," and "savings." The word "causality" is no exception.

It is generally agreed that a definition is meaningful or "convenient" in terms of the "prescientific" choice of the question or theory in which the economist is interested [18, p. 65]. Definitions must be clearly stated. What is to be included in the domain of a definition should be stated as well as what is to be excluded; otherwise the definition will appear to contain persuasive or evaluative overtones.

> When a scientist introduces a technical term, in no matter how detached a manner, he indicates his interest in what he names — his estimation of the importance of talking about it, or of predicting its occurrence—and he often leads his readers to have a similar interest ... When a definition is given mainly for the purposes of distinction or classification, when it is used to guide only those interests which (like

curiosity) are involved in making the classification understood, and when it in no way suggests that this is the one legitimate sort of classification, then the definition will not be called "persuasive" [32, p. 336].

A lucid discussion of "persuasive" definitions and "value-loaded" concepts in economics is given by Hutchison [18, pp. 64-73]. To be sure, the word "causality" has been used by the recursivists for distinction and classification. While they recognize that their definition of causality is not the only one of use to economists, they nonetheless argue that it is superior to any other used in economics, and, hence, prescribe recursive systems as the legitimate description of economic phenomena.

Except for the Strotz-Wold discussion of causality, very few attempts have been made to define causality as a useful and meaningful concept for economists. Before we discuss these other concepts, let us further examine the Strotz-Wold notion of causality.

Wold, well aware of the philosophical difficulties in defining causality, argues that a notion of causality, adequate from both a common sense and scientific viewpoint, can be defined in the context of a controlled experiment. Specifically, he states that "one or more variables are under the experimenter's control, and for suitably chosen values of these he observes the values of one or more other variables in whose variation he is interested. Then if the experiment reveals that an observed variable varies systematically as the controlled variables are allowed to vary, this relationship is a type case of a causal relation" [40, p. 165].

This notion of causality remains unchanged in a later article by Strotz and Wold [35]. They point out that their intention is to define causality, not precisely but in a "primitive" way.[8] The broad spectrum of their definition of causality permits causal interpretations of interdependent (defined as *vector causality*) as well as recursive systems. For example, given the following interdependent system where y is a vector of endogenous variables and z, a vector of exogenous variables

$$B \, y + \Gamma \, z = u$$

it can be said that the vector z *causes* the vector y. But this usage of causality, they assert, is nothing more than an "abstract terminological extension of the usual notion of causality" [35, p. 421]. It is, in other words, the vernacular use of the word "causality."

It should be emphasized that the Strotz-Wold definition of causality consists of a hierarchy of definitions of causality. At the top is the notion of causality contained in a stimulus-response relationship measured as a controlled experiment. In fact, Wold claims that "The supreme tool . . . for establishing a causal relationship . . . is the *controlled experiment*" [40, p. 165]. A distinctly lower-order notion of causality applies to interdependent systems. Unless otherwise stated, I shall discuss the former notion of causality as the Strotz-Wold definition of causality.

Their concept of causality is intended to be that of everyday usage in the laboratory, and emphasizes the notion of control. The meaning of causality is the following: "z is the cause of y if by hypothesis, it is 'or would' be possible by *controlling* z indirectly to control y, at least stochastically. But it may or may not be possible by controlling y indirectly to control z" [35, p. 418]. Only in special cases may a causal relation be reversible and symmetric. Furthermore, they stress that y and z cannot both be subjected to simultaneous control changes independent of each other without the causal relationship between them being violated.

Strotz and Wold discuss other kinds of causality contained in their taxonomy of econometric models: causal circles, bicausal chains, and interdependent systems. The notion of causality as it applies to the interpretation of a coefficient in all of these models "is to be found in the underlying dynamic model which, *if the laboratory notion of causality is to be sustained*, will be recursive in character" [35, p. 426].

The Strotz-Wold definition of causality, however "primitive" they may regard it, is an intuitively appealing one. It emphasizes the notion of control, and, therefore, has an advantageous stochastic use—it is the *raison-d'être* for a conditional expectation whose coefficients can be estimated by ordinary least squares. Moreover, the importance of a controlled experiment of "cause-effect" is apparent to any scientist. It is, however, a definition containing some conceptual difficulties which limit its usefulness in economics.

The distinction, however, between cause and effect in economics is often vague and difficult to define not merely because of measurement problems, but because of large numbers of interacting groups of persons and institutions. Furthermore, a cause-effect involving only a z and a y is a gross oversimplification of an economic phenomenon. When causality in economics is more accurately regarded as a process, i.e., a string of causes and effects, not a controlled experiment involving only a z and y [8, p. 190], it becomes increasingly difficult to distinguish causes from effects.

An additional difficulty of any causal chain as an empirical proposition lies in finding the ultimate cause [7, pp. 89-90]. How far an investigator should extend the causal sequence is a problem that is best solved by defining a subcycle, which distinguishes relevant from irrelevant variables. The Strotz-Wold definition of causality subsumes irrelevant variables[9] as part of the experimental conditions. Yet, it is not entirely clear, at least to this reviewer, what criteria Strotz and Wold would suggest for distinguishing relevant from irrelevant variables. This point cannot be overemphasized. To say that X causes Y one must specify the conditions under which X will be followed by a Y. As Hempel [16, p. 348] clearly states ". . . to the extent that those conditions remain indeterminate, a general statement of causal connection amounts at best to the vague claim that *there are* certain further unspecified background conditions whose explicit mention in the given statement would yield a truly general law connecting the 'cause' and the 'effect' in question."

With few exceptions, economics is a nonexperimental science.[10] For example, in studying consumption behavior in the context of a macroeconomic model, most investigators have regarded consumption and personal income as interacting variables, recognizing that either variable can be the cause of the other. Both variables can be subjected to simultaneous controlled changes and still have a causal relationship between them. Suppose consumption and personal income are controlled by changes in taxes. Within a given time period the effect of a change of taxes on consumption and personal income can be measured as well as the effects of changes that consumption and personal income have on each other. Most economists, I surmise, would agree with D. B. Suits that the position of an economist is quite different from that of an experimental scientist. He states "that the phenomena our economist wants to isolate and study cannot be brought into a laboratory and manipulated at will. He cannot put a family in a test tube and observe its behavior when various levels of income are injected, nor can he manipulate price to see how a market responds" [37, pp. 2-3].

Strotz and Wold consider one domain of causal laws. A rubric of laws of causality according to type and form of law and domain, and level of application is given by Feigl [10]. In formulating their notion of causality they are essentially concerned with sequential events. According to their hierarchy of notions of causality the temporal succession of events in economics has a higher order of aspiration and importance than the simultaneous occurrence of such events. Accordingly, their notion is a restrictive one for it is dependent on sequential events and does not (except for vector causality) allow for simultaneous occurrences of events that are interrelated.

This point is closely associated with the aim of model building in economics, which is the same as the aim of any scientific discipline—the understanding of scientific laws governing economic phenomena. The more fundamental the law, the more irrelevant absolute time and space coordinates become. Many philosophers of science agree with Russell that *"time* must not enter explicitly into our formulae. All mechanical laws exhibit acceleration as a function of configuration, not of configuration and time jointly; and this principle of the irrelevance of the time may be extended to all scientific laws . . ." [28, pp. 401-402].[11]

The notion of causality presented by Strotz and Wold is not intended to "straitjacket" theorists to one interpretation. Nonetheless, they argue that their notion of causality is the one used in economics. It appears that economists have not been too cognizant of the notion of causality which they employ.[12] To pin such a label on economists is, at best, an uncertain blessing, or worse, ascribes to them a perfunctory usage of the "notion of causality."

Contrary to the Strotz-Wold argument "that the notion of causality in economics is the one we have presented" [35, p. 420], a notion of causality that is perhaps more compatible with the nature of econometric models is the idea of a functional relationship for explanation and prediction. The notion of causality in this sense is simply a working assumption, broad enough to include interdependent as well as recursive systems, without asserting that the notion itself is a verifiable statement about reality [14]. But more about this later.

In summary, the principle of causality may take on various forms: "an empirical generalization, an a priori truth, a concealed definition, a convention that may be accepted or not as one pleases" [23, p. 323]. Strotz and Wold [35] have adopted the form of an empirical generalization that is applicable to certain economic situations, but it is not general enough for a broad range of economic problems. Had Strotz and Wold represented their definition of causality in a less persuasive way (not as an empirical generalization) without claiming it to be the one used in economics, or relegated to second-class scientific status, a notion of causality (defined by them as vector causality) contained in interdependent systems, their prescription for empirical work in economics could have been taken at face value. But their notion of causality strongly suggests that recursive systems are the legitimate descriptions of the economic world.[13] Their arbitrarily defined hierarchy of models is not to be taken as *the* one applicable to the economic world. An open question in economics is still, "Which notion of causality is the most useful in an operational sense?"

In a subsequent article by Wold [46] causality concepts including his earlier ones are discussed and modified. He reaffirms his position regarding the controlled experiment—it is "the supreme tool which the scientist has at his disposal to establish a causal relationship" [46, p. 270]. Nonetheless, there is a discernible shift in Wold's position. What is now needed is an operational notion of causality applicable to interdependent systems but one that recognizes the supremacy of the controlled experiment. Since interdependent systems are generally regarded as models of non-experimental situations, the above need may, at first reading, seem contradictory. Wold's answer is to (1) expand the concept of stimulus-response as used in experimental situations to include a common sense understanding of "cause" and "effect." He labels the new notion a "generalized stimulus-response" definition of causality which is applicable to fictitious as well as real experiments and (2) partially reinterpret interdependent systems [48, pp. 144-150] in the following manner: let an interdependent system be represented by the following asymmetric form.

$$y = By + \Gamma z + u$$

This can be rewritten as

$$y = By^* + \Gamma z + u^*$$

where y^* is the systematic part of the vector of the endogenous variable y. Here the expected values of the current endogenous variables enter as causal variables, but not their observed values. The parameters are estimated by a fixed point estimator.[14]

For Wold the importance of the controlled experiment cannot be overemphasized. Yet, the controlled experiment performed in a laboratory is neither a necessary nor a sufficient condition for establishing the causality of a relationship. If a causal relationship can be deduced explaining the movement of a planet, it will be established on the relationship's ability to predict the position of the planet, not on the performance of a controlled experiment. Prediction is a more important consideration for establishing a causal relationship than the fact that a controlled experiment can be conducted. The laboratory notion of a controlled experiment, to be sure, is a useful concept for making specific the conditions under which the cause will be followed by the effect. The essential connection between causality and prediction will be discussed later on.

A few other notions of causality have been developed for economists. H. A. Simon [30, 31] conceptualizes causality in terms of a model. He defines causality as "an asymmetrical relation among certain variables, or subsets of variables, in a self-contained structure" [31, p. 73]. (A self-contained structure is defined as a linear structure in which the number of equations is equal to the number of variables.) For example [31, p. 57 and 17, p. 238], suppose we have the following simple model:

$$X_1 + a_{12}X_2 - b_1 = 0, \quad a_{21}X_1 + X_2 - b_2 = 0.$$

The variable X_1 is said to be directly causally dependent on X_2 if and only if $a_{21} = 0$ and $a_{12} \neq 0$. Simon points out that there is no necessary connection between the asymmetry of the relation and asymmetry in time. The model can be recursive among subsets of dependent variables and have interdependence within a subset of dependent variables. Fisher [12] describes this model as a block recursive system [10] and also illustrates the use of Simon's notion of causality.[15]

Orcutt [24, 25] offers a straightforward, pragmatic notion of causality that is similar to Simon's. A causal relation is an asymmetrical or unidirectional relation. The unidirectional aspect of a causal relation is critically important for making meaningful economic policy statements. To be sure, the direction of causation is an empirical question, but the search should be for unidirectional relationships.

Basmann, critical of the Strotz-Wold definition of causality, offers his definition of the "classical principle of causality." He says,

> Assume that a mechanism under investigation can be isolated from all systematic, i.e., nonrandom, external influences; assume that the mechanism can be started over repeatedly from any definite initial condition. If every time the mechanism is started up from approximately the same initial condition, it tends to run through approximately the same sequence of events, then the mechanism is said to be causal [2, p. 442].

This definition leans heavily on notions of causality discussed by Frank [13]. They arise out of astronomy and Newtonian physics. The principle of causality as it pertains to observations of state variables, i.e., the variables of a mechanical system is ". . . that all observable facts are governed by causal laws that allow us to predict measurable values of the *state variables* from their measured values at the present" [13, p. 269].

The causal laws themselves are of the differential form

$$\frac{d\xi}{dt} = F_k(\xi_1, \xi_2, ..., \xi_n) \quad \text{where } k = 1, 2, ...,$$

where the ξ's are the state variables, and t is time. Given values of the state variables for one instant of time, we can find values of the ξ's for any other time from the above expression. Frank formulates a principle of causality that perhaps could be tested by experiments as follows:

> Whatever the specific form of F_k may be, one thing is certain: The changes of the variables in time $d\xi_k/dt$ are dependent upon the present values of $\xi_1, ..., \xi_n$ only. Whenever these variables reassume their original values, the changes in time preassume their values too. In other words, if a state or the system repeats itself, all following states repeat themselves too. If we call a value system of the ξ_k the "state A" of our system, we can say: If a state A of our system is followed by a state B, every time that A returns it is followed by B. This is a formulation of the principle of causality which does not make use of expressions like "simple formula." We must keep in mind that saying that the system "has a state A" or "a state B" means only that the ξ_k have certain numerical values. The statement "A returns" or "B returns" refers only to the numerical values of the state variables, not to observable facts [12, p. 269].

This principle of causality can be "tested" by defining "state A" as consisting of a relevant group of ξ_k having specific values, while values of other ξ_k are irrelevant. What is actually "tested" is the specification of the set variables that one can consider "relevant" in the sense that the "return of a small number of variables to their original values would imply that 'state A' has returned... implying...that 'state B' will also return" [13, p. 271].

Causality, as a recurrence of a sequence of events divided into two states, A and B where A follows B, has a useful meaning for economists. Even if there is no recurrence of the same state A, the principle is still valid. If we exclude state A of the universe, we must consider incomplete or approximate, cycles [13, p. 282]. An example is recurrence of the business cycle in the milieu of changing political environments.

We can regard state A at an initial $t = t_0$ as consisting of a set of economic conditions—measurable economic variables, assumed to be the relevant ones. An incomplete cycle is so defined by determining what state variables can and must be disregarded. Economic systems are seen as incomplete cycles. In studying the recurrence of states (as incomplete cycles) economists generally work with a small number of variables.[16]

Basmann's mechanism can be explained (in a more meaningful way to economists) as a recurrence of a set of economic variables within the context of a larger economic system. A causal hypothesis refers to the set in *isolation* from the remaining parts of the larger system. The concept of *ceteris paribus* is used by economists to describe the isolation of a submechanism, e.g., a partial equilibrium model, in which the behavior of certain economic variables is isolated from the influence of other variables.

A Causal Interpretation of a Nontriangular System—The difference between Basmann's notion of causality and that of Strotz and Wold is revealed in a sharp exchange between them. Basmann [2] constructs a model of economic behavior that is recursive and nontriangular and has structural relations which he claims to be causal according to the "classical principle of causality." His notion of recursiveness allows for nontriangular as well as triangular systems, whereas Strotz and Wold restrict recursiveness to triangular systems. Basmann [2, p. 439] considers any system to be *recursive* if it can be equivalently expressed by a set of ordinary difference equations.

Basmann sets up conditions for performing a stimulus-response experiment for the consumer sector by observing consumer response to controlled values of p'_t and m'_t in the following equation:

$$(8) \quad d(p'_t, m'_t) = \beta_1 p'_t + \gamma_1 m'_t + \gamma_2 + u_t.$$

Classical least squares regression will give unbiased estimates of β_1, γ_1, and γ_2. Similarly for the production sector two stimulus-response experiments are given in the form of a causal output relation,

$$(9) \quad s(p'_{t-1}) = \beta_2 p'_{t-1} + \gamma_3 + v_t,$$

and a causal inventory-supply relation,

$$(10) \quad i(p'_t - p'_{t-1}) = \beta_3 (p'_t - p'_{t-1}) + w_t.$$

The random disturbances are denoted as u_t, v_t, and w_t.

Coupled with (8), (9), and (10) are two assumptions implying "that the consumer sector and supply sector exert systematic influences on each other and *jointly* determine market p^*_t and market q^*_t." [2, p. 444]. The assumptions are that 1) the observed market price, p^*_t, and the observed disposable consumer income, m^*_t, satisfy for every t:

$$(11) \quad d(p^*_t, m^*_t) = s(p^*_{t-1}) + i(p^*_t - p^*_{t-1})$$

and that 2) the market price, p^*_t, and the observed market quantity, q^*_t, satisfy for every t:

$$(12) \quad s(p^*_{t-1}) + i(p^*_t - p^*_{t-1}) = q^*_t.$$

The observed price p^*_t is assumed to clear the market. Furthermore, the observed q^*_t, quantity sold to consumer, is assumed to be equal to total supply. This is done by specifying p_t and p_{t-1} to be equal to the observed prices p^*_t, p^*_{t-1}.

From (11), (12) and (8), (10) the following equivalent interdependent system of structural equations can be deduced:

$$(13) \quad q^*_t = \beta_1 p^*_t + \gamma_1 m^*_t + \gamma_2 + u_t$$

$$(14) \quad q^*_t = \beta_1 p^*_t + (\beta_2 - \beta_3) p^*_{t-1} + \gamma_3 + (v_t + w_t)$$

The individual equations, which are the structural equations of a *nontriangular* system, do not embody the notion of causality contained in the stimulus-response relationships (8) and (10). The physical extension of this system (not its representation as a mathematical model, nor the rule for translating the structural equations into the reduced form) can be given a causal interpretation according to the classical notion of causality. Furthermore, the interdependent system (13)-(14) can be transformed into a system of the ordinary difference equations representing the reduced form.

In summary, the interdependent system (13) and (14) represents a mechanism in isolation from all systematic (nonrandom external) influences. It can be started up from approximately the same initial values of price and quantity, and the time sequence of prices always converges[17] to a dynamic equilibrium path given initial values of price, quantity and the values of the exogenous variable m^*.

Strotz and Wold [36] reply that Basmann's interpretation of the classical principle of causality falls within their notion of *vector causality*, and suggest that (13) and (14) present an equilibrium model displaying bicausality [35, p. 425]. Since (13) and (14) are not an explicit causal chain, no causal interpretation in the sense of *explicit* causality can be made of, say, β_1 in (13).

The crux of the argument between Strotz and Wold, and Basmann lies in a notion of causality that is adequate for explaining the rationale of an economic model. All recognize the importance of the underlying dynamic model[18] in attributing causality to the parameters of model, but Strotz and Wold differ from Basmann in their use of the controlled experiment as *the* criteria for establishing a causal relationship. They regard the controlled experiment as the supreme tool for establishing such a relationship. Basmann's criteria do not lie in the controlled experiment, but whether the model satisfies the classical notion of causality. The test for causality is essentially a forecasting one. For Basmann a controlled experiment is important as a way to construct the autonomous component parts of an economic model. To these parts he adds a relationship explaining how the consumer and output interact with each other in the determination of the price and quantity. Because Strotz and Wold adhere to a unidirectional "cause and effect" notion of causality (the notion of *explicit* causality), they deny the fact that a causal interpretation can be made of the coefficients of an interdependent system (except in the sense of vector causality).

Basmann, on the other hand, allows interaction to occur among the dependent variables in his model of the economic world; hence the B matrix (2) can be nontriangular and its elements be given a causal interpretation if the reduced form of the system (13)-(14) satisfies the "classical principle of causality."

In summary: the issues between Strotz and Wold, and Basmann involve different interpretations of recursiveness and operational notions of causality.

Causality and Time

So far, we have skirted the issue of causality and time in economics. What is the relevance of time to economists? Most economists have a notion of cause and effect as discrete events over time. But can effect be contemporaneous with cause in economics? Lenzen [19, p. 8] points out that whether cause or effect is successive or contemporaneous depends on the use of an integral or differential mode of description. The use of the former allows us to find values of the state variables at any time t if the value for t=0, for example, and the differential equations are given. In this case the state variable is a function of time. On the other hand, the differential equation expresses the rates of change of state variables as functions of the state. This means, of course, that an economic theory in the form of a differential equation in which time appears as an argument can be transformed in such a way that time is eliminated [23, pp. 320-321 and 29, p. 285].

For example, in the mathematical formulation of investment behavior we may describe the causal process as a successive one by an integral equation whereby the stock of capital at time t can be found, given values of the state variable at an instant of time (e.g., t=0) and the differential equation. Also, a higher order derivative of investment with respect to time can be made equal to the value of a state variable.

The question of cross-section analysis arises. What are the causal implications of such an analysis at a single point in time? The "classical notion of causality," independent of both explicit time and the functional form of the relationship, is applicable here. But it seems to me that economists have not been very careful in maintaining the set of relevant variables derived from a cross-sectional analysis in answering policy questions involving time. For example, a cross-sectional study of consumption and income has different causal implications than a time-series study of the same variables. Yet to use the former for forecasting consumption as aggregate income changes over time entails satisfying a number of crucial assumptions. Otherwise, what were hitherto considered irrelevant variables now become relevant ones.

Causality and Prediction

Economists have contradictory notions about the relationship of prediction and causality. Yet most of them would agree with Milton Friedman's dictum that "the ultimate goal of a positive science is the development of a 'theory' or 'hypothesis' that yields valid and meaningful (i.e., not truistic) predictions about phenomena not yet observed" [15, p. 7].

Like many economists, Wold [46] makes a distinction between prediction and causality. In particular, he maintains that interdependent systems purport to explain by predicting. Causal chains, he claims, also purport to predict, but do so in a more scientific way than interdependent systems because they establish a stimulus-response relationship. Therefore, causal chains aspire to the role of *scientific prediction*, because the establishment of a stimulus-response relationship has, in some ways, the character of *scientific explanation*. According to Hempel [16, p. 234], scientific prediction in empirical sciences consists in making a statement about a future event from 1) statements about the initial conditions, e.g., current level of gross national product and 2) suitable general laws. The distinction between explanation and prediction is a pragmatic one. In the case of explanation the determining conditions are sought for the known final event. In the case of prediction the initial conditions are given and their effect is to be determined.

The confusion about the connection between causality and prediction stems from the practice of making predictions outside the range of tested scientific laws and theories.[19] The difficulty lies in distinguishing such predictions from those based on tested scientific laws. The line of demarcation, to be sure, is vague. However, "scientific prognoses"—prediction based on scientific law or theory —illustrate the essential connection between causality and prediction.

Most philosophers of science [e.g., 8, p. 192; 10, p. 408; and 27, p. 60] would agree that the essence of causality is prediction. Feigl, in particular, states that "clarified (purified) concept of causation is defined in terms of *predictability according to a law* (or, more adequately, according to a set of laws)" [10, p. 408]. The essential connection between causality and prediction has been succinctly expressed by K. Popper [26, pp. 59-60].

> To give a *causal explanation* of an event means to deduce a statement which describes it, using as premises of the deduction one or more *universal laws, together with certain singular statements of the initial conditions*. For example, we can say that we have given a causal explanation of the breaking of a certain piece of thread if we have found that the thread has a tensile strength of 1 lb. and that a weight of 2 lbs. was put on it. If we analyze this causal explanation we shall find several constituent parts. On the other hand there is the hypothesis: "Whenever a thread is loaded with a weight exceeding that which characterizes the tensile strength of the thread, then it will break"; a statement which has the character of a universal law of nature. On the other hand, we have singular statements (in this case two) which apply only to the specific event in question: "The weight characteristic for this thread is 1 lb." and "The weight put on this thread was 2 lbs."
>
> We have thus two different kinds of statement, both of which are necessary ingredients of a complete causal explanation. They are (1) *universal statements*, i.e., hypotheses of the character of natural laws, and (2) *singular statements*, which apply to the specific event in question and which I shall call "initial conditions." It is from universal statements in conjunction with initial conditions that we *deduce* the singular statement, "This thread will break." We call this statement a specific or singular *prediction*.

This view is similar to Hempel's notion of *scientific prediction* [16, p. 234]. A causal explanation is a special kind of explanation in the following sense: an event is said to have caused an effect only if "there are general laws connecting the former with the latter in such a way that, given a description of the antecedent events, the occurrence of the effect can be deduced with the help of the laws," Hempel [16, p. 301].

Unfortunately, the science of economics is too immature to have a set of universal laws that are well tested and confirmed. Besides, there is the difficulty of ascertaining the relevant set of initial conditions. Moreover, most explanations offered for the occurrence of economic events are incomplete. Too often in economics prediction is based on vague generalizations and incomplete with little or no recognition of the initial conditions. In practice the inexorable demand for economic forecasts has produced too many that are based on hunch, judgment, and outright guesswork. In addition, many of them are tinged by political and ideological suppositions [18, pp. 89-102].

Causality and Identification

Observational equivalence (12) is said to arise when two or more theories have the same implications about an observable phenomenon. The observations, however rich and extensive, cannot distinguish the parameters of one theory from those of another. The question of identification in economics is concerned with distinguishing one theory from another in terms of the way each theory generates the observations as the true ones.

Identification is interlinked with notions of causality for the following reasons:

a. Tests of identification are formulated, in part, in terms of excluded variables, the set of irrelevant (or relevant) ones crucial in "testing" a notion of causality discussed earlier.

b. The identification problem was, until recently, considered a part of the general problem of building interdependent but not recursive systems. The problem did not arise, as Wold points out, in recursive systems because "the parameters are here estimated directly on the basis of the behavior relations of the system in *its* original, unreduced form" [41, p. 368].

Yet, later in the same article Wold mentions the formal equivalence of the two systems [41, pp. 410-412]. It is an equivalence, however, that is limited to the formal mathematical properties of the model. Nonetheless, one must distinguish between the two systems as operative or explanatory mechanisms. Wold reasserts that "...the parting of the ways (between interdependent and recursive systems) is linked up with the specification of behavior relations in terms of conditional expectations and cause-effect patterns" [41, p. 412]. The wavering of Wold's position becomes evident toward the end of the same article where he observes that the aforementioned equivalence poses a new type of identification problem.

What Wold is alluding to is revealed by Basmann (5) who shows the observational equivalence of explicit causal chains and interdependent systems. He points out that both an interdependent representation and an explicit causal chain one "define one and the same statistical hypothesis" [5, p. 1089].

Basmann concludes that "if an 'explicit causal chain' with premise $\bar{\beta_1}$ is found to be in better agreement with observation than an 'interdependent' model with premise β_1 we must attribute that state of affairs to the better agreement of the premise $\bar{\beta_1}$ with observations and not to the fact that the 'explicit causal chain' has the 'explicit causal chain' property" [5, p. 1089].

The observational equivalence of the two systems has particular relevance to a claim put forth by Wold regarding tests of the direction of the causality in explicit causal chains. Wold points out that "causal directions are part of the model, with implications that are liable to empirical tests just as any other part of the hypothetical setup" [45, p. 756]. The model to which Wold refers is an explicit causal chain. He tests the hypothesis, x→y, x influences y, against the alternative one, y→x, y influences x. The theorem on the observational equivalence of interdependent and explicit causal chain systems states that there exists an interdependent representation of each of these hypotheses. Furthermore, both representations, interdependent and explicit causal chain, contain the same statistical hypothesis. The significance of the theorem lies in the fact that it is not possible to statistically test in the context of either kind of econometric model the direction of causation because the hypothesis x→y and the alternative one y→x are each equivalent to neither x→y nor x←y which means that x and y mutually influence each other, or that x and y do not influence each other, but both are influenced by a third variable.

The issue of tests of the direction of causality needs further clarification[20] about what is "causal." Basmann [2] in constructing a nontriangular recursive system uses the term "causal" to refer to the physical extension of the system as a combination of symbols in the mathematical language, not to the mathematical language and symbols themselves. Furthermore, he uses the word "causal" to describe the *system;* not in reference to either a coefficient or an equation of the system. When Wold discusses the "causal interpretation" of numerical coefficients, it is not clear to this reviewer, whether he refers to the coefficients as physical extensions of his system, or as verbal symbols explaining his notion of causality. If the former, then there is no test because of the aforementioned theorem on the observational equivalence of interdependent and recursive systems that can ascribe causality to coefficients of either system. If the latter, then no question about the physical system is involved.

4. CONCLUSION

Which operational notion of causality is most useful to economists is still an open question. While there are circumstances calling for the Strotz-Wold notion of causality, it is neither a notion that economists generally employ, because of its restricted domain, nor a notion sufficiently well defined in terms of theory construction and hypothesis testing. Furthermore, the issue is muddled by the observational equivalence of explicit causal chains and interdependent systems.

More general tests of identification are needed in addition to an operational notion of causality in economics, that deals explicitly with time, prediction, and a conceptualization of how fundamental economic laws are to be found.

NOTES

[1]In the early 1950s the debate centered on simultaneous versus single equation estimation. Later, it evolved into two debates: a broad one of interdependent versus recursive systems—essentially a debate about how the economic world should be conceptualized for hypothesis testing. This debate is not particularly concerned with the mathematical or statistical properties of either system, but is about the methodological and philosophical aspects of the meaning of causality in economics. The second debate is still about the relative merits of single and simultaneous equation estimators in connection with the problem of identification [22].

[2]Strictly speaking the system should be called triangular-recursive in order to differentiate it from any system (triangular or nontriangular) said to be *recursive* if it can be equivalently expressed by a set of ordinary differential equations [9, pp. 52-54; also 2, p. 439]. Unless otherwise mentioned in this paper, the common usage of the word "recursive" in economics as referring to triangular systems will be maintained.

[3]Strotz differs with Wold. He feels that stipulation (b) is too restrictive and unnecessary [35, p. 420 fn. 5 and p. 430, fn. 6]. However Fisher [12, pp. 96-97] points out that the variance-covariance matrix of random disturbances of a recursive system must be diagonal in order to obtain consistent least-squares estimates.

[4]In an earlier study Wold [39] took a more tentative position regarding the relative merits of both systems than he does here. He states, "From the viewpoint of dynamic analysis, a structural system (an interdependent system) is a mixed type of approach, since static hypotheses are permitted in the form of equilibrium relations. This in itself is no disadvantage, quite the contrary. By introducing other types of relations than causal dependences the approach becomes more flexible, and, therefore, opens up new possibilities for econometric anaysis" [39, p. 53].

[5]Aggregation over time may lead to interdependency as a solution to the problem where the time periods of the data are larger than the unit period of the dynamic theory. The smaller the time periods for which data are available, given the unit period of the dynamic theory, the greater the likelihood of using a recursive system. A demonstration of this is given by Benzil and Hansen [6, pp. 163-164].

[6]According to Strotz the investigator "constructs what is essentially an equilibrium version of the recursive system. The specification error is introduced because the probability characteristics of the recursive model do not guarantee that the system will be always in equilibrium when observed, so that equilibrium obtained is but a chance and not a specification" [34, p. 428].

[7]Such controversies involved the fallacy of "essentialism." It refers to an ultimate explanation, a truism, such that further explanation becomes unnecessary and impossible. This is not consistent with the aims of science [26, p. 431].

[8]I am indebted to R. Strotz for pointing out to me that the word "primitive" was used in the Strotz-Wold article [35, p. 420] to mean "undefined within the context of the theory."

[9]The frequent use of the term *ceteris paribus* by economists is an alternate way of defining a subcycle. Practical considerations in specifying a subcycle are discussed by Hutchison [18, pp. 86-87].

[10]Examples of exceptions are the controlled experiments to test micro-economic hypotheses. See Sidney Siegel and Lawrence A. Fouraker, *Bargaining and Group Decision Making. Experiments in Bilateral Monopoly* (New York, McGraw-Hill, 1960) and Lawrence A. Fouraker and Sidney Siegel, *Bargaining Behavior* (New York, McGraw-Hill, 1963). Also, James L. Murphy, "Effect of the Threat of Losses on Duopoly Bargaining," *Quarterly Journal of Economics,* LXXX (1966), pp. 296-313.

[11]Similar views are given by H. Margenau, "Meaning and Scientific Status of Causality," *Philosophy of Science,* Vol. 1, No. 2 (April, 1934), p. 142 and H. Feigl [10], p. 412.

[12]Few economists used the word "causality" except in a vernacular sense. An example of the use of causality in the Strotz-Wold sense appears in a paper, by F. A. Lutz, "Politische Uberzeugungen and Nationalokonomische Theorie," *Ordo,* Bd. IX, 1957, p. 15. Hutchison translates it [18, pp. 86-87]. Other examples are given in Part IV of *Econometric Model Building, Essays on the Causal Chain Approach,* edited by H. O. A. Wold (Amsterdam: North Holland Publishing Co., 1964).

Uses of the word "cause" in the history of economic thought is well documented by Gerald Garb, "The Problem of Causality in Economics," *Kyklos,* Vol. 17, 1964, pp. 594-609.

[13]Wold states that empirical evidence will settle the issue between interdependent and recursive systems. Apparently having some forethought about the empirical results, Wold alludes to a verdict of applied work. He states that "It is still too early to attempt a comparative appraisal of the empirical results" [47, p. 32]. Nevertheless, he conjectures "that the time will soon be ripe for a verdict" [47, p. 33]. In a review appearing a year later Wold reaffirms his optimism regarding the verdict of applied work. "There is still no verdict, but it seems safe to say that the recent results on models specified in terms of conditional expectations pave the way toward a verdict" [49, p. 1215].

Whether empirical evidence can, in principle, even settle the issue is a question we shall delay answering until p. 140 under *Causality and Identification.*

[14]Evidence on the forecasting efficiency and other properties of this estimator is given by [22], and E. J. Mosbaek and H. O. A. Wold, *Interdependent Systems, Structure and Estimation,* Amsterdam: North Holland Publishing Co., 1970.

[15]Another illustration of Simon's concept of causality is given by Karl Fox, "A Submodel of the Agricultural Sector," *The Brookings Quarterly Econometric Model of the United States,* edited by J. S. Duesenberry *et al.,* Chicago, Rand McNally & Co., 1965, pp. 409-461.

[16]How small the number of variables should be is a bone of contention in economics. The arguments of T. C. Lui are relevant here. He is critical of how economists distinguish relevant from irrelevant variables, particularly in the context of identifying a system of simultaneous equations (T. C. Lui, "A Simple Forecasting Model for the U. S. Economy," *International Monetary Fund Staff Papers,* IV, August, 1955, pp. 434-466).

[17]The condition for convergence is given by Basmann [2, p. 445].

[18]Basmann adds that according to the classical *Principle* the system must be dynamically stable, i.e., the endogenous variables must be theoretically constrained from diverging to infinity. He states that the constraint "might take the form of a requirement that the roots of the corresponding auxiliary equation be constrained to the interior of the unit circle in the complex plane, or it might take the form of some special mechanism to halt the divergence if the roots are not so constrained" [3, p. 242].

[19]Though there are some economists who maintain that behind every prediction, "there is always some theory, however, naive it may be," H. Theil, *Applied Economic Forecasting,* North Holland, Amsterdam, p. 2.

[20]I am indebted to R. L. Basmann for pointing this out to me.

REFERENCES

1. Anderson, W. H. L. and W. L. L'Esperance. "An Econometric Model of the Market for Yellow Perch," Abstract, *Proceedings of the 26th Annual Meeting of the American Society of Limnology and Oceanography in Conjunction with the Sixth Conference on Great Lakes Research,* June, 1963.

2. Basmann, R. L. "The Causal Interpretation of Nontriangular Systems of Economic Relations," *Econometrica,* 31 (July, 1963), 439-448.

3. ————. "Reply to R. W. Clower," *Econometrica,* 33, No. 1 (January, 1965), 242.

4. —————. "Review of Econometric Model-Building: Essays on the Causal Chain Approach," edited by H. O. A. Wold, *Journal of the American Statistical Assocation,* (September, 1965), 924-927.
5. —————. "A Note on the Statistical Testability of 'Explicit Causal Chains' Against the Class of 'Interdependent' Models," *Journal of the American Statistical Association,* (December, 1965), 1080-1093.
6. Bentzel, R. and B. Hansen. "On Recursiveness and Interdependency in Economic Models," *Review of Economic Studies,* 22, No. 59 (1954), 153-168.
7. Bridgman, P. W. *The Logic of Modern Physics.* New York: MacMillan Co., 1949.
8. Carnap, R. *Philosophical Foundations of Physics.* New York: Basic Books, Inc., 1966.
9. D'Abro, A. *The Rise of the New Physicis, Its Mathematical and Physical Theories.* Dover Publications, 1951.
10. Feigl, H. "Notes on Causality," *Readings in the Philosophy of Science,* edited by H. Feigl and M. Brodbeck, New York: Appleton-Century-Crofts, 1953, 408-418.
11. Fisher, F. M. "Dynamic Structure and Estimation in Economy-wide Econometric Models," *The Brookings Quarterly Econometric Model of the United States,* edited by J. S. Duesenberry, G. Fromm, L. R. Klein, and E. Kuh. Chicago: Rand McNally & Company, 1965, 589-635.
12. —————. *The Identification Problem in Econometrics.* New York: McGraw-Hill, 1966.
13. Frank, P. *Philosophy of Science: The Link between Science and Philosophy.* Englewood Cliffs, N.J.: Prentice-Hall, Inc., 1957.
14. —————. *Modern Science and Its Philosophy.* New York: Collier Books, 1961, Chap. 1.
15. Friedman, M. "The Methodology of Positive Economics," in *Essays in Positive Economics,* The University of Chicago Press, 1953.
16. Hempel, C. G. *Aspects of Scientific Explanation and Other Essays in the Philosophy of Science.* New York: The Free Press, 1965.
17. Hurwicz, L. "On the Structural Form of Interdependent Systems," *Logic, Methodology and Philosophy of Science,* Proceedings of the 1960 International Congress, edited by E. Nagel, P. Suppes, and A. Tarski, Stanford University Press, 1962, 232-239.
18. Hutchison, T. W. *"Positive" Economics and Policy Objectives.* Cambridge, Mass.: Harvard University Press, 1964.
19. Lenzen, V. F. *Causality in Natural Science.* Springfield, Illinois: Charles Thomas, 1954.
20. L'Esperance, W. L. "A Case Study in Prediction: the Market for Watermelons," *Econometrica,* 32, No. 1-2 (January-April, 1964), 163-173.
21. —————. "A Case Study in Prediction: A Reply," *Econometrica,* 32, No. 3 (July, 1964), 428-430.
22. —————. "Further Evidence on the Predictive Power of Various Estimators," *International Economic Review,* 8, No. 1 (February, 1967), 45-66.
23. Nagel, E. *The Structure of Science.* New York: Harcourt, Brace and World, Inc., 1961.
24. Orcutt, G. H. "Toward Partial Re-Direction of Econometrics," *The Review of Economics and Statistics,* (August, 1952), 211-213.
25. —————. "Actions, Consequences, and Causal Relations," *The Review of Economics and Statistics,* (November, 1952), 305-313.
26. Popper, K. *The Logic of Scientific Discovery.* New York: Harper & Row, 1959, 59-60.
27. Rudner, R. S. *Philosophy of Social Science.* Englewood Cliffs, N.J.: Prentice-Hall, Inc., 1966.
28. Russell, B. "On the Notion of Cause with Applications to the Free-Will Problem," *Readings in the Philosophy of Science,* edited by H. Feigl and M. Brodbeck. New York: Appleton-Century-Crofts, 1953, 387-407.
29. Samuelson, P. A. *Foundations of Economic Analysis.* Cambridge, Mass.: Harvard University Press, 1947.
30. Simon, H. A. "On the Definition of the Causal Relation," *Journal of Philosophy,* 49 (July, 1952), 517-528.
31. —————. "Causal Ordering and Identifiability," Chapter III of *Studies in Econometric Method,* Cowles Commission for Research in Economics, Monograph No. 14, New York: John Wiley & Sons, 1953. Reprinted as Chap. 1 of H. A. Simon, *Models of Man,* New York: John Wiley & Sons, 1957; and as Chap. 3 of A. Ando, F. M. Fisher, and H. A. Simon, *Essays on the Structure of Social Science Models,* Cambridge, Mass.: M.I.T. Press, 1963.
32. Stevenson, C. L. *Mind.* July, 1938.
33. Stojkovic, G. "Comments on a Case Study in Prediction," *Econometrica,* 32, No. 3 (July, 1964), 425-427.
34. Strotz, R. H. "Interdependence as a Specification Error," *Econometrica,* 28, No. 2 (April, 1960), 428-442.

35. Strotz, R. H. and H. O. A. Wold. "Recursive vs. Nonrecursive Systems: An Attempt at Synthesis," *Econometrica*, 28, No. 2 (April, 1960), 417-427.
36. ————— and —————. "The Causal Interpretability of Structural Parameters: A Reply," *Econometrica*, 31, No. 3 (July, 1963), 449-450.
37. Suits, D. B. *Statistics: In Introduction to Quantitative Economic Research.* Chicago: Rand McNally and Company, 1963.
38. Valavanis, S. *Econometrics, An Introduction to Maximum Likelihood Methods.* New York: McGraw-Hill, 1959, 83-84.
39. Wold, H. O. A. and L. Jureen. *Demand Analysis, Study in Econometrics.* New York: John Wiley and Sons, 1953.
40. Wold, H. O. A. "Causality and Econometrics," *Econometrica*, 22, No. 2 (April, 1954), 162-177.
41. —————. "Ends and Means in Econometric Model Building. Basic Considerations Reviewed," in U. Grenander, ed., *Probability and Statistics* (The Harald Cramer Volume). Stockholm: Almquist and Wiksell, 1959, 355-434.
42. —————. "A Case Study of Interdependent Versus Causal Chain Systems," *Review of the International Statistical Institute*, 26 (1959), 5-25.
43. —————. "A Generalization of Causal Chain Models," *Econometrica*, 28, No. 2 (April, 1960), 443-463.
44. —————. "Construction Principles of Simultaneous Equations Models in Econometrics," L'Institut International de Statistique, 32nd Session, May 30-June 9, 1960, Tokyo.
45. —————. "Unbiased Predictors," *Proceedings of the Fourth Berkeley Symposium on Mathematical Statistics and Probability.* Berkeley and Los Angeles: University of California Press, 1961, 719-761.
46. —————. "On the Definition and Meaning of Causal Concepts," *The Approach of Model Building in the Human Sciences*, Entretien de Monaco en Sciences Humaines, 1964, 265-295.
47. ————— (editor). *Econometric Model-Building: Essays on the Causal Chain Approach.* Amsterdam: North Holland Publishing Co., 1964.
48. —————. "Toward a Verdict on Macroeconomic Simultaneous Equations," *The Econometric Approach to Development Planning*, Pontificia Academia Scientiarvm, Amsterdam: North Holland Publishing Co., 1965, 115-166.
49. —————. Review of *Methodes statistiques de l'econometrie* by Edmond Malinvaud, Paris, France: Dunod, 1964. *Journal of the American Statistical Association*, December, 1965, 1213-1215.

Letter to Professor Wilford L. L'Esperance, December 13, 1967
by
Robert H. Strotz, Dean
College of Arts and Sciences
Northwestern University, Evanston, Illinois

Dear Professor L'Esperance:

It was a pleasure to receive and to read your manuscript, "Interdependence vs Recursiveness: A Review of the Debate and Notions of the Causality in Economics," except that it made me regret all the more that I did not attend the conference last May.

Let me take up your invitation to comment on your interpretation of the Strotz-Wold "notion of causality," and apologize in advance if I seem to focus on things that I may be critical of rather than to applaud the many fine insights in your paper.

I believe I should begin by commenting on your use of the word "primitive" on page 128, line 28. You may perhaps be playing on words here, but I should make doubly sure that you understand how this word was used in the Strotz-Wold article. It means "undefined within the context of the theory." The starting point in my understanding of what the Strotz-Wold article says is that the central task is to define within the analysis the term "causally interpretable parameter." This definition proceeds in terms of the undefined or primitive term "cause," and others.

Now, to say that "cause" is not defined within the analysis is not to say that we are not communicating with it. As with all such primitive terms, the presumption is that all readers have a common understanding of what that term means as it is used. To provide this understanding, we point to its usage in the laboratory, and pretty much let it go at that. The definition of "casually interpretable parameter" is given in Section 2, and it is, as stated in our reply to Basmann, essentially a "real" definition, having empirical content. That it has empirical content, of course, has nothing to do with empirical generalization; this simply means . . . there exists in principle an observational test to ascertain whether or not a particular parameter in a simultaneous model does or does not fall within the category of "causally interpretable parameters."

The central contribution of the paper is, I believe, in its *assertion* that

(a) causal-chain systems have parameters that are "causally interpretable," and this is a nice thing about them;

(b) non-causal-chain or interdependent systems may (or may not) also have "causally interpretable parameters;" when they do, the interpretation is to be found in an underlying causal-chain system to which the interdependent system is an approximation or, in its exact form, an equilibrium state.

I have often wondered, in my contribution to the writing of this paper, if it might have been better had we used a term that I like in this context, namely, *autonomy*. My fear was that the conceptualization of the relations in a simultaneous equation system as having autonomy or not also poses semantic issues which might only have complicated the discussion. But what it means to me to say that a relation in the system has *autonomy* is that other relations can be altered without affecting this particular one. This, I believe, is to say that an autonomous relation is one whose parameters are "causally interpretable."

I am frankly troubled as to just how "persuasive" our definition of "causally interpretable parameter" actually was. When assigning meaning ostensively to the word "cause," we clearly repudiated "monopoly rights" (your ref. 35, page 418) or a desire for "strait-jacketing" (page 420). What "persuasive" element there might be must reside in the presumption that autonomy or causal interpretability is a *good* feature of a model. Hence, there is clearly a recommendatory tone in our article for we are in effect saying that, unless data limitations, etc., mitigate against it, economists are well-advised to use causal-chain systems because they have this *good* property or, alternatively, to use interdependent systems which they are prepared to interpret in terms of an underlying causal-chain system because they, too, have this *good* property.

Note that in my last sentence I am clearly not embracing only causal-chain systems and rejecting interdependent systems. In fact, my feeling is that what the Strotz-Wold article accomplished was to show how parameters in an interdependent system may be causally interpretable as well as those in a causal-chain system.

What about our argument that "the notion of causality in economics is the one we have presented"? Is this a valid empirical generalization? I think the real question here is whether or not most economists are content with such non-laboratory notions as those of bi-causality or causal circles. I think (though, having conducted no survey, this can only be a conjecture) that most economists would not embrace these notions unless they felt that this was the only way in which they could justify their use of interdependent systems. My view is that interdependent systems can be justified as approximations to causal-chain systems; consequently, bi-causality and causal circles are unnecessary. I feel the profession hasn't wanted these concepts anyway.

Of course, the conventional notion would embrace both explicit causality and vector causality; and, I may comment, both of these are consistent with the classical definition as given by Basmann. In fact, I believe that there is little disagreement between Basmann and me. In my judgment, his critique of the Strotz-Wold paper essentially misfired. This was because he did not maintain the distinction you so clearly make between triangular recursiveness, on the one hand, and recursiveness in the sense of a system of differential equations, on the other. Having obfuscated this distinction, his "counter-example" missed the point.

May I call your attention to the italized word *assertion* that occurred earlier in this letter. I fear that this may be all that our essential contribution is. The propositions (a) and (b), above, are not *demonstrated*. We could be wrong. To show this, I can dream up a counter-example that puts the issue squarely. Consider a recursive model in which quantity demanded is a function of price and exogenous variables, and in which price is a function of past quantities demanded and supplied and past price. Suppose now that government price setting is initiated so that the causal relationship determining price is no longer valid and price now enters as an exogenous variable. Will the coefficient of price in the demand function change? I think not, but that is an empirical question. If people resent paying prices that are set by the government instead of determined by the market, the demand function might shift. Indeed, I remember some years ago that Professor Marschak reported on a study that found this phenomenon for the demand for gasoline. It appeared to depend upon what component of the price (including tax) the tax amounted to. My guess is that this was a spurious statistical finding, but it cannot be ruled out a priori. Again, this is a matter of autonomy. Is the demand function an autonomous relationship? Or does it depend on the nature of other behavioral relationships within the system? In the latter case, even the parameters of a causal-chain system will not be "causally interpretable." Accumulation of good evidence that this is a common situation would be a better rebuttal to our paper than any I have encountered so far. A rebuttal to the rebuttal, of course, might be that the problem would disappear if the model were properly specified.

May I now mention a few minor matters:

(1) In note 3 on page 142, I squirm a little when I see the word "However." This seems to suggest that what Fisher has pointed out is some sort of qualification of what I believe, as reported in the previous sentence. This is, of course, not so, because what Fisher has pointed out must always have been obvious to everybody.

(2) With reference to the bottom of page 126, "Basmann's proof (4) of the observational equivalence of explicit causal-chains and interdependent systems" is also terribly obvious. The point of interest is that the property of causal interpretability is not invariant with respect to transformations. Consider a triangular system S and a non-triangular system S' related by a linear transformation. Now

let y_g become an exongenous variable, strike out the g-th equation in each of these two systems to obtain two *new* systems describing the *new* reality and ask whether the coefficients y_g in the remaining equations will be the same as before. Our assertion is that for the system S they will be, for S' they will not.

(3) On page 129 you state that "it is the *raison-d'etre* for a conditional expectation whose coefficients can be estimated by ordinary least squares." I believe the raison-d'etre for causal-chain systems is autonomy of relationships and not the applicability of any particular estimation procedure.

(4) On page 130, you state "yet, it is not entirely clear, at least to this reviewer, what criteria Strotz and Wold suggest for distinguishing relevant from irrelevant variables." My feeling is that we have suggested none because this is a problem in application and lies outside the rather formal framework of the discussion. It would, of course, be methodologically useful to have such criteria.

Again, let me express my gratitude to you for having produced so interesting a paper. I hope you will excuse me for having focused on points of difference rather than points of agreement.

Best regards.

Sincerely yours,
Robert H. Strotz

RHS/1b
cc: Professor H. O. A. Wold

Letter to Professor Wilford L. L'Esperance, November 21, 1967
by
Herman O. Wold
University Institute of Statistics, Uppsala

(Editor's note: H. Wold's original letter, 11/21/67 was based on an earlier version of W. L'Esperance's paper. All of the footnotes of the letter and the postscript of 1/13/68 are based on the final version of W. L'Esperance's paper).

Dear Les:[1]

I have read your paper with interest and appreciation. It brings in vivid memory the period when I struggled very hard with the definition and meaning of causal concepts and with their operative use in economics and other fields of application.[2] I take pleasure in commenting upon your paper.

[1]When you and.Professor Brunner, editor of this volume, asked me for permission to publish the following letter, I was pleased to get this opportunity to present a brief recount of thoughts developing over many years and scattered over many papers. In stating my grateful agreement I asked for permission to include some footnotes and references, leaving the original text of the letter intact, and making for easier access to the general reader. The references are given at the end of the postscript (1/13/68) and are numbered (1) through (7).

[2]Strictly speaking, the period divides in two: One from around 1950 into 1958 when it gradually dawned upon me that the relation between stimulus and response in controlled experiments is a special case of cause-effect relationships, and that the definition extends to non-experimental and mixed experimental—nonexperimental relationships by way of ficticious stimulus-response experiments; the second from 1958 through 1963 when the problems A and B referred to in point 2, p. 149, were taken up from the point of view of predictors (equals conditional expectations) and I soon discovered that Problem B has no answer in terms of unbiased predictors when it comes to the structural relations of interdependent systems, and that a clear-cut answer can be given after a suitable respecification of the structural relations.

1. To begin by a general appraisal, I am impressed by your objective attitude, and by your keen desire to come to grips with the problems, a difficult problem area about which there has been so much controversial and partly confused debate.

2. Part of the difficulty is that causality is a concept at the fundamental level of knowledge and therefore is tied up with a great many other fundamental notions, such as unirelational vs. multirelational models, deterministic vs. stochastic models, descriptive vs. explanation. Hence for a definition of causation to be useful it must fit in with the current use of these other concepts, and this is a rich source of confusion. It so happened that I ran into these problems in connection with unirelational models, the famous "problem of the choice of regression" (Problem A). This was in the early 1940's and it was only later that I ran into related problems concerned with multirelational models, and in particular the famous "problem of the causal interpretation of individual parameters in simultaneous equations" (Problem B).

3. Dealing first with unirelational and then with multirelational models, I had the good luck of going from simpler to more difficult problems. In your presentation you start with multirelational models, arguing in the opposite direction, and this makes it somewhat difficult to assess how your review stands relative to my actual position. Starting off with multirelational models, you begin as it were to build the upper floor of the house before you have the foundation in terms of unirelational models. As to unirelational models, your key argument refers to the situation in controlled experiments. This is however too narrow, for econometric models are nonexperimental. A general definition is needed that covers both experimental and nonexperimental situations. My approach toward such a generalization is to define causal relations as stimulus-response relations in real or ficticious experiments. The key reference is my paper "On the definition and meaning of causal concepts."

4. This last paper is missing in your original manuscript. I do not complain, but since the paper marks a switch in the orientation of my research I take the opportunity to adduce some remarks.[3]

The first draft of the paper was written in 1956-57, and to some extent inspired by the exchanges of thought with Bob Strotz when he was here for some six months in the mid-fifties. It was by then it dawned upon me how fundamental and consequential the notion of causation is for econometrics and scientific method in general. Hence I decided to write a paper on these matters that takes up the questions from the general point of view of scientific method, and with the intention to test my approach by publishing the paper in a journal specializing in scientific method and philosophy of science.

The mimeographed manuscript was circulated rather widely from 1957 and onwards. Then came a switch in my orientation, and I got so busy that I had no time to pursue the publication of the paper. Only much later I took it up again, namely at the *Entretiens de Monaco 1964*, where I served as scientific organizer at the request of the *Centre International d'Etude des Problemes Humains*, a small academy where I happen to be a member from its start in 1961. The transactions of the *Entretiens 1964* were not published until the end of 1966, a delay largely due to the death of Prince Pierre, the Honorary President of the *Centre*.

[3]The final edition of your paper takes up and discusses this and more recent papers of mine. The revision of your paper will be briefly commented upon at the end of this letter; see the postscript of 1/13/68.

The published version is essentially the same as the mimeographed version of 1956-57. The main difference is that I organized the definition in terms of model building, to emphasize that causal hypotheses enter as assumptions in the construction of cognitive models.[4]

5. The switch in my orientation was that I began to focus my interest on the specification of econometric and other models in terms of *predictors,* i.e. relations specified in terms of conditional expectations. The new orientation did not interfere with my views on causation and on the causal specification of models, for predictors are very suitable as representation of causal relations inasmuch as they follow much the same rules of operation, and in particular they are (a) irreversible, and (b) under general conditions admissible to substitution.

The new orientation is primarily concerned with probability concepts, not with causal specification, but I take the opportunity to follow up by some references, partly for the sake of completeness, partly because predictors and causal relations are so closely related.

Thanks to the new orientation, the obscure questions about interdependent systems that had been in the back of my mind such a long time gradually dissolved, and I got clearcut answers to the questions. My first results were reported in the Harald Cramer volume, your ref. 41, published in Sweden at the end of 1958 and in the United States in early 1959, and further contributions followed in a sequence of papers, including your references 46 and 47 (but not 45 which is my last paper before the switch). This line of research was rounded off by my report to the study week on econometrics, October 1963, organized by the Pontifical Academy of Sciences and published in 1965. My answer to the obscure problems, including Problem B, involved a partial reinterpretation and respecification of interdependent systems. For a brief summary, let us consider an interdependent system as written in the asymmetric form

$$(5.1) \quad y = By + \Gamma z + \varepsilon$$

Letting the parameters-matrices B and Γ be numerically the same, we rewrite the system as

$$(5.2) \quad y = By^* + \Gamma z + \varepsilon^*$$

where the vector y^* is the systematic part of the vector of endogenous variables y as resulting from the reduced form, which is the same both in (1) and (2), namely

$$y = (I-B)^{-1}\Gamma z + \varepsilon^*$$

The individual parameters in (2) but not in (1) allow a causal interpretation in the sense of Problem B. The salient point thus is that in (2) it is the *expected* values of the current endogenous variables that enter as causal variables, not their *observed* values. In this light I soon found the fix-point method, which started a line of research outside the scope of your paper.[5]

The fix-point method brought me into contact wth Ernie Mosbaek. Then followed our joint paper at the Rome meeting, where causal concepts and Problem B again are placed in focus, this time from the point of view of relaxation of the *ceteris paribus* clause.

[4]For further development of this order of ideas, see Refs. (2) and (5).

[5]See the introductory Chapter 1.4 in Ref. (7), a Monte Carlo study of the performance of the fix-point method as compared with other methods for the estimation of interdependent systems.

6. In my opinion Part 3 is the most ambitious and most interesting part of your paper. After the detailed discourse above, I see no point in aiming at a complete report of agreements and disagreements with your paper page by page; the best I can do is to venture some comments on a number of specific points.

a. To begin by a semantic issue: I see the controversial questions about causality not as a semantic issue, but as one at the level of substance of scientific method — a matter of appropriate specification of explanatory models. It is not clear to me whether this remark applies to the heading of your Part 3 or to the substance of your argument.

b. By referring to me as the "leading proponent of recursive systems" (your page 120), the general reader will include me in your sweeping references on page 119 when talking about "claims for the superiority" (second para)[6] and "narrow definition of causality" (p. 120). In the first respect your statement is unfounded (see point c below); as to the second I have found nothing in your paper to bring in evidence that my definition is too narrow.

c. Page 120: Your references to "Demand Analysis" are O.K., but in this book (1952, 1953) you cannot find any claim to the effect that recursive systems are superior to interdependent systems. My position, clearly stated on page fifty-three, was an awaiting attitude, pointing at the obscure questions about interdependent systems, and saying "Maybe these questions can be cleared up." It is true that I said that these obscurities do not exist in recursive systems, but this is not equivalent to a claim of superiority. Actually, all the time I had a feeling that a clearcut answer to the obscure questions were around the corner, but it was not until some ten years later that I found such answers in terms of predictors.

d. Page 122: I am not very happy with the causal interpretation of interdependent system ventured by Strotz and myself in our joint paper, your ref. 30. Incidentally, that paper was drafted in the mid-1950s during Bob's visit in Uppsala; we discussed it now and then when we met; and then we dug up the manuscript to serve as the first part of our triptych paper in the Festschrift issue of Econometrica 1960 in honour of Ragnar Frisch. I have checked with Bob that the causal interpretation we gave is based on (5.1) as given above. Hence it is not equivalent to the interpretation in terms of predictors—briefly summarized in (5.2) above—that I reached somewhat later; see especially the Vatican paper referred to above.

e. Page 125, third para: Again a disclaimer. I have always held the view that it is a positive feature of interdependent systems that they involve a generalization so as to include identities, equilibrium, conditions, etc. It is quite another matter that this generalization brings difficulties—and it was in the hope to dissolve these difficulties that I was so interested in interdependent systems!

f. Page 126: Much of the confusion about causal concepts is due to the fact that there are two concepts to keep apart:

(i) Causation as specified by cause-effect relationships; this is the object of my definition.

(ii) Causation as a general principle; a typical statement in this vein is the classical tenet "Everything has a cause."

This distinction is emphasized in my Monaco paper, and in the context I refer to earlier authors, e.g. Braithwaite.

[6] I am glad to find that in the final version you write "legitimacy" instead of "superiority." My comment 6c refers to the previous phrasing.

g. Page 133: The reference to Orcutt is excellent. If I understand him correctly, his views about causation are closely related to mine, especially as they had emerged in the early 1950s. They are, however, independent—I see this as an indication that unprejudiced minds with more or less the same general experience tend to see the questions about causation in the same way. Clearly, the interpretation in terms of (5.2) is not embodied in Orcutt's paper.[7]

h. Page 138: The distinction prediction-causation is discussed in detail in my Monaco paper; see point 4 above. I give examples to show the conceptual difference between the two notions. I refer to Feigl in the context, and also to the fact that he touches upon controlled experiments as the key to the distinction between the two concepts.

My views on the distinction lie behind the joint paper Mosbaek-Wold (1965); see point 6 above. It is my understanding that our argument involves some further elaboration of my conceptual views relative to the Monaco paper. I should like to check to what extent these same views are apparent in Orcutt's paper, your refs. 24, 25.

7. Well, this has become a long letter. To me, it has been quite interesting to review my arguments on causation relative to your discourse. My main incentive has been, of course, that since you have honoured my views by a serious discourse, then I should in my turn do my best to report whether or not I agree with your exposition of my views. My reporting was complicated by the fact that your main reference to my work is the Strotz-Wold paper (1960), and this paper happens to be in the midst of the evolution of my analysis: Our joint paper essentially belongs to the period when I focussed on causal interpretation by way of (5.1) above, whereas my own paper in the same triptych belongs to the later period when I had switched the focus to an interpretation of multirelational models in terms of predictors, arguing in terms of the respecified system (5.2). Thus the Strotz-Wold paper is not based on the interpretation which was first brought to full significance in my Vatican paper 1963.

8. To sum up my present position briefly, the interdependent systems are still in a dilemma. The essence of the dilemma, however, is not the nature of a question of causal specification, for this is possible by way of (5.2), but rather with regard to the dualism of apparent scatter vs. genuine scatter. Here I refer to my recent papers, most recently my invited paper at the Sydney session of ISI, September 1967.

Even the longest letters have an end, as H. C. Andersen might have said. The Sydney session of ISI gave me an opportunity to travel around the world for two months, including one month in Latin America together with. . . .

Sincerely yours,
H. Wold

Postscript (11/21/67): Rereading my letter and checking against my notes in the margin of your paper, there remain some minor points, and I feel inclined to take up one of them. On page 131 you criticize our argument as too "persuasive." This is not very well in line with what you admit on page 131, namely that it is not our intention to "straitjacket" theorists. Nor is it in line with the title of our paper: "An attempt . . . ." As is clear

[7]For further clarity, this last sentence should be elaborated as follows: ". . . Orcutt's paper, nor is the ensuing answer to Problem B as restated in point 2 of my letter."

from my letter, the actual situation was that there had been practically no response from the interdependent camp to my pleas for clarity from 1945 up to 1960, and Strotz was the first one to take up the matter for a serious discourse, so I was delighted to enter upon a collaboration to *attempt* to clear up the obscure issues. Now in hindsight, I think that the attempt in our joint paper was not very successful. As to my own paper in the same triptych I was on the move in a new direction, but I had not as yet found in full clarity the answer stated in my Vatican paper 1963 and quoted above in (5.2).

Another comment in hindsight: I do not at all complain about the period in the 1950's when I worked rather alone with these matters. It gave me an insight into the foundations of scientific method that has been an asset for my work ever since, and in particular for my "Time" and "Sydney" papers.

Postscript (1/13/68): When it comes to the final version of your paper, my comments must begin by stating a feeling of ambivalence. On the one hand I am happy to find that you have included "On the definition and meaning of causal concepts" and later papers of mine up to 1966 (your refs. 46-49). On the other hand I am sorry to find that the key features of my argument have not come through in your review. I see this largely as a failure on my part to set forth my arguments in a manner which is enough lucid and convincing. Hence I shall not enter on a detailed discussion of the revised version page by page, but instead restate the following points which have not come through in your treatment.

(i) It is essential to keep apart the questions (a) how to *define* a cause-effect relationship, and (b) how to *establish* a cause-effect relationship in a given situation.

Controlled experiments are the scientist's supreme tool to *establish* cause-effect relations. In nonexperimental situations it is more difficult.

The *definition* of cause-effect relations is, or should be, the same in experimental and nonexperimental situations, including interdependent systems. My definition (your ref. 46) is perfectly general in this respect, inasmuch as it first starts with controlled experiments as a special case, and then extends the definition to nonexperimental situations.

(ii) With reference to point 2 and formulas (5.1) and (5.2) of my letter, Problem B has no general answer when it comes to the structural relations (5.1) of interdependent systems, but it can be given a clearcut answer if the structural relations are respecified by way of (5.2). The first part of this proposition had not dawned upon me when Bob Strotz and I drafted our joint paper (1960, ref. 35 in the revised version of your paper), but it did by the time the paper was published, and rather soon I arrived at the second part of the proposition (my struggles can be followed up to my Vatican paper, your ref. 48, where I feel that I had at last managed to give a reasonably clearcut exposition of the probability arguments involved).

For example, let us assume that the structural form (5.1) of an interdependent system involves a demand relation in logarithmic variables where the coefficient of the price variable is $-.8$. Strotz and I in our joint paper (your ref. 35) tried to interpret the coefficient $-.8$ as a price elasticity of .8 in the sense of Marshall's classical definition of demand elasticities. To repeat, I found later on that this interpretation is untenable, whereas a related interpretation is possible on the basis of the respecification (5.2), namely that the demand elasticity is .8 when formed with regard to the expected price, not with regard to the *observed* price.

In your review of my attempts to clarify the definition and meaning of causal concepts I cannot find a trace of the transition from (5.1) to (5.2). You lean heavily on Basmann's theorem on "the observational equivalence of interdependent and recursive systems", but if I understand correctly this theorem refers to interdependent system of type (5.1) not to the respecified and generalized systems (5.2).

(iii) The specific problems of econometrical model building merge with general problems of scientific method. Causal aspects of model building are a typical case in point, others are the distinction between experimental and nonexperimental model building, and—merging with technical problems of probability theory—the distinction between apparent scatter and genuine scatter. In recent years my studies have often focussed on problems at this fundamental level. Although these problem areas are largely ignored in current literature it is my understanding that they are of fundamental importance; in particular I am thinking of the distinction between apparent scatter and genuine scatter, and the question about causal reversibility. To some extent these issues linked up with the problems dealt with in your paper, but to a large extent they are concerned with other orders of ideas. Hence it would carry me too far to enter here on these matters; I should like however to conclude my comments with a list of references to these recent studies.

(1) Time as the realm of forecasting. Pages 525-560 in "Interdisciplinary Perspectives of Time," eds. E. M. Weyer and R. Fischer. New York: The New York Academy of Sciences, 1967.

(2) Forecasting and scientific method. Pages 1-66 in "Forecasting on a scientific basis," ed. H. Wold. Lisbon: Gulbenkian Foundation, 1967.

(3) Nonexperimental statistical analysis from the general point of view scientific method. Bull. Intern. Statist. Inst., 42 (1968).

(4) Review of Carl F. Christ: *Econometric Models and Methods*. Review Intern. Statist. Inst., 36 (1968) 100-103.

(5) Ends and means of scientific method, with special regard to the social sciences. Pages 96-140 in "Universitetet och forskningen," ed. B. Lindskog. Acta Universitatis Upsaliensis, 17 (1968).

(6) Econometrics as pioneering in nonexperimental model building. Presidential Address, Econometric Society: Econometrica, 1969.

(7) With E. J. Mosbaek: Interdependent systems. Structure and estimation. Amsterdam: North-Holland Publ. Co., 1970.

AN EMPIRICAL EVALUATION OF ALTERNATIVE THEORIES OF CORPORATE INVESTMENT*

Dale W. Jorgenson
Harvard University

Calvin D. Siebert
University of Iowa

1. INTRODUCTION

The purpose of this paper is to compare alternative theories of investment behavior with regard to their ability to explain the investment activity of corporations. The theories we consider have already undergone substantial empirical testing and all of them deserve careful consideration as possible explanations of investment behavior. Unfortunately, the evidence already available is not sufficient to provide an adequate comparison of the alternative theories. Given a correct specification of the lag structure underlying the investment process, time-series data for industry aggregates do not provide sharp discrimination among alternative explanations of investment behavior.[1] Studies of cross-section data on the investment activity of individual firms exhibit little stability over time so that any comparisons based on observations for corporations must first provide a satisfactory explanation of the observations for individual firms over time.[2] In this study we concentrate on time-series data for a small but representative sample of firms selected from the *Fortune* Directory [14] of the 500 largest United States industrial corporations for 1962. For each individual firm we determine an appropriate specification of

*Support for this research was provided by the National Science Foundation.

the lag between changes in demand for capital and investment expenditures under each of five alternative theories of the demand for capital. We find that the results enable us to discriminate quite sharply among alternative theories of investment.

The point of departure for this study is the flexible accelerator model of investment behavior originated by Chenery [2] and Koyck [29]. In this model attention is focused on the time pattern of investment behavior. The firm is taken to have a desired level of capital, determined by long-run considerations. The precise specification of the desired level of capital has been the subject of a wide variety of alternative theories of investment behavior. The alternative theories do agree, however, on the validity of the fundamental flexible accelerator mechanism for translating changes in desired capital into actual investment expenditures. Denoting the actual level of capital in period t by K_t and the desired level by K_t^*, capital is adjusted toward its desired level by a certain proportion of the discrepancy between desired and actual capital stock in each period,

$$(1) \quad K_t - K_{t-1} = [1-\lambda] [K_t^* - K_{t-1}].$$

Alternatively, actual capital may be represented as a weighted average of all past levels of desired capital,

$$(2) \quad K_t = [1-\lambda] \sum_{\tau=0}^{\infty} \lambda^\tau K_{t-\tau}^*.$$

We refer to the latter form of the flexible accelerator as a distributed lag function with actual capital in period t a function of desired levels of capital. The average lag of adjustment is $\lambda/[1-\lambda]$. This lag represents the average time required for a change in desired capital that persists indefinitely to be translated into a change in actual capital stock.

The adjustment mechanism that underlies the flexible accelerator may be interpreted as a result of gestation lags or as the result of an expectation formation process or both as Nerlove [45] has demonstrated. By permitting discrepancies between desired and actual levels of capital the effects of gestation lags and lags between the actual and expected values of the alternative determinants of investment are incorporated into the theories.

The flexible accelerator mechanism can be transformed into a complete theory of investment behavior by adding a model of replacement investment and a specification of the desired level of capital. By accounting definition the change in capital from period to period is equal to gross investment less replacement investment. The flexible accelerator provides an explanation of change in capital, but not of gross investment. The choice of a model of replacement is important since replacement investment predominates in investment expenditures, at least at the aggregate level.[3] A simple model that has been widely adopted for empirical work is that replacement is proportional to actual capital stock. Under this assumption the accounting definition for change in capital may be written,

$$(3) \quad K_t - K_{t-1} = I_t - \delta K_{t-1},$$

where δ is the rate of replacement, a fixed constant. This model of replacement investment can be supported on grounds of empirical validity. In repeated tests on the aggregate level[4] and for individual firms[5] this theory has been proved satisfactory as a representation of replacement investment. These empirical results support the validity of the asymptotic approximation that replacement is proportional to capital stock for populations of investment goods whatever the underlying distribution of replacements for individual items.[6] Combining the accounting identity given above with the flexible accelerator mechanism,

$$I_t - \delta K_{t-1} = [1 - \lambda] [K_t^* - K_{t-1}],$$

we obtain a model of investment expenditures,

$$(4) \quad I_t = [1 - \lambda] [K_t^* - K_{t-1}] + \delta K_{t-1}.$$

To complete the theory of investment behavior it is necessary to add to the flexible accelerator mechanism and the model of replacement investment a specification of the desired level of capital stock. At this point alternative theories of investment behavior diverge. In the empirical studies of Chenery and Koyck the level of desired capital was assumed to be proportional to output. The corresponding theory of investment is often referred to as the capacity utilization theory since high levels of investment expenditure are associated with high ratios of output to capital and low levels of investment with low ratios of output to capital. An alternative theory of investment is that desired capital is proportional to profit. Two alternative rationalizations of this theory have been offered. First, Tinbergen argues that realized profits measure expected profits and that "it is almost a tautology to say that investment is governed by profits expectations."[7] Secondly, the rate of investment may be constrained by the supply of funds. In the strong version of this theory the financial constraint operates at all times; the cost of funds schedule becomes highly inelastic where internal funds are exhausted. In a weaker version of the theory the financial constraint operates at low rates of

capacity utilization while extreme pressure on capacity may result
in the use of outside sources of finance.[8] Both the capacity utilization and profits theories of investment were originally propounded
as alternatives to the rigid accelerator theory. In this theory investment is simply proportional to changes in output. The rigid
accelerator was disconfirmed in tests by Kuznets [32], Tinbergen
[51], Chenery [2], Koyck [29], and Hickman [20].

Much effort has been devoted to comparison of profits and
capacity utilization theories of investment behavior. The culmi-
nation of this work is Kuh's intensive study of some thirty different
equation forms for the two theories and for combinations of both.
Kuh found negative results for nearly all tests of intertemporal
homogeneity of cross sections and homogeneity across firms for
time series.[9] He emphasizes the results from time series, concluding,

> Since the major objective is to improve understanding of dynamic,
> time-series behavior, it should be pointed out that no matter how the
> contrasts are drawn from time series, the acceleration sales model is
> superior to the internal fund flow, profit model.[10]

An alternative attack on the use of current profits has been made
by Grunfeld. He incorporates profits into a flexible accelerator
model and finds that the partial correlation of profits and investment, given capital stock, is insignificant:

> Our results do not confirm the hypothesis that profits are a good
> measure of those expected profits that will tend to induce investment
> expenditures. The observed simple correlation between investment and
> profits seems to be due to the fact that profits are just another measure
> of the capital stock of the firm and one that is in most cases inferior
> to the measure that we have constructed.[11]

Grunfeld suggests that discounted future earnings less the costs of
future additions to capital provides a better measure of expected
profits than current realized profits. In Grunfeld's theory desired
capital is proportional to the market value of the firm in the
securities markets. Grunfeld proposes this measure of discounted
future earnings less the costs of future additions to capital since
presumably stock market participants have available nearly as
much relevant information about the future as the managers of
the firms. They have information on changes in supply and demand conditions such as technological change, anticipated movement into new products and new markets, and forecasts of future
demand conditions. In addition, the participants in the securities
market have strong economic incentives to carefully analyze all
the relevant information to make the most accurate forecasts of

the future profitability of the firms possible. Combining Koyck's specification of distributed lags with Tinbergen's profits model, Grunfeld was able to show that realized profits are not an adequate measure of expected profits. An implication of Grunfeld's results is that previous empirical tests of the determinants of investment expenditures should be reevaluated in the light of Koyck's superior treatment of the time structure of investment behavior.

At the outset of econometric studies of investment behavior in Tinbergen's monograph, *Statistical Testing of Business Cycle Theories*, the neoclassical theory of optimal capital accumulation was considered a serious alternative to the rigid accelerator as an explanation of investment. Explanations based on the neoclassical theory were tested by Tinbergen, subsequently by Roos [46, 47], and by Klein [27, 28]. In these studies the theory of optimal capital accumulation was employed primarily as a source of possible explanatory variables—interest rates, relative prices, and so on. Tinbergen found a significant effect for interest rates in only one of five sets of data he examined.[12] Negative results were also reported by Klein.[13] In these tests of the neoclassical theory little attention was paid to the measurement of the cost of capital, the tax treatment of business income, or to the way that the cost of capital, the tax structure, and the price of capital goods enter the demand for capital services. Perhaps most important, none of these tests was based on a proper specification of the lag structure from changes in desired capital to investment expenditures. A reevaluation of the neoclassical theory of optimal capital accumulation as an explanation of investment behavior has been undertaken by Jorgenson and Stephenson [25].[14] Their results suggest that the neoclassical theory of investment merits consideration as an alternative to the capacity utilization and profits theories.

Given that profit expectations determine investment behavior, the empirical results of Grunfeld and Kuh suggest that profit expectations cannot be adequately represented by current realized profits. Kuh points out that,

> . . . the expectational hypothesis for profits cannot, and perhaps should not, be distinguished from the sales level or capacity accelerator hypothesis. The main candidate variable for the expectational hypothesis is simply net income after tax, a secondary candidate being gross operating profit. Both variables will have strong correlations with the level of sales.[15]

In this study we retain the profits model as a possible specification of the desired level of capital; however, we choose as our measure of profits the flow of internal funds available for investment. The basic premise of the corresponding theory of investment behavior is that the supply of funds schedule rises sharply at the point where internal funds are exhausted. We call this the Liquidity theory of investment. In view of the strong empirical support for the capacity utilization theory from the results of Kuh and from those of Eisner [8-12] and Hickman [21], we take desired capital to be proportional to output as a possible explanation of investment expenditures. We call this the Accelerator theory of investment. Finally, the results of Grunfeld suggest that profit expectations can best be measured by the market value of the firm, so that desired capital is proportional to market value. We call this the Expected Profits theory of investment. All three theories will be included in our comparison of alternative explanations of investment behavior.

The neoclassical theory of investment behavior is based on an optimal time path for capital accumulation. It also implies a theory of the cost of capital. This theory has been developed by Modigliani and Miller [38-43]. In the Modigliani-Miller theory the cost of capital is shown to be independent of the financial structure of the firm or of dividend policy; this view contrasts sharply with the theory of the cost of capital underlying the liquidity theory of investment behavior. In the liquidity theory the supply schedule is horizontal up to the point at which internal funds are exhausted and vertical at that point. If interest payments are deductible for tax purposes, the Modigliani-Miller view must be qualified.[16] The appropriate cost of capital for investment decisions is still a weighted average of the expected return to equity and the return to debt. Return to equity can be measured in a number of alternative ways. In this study we consider two possibilities: First, capital gains on assets held by the firm may be regarded as transitory so that return to equity and the price of capital services should be measured excluding capital gains; secondly, capital gains on assets may be regarded as part of the return to investment so that return to equity and the price of capital services should include capital gains. We refer to the theory of investment behavior incorporating capital gains as Neoclassical I and the theory excluding capital gains as Neoclassical II. These two theories of investment behavior, differing in their treatment of the cost of capital but based on optimal capital accumulation, complete the list of five alternative explanations of investment behavior to be included in our comparison.

To summarize: We compare the following alternative theories of investment behavior: Neoclassical, Accelerator, Expected

Profits, and Liquidity. These theories have been tested on widely varying bodies of data for different time periods and for different specifications of the time structure of investment behavior. Koyck has demonstrated the importance of the lag structure between changes in desired capital and the actual level of capital stock. To evaluate alternative theories of investment behavior it is essential to choose a lag structure that is appropriate for each theory and to compare the resulting explanations of investment expenditures. We take the flexible accelerator model as a point of departure for our study; we assume that replacement is proportional to capital stock. The alternative theories of investment behavior differ in specification of the desired level of capital. Given a proper specification of the lag structure for each theory, we are able to discriminate among the alternative specifications of desired capital and thereby among alternative theories of investment behavior.

In the following section we describe the basic flexible accelerator model in more detail and generalize it to permit a wider range of alternative lag structures. In Section 3 we describe the measurement of variables that enter into the Accelerator, Liquidity, Expected Profits, and Neoclassical theories of investment behavior. We then turn to the empirical results. Explanations of investment behavior based on each of the alternative theories are compared for each of the corporations included in our sample. The relative performance of the alternative explanations is assessed. We conclude with the implications of our study for the theory of investment and, more generally, for the theory of the firm.

2. FRAMEWORK OF THE STUDY

The studies of Accelerator, Expected Profits, and Liquidity theories of investment behavior by Grunfeld and Kuh are based on the flexible accelerator mechanism. While this mechanism represents a considerable generalization of the rigid accelerator, the resulting empirical characterization of the time structure of investment behavior is implausible. Kuh finds that the average lag between changes in desired capital and actual expenditures ranges from five to ten years or more.[17] Similar results were obtained by Grunfeld[18] and Koyck.[19] These results conflict sharply with survey results for new manufacturing plants obtained by Mayer [35]. Mayer finds that the average time required from the decision to undertake investment to the completion of construction is less than two years.[20] Using a generalization of

Koyck's distributed lag function, Jorgenson and Stephenson [26] have corroborated Mayer's survey results. For manufacturing and its subindustries they obtain average lags between changes in desired capital and actual expenditures ranging from a year and a half to three years.[21] These results suggest that a generalization of the flexible accelerator mechanism is required for a valid comparison among alternative theories of investment behavior.

In the original flexible accelerator model (2), actual capital may be represented as a weighted average of all past levels of desired capital with geometrically declining weights. To generalize this assumption we let μ_τ be the weight of desired capital of period t-τ in determining the level of actual capital in period t, obtaining the distributed lag function,

$$(5) \quad K_t = \sum_{\tau=0}^{\infty} \mu_\tau K^*_{t-\tau}.$$

In this version of the distributed lag function the weights are non-negative and sum to unity,

$$\mu_\tau \geqq 0, \qquad\qquad (\tau = 0, 1 \ldots),$$

$$\sum_{\tau=0}^{\infty} \mu_\tau = 1.$$

The weights appropriate for the original flexible accelerator decline geometrically,

$$\mu_\tau = (1-\lambda)\lambda^\tau, \qquad\qquad (\tau = 0, 1 \ldots).$$

To generalize the flexible accelerator mechanism we first difference both sides of the distributed lag function (5),

$$K_t - K_{t-1} = \sum_{\tau=0}^{\infty} \mu_\tau [K^*_{t-\tau} - K^*_{t-\tau-1}],$$

and add the model of replacement (3),

$$I_t - \delta K_{t-1} = \sum_{\tau=0}^{\infty} \mu_\tau [K^*_{t-\tau} - K^*_{t-\tau-1}],$$

so that,

$$(6) \quad I_t = \sum_{\tau=0}^{\infty} \mu_\tau [K^*_{t-\tau} - K^*_{t-\tau-1}] + \delta K_{t-1}.$$

To complete the theory of investment behavior we must adopt a specification of the desired level of capital; we combine the generalized accelerator mechanism with each of the five alternative specifications of the desired level of capital described in the preceding section.

To estimate the parameters of a theory of investment behavior based on the generalized accelerator mechanism (6) the sequence of weights $\{\mu_\tau\}$ must be approximated by a sequence generated by a finite number of parameters. In the Chenery-Koyck model the weights decline geometrically; Solow [49] has proposed that the weights be taken to correspond to the Pascal probability distribution. Jorgenson [24] has proposed a class of distributed lag functions based on the general Pascal probability distribution. This class of distributed lag functions includes those of Koyck and Solow as special cases; an arbitrary distributed lag function may be approximated to any desired degree of accuracy by a member of this class.[22] To compare alternative theories of investment behavior we must discriminate among alternative specifications of desired capital. Misspecification of the lag distribution for a given theory of investment behavior may bias the results of our comparison. Accordingly, we choose the best lag distribution for each alternative specification of desired capital from among the class of general Pascal distributed lag functions. Differences in the resulting explanations of investment behavior may then be attributed to the specification of the desired level of capital rather than to the specification of the lag distribution.

In the final form[23] of the general Pascal distributed lag function, gross investment is a function of changes in desired capital, lagged values of net investment, and the level of capital stock. As an example, suppose that the best lag distribution requires current and lagged changes in desired capital and lagged net investment; the final form of the distributed lag function may be written,

$$I_t = \gamma_0 [K_t^* - K_{t-1}^*] + \gamma_1 [K_{t-1}^* - K_{t-2}^*] - \omega_1 [I_{t-1} - \delta K_{t-2}] + \delta K_{t-1}.$$

Under the Accelerator theory of investment behavior desired capital is proportional to output,

$$K_t^* = \alpha Q_t$$

where α is the desired capital-output ratio. For the lag specification we have given, the complete Accelerator theory of investment behavior may be written,

$$I_t = \alpha \gamma_0 [Q_t - Q_{t-1}] + \alpha \gamma_1 [Q_{t-1} - Q_{t-2}] - \omega_1 [I_{t-1} - \delta K_{t-2}] + \delta K_{t-1},$$

where the parameters—α, γ_0, γ_1, ω_1, δ—are estimated from data on output, capital stock, and investment expenditures. Since the weights in the distributed lag function must sum to unity the coefficients of this function must satisfy,[24]

$$\gamma_0 + \gamma_1 = 1 + \omega_1.$$

This restriction enables us to estimate the parameters—α, γ_0, γ_1, ω_1—from estimates of $\alpha\gamma_0$, $\alpha\gamma_1$, and ω_1. The rate of replacement may be estimated directly in calculating capital stock; as a check on the results, the rate of replacement may also be estimated as the coefficient of capital stock.

To estimate the parameters of the distributed lag function for each theory of investment behavior, an error term must be added to the final form of the distributed lag function as given above. We adopt the specification that the error term is distributed independently on successive observations with zero mean and constant variance. This specification has been employed by Chenery, Grunfeld, Jorgenson and Stephenson, and Kuh in studies based on the flexible accelerator mechanism and its generalization. Letting $\{\varepsilon_t\}$ denote the sequence of random errors, we assume that:

$$E(\varepsilon_t) = 0, \quad V(\varepsilon_t) = \sigma^2, \qquad (t=1 \ldots n),$$

where σ^2 is a constant, and:

$$C(\varepsilon_t, \varepsilon_{t-\tau}) = 0, \qquad (t, t-\tau = 1 \ldots n; \ \tau \neq 0).$$

Gross investment has considerable serial correlation due to the continuity of investment programs internal to the firm, the effects of the business cycle, and the possibility of trends in investment expenditures. It might be argued that the "true" disturbances in the explanation of investment behavior are also serially correlated. This view is deficient for the following reasons: First, all variables are deflated in order to remove the influence of common price trends; secondly, the investment series is in the main a first difference series so that trends in the underlying capital stock data are largely eliminated; finally, any remaining trend in the observations on investment may be explained by rising replacement requirements as represented by the capital stock variable. The distributed lag function itself fully accounts for serial correlation in the dependent variable since investment is represented as a weighted average of past changes in desired capital. Errors in the explanation may be accounted for by random variations in forces that are independent of the process translating changes in desired capital into actual investment expenditures.

Given a correct specification of the lag structure between changes in desired capital and actual investment expenditures, time-series data for industry aggregates do not provide sharp discrimination among alternative explanations of investment behavior. Griliches and Wallace [16] have compared models similar to our Expected Profits and Neoclassical II models using quarterly time series for all of manufacturing. While the Neoclassical model is superior to the Expected Profits model on the basis of their empirical results, both models perform well.[25] On the basis of data for individual firms Grunfeld and Kuh were able to discriminate between the Liquidity model and the Expected Profits and Accelerator models. Accordingly, we employ data on the investment behavior of individual firms as the basis for our comparison of alternative theories. Data on individual firms have been analyzed through both time-series and cross-section models. The study of Meyer and Kuh [37] relied primarily on cross sections. Kuh has shown that cross sections for successive years do not provide a stable explanation of investment behavior. The intercepts for cross sections exhibit a strong pattern of cyclical variation, suggesting that the dynamic specification of the models used for cross sections is incorrect.[26] Kuh also rejects the hypothesis that the parameters of successive cross sections are the same.[27] In order to specify the lag structure correctly we concentrate on time-series data for individual firms. We do not assume that parameters for all firms are the same for cross sections at a given point in time. Our results are thus free of biases that could result from inappropriate assumptions about the homogeneity of investment behavior across firms in cross sections. We do not assume that the parameters are the same for different firms. The framework of our study is similar in this respect to that of Grunfeld. Our results are free of biases that could result from aggregation across firms in time series for industry groups. In a subsequent paper we will study possible sources of aggregation bias in distributed lag functions estimated from data on industry groups.

To summarize: In order to provide better discrimination among alternative theories of investment behavior our comparison is based on observations for individual firms rather than for industry aggregates. We determine an appropriate lag specification for each firm under each alternative specification of the desired level of capital stock. Each theory of investment behavior is based on a generalized accelerator mechanism and on the assumption that replacement investment is proportional to capital stock. Alternative theories differ in the specification of desired levels of capital stock. To compare alternative theories we first select the best lag distribution for each firm under each specification of desired capital among the class of general Pascal distributed lag functions. Our results are free of biases that could result from misspecification of the lag distribution or from inappropriate assumptions about the homogeneity of investment behavior across firms.

3. MEASUREMENT

The purpose of this section is to describe the accounting measurements that underlie our empirical evaluation of alternative theories of investment behavior. To provide a valid comparison among alternative explanations of investment expenditures the variables that enter each of the competing theories must be measured with as much precision as accounting data permit. For each firm the data must be available on a consistent basis over a substantial period of time. All firms whose stock is traded publicly have had to file annual reports with the Securities and Exchange Commission since 1934. These annual reports, consisting of complete income and balance sheet statements, are published in *Moody's Industrial Manual* [44] for the larger corporations. It was impossible to include firms in our sample that lost their identity through mergers during the period since 1934. Firms that shifted fiscal accounting years or changed their practices in the consolidations of accounting reports also failed to satisfy the criteria for inclusion in our sample. Limitations in the availability of detailed accounting data resulted in concentration on larger firms. A second justification for concentration on larger firms is the importance of their activity. At least two of the firms in our sample have investment programs that rival those of entire industry groups as reported in the Office of Business Economics (OBE) and Securities and Exchange Commission (SEC) Quarterly Investment Survey [54]. In any case our primary interest is in the investment activity of the individual corporation. Stochastic elements in the empirical investment functions are to be attributed to variations in the behavior of individual firms rather than to sampling variation.

In order to provide a wide range of industrial activity, we chose a sample of fifteen firms from the *Fortune* Directory of the 500 largest United States industrial corporations for 1962, using the industrial classification of the OBE-SEC Investment Survey in the selection of individual firms. The firms are selected from fourteen different OBE-SEC industry groups. The only industry group not represented is Textiles. In many cases the largest firm in the OBE-SEC industry group was selected. In some cases appropriate data were not available for the largest firm; we then attempted to compile data for the second largest firm, and so on. Although all the firms included in our sample are large, there is considerable variation among them as to size and rate of growth. The firms included are listed in Table 1; the average amount of investment and the capital stock of each firm are given in the table along with the OBE-SEC industry classification of the firm. The average rate of investment in the post-war period for the firm with the largest level of investment activity, General Motors, was 200 times the rate for the firm with the smallest level, Westinghouse Air Brake. Capital stock for the firm with largest net fixed assets in 1961, Standard Oil of New Jersey, was approximately 160 times the capital stock of Westinghouse Air Brake. IBM, the firm with the most rapid rate of growth, had capital stock in 1961 twelve times larger than its 1937 capital stock. At the other extreme, Anaconda Company's 1961 capital stock declined in size by a third from the 1937 level. While it must be emphasized that our sample of firms should not be considered a probability sample of large United States corporations, the sample provides sufficient heterogeneity to serve as an adequate test of alternative theories of in-

TABLE 1

No.	Firm	Average Amount of Investment[a]	Capital Stock[b]	OBE-SEC Industry
1	General Motors	.7670	3.1225	Motor Vehicles and Equipment
2	Goodyear Tire and Rubber	.0554	.3616	Rubber Products
3	American Can	.0414	.5374	Other Durables
4	Pittsburgh Plate Glass	.0345	.3128	Stone, Clay, and Glass
5	United States Steel	.2980	2.9437	Primary Iron and Steel
6	General Electric	.1190	.7247	Electrical Machinery and Equipment
7	Reynolds Tobacco	.0127	.1267	Other Non-durables
8	Dupont	.1540	.9404	Chemicals and Allied Products
9	Anaconda Company	.0511	.7077	Primary Non-ferrous Metal
10	Standard Oil, N. J.	.6274	6.3560	Petroleum and Coal Products
11	International Paper	.0563	.4780	Paper and Allied Products
12	Westinghouse Air Brake	.0038	.0393	Transportation Equipment, excluding Motor Vehicles
13	International Business Machines	.1839	.9492	Machinery, except Electrical
14	Swift and Company	.0266	.2467	Food and Beverage
15	Westinghouse Electric	.0497	.3841	Electric Machinery and Equipment

SOURCE: See Statistical Appendix.

[a]Mean annual gross investment for the post-war period, 1946-1963, in billions of 1954 dollars.

[b]End of year net fixed assets for 1961 in billions of 1954 dollars.

vestment behavior. A larger sample would have made it difficult for us to give proper attention to compilation of accurate and consistent data for each individual firm. Of course, considerable care should be taken in extrapolating the results of the present study to small firms or to closely held corporations.

Turning to the measurement of individual variables, we give a brief outline of the procedure followed for deriving each variable from accounting reports for an individual corporation. The Statistical Appendix gives a more detailed discussion of our empirical measures, the problems of deriving the empirical counterparts of certain variables, and a more complete listing of the sources of the data. The dependent variable, gross investment, denoted I_t, is the current value of investment in plant and equipment deflated by the investment goods price index for manufacturing, denoted q_t, to obtain the value of investment in constant dollars of 1954. The gross investment data are obtained from Form 10K reports of companies registered with the Securities and Exchange Commission as reported in *Moody's Industrial Manual*. These data are listed under additions at cost in *Moody's* and, following normal tax accounting procedure, include any additions which have an expected life of more than one year. Comparable data on investment are not available for the firms included in our sample for years earlier than 1934. Calculation of capital stock by the perpetual inventory method was not feasible. The method we employed was to select an initial and terminal date of net capital stock from each firm's balance sheet reports. These benchmark figures were deflated by the National Industrial Conference Board [4,6] fixed capital stock deflators for the firm's industry group. These deflated stock figures were interpolated by gross investment in constant prices,[28] resulting in capital stock values for each year and an estimate of replacement in constant prices for each year.

The independent variables for alternative specifications of desired capital were measured as follows: The value of output, denoted by $p_t Q_t$, was measured by sales plus the change in inventory stock. Output in constant dollars of 1954, denoted Q_t, was measured by the value of output deflated by the Wholesale Price Index [56] of the firm's industry group, denoted p_t. A more accurate measure of output would be sales plus the change in finished goods inventory.[29] Unfortunately, a breakdown of inventory into finished goods, goods in process, and raw materials was not available for all firms. In the Accelerator theory of investment behavior, desired capital is assumed to be proportional to output,

$$\text{Accelerator: } K_t^* = \alpha Q_t,$$

where α is the desired capital-output ratio.

Internal funds available for investment expenditures are measured by profits after taxes plus depreciation less dividends paid. This liquidity measure was converted into constant prices of 1954 by dividing the current value of internal funds by the investment goods price index, q_t. The resulting measure of liquidity, denoted L_t, was suggested as the appropriate measure by Kuh on the grounds that the effects of liquidity can be distinguished from those of output while expected profits as measured by profits after taxes cannot be distinguished from output. Since changes in desired capital are employed to explain investment for changes in capacity with replacement accounted for separately, an alternative liquidity measure would be to subtract replacement in constant prices from the liquidity measure suggested by Kuh. A trial of this measure for several firms gave nearly the same results as those for the liquidity variable suggested by Kuh.[30] In the Liquidity theory of investment behavior, desired capital is proportional to liquidity,

$$\text{Liquidity: } K_t^* = \alpha L_t,$$

where α is the desired ratio of capital to the flow of internal funds available for investment.

The market value of the firm was measured as the market value of stocks outstanding plus the book value of debt including short-term liabilities at the beginning of the period. This measure was reduced to constant prices of 1954 by dividing the current market value of the firm by the implicit deflator for gross national product. The resulting measure, denoted V_t, was suggested by Grunfeld as an approximation to the discounted value of expected future cash flow net of future investment expenditures.[31] Since a large part of a corporation's debt is not publicly traded and no selling prices are quoted on some issues for months at a time, our only recourse was to use the book value of debt. The error introduced by this limitation of the data is relatively small both because book value and market value of debt are quite close and because debt is a very small fraction of the market value of the firm for the corporations included in our sample. In the Expected Profits theory of investment behavior, desired capital is proportional to the market value of the firm,

$$\text{Expected Profits: } K_t^* = \alpha V_t,$$

where α is the desired ratio of capital to market value of the firm.

In the Neoclassical theory of investment behavior, desired capital stock is equal to the value of output deflated by the price of capital services, denoted c_t. We have already discussed measurement of the value of output. The price of capital services depends on the price of investment goods, the cost of capital, and the tax structure,

$$c_t = \frac{q_t}{1-u_t}[(1-u_t w_t)\delta + r_t - \frac{q_t - q_{t-1}}{q_t}],$$

where q_t is the investment goods price index, δ the rate of replacement, r_t the cost of capital, u_t the rate of taxation of corporate income, and w_t the proportion of depreciation at replacement cost deductible from income for tax purposes. The rate of replacement is obtained in the calculation of capital stock. The rate of taxation of corporate income is the ratio of profits before taxes less profits after taxes to profits before taxes. The variable w_t, describing depreciation deductions, is the ratio of depreciation for tax purposes to depreciation at current replacement cost.

To measure the rate of return we define gross business income as the sum of profits before taxes, depreciation, and interest. Gross business income is equal to the value of capital services for all classes of assets. From balance sheet data we were able to obtain data on the value of depreciable and depletable assets and the value of inventories and cash plus accounts receivable. We derived an expression for the price of capital services for each of the four classes of assets, using the formula given above with appropriate specializations; for example, for nondepreciable assets the rate of replacement, δ, is zero. The price of capital services for each asset class depends on the cost of capital; given the fact that gross business income is the sum of the values of capital services, we were able to solve for the cost of capital. Two formulations were employed: First, the cost of capital was taken to be profits after taxes plus depreciation for tax purposes less depreciation at current replacement cost plus accrued capital gains on depreciable assets, depletable assets, and inventories, all divided by the market value of the firm in current prices. Secondly, the cost of capital was measured excluding all accrued capital gains.

For all firms included in the sample, interest payments deducted for tax purposes were negligible so that we excluded them from gross business income in both measures of the cost of capital. Similarly, realized capital gains on assets were essentially zero for depreciable and depletable assets. For a number of firms capital

gains on inventories are included in recorded profits. This is especially true for firms pricing ending inventory stock on the FIFO
(first-in,first-out) method. For the firms using FIFO methods no
adjustment of recorded profits for capital gains was made; this
practice was also followed for firms following average-cost pricing
of ending inventories. Profits were adjusted for inventory capital
gains for firms that employed LIFO (last-in, first-out) inventory
pricing.[32] In the first version of the Neoclassical theory, capital gains
are assumed to be taken into account in investment decisions;
desired capital is proportional to the value of output divided by
the price of capital services including capital gains,

$$\text{Neoclassical I: } K_t^* = \alpha \frac{p_t Q_t}{c_t}, \quad c_t = \frac{q_t}{1-u_t}[(1-u_t w_t)\delta + r_t - \frac{q_t - q_{t-1}}{q_t}],$$

where α is the elasticity of output with respect to capital input. In
the second version of the Neoclassical theory, capital gains are
assumed to be transitory; they are ignored in assessing the appropriate cost of capital for investment decisions and in the price of
capital services; desired capital stock is again proportional to the
value of output divided by the price of capital services,

$$\text{Neoclassical II: } K_t^* = \alpha \frac{p_t Q_t}{c_t}, \quad c_t = \frac{q_t}{1-u_t}[(1-u_t w_t)\delta + r_t],$$

where, as before, α is the elasticity of output with respect to capital
and the price of capital services and cost of capital are measured
with capital gains set equal to zero.[33]

4. EMPIRICAL RESULTS

To provide a basis for comparing alternative theories of investment behavior, we first determine an appropriate specification
of the lag between changes in desired capital and investment expenditures under each specification of desired capital. We choose
the best lag distribution for each firm from among the class of general Pascal distributed lag functions. In each case the appropriate
specification of the distributed lag function is selected from those
with current and two lagged changes in desired capital and two
lagged values of net investment. These limitations are not very
restrictive since annual data are employed for each firm. A very
large variety of alternative lag distributions can be represented in
this way, including the geometric distribution proposed by Koyck.
Changes in desired capital and lagged net investment were al-

lowed to enter the distributed lag function so long as they lowered the residual variance around the regression. The final set of values of current and lagged changes in desired capital and lagged net investment gives the minimum residual variance subject to the restrictions we have indicated. Given the best specification of the generalized accelerator mechanism for each alternative specification of desired capital, we can compare alternative theories of investment behavior with regard to their ability to explain the investment activity of corporations.

The best distributed lag function for each of the five alternative theories of investment behavior included in our comparison is presented for each of the fifteen firms of our sample in Table 2. Distributed lag functions were fitted to data for the post-war period, 1949-63, and for the post-war and pre-war period, 1937-41 and 1949-63, combined. For purposes of policy and prediction the explanation of investment behavior under post-war conditions is the most relevant. Data for the pre-war period were included in order to examine the effects of adding observations from a period with quite different economic conditions. The war years, 1942-5, were not included on the grounds that investment decisions during that period were not based on the usual economic criteria. Since some of the distributed lag functions employ as many as three lagged changes in desired capital and since data are available only since 1934, the years 1934-6 and 1946-8 could not be used for unlagged variables. Finally, two firms include one less observation; data for United States Steel are not available for 1934, and 1963 data for Pittsburgh Plate Glass are not comparable with those of previous years.

The estimated coefficients of each distributed lag function are listed in Table 2 with estimated standard errors given in parentheses. The results for each firm are arranged in the following format: The column labeled X_1 contains the intercept coefficient. The coefficient of capital stock, an estimate of the rate of replacement, is given in the column labeled X_7. Columns headed X_2, X_3, and X_4 contain estimates of the parameters—$\alpha\gamma_0$, $\alpha\gamma_1$, $\alpha\gamma_2$—associated with changes in desired capital. Columns headed X_5 and X_6 give estimates of the parameters corresponding to lagged net investment—ω_1, ω_2. The rows of Table 2 correspond to the alternative specifications of desired capital. A blank row indicates that none of the changes in desired capital lowered the residual variance around the regression. In Table 2 the post-war results for the best distributed lag function for each firm and each specification of desired capital are presented first.

TABLE 2

Regression Coefficients. Estimates, 1949 - 1963. General Motors

Model	X_1	X_2	X_3	X_4	X_5	X_6	X_7
Neoclassical I	.2449	.0160 (.0063)	.0150 (.0066)		−.3444 (.2061)		.1794 (.0540)
Neoclassical II	.1231	.0411 (.0094)	.0654 (.0105)	.0202 (.0089)		−.3732 (.1311)	.1826 (.0361)
Accelerator	.1963		.0666 (.0327)		−.4780 (.2115)		.1878 (.0593)
Expected Profits	.2793	.0858 (.0267)	.0610 (.0268)				.1493 (.0571)
Liquidity Model	.2345	.3032 (.2710)	.4941 (.2743)		−.3989 (.2279)		.1712 (.0620)

Regression Coefficients. Estimates, 1937-1941, 1949-1963. General Motors

Model	X_1	X_2	X_3	X_4	X_5	X_6	X_7
Neoclassical I	.0800	.0162 (.0056)	.0152 (.0060)		−.2963 (.2221)	−.2415 (.2160)	.2246 (.0403)
Neoclassical II	.0438	.0386 (.0087)	.0485 (.0093)		−.2269 (.1540)	−.3429 (.1535)	.2122 (.0290)
Accelerator	.0426	.0400 (.0283)	.0838 (.0283)		−.4083 (.2060)	−.2721 (.2181)	.2194 (.0498)
Expected Profits	.0973	.0488 (.0185)			−.5189 (.1813)		.2156 (.0398)
Liquidity Model	.0846	.3554 (.2341)	.5468 (.2372)		−.4527 (.1946)		.2171 (.0418)

Regression Coefficients. Estimates, 1949-1963. Goodyear

Model	X_1	X_2	X_3	X_4	X_5	X_6	X_7
Neoclassical I	−.0164	.0113 (.0035)	.0061 (.0032)	.0076 (.0042)		.5592 (.2897)	.2449 (.0637)
Neoclassical II	.0047	.0148 (.0066)			−.5397 (.2481)	.7137 (.2651)	.1642 (.0695)
Accelerator	.0117	.0582 (.0316)			−.4529 (.2588)	.5121 (.2738)	.1365 (.0743)
Expected Profit	.0011	.0533 (.0192)			−.6175 (.2341)	.7375 (.2448)	.1704 (.0622)
Liquidity Model							

Regression Coefficients. Estimates, 1937-1941, 1949-1963. Goodyear

Model	X_1	X_2	X_3	X_4	X_5	X_6	X_7
Neoclassical I	−.0236	.0124 (.0028)	.0062 (.0027)	.0078 (.0034)		.4552 (.2387)	.2629 (.0442)
Neoclassical II	−.0120	.0168 (.0068)		.0076 (.0073)	−.5097 (.2398)	.6395 (.2688)	.2091 (.0589)
Accelerator	−.0114	.0582 (.0278)			−.4252 (.2411)	.3884 (.2472)	.2044 (.0600)
Expected Profits	−.0117	.0591 (.0172)			−.6396 (.2146)	.6268 (.2207)	.2033 (.0510)
Liquidity Model							

TABLE 2—CONTINUED

Regression Coefficients. Estimates, 1949-1963. American Can

Model	X₁	X₂	X₃	X₄	X₅	X₆	X₇
Neoclassical I	.0035	.0022 (.0016)	.0104 (.0029)	−.0021 (.0013)		−.8988 (.4010)	.0486 (.0324)
Neoclassical II	.0254	.0102 (.0055)	.0147 (.0054)				.0235 (.0349)
Accelerator	.0307	.0881 (.0396)				.2491 (.2441)	.0277 (.0363)
Expected Profits	.0320		.0426 (.0207)				.0181 (.0379)
Liquidity Model							

Regression Coefficients. Estimates, 1937-1941, 1949-1963. American Can

Model	X₁	X₂	X₃	X₄	X₅	X₆	X₇
Neoclassical I	.0112	.0024 (.0014)	.0068 (.0017)			−.4998 (.2518)	.0468 (.0240)
Neoclassical II	.0146	.0115 (.0041)	.0152 (.0042)				.0460 (.0218)
Accelerator	.0051	.0921 (.0366)	.0491 (.0395)				.0708 (.0251)
Expected Profits	.0095		.0414 (.0176)				.0671 (.0250)
Liquidity Model	.0090		−.5213 (.3912)				.0738 (.0276)

Regression Coefficients. Estimates, 1949-1962. Pittsburgh Plate Glass

Model	X₁	X₂	X₃	X₄	X₅	X₆	X₇
Neoclassical I	.0241	.0064 (.0021)	.0028 (.0013)		−.5431 (.1988)		.0130 (.0437)
Neoclassical II	.0218	.0181 (.0143)			−.4847 (.2797)	.3884 (.2888)	.0339 (.0603)
Accelerator	.0094	.0906 (.0598)	.1245 (.0549)		−.5716 (.2525)		.0554 (.0570)
Expected Profits	.0114	.0849 (.0399)			−.3681 (.2308)		.0623 (.0585)
Liquidity Model							

Regression Coefficients. Estimates, 1937-1941, 1949-1962. Pittsburgh Plate Glass

Model	X₁	X₂	X₃	X₄	X₅	X₆	X₇
Neoclassical I	.0031	.0082 (.0018)	.0042 (.0016)	−.0010 (.0005)	−.6511 (.1524)		.0825 (.0295)
Neoclassical II	.0063	.0192 (.0117)			−.5880 (.2336)	.3787 (.2526)	.0833 (.0443)
Accelerator	.0005	.1053 (.0440)	.1283 (.0421)		−.6318 (.1890)		.0831 (.0358)
Expected Profits	.0033	.0630 (.0266)			−.5685 (.2153)	.2579 (.2327)	.0947 (.0412)
Liquidity Model	.0046		.4484 (.3547)	.6578 (.3786)	−.6391 (.2332)	.2906 (.2571)	.0827 (.0497)

TABLE 2—CONTINUED

Regression Coefficients. Estimates, 1949-1963. United States Steel

Model	X_1	X_2	X_3	X_4	X_5	X_6	X_7
Neoclassical I	.3535	.0090 (.0065)	.0176 (.0067)		−.4869 (.2204)		−.0334 (.0845)
Neoclassical II	.4325	.0113 (.0094)	.0129 (.0103)		−.4062 (.2437)	.3546 (.3014)	−.0538 (.0962)
Accelerator							
Expected Profits	.3446	.0262 (.0224)	.0712 (.0271)		−.4940 (.1864)	.4085 (.2378)	−.0253 (.0726)
Liquidity Model	.4129		−.3105 (.2694)		−.4975 (.2310)	.5724 (.2683)	−.0403 (.0897)

Regression Coefficients. Estimates, 1938-1941, 1949-1963. United States Steel

Model	X_1	X_2	X_3	X_4	X_5	X_6	X_7
Neoclassical I	.4017	.0106 (.0044)	.0057 (.0033)	.0032 (.0011)	−.5471 (.1993)	.4147 (.2151)	−.0426 (.0830)
Neoclassical II	.4645	.0127 (.0050)	.0066 (.0036)	.0039 (.0013)	−.4331 (.2162)	.4392 (.2170)	−.0644 (.0831)
Accelerator							
Expected Profits	.4585		.0820 (.0264)		−.5183 (.1552)		.0838 (.0750)
Liquidity Model							

Regression Coefficients. Estimates, 1949-1963. General Electric

Model	X_1	X_2	X_3	X_4	X_5	X_6	X_7
Neoclassical I	.0626	.0025 (.0009)			−.8927 (.2049)	.4317 (.1928)	.0740 (.0578)
Neoclassical II	.1108	.0124 (.0032)	.0126 (.0037)	.0056 (.0033)	−.2758 (.1442)		−.0199 (.0552)
Accelerator	.0527	.0322 (.0255)			−.8627 (.2484)	.3755 (.2336)	.0819 (.0722)
Expected Profits	.0938	.0170 (.0096)	.0158 (.0093)		−.8451 (.2258)	.4612 (.2191)	.0164 (.0644)
Liquidity Model	.1153	−.3872 (.2715)	−.7531 (.3032)	−.5652 (.1916)	−.8013 (.1857)		.0007 (.0634)

Regression Coefficients. Estimates, 1937-1941, 1949-1963. General Electric

Model	X_1	X_2	X_3	X_4	X_5	X_6	X_7
Neoclassical I	.0115	.0010 (.0004)		−.0012 (.0009)	−.8758 (.2074)	.3287 (.1893)	.1449 (.0231)
Neoclassical II	.0149	.0064 (.0021)	.0070 (.0038)		−.4471 (.1630)		.1272 (.0214)
Accelerator	.0142	.0495 (.0186)	.0235 (.0223)		−.7521 (.2266)	.2745 (.2091)	.1275 (.0224)
Expected Profits	.0308	.0163 (.0088)			−.9036 (.2220)	.4973 (.2149)	.1148 (.0243)
Liquidity Model							

TABLE 2—CONTINUED

Regression Coefficients. Estimates, 1949-1963. Reynolds Tobacco

Model	X₁	X₂	X₃	X₄	X₅	X₆	X₇
Neoclassical I	.0085	.0012	.0015		−1.0387		−.0325
		(.0007)	(.0010)		(.3338)		(.0794)
Neoclassical II	.0132	.0026	.0050		−1.1316		−.1353
		(.0008)	(.0025)		(.3160)		(.1090)
Accelerator	.0040		.0470		−.7709		.0278
			(.0104)		(.2297)		(.0463)
Expected Profits	.0026	.0049			−.8287		.0579
		(.0022)			(.3185)		(.0647)
Liquidity Model	.0048			.3595	−.9936		.0031
				(.2527)	(.3533)		(.0762)

Regression Coefficients. Estimates, 1937-1941, 1949-1963. Reynolds Tobacco

Model	X₁	X₂	X₃	X₄	X₅	X₆	X₇
Neoclassical I	.0051	.0012	.0008		−1.0057		.0096
		(.0005)	(.0005)		(.2576)		(.0552)
Neoclassical II	.0096	.0028	.0041		−.9684		−.0729
		(.0007)	(.0017)		(.2279)		(.0697)
Accelerator	.0023		.0479		−.7163		.0491
			(.0094)		(.1961)		(.0401)
Expected Profits	.0065	.0069	.0089		−.9320		−.0302
		(.0025)	(.0084)		(.2944)		(.1089)
Liquidity Model	.0012		.2177		−.8350		.0649
			(.1857)		(.3027)		(.0623)

Regression Coefficients. Estimates, 1949-1963. Dupont

Model	X₁	X₂	X₃	X₄	X₅	X₆	X₇
Neoclassical I	−.1940		.0020				.4203
			(.0018)				(.1029)
Neoclassical II							
Accelerator	−.2095		.0749				.4291
			(.0498)				(.0991)
Expected Profits							
Liquidity Model							

Regression Coefficients. Estimates, 1937-1941, 1949-1963. Dupont

Model	X₁	X₂	X₃	X₄	X₅	X₆	X₇
Neoclassical I	−.1357		.0020				.3515
			(.0018)				(.0589)
Neoclassical II							
Accelerator	−.1597	.0726	.0874			.5300	.3725
		(.0494)	(.0477)			(.2870)	(.0583)
Expected Profits							
Liquidity Model	−.1509		.4253			.5016	.3769
			(.3578)			(.2780)	(.0613)

TABLE 2—CONTINUED

Regression Coefficients. Estimates, 1949-1963. Anaconda Company

Model	X_1	X_2	X_3	X_4	X_5	X_6	X_7
Neoclassical I	.0346	.0199		.0092	−.9476	.5945	.0174
		(.0043)		(.0042)	(.1475)	(.1657)	(.0492)
Neoclassical II	.0352	.0167	−.0128		−1.0615	.5281	.0172
		(.0064)	(.0088)		(.2544)	(.2222)	(.0656)
Accelerator	.0708		.0956	.0353	−.9639	.4188	−.0332
			(.0316)	(.0351)	(.2136)	(.2242)	(.0627)
Expected Profits	.0036	.1126	.0415	.0664	−.9997	.9355	.0637
		(.0282)	(.0189)	(.0233)	(.1827)	(.2155)	(.0590)
Liquidity Model	.0385		.4429		−1.1829	.6953	.0124
			(.1000)		(.1677)	(.1659)	(.0502)

Regression Coefficients. Estimates, 1937-1941, 1949-1963. Anaconda Company

Model	X_1	X_2	X_3	X_4	X_5	X_6	X_7
Neoclassical I	.0686	.0042			−.8294	.3617	−.0300
		(.0029)			(.1975)	(.1679)	(.0274)
Neoclassical II	.0656	.0146			−.8360	.3638	−.0207
		(.0048)			(.1661)	(.1409)	(.0234)
Accelerator	.0744		.0525	.0298	−.8302	.3286	−.0379
			(.0240)	(.0259)	(.1972)	(.1692)	(.0259)
Expected Profits	.0718	.0295			−.9410	.4870	−.0347
		(.0145)			(.1920)	(.1652)	(.0276)
Liquidity Model	.0638		.2951	.1113	−.9601	.4376	−.0240
			(.1113)	(.1077)	(.1924)	(.1631)	(.0246)

Regression Coefficients. Estimates, 1949-1963. Standard Oil, N. J.

Model	X_1	X_2	X_3	X_4	X_5	X_6	X_7
Neoclassical I	−.0669	.0116	.0097	.0067			.1227
		(.0027)	(.0026)	(.0027)			(.0211)
Neoclassical II	.0685	.0226		.0154	−.5541	.4927	.0914
		(.0064)		(.0078)	(.1768)	(.2110)	(.0217)
Accelerator	−.0147	.1084	.0548		−.5115		.0915
		(.0494)	(.0517)		(.2512)		(.0319)
Expected Profits	.0321	.0423		.0361	−.5595	.5089	.1035
		(.0199)		(.0222)	(.2393)	(.2442)	(.0300)
Liquidity Model	.0451		.4302		−.4661		.0921
			(.3250)		(.2432)		(.0359)

Regression Coefficients. Estimates, 1937-1941, 1949-1963. Standard Oil, N. J.

Model	X_1	X_2	X_3	X_4	X_5	X_6	X_7
Neoclassical I	.0284	.0104	.0064	−.0036	−.3602		.0957
		(.0031)	(.0037)	(.0014)	(.1859)		(.0169)
Neoclassical II	.2306	.0279	.0140				.0617
		(.0078)	(.0081)				(.0213)
Accelerator	.1190	.1163	.0555		−.4098		.0701
		(.0526)	(.0538)		(.2411)		(.0223)
Expected Profits	.1477	.0510		.0347	−.3574	.3879	.0844
		(.0216)		(.0249)	(.2157)	(.2267)	(.0216)
Liquidity Model	.0813	.5532	.6584		−.5330		.0796
		(.4845)	(.3636)		(.2775)		(.0253)

TABLE 2—CONTINUED

Regression Coefficients. Estimates, 1949-1963. International Paper

Model	X_1	X_2	X_3	X_4	X_5	X_6	X_7
Neoclassical I	.0047	.0102	.0083				.1248
		(.0025)	(.0025)				(.0357)
Neoclassical II	.0096	.0256	.0361				.0860
		(.0071)	(.0080)				(.0342)
Accelerator	.0031	.1218	.1912				.1137
		(.0514)	(.0513)				(.0407)
Expected Profits	−.0036	.0489	.0580				.1399
		(.0145)	(.0151)				(.0386)
Liquidity Model	−.0027		1.5390		−.3536		.1377
			(.2811)		(.1573)		(.0331)

Regression Coefficients. Estimates, 1937-1941, 1949-1963. International Paper.

Model	X_1	X_2	X_3	X_4	X_5	X_6	X_7
Neoclassical I	.0116	.0059		.0031	−.4285		.0882
		(.0029)		(.0017)	(.1904)		(.0582)
Neoclassical II	.0140	.0045		.0052	−.3469		.0879
		(.0043)		(.0029)	(.2238)		(.0610)
Accelerator	−.0097	.1494	.1682		−.5002		.1192
		(.0594)	(.0519)		(.1655)		(.0504)
Expected Profits	−.0117	.0629	.0492		−.3319		.1380
		(.0182)	(.0215)		(.1716)		(.0496)
Liquidity Model	−.0148	.3932	1.6875		−.3442		.1405
		(.3159)	(.3182)		(.1739)		(.0422)

Regression Coefficients. Estimates, 1949-1963. Westinghouse Air Brake

Model	X_1	X_2	X_3	X_4	X_5	X_6	X_7
Neoclassical I	.0006	.0047	.0028				.0998
		(.0014)	(.0013)				(.0453)
Neoclassical II	−.0006	.0073	.0062				.1251
		(.0014)	(.0013)				(.0298)
Accelerator	.0009	.0164	.0367		−.2350		.0739
		(.0132)	(.0138)		(.2294)		(.0516)
Expected Profits	.0008	.0515	.0415				.0993
		(.0162)	(.0161)				(.0455)
Liquidity Model	.0008	.2724	.6305		−.3264	.5982	.1088
		(.2366)	(.2256)		(.2780)	(.3347)	(.0590)

Regression Coefficients. Estimates, 1937-1941, 1949-1963. Westinghouse Air Brake

Model	X_1	X_2	X_3	X_4	X_5	X_6	X_7
Neoclassical I	−.0001	.0040	.0013		−.3028		.1058
		(.0011)	(.0012)		(.2248)		(.0423)
Neoclassical II	−.0013	.0075	.0062				.1418
		(.0011)	(.0011)				(.0243)
Accelerator	−.0002	.0157	.0319		−.3202		.1001
		(.0112)	(.0119)		(.2086)		(.0469)
Expected Profits	.0006	.0382	.0216		−.2522		.0907
		(.0117)	(.0110)		(.2031)		(.0435)
Liquidity Model	.0005	.1084	.1271		−.3053		.0872
		(.0999)	(.0915)		(.2439)		(.0543)

TABLE 2—CONTINUED

Regression Coefficients. Estimates, 1949-1963. International Business Machines

Model	X_1	X_2	X_3	X_4	X_5	X_6	X_7
Neoclassical I	.0269	.0210	.0193				.2793
		(.0078)	(.0079)				(.0263)
Neoclassical II	.0262	.0825	.0576				.2177
		(.0169)	(.0248)				(.0295)
Accelerator	.0223	.5503					.1948
		(.1195)					(.0296)
Expected Profits	.0312	.0094					.2849
		(.0046)					(.0300)
Liquidity Model	.0253	1.3546					.2515
		(.6170)					(.0345)

Regression Coefficients. Estimates, 1937-1941, 1949-1963. International Business Machines

Model	X_1	X_2	X_3	X_4	X_5	X_6	X_7
Neoclassical I	.0105	.0224	.0197				.3021
		(.0070)	(.0072)				(.0192)
Neoclassical II	.0117	.0869	.0561				.2376
		(.0158)	(.0233)				(.0254)
Accelerator	.0094	.5809					.2074
		(.1071)					(.0257)
Expected Profits	.0130	.0097					.3110
		(.0040)					(.0217)
Liquidity Model	.0108	1.4881					.2676
		(.5395)					(.0810)

Regression Coefficients. Estimates, 1949-1963. Swift

Model	X_1	X_2	X_3	X_4	X_5	X_6	X_7
Neoclassical I	.0277	.0007		.0005	−.7229	.3825	−.0051
		(.0003)		(.0004)	(.2684)	(.2604)	(.0979)
Neoclassical II	.0368	.0007			−.6777	.2953	−.0428
		(.0006)			(.2616)	(.2355)	(.1049)
Accelerator							
Expected Profits	.0208	.0882		.0667	−.5122		.0195
		(.0453)		(.0393)	(.1752)		(.1029)
Liquidity Model	.0341		.2554		−.6591		−.0349
			(.1886)		(.2059)		(.1039)

Regression Coefficients. Estimates, 1937-1941, 1949-1963. Swift

Model	X_1	X_2	X_3	X_4	X_5	X_6	X_7
Neoclassical I	.0188	.0003			−.6014		.0245
		(.0001)			(.1294)		(.0710)
Neoclassical II	.0231	.0003			−.6088		.0067
		(.0002)			(.1382)		(.0810)
Accelerator							
Expected Profits	.0219	.0367		.0431	−.5820		.0117
		(.0355)		(.0325)	(.1523)		(.0889)
Liquidity Model	.0169		.1556		−.8645	.2239	.0344
			(.1056)		(.2518)	(.2101)	(.0873)

TABLE 2—CONTINUED

Regression Coefficients. Estimates, 1949-1963. Westinghouse Electric

Model	X_1	X_2	X_3	X_4	X_5	X_6	X_7
Neoclassical I	.0454		.0009	.0007	−.6319	.3959	.0166
			(.0006)	(.0005)	(.2279)	(.2382)	(.0603)
Neoclassical II	.0415	.0086	.0052	.0045	−.4924	.5668	.0114
		(.0033)	(.0043)	(.0038)	(.2395)	(.2102)	(.0547)
Accelerator	.0148	.0511	.0440		−.5646		.0745
		(.0254)	(.0242)		(.2232)		(.0589)
Expected Profits	.0270	.0197			−.7072	.5626	.0670
		(.0134)			(.2263)	(.2349)	(.0587)
Liquidity Model							

Regression Coefficients. Estimates, 1937-1941, 1949-1963. Westinghouse Electric

Model	X_1	X_2	X_3	X_4	X_5	X_6	X_7
Neoclassical I	.0070		.0007		−.7932	.4433	.1194
			(.0006)		(.2230)	(.2288)	(.0379)
Neoclassical II	.0078	.0085			−.7567	.4652	.1094
		(.0032)			(.1939)	(.1976)	(.0312)
Accelerator	.0017	.0534	.0431		−.6192		.1110
		(.0178)	(.0186)		(.1759)		(.0296)
Expected Profits	.0046	.0202			−.7707	.5025	.1279
		(.0121)			(.2145)	(.2198)	(.0365)
Liquidity Model							

To illustrate the interpretation of the fitted distributed lag functions presented in Table 2, we take the post-war results for General Motors as an example. For the Neoclassical I theory of investment desired capital stock is proportional to the value of output, $p_t Q_t$, divided by the price of capital services, c_t, including capital gains. For the post-war period the form of the distributed lag function selected for General Motors includes current and lagged changes in desired capital and lagged net investment. The final form of the distributed lag function may be written,

$$I_t = \beta + \alpha\gamma_0 \left[\frac{p_t Q_t}{c_t} - \frac{p_{t-1} Q_{t-1}}{c_{t-1}} \right] + \alpha\gamma_1 \left[\frac{p_{t-1} Q_{t-1}}{c_{t-1}} - \frac{p_{t-2} Q_{t-2}}{c_{t-2}} \right]$$
$$- \omega_1 [I_{t-1} - \delta K_{t-2}] + \delta K_{t-1}.$$

From Table 2 the numerical values for each estimate may be substituted for the unknown parameters—β, $\alpha\gamma_0$, $\alpha\gamma_1$, ω_1, δ. These values are given in the first row of the table, labeled Neoclassical I. Substituting these values into the distributed lag function, we obtain:

$$I_t = .2449 + \underset{(.0063)}{.0160} \left[\frac{p_t Q_t}{c_t} - \frac{p_{t-1} Q_{t-1}}{c_{t-1}} \right] + \underset{(.0066)}{.0150} \left[\frac{p_{t-1} Q_{t-1}}{c_{t-1}} - \frac{p_{t-2} Q_{t-2}}{c_{t-2}} \right]$$
$$+ \underset{(.2061)}{.3444} \ [I_{t-1} - \delta K_{t-2}] + \underset{(.0540)}{.1794} \ K_{t-1}.$$

For the Neoclassical II theory of investment desired capital is analogous to that in Neoclassical I, except that capital gains are set equal to zero for the price of capital services and the cost of capital. For the post-war period the form of the distributed lag function selected for General Motors includes three values of change in desired capital and two lagged values of net investment. The estimated distributed lag function with numerical values from the row of Table 2 labeled Neoclassical II is:

$$I_t = .1231 + \underset{(.0094)}{.0411} \left[\frac{p_t Q_t}{c_t} - \frac{p_{t-1} Q_{t-1}}{c_{t-1}} \right] + \underset{(.0105)}{.0654} \left[\frac{p_{t-1} Q_{t-1}}{c_{t-1}} - \frac{p_{t-2} Q_{t-2}}{c_{t-2}} \right]$$
$$+ \underset{(.0089)}{.0202} \left[\frac{p_{t-2} Q_{t-2}}{c_{t-2}} - \frac{p_{t-3} Q_{t-3}}{c_{t-3}} \right] + \underset{(.1311)}{.3732} \ [I_{t-2} - \delta K_{t-3}] + \underset{(.0361)}{.1826} \ K_{t-1}.$$

In the Accelerator theory of investment, desired capital is proportional to output, Q_t. The best distributed lag function for General Motors for the post-war period includes lagged change in desired capital and lagged net investment. The final form of the distributed lag function may be represented as:

$$I_t = \beta + \alpha \gamma_1 [Q_{t-1} - Q_{t-2}] - \omega_1 [I_{t-1} - \delta K_{t-2}] + \delta K_{t-1}.$$

The numerical values for each parameter estimate are given in the third row of Table 2, labeled Accelerator; substituting these values into the distributed lag function, we have:

$$I_t = .1963 + \underset{(.0327)}{.0666} \ [Q_{t-1} - Q_{t-2}] + \underset{(.2115)}{.4780} \ [I_{t-1} - \delta K_{t-2}] + \underset{(.0593)}{.1878} \ K_t.$$

Similarly, for the Expected Profits theory of investment, desired capital is proportional to the market value of the firm, V_t. The best distributed lag function for General Motors in the post-war period includes current and lagged changes in desired capital and no lagged values of net investment. The final form of the distributed lag function is:

$$I_t = \beta + \alpha \gamma_0 [V_t - V_{t-1}] + \alpha \gamma_1 [V_{t-1} - V_{t-2}] + \delta K_{t-1}.$$

Substituting the numerical values from the fourth row of Table 2, labeled Expected Profits, the estimated distributed lag function becomes:

$$I_t = .2793 + \underset{(.0267)}{.0858} \; [V_t - V_{t-1}] + \underset{(.0268)}{.0610} \; [V_{t-1} - V_{t-2}] + \underset{(.0571)}{.1493} \; K_{t-1}.$$

For the Liquidity theory of investment behavior the best distributed lag function includes current and lagged changes in desired capital and lagged net investment; after appropriate substitutions, we obtain:

$$I_t = .2345 + \underset{(.2710)}{.3032} \; [L_t - L_{t-1}] + \underset{(.2743)}{.4941} \; [L_{t-1} - L_{t-2}]$$

$$+ \underset{(.2279)}{.3989} \; [I_{t-1} - \delta K_{t-2}] + \underset{(.0620)}{.1712} \; K_{t-1}.$$

5. COMPARISON

We have determined the best specification of the distributed lag between changes in desired capital and investment expenditures for each of five alternative theories of investment behavior and for each of fifteen corporations included in our sample. We can compare the alternative specifications of desired capital with respect to the explanation of investment behavior for the fifteen corporations. The relative performance of the alternative specifications provides our criterion for comparison of alternative theories of investment behavior. Relative performance may be measured in many ways. The best measure of performance is the residual variance for the best fitted distributed lag function corresponding to each theory. The theory of investment behavior that results in the least residual variance provides the best explanation of investment behavior. Performance as measured by residual variance can usefully be supplemented by an analysis of the fitted coefficients. The coefficients associated with changes in desired capital are of particular interest. Without these terms, the fitted distributed lag functions contain only lagged net investment and capital stock, so that the resulting explanation of investment expenditures cannot be attributed to a theory of investment behavior. Finally, an alternative measure of goodness of fit based on the qualitative characteristics of the fitted distributed lag functions is the number of "right" and "wrong" changes in direction for the fitted values of investment by comparison with the actual values.

First, we consider the number and significance of coefficients of changes in desired capital stock entering each fitted distributed lag function. A summary of the evidence is provided by Table 3. The first half of the table gives the number of coefficients of changes in desired capital that enter the fitted distributed lag functions for all firms. In selecting an appropriate form for the lag distribution a value of change in desired capital was allowed to enter the regression if it lowered the residual variance around the regression. The column labeled X_2 gives the number of values of current changes in desired capital for all firms, the column X_3 the number of lagged changes in desired capital, and the column X_4 the number of changes in desired capital lagged twice. The second half of the table presents the number of coefficients of changes in desired capital stock whose fitted values are twice their estimated standard errors or more. For example, in the fitted distributed lag functions for the Neoclassical I theory of investment, 13 of a possible 15 coefficients of current changes in desired capital enter the regressions for post-war data. Of these, 10 have coefficients that are twice their standard errors or more. For this same theory, 12 of a possible 15 coefficients of lagged changes in desired capital enter the regressions for post-war data; six of 15 coefficients of changes in desired capital lagged twice enter these regressions. The total number of coefficients for all lags and all firms is 31, or an average of slightly over two per firm; the total number of these coefficients twice their standard errors or more is 20 or between one and two per firm.

TABLE 3

Number of Desired Capital Stock Coefficients

MODEL	1949-1963				1937-1941, 1949-1963			
	X_2	X_3	X_4	Total	X_2	X_3	X_4	Total
Neoclassical I	13	12	6	31	13	11	6	30
Neoclassical II	14	10	4	28	14	8	3	25
Accelerator	9	9	1	19	11	11	1	23
Expected Profits	13	7	3	23	12	5	2	19
Liquidity Model	4	8	2	14	5	10	2	17

Number of Coefficients Twice Their Standard Errors

MODEL	1949-1963				1937-1941, 1949-1963			
	X_2	X_3	X_4	Total	X_2	X_3	X_4	Total
Neoclassical I	10	8	2	20	11	5	4	20
Neoclassical II	10	7	1	18	11	5	1	17
Accelerator	5	6	0	11	8	7	0	15
Expected Profits	9	6	1	16	9	3	0	12
Liquidity Model	1	4	1	6	1	3	0	4

The tabulation of coefficients given in Table 3 supports the following conclusions: First, the results are generally similar for post-war data and for combined pre-war and post-war data. The Neoclassical I theory of investment, including capital gains in the price of capital services and the cost of capital, has the largest number of coefficients entering the fitted distributed lag functions and the largest number of coefficients twice their standard errors or more for both post-war and combined pre-war and post-war data. The Neoclassical II theory of investment, excluding capital gains, has the second largest number of coefficients in both groups for both sets of data. The Accelerator and Expected Profits theories of investment stand next in order of the number of coefficients entering the fitted distributed lag functions and the number of coefficients that are twice their standard errors or more. The Expected Profits theory has a large number of coefficients in each category for the post-war data while the ordering of the two theories is reversed for the pre-war and post-war data combined. The Liquidity theory of investment has fewer coefficients entering the fitted distributed lag functions than any other theory and fewer coefficients twice their standard errors or more. For the post-war data only 14 changes in desired capital enter the fitted regressions or less than one per firm. Only six of these coefficients are twice their standard errors or more for the post-war data and only four for the combined pre-war and post-war data.

We turn next to the direct measurement of the relative performance of the alternative theories of investment in the explanation of corporate investment behavior. As a standard for evaluation of the performance of all models, we have fitted two "naive" models to the same data. The first naive model is a simple regression of investment against its own lagged value,

$$I_t = \beta_0 + \beta_1 I_{t-1}.$$

The second naive model is the best autoregressive scheme for investment; as many as three lagged values of investment are allowed to enter so long as they reduce the residual variance around the fitted autoregression. The second naive model may be written,

$$I_t = \beta_0 + \beta_1 I_{t-1} + \beta_2 I_{t-2} + \beta_3 I_{t-3}.$$

We refer to these models as Naive Model I and Naive Model II, respectively.

Goodness of fit statistics for all theories of investment behavior and for the two naive models are given for each corporation included in our sample in Table 4. The coefficient of multiple determination, R^2, is given in the first column of this table; the standard error of the regression, s, is given in the second column; and the third column gives the Durbin-Watson ratio, d. The standard error of the regression is corrected for degrees of freedom while the coefficient of multiple determination is not. Accordingly, comparison of the relative performance of the different models is based on the standard error. For comparison of the various models on the basis of standard error the random error for the underlying distributed lag model must be serially independent. To provide some evidence on this assumption, we employ the Durbin-Watson statistic. This statistic is biased toward randomness when lagged values of net investment are included in the fitted distributed lag function.[34] However, this bias affects all the distributed lag functions equally so that values of the Durbin-Watson statistic provide useful information about the relative presence or absence of autocorrelation. Employing the tables of Durbin and Watson the hypothesis of randomness cannot be rejected in favor of either positive or negative autocorrelation for any model for any firm for any time period. This evidence points to lack of substantial serial correlation.

The tabulation of goodness of fit statistics given in Table 4 reveals that for every fitted distributed lag function with at least one change in desired capital, the resulting goodness of fit is superior to that of Naive Model I. Where no change in desired capital enters the fitted distributed lag function we obtain, of course, a type of naive model. The seventeen instances where this occurs are indicated in Table 4 by an asterisk. In 18 of 30 cases for postwar and combined pre-war and post-war data Naive Model II provided a better explanation of investment than Naive Model I. In most of these cases only two lagged values of investment reduce the standard error of the regression. For nearly every firm the fitted distributed lag functions were superior to Naive Model II on the basis of goodness of fit for both post-war and combined pre-war and post-war data, except for the Liquidity theory of investment. For the post-war data the Liquidity theory is superior to Naive Model II for nine of the 15 firms. For the combined data the Liquidity theory is superior to Naive Model II for only seven of the 15 firms.

Our comparison of alternative theories of investment behavior is based on the criterion of minimum standard error for the fitted distributed lag functions. All possible two-way comparisons of the

TABLE 4

Goodness of Fit Statistics

Firm and Model	1949-1963			1937-41, 1949-63		
	R^2	s	d	R^2	s	d
General Motors						
Neoclassical I	.70	.1765	2.03	.83	.1650	1.44
Neoclassical II	.89	.1148	2.32	.91	.1190	1.91
Accelerator	.62	.1920	2.21	.82	.1681	1.98
Expected Profits	.64	.1852	1.36	.79	.1705	2.19
Liquidity Model	.61	.2037	2.29	.79	.1791	2.28
Naive Model I	.47	.2072	2.22	.70	.1937	2.28
Naive Model II	.47	.2072	2.22	.70	.1937	2.28
Goodyear						
Neoclassical I	.73	.0119	2.71	.83	.0104	2.75
Neoclassical II	.66	.0127	2.14	.74	.0128	2.55
Accelerator	.61	.0135	1.61	.71	.0130	1.49
Expected Profits	.71	.0118	2.16	.79	.0110	1.90
Liquidity Model	—*	—	—	—*	—	—
Naive Model I	.30	.0159	1.78	.55	.0149	1.81
Naive Model II	.38	.0157	2.02	.55	.0149	1.81
American Can						
Neoclassical I	.66	.0087	2.21	.66	.00874	2.16
Neoclassical II	.44	.0101	2.16	.64	.00875	2.10
Accelerator	.39	.0105	1.73	.48	.01049	2.01
Expected Profits	.27	.0110	2.15	.45	.01050	1.95
Liquidity Model	—*	—	—	.33	.0116	1.86
Naive Model I	.00002	.0123	1.97	.14	.0127	2.04
Naive Model II	.04	.0121	1.76	.34	.0112	2.04
Pittsburgh Plate Glass						
Neoclassical I	.72	.0089	2.16	.80	.0078	2.15
Neoclassical II	.41	.0129	1.86	.53	.0116	1.83
Accelerator	.51	.01178	2.36	.66	.0099	2.43
Expected Profits	.45	.01180	1.91	.60	.0107	2.17
Liquidity Model	—*	—	—	.55	.0117	1.80
Naive Model I	.18	.0131	1.58	.36	.0121	1.68
Naive Model II	.30	.0127	1.83	.36	.0121	1.68
U.S. Steel						
Neoclassical I	.51	.0801	1.46	.64	.0800	2.32
Neoclassical II	.50	.0854	1.63	.66	.0783	2.21
Accelerator	—*	—	—	—*	—	—
Expected Profits	.69	.0676	1.42	.59	.0762	1.25
Liquidity Model	.46	.0841	1.57	—*	—	—
Naive Model I	.11	.0948	1.47	.25	.0971	1.41
Naive Model II	.39	.0818	1.70	.44	.0891	1.73
General Electric						
Neoclassical I	.72	.0227	1.80	.79	.0237	1.71
Neoclassical II	.85	.0173	1.37	.79	.0225	1.13
Accelerator	.58	.0276	1.89	.78	.0239	1.81
Expected Profits	.71	.0244	2.27	.73	.0258	2.20
Liquidity Model	.71	.0240	2.58	—*	—	—
Naive Model I	.37	.0296	1.14	.60	.0285	1.65
Naive Model II	.51	.0272	1.71	.64	.0279	1.95
Reynolds Tobacco						
Neoclassical I	.85	.0040	2.20	.86	.00355	2.27
Neoclassical II	.89	.0034	2.28	.89	.0031	2.02
Accelerator	.92	.0028	1.98	.91	.0027	1.85
Expected Profits	.84	.0039	1.87	.85	.00354	1.71
Liquidity Model	.80	.0043	2.03	.79	.0042	1.71
Naive Model I	.76	.0044	1.73	.76	.0041	1.66
Naive Model II	.76	.0044	1.73	.76	.0041	1.66
Dupont						
Neoclassical I	.60	.0321	1.55	.68	.0324	1.71
Neoclassical II	—*	—	—	—*	—	—
Accelerator	.63	.0309	1.38	.77	.0290	1.72
Expected Profits	—*	—	—	—*	—	—

TABLE 4—CONTINUED

Goodness of Fit Statistics

Firm and Model	1949-1963			1937-41, 1949-63		
	R^2	s	d	R^2	s	d
Liquidity Model	—*	—	—	.73	.0305	1.59
Naive Model I	.30	.0407	1.42	.47	.0405	1.75
Naive Model II	.30	.0407	1.42	.55	.0385	1.68
Anaconda Company						
Neoclassical I	.87	.0078	1.06	.81	.0109	1.93
Neoclassical II	.78	.0102	1.65	.87	.0092	1.61
Accelerator	.80	.0098	2.48	.85	.01028	2.23
Expected Profits	.87	.0084	2.83	.83	.01034	1.84
Liquidity Model	.85	.0080	1.98	.86	.0097	2.05
Naive Model I	.30	.0151	1.25	.61	.0144	1.32
Naive Model II	.54	.0128	1.93	.70	.0134	2.14
Standard Oil, N.J.						
Neoclassical I	.86	.0736	2.48	.84	.0889	1.85
Neoclassical II	.86	.0755	2.25	.73	.1085	1.27
Accelerator	.69	.1083	1.79	.68	.1202	1.60
Expected Profits	.75	.1022	2.24	.70	.1205	1.92
Liquidity Model	.55	.1249	1.62	.61	.1336	1.78
Naive Model I	.43	.1285	1.43	.44	.1454	1.55
Naive Model II	.50	.1258	1.67	.44	.1454	1.55
International Paper Company						
Neoclassical I	.74	.0105	2.01	.50	.0177	1.96
Neoclassical II	.77	.0100	2.02	.44	.0186	2.01
Accelerator	.66	.0121	1.72	.63	.0151	1.86
Expected Profits	.72	.0109	1.39	.66	.0145	1.36
Liquidity Model	.79	.0096	2.37	.78	.0122	2.01
Naive Model I	.14	.0177	1.79	.32	.0187	1.81
Naive Model II	.14	.0177	1.79	.41	.0180	1.70
Westinghouse Air Brake Corp.						
Neoclassical I	.61	.00135	1.87	.65	.00129	2.08
Neoclassical II	.84	.0009	1.76	.86	.0008	1.61
Accelerator	.55	.0015	1.66	.55	.0015	1.70
Expected Profits	.60	.00137	2.08	.62	.00134	2.30
Liquidity Model	.57	.0016	1.71	.40	.00170	1.83
Naive Model I	.19	.0018	2.01	.28	.001696	2.00
Naive Model II	.19	.0018	2.01	.34	.00167	1.82
International Business Machine						
Neoclassical I	.93	.0271	1.27	.96	.0247	1.10
Neoclassical II	.96	.0208	2.57	.97	.0196	2.09
Accelerator	.95	.0218	2.53	.97	.0199	2.25
Expected Profits	.89	.0313	1.91	.93	.0287	1.68
Liquidity Model	.90	.0306	2.38	.94	.0274	2.26
Naive Model I	.83	.0384	2.17	.90	.0339	2.17
Naive Model II	.89	.0324	1.90	.94	.0277	2.21
Swift						
Neoclassical I	.65	.0049	1.37	.65	.0046	1.47
Neoclassical II	.53	.00543	1.83	.60	.0049	1.51
Accelerator	—*	—	—	—*		
Expected Profits	.59	.0051	1.60	.56	.0053	1.87
Liquidity Model	.49	.00538	1.59	.58	.00520	2.01
Naive Model I	.36	.0055	1.54	.49	.00519	1.73
Naive Model II	.42	.0055	2.07	.49	.00519	1.73
Westinghouse Electric						
Neoclassical I	.64	.0125	2.06	.65	.0131	1.87
Neoclassical II	.75	.0110	1.56	.73	.0114	1.71
Accelerator	.58	.01289	1.64	.76	.0108	1.74
Expected Profits	.57	.01293	1.70	.67	.0126	1.70
Liquidity Model	—*	—	—	—*		
Naive Model I	.25	.0150	1.37	.51	.0140	1.69
Naive Model II	.47	.0131	1.78	.64	.0129	2.18

*No K_t^* variable reduces the standard error of the regression.

alternative theories are presented in Table 5 for both post-war and combined pre-war and post-war data. The numbers listed in each row give the number of firms out of fifteen for which the theory listed at the left hand side of the table has a lower standard error than the theory listed at the top of the table. As an example, considering the post-war results listed in the first half of the table, the Accelerator theory has a lower standard error than Neoclassical I for three out of 15 firms; the Accelerator has a lower standard error than Neoclassical II for four out of 15 firms and a lower standard error than the Expected Profits theory for five out of 15 firms with two ties. Finally, the Accelerator theory has a lower standard error than the Liquidity theory for 10 out of 15 firms.

The tabulation presented in Table 5 supports the following ranking of the alternative theories of investment behavior: For post-war data the Neoclassical I theory of investment, including capital gains in both the price of capital services and the cost of capital, is slightly superior to the Neoclassical II theory, excluding capital gains. It is strongly superior to the Accelerator theory with a lower standard error for 12 of 15 firms. It is also superior to the Expected Profits theory with a lower standard error for 12 of 15

TABLE 5

Model Ranking on Minimum Residual Variance Criterion, 1949-1963

Model \ Model	Neoclassical I	Neoclassical II	Accelerator	Expected Profits	Liquidity Model
Neoclassical I		8	12	12	14
Neoclassical II	7		11	9, tie	10, tie
Accelerator	3	4		6	10
Expected Profits	3	5, tie	9		10, tie
Liquidity Model	1	4, tie	5	4, tie	

Model Ranking on Minimum Residual Variance Criterion, 1937-1941, 1949-1963

Model \ Model	Neoclassical I	Neoclassical II	Accelerator	Expected Profits	Liquidity Model
Neoclassical I		7	9	10	12
Neoclassical II	8		10	10, tie	13
Accelerator	6	5		10	11, tie
Expected Profits	5	4, tie	5		10
Liquidity Model	3	2	3, tie	5	

firms. Finally, Neoclassical I is superior to the Liquidity theory for 14 of 15 firms. Continuing the ranking for post-war data, the Neoclassical II theory of investment behavior is superior to the Accelerator theory for 11 of 15 firms. It is superior to the Expected Profits theory for nine of 15 firms with one tie. Finally, Neoclassical II is superior to the Liquidity theory for 10 of 15 firms with two ties. The Expected Profits theory is superior to the Accelerator theory for eight of 15 firms with two ties. Expected Profits is superior to the Liquidity theory for 10 of 15 firms with one tie. Finally, the Accelerator theory is superior to the Liquidity theory for 10 of 15 firms. We conclude that for the post-war data the alternative theories may be ranked as follows:

1. Neoclassical I.
2. Neoclassical II.
3. Expected Profits.
4. Accelerator.
5. Liquidity.

A similar analysis of the results for combined pre-war and post-war data supports the following ranking of alternative theories of investment behavior: The Neoclassical II theory of investment is superior to the Neoclassical I theory for eight of 15 firms. Neoclassical II is superior to the Accelerator in 10 of 15 firms, Expected Profits in 10 of 15 firms with one tie, and the Liquidity theory in 13 of 15 firms. The Neoclassical I theory of investment is superior to the Accelerator for nine of 15 firms, the Expected Profits theory for 10 of 15 firms, and the Liquidity theory for 12 of 15 firms. The Accelerator is superior to the Expected Profits theory for 10 of 15 firms and the Liquidity theory for 11 of 15 firms with one tie. Finally, the Expected Profits theory is superior to the Liquidity theory for 10 of 15 firms. The resulting ranking of alternative theories of investment behavior is:

1. Neoclassical II.
2. Neoclassical I.
3. Accelerator.
4. Expected Profits.
5. Liquidity.

Our first conclusion is that the Liquidity theory of investment can be dismissed from serious consideration as an explanation of corporate investment behavior. As one might suspect, financial constraints play a very minor role in the explanation of investment behavior for large firms. Our results strongly corroborate the previous findings of Grunfeld and Kuh. For eight corporations for the period 1935-54, Grunfeld found that the partial correlation between profits and investment given capital stock was insignificant for six of the eight corporations.[35] Four of the firms in Grunfeld's sample are included in our sample of 15 firms so that the results are not completely independent. Nevertheless, the differences between the two studies are sufficiently great that the results can be taken to reinforce each other. Kuh's study is based on 60 corporations in the capital goods industry for the period 1935-56. None of the firms in Kuh's sample are included in our sample; furthermore, his sample is concentrated on firms that are considerably smaller than those we have analyzed. Kuh concludes that the results from time series fail to support the internal funds or profits model.[36]

Our second conclusion is that Expected Profits and Accelerator models perform about equally well. The results for the post-war period favor the Expected Profits model while the results for combined pre-war and post-war data favor the Accelerator model. The goodness of fit comparison of the two theories is reinforced by the enumeration of the number of coefficients that enter the fitted distributed lag functions for each theory, presented in Table 3. Again, the results favor the Expected Profits theory for the post-war period and the Accelerator theory for the combined data. Our findings reinforce and extend Kuh's identification of expected profits with the capacity utilization theory or accelerator. No doubt information about profit expectations may be obtained from stock market data; however, this same information is adequately represented by levels of output or sales. Just as changes in profits before and after taxes are determined primarily by sales changes, alterations in the market value of the firm are adequately accounted for, so far as the determination of investment behavior is concerned, by alterations in output levels. Expected profits, whether measured by realized profits or the market value of the firm, may be represented by output levels. We conclude that a theory of investment behavior based on profit expectations may be identified with the capacity utilization theory so far as empirical results are concerned.

Our final conclusion is that either of the versions of the neoclassical theory of investment behavior we have examined is clearly superior to capacity utilization or profit expectations theories of investment. The neoclassical theory is far superior to internal funds theories of investment. Our findings thus corroborate the conclusions of Griliches and Wallace,[37] based on an analysis of quarterly time-series data for all of manufacturing. Of course, our results provide a much sharper discrimination among alternative theories of investment behavior as our comparison of results from aggregate time series and time series for individual firms led us to expect. Between the two versions of the neoclassical theory of investment our results suggest that a better explanation of post-war corporate investment behavior is provided by the Neoclassical I theory, incorporating capital gains in the price of capital services and the cost of capital. For the combined pre-war and post-war data the results are reversed. In any case the two theories are remarkably similar in performance for the two sets of data.

Diagrams of fitted versus actual values of investment for the post-war period for each of the alternative theories of investment behavior in our comparison are presented for our sample of fifteen corporations in Figures 1 through 15; each figure gives the pattern of investment for all theories for each firm. Fitted distributed lag functions with no changes in desired capital are omitted from the figures. Corresponding results for Naive Model II are plotted for all firms, except American Can. For American Can Naive Model II did not lower the residual variance around the regression. In this case the mean level of investment provides the "best" naive model explanation of investment.

An alternative method for assessing the goodness of fit of the distributed lag functions corresponding to each theory of investment behavior is the number of "right" and "wrong" changes in direction for the fitted values of investment by comparison with the actual values. The number of correct changes in direction, the number of incorrect changes, and the number of extra turning points for the fitted values of investment are recorded in Table 6. Results are tabulated separately for peaks and troughs. The direction of change at a peak or trough is correct if the fitted value of investment at time t+1 is less than the fitted value at time t for a peak of actual investment and greater than the fitted value at time t for a trough. The results in Table 6 are derived from the diagrams for the post-war period. Where no changes in desired capital enter a fitted distributed lag function, results from Naive Model II are substituted for those of the distributed lag function except for American Can. In the case of American Can since the mean level of investment provides the "best" naive model explanation of investment, it was used when no changes in desired capital enter a fitted, distributed lag function. As an example, we consider the results for the Neoclassical I theory of investment behavior for General Motors. The distributed lag function was correct for one of three peaks and two of three troughs; it indicated one extra peak.

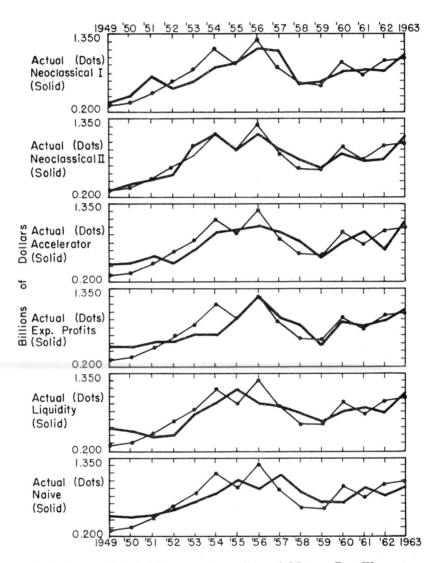

FIGURE 1—Model Comparison: General Motors, Post-War

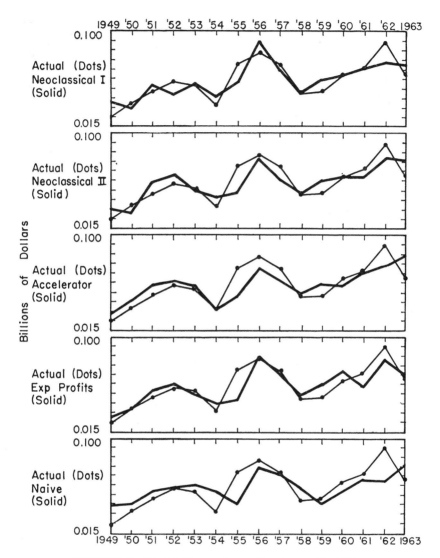

FIGURE 2—Model Comparison: Goodyear, Post-War

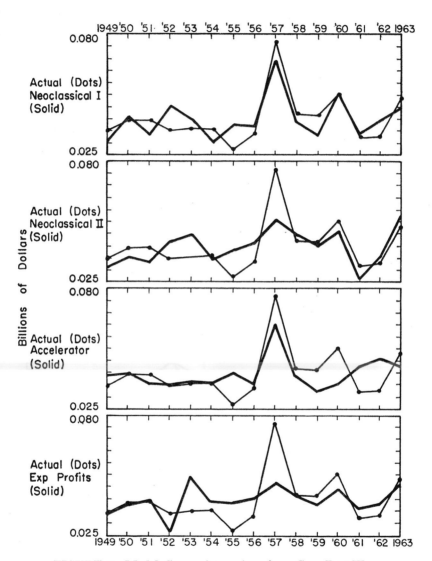

FIGURE 3—Model Comparison: American Can, Post-War

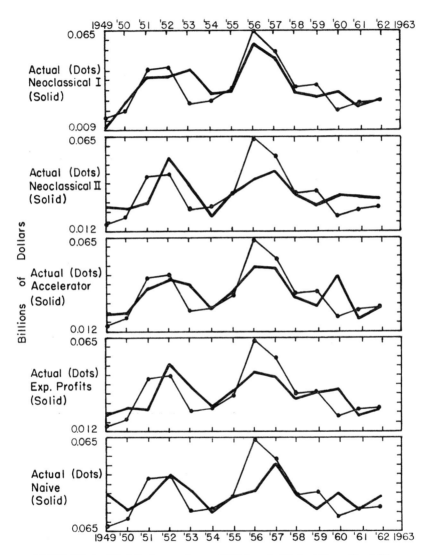

FIGURE 4—Model Comparison: Pittsburgh Plate Glass, Post-War

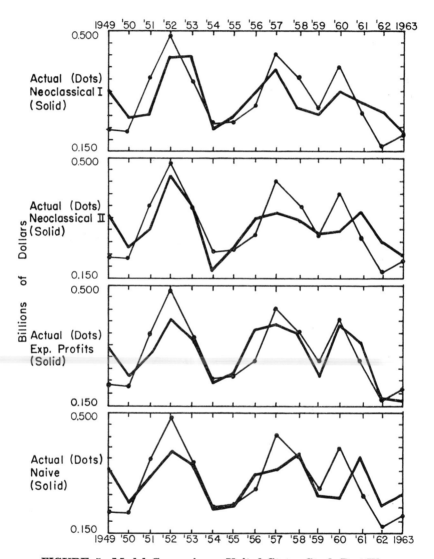

FIGURE 5—Model Comparison: United States Steel, Post-War

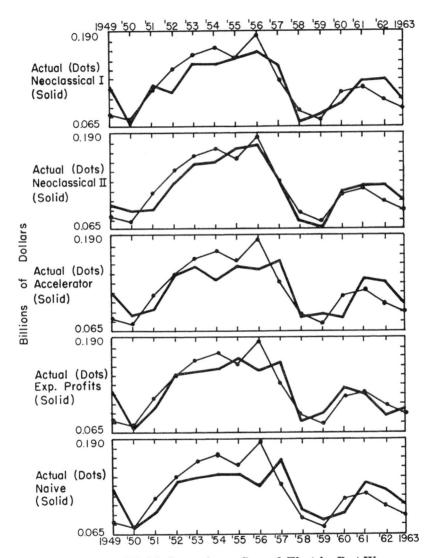

FIGURE 6—Model Comparison: General Electric, Post-War

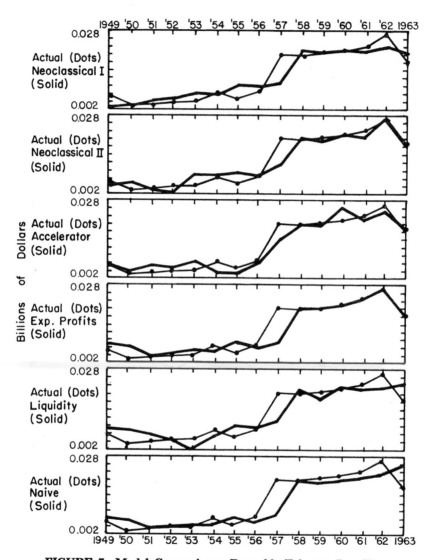

FIGURE 7—Model Comparison: Reynolds Tobacco, Post-War

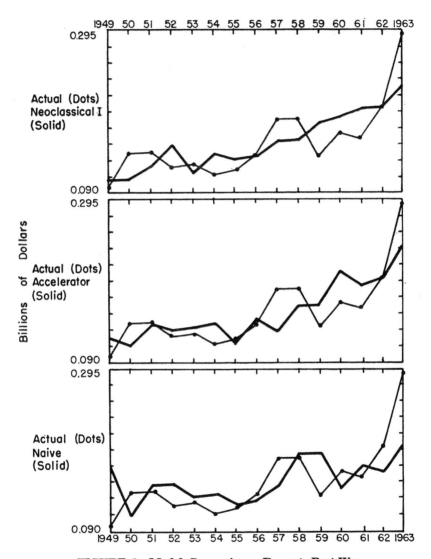

FIGURE 8—Model Comparison: Dupont, Post-War

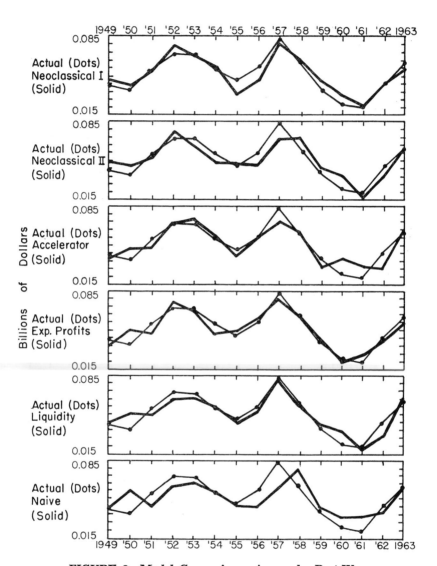

FIGURE 9—Model Comparison: Anaconda, Post-War

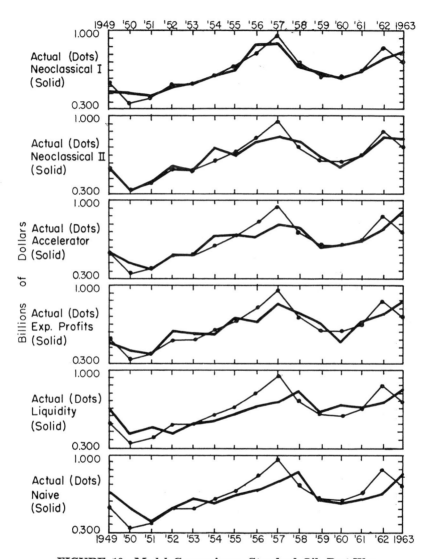

FIGURE 10—Model Comparison: Standard Oil, Post-War

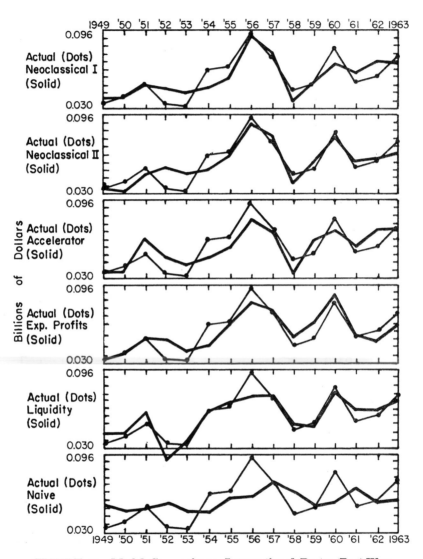

FIGURE 11—Model Comparison: International Paper, Post-War

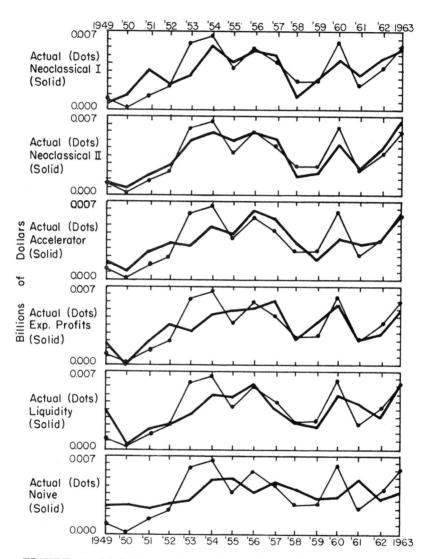

FIGURE 12—Model Comparison: Westinghouse Air Brake, Post-War

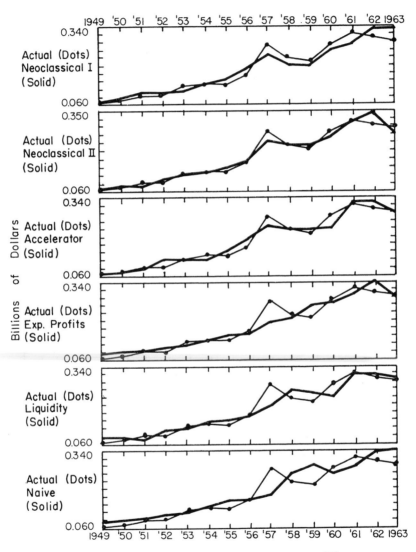

FIGURE 13—Model Comparison: IBM, Post-War

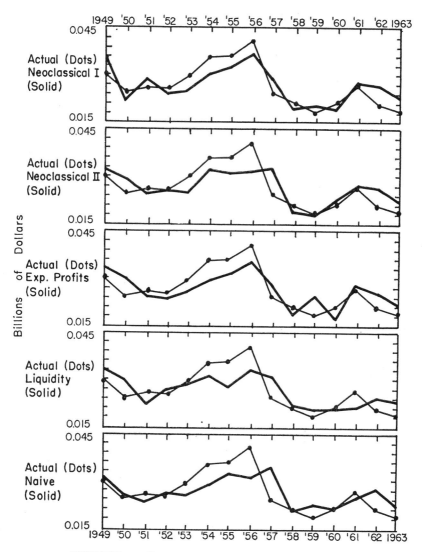

FIGURE 14—Model Comparison: Swift, Post-War

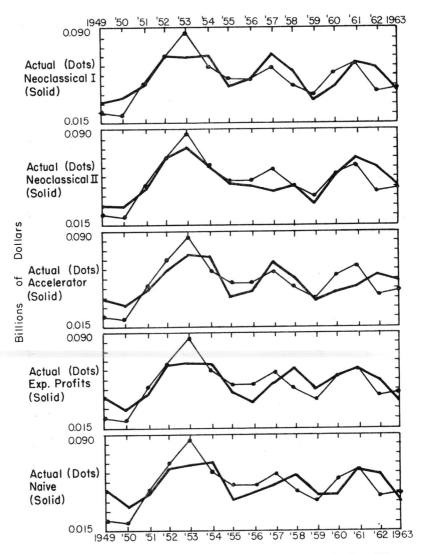

FIGURE 15—Model Comparison: Westinghouse Electric, Post-War

On the basis of the number of correct turning points, the alternative theories may be ranked as follows:

1. Neoclassical I.
2. Neoclassical II.
3. Accelerator.
4. Expected Profits.
5. Liquidity.

Naive Model II ranks last by a considerable margin on the turning point criterion. The Liquidity theory of investment ranks lowest among the alternative theories of investment behavior. Expected Profits and Accelerator theories have nearly identical performance on turning points. Neoclassical I theory is slightly superior to Neoclassical II and both have a better performance record than the Accelerator or Expected Profits theories. We conclude that the ranking produced by an examination of turning points is substantially the same as that produced by the criterion of minimum residual variance.

TABLE 6
Prediction of Direction of Change of Investment at Turning Points, Post-War

Model	Firm	G.M.[1]		G.T.R.		Am. Can		P.P.G.		U.S.S.		G.E.		R.T.		Dupont	
		P[2]	T[3]	P	T	P	T	P	T	P	T	P	T	P	T	P	T
Neoclassical I	R[4]	1	3	2	2	3	2	1	0	2	3	1	3	1	2	0	2
	W[5]	2	0	1	0	0	1	1	2	1	1	2	0	1	0	3	1
	E[6]	1	0	1	1	1	0	0	0	0	0	1	0			0	0	1
Neoclassical II	R	3	3	3	2	3	3	1	0	2	3	1	3	1	0	0	0
	W	0	0	0	0	0	0	1	2	1	1	2	0	1	2	3	3
	E	0	0	0	1	1	0	0	1	0	0	0	0	0	0	1	0
Accelerator	R	1	2	2	2	2	1	2	0	1	3	1	1	2	2	2	2
	W	2	1	1	0	1	2	0	2	2	1	2	2	0	0	1	1
	E	1	0	0	0	1	0	0	1	0	0	1	0	1	0	1	1
Expected Profits	R	2	3	3	2	3	3	2	0	3	3	1	2	1	0	0	0
	W	1	0	0	0	0	0	0	2	0	1	2	1	1	2	3	3
	E	0	0	0	0	0	0	0	0	0	0	0	1	0	0	1	0
Liquidity Model	R	1	1	1	0	0	0	1	0	1	3	1	2	0	0	0	0
	W	2	2	2	2	3	3	1	2	2	1	2	1	2	2	3	3
	E	1	0	0	0	0	0	1	1	0	0	0	0	1	0	1	0
Naive Model	R	0	0	1	0	0	0	1	0	1	3	1	2	0	0	0	0
	W	3	3	2	2	3	3	1	2	2	1	2	1	2	2	3	3
	E	0	0	0	0	0	0	1	1	0	0	0	0	0	0	1	0

TABLE 6—CONCLUDED
Prediction of Direction of Change of Investment at Turning Points, Post-War

Model	Firm	An. Co.		S.O.		I.P.		West. Air B.		I.B.M.		Swift		W. El.		Totals	
		P	T	P	T	P	T	P	T	P	T	P	T	P	T	P	T
Neoclassical I	R	2	3	1	1	3	3	3	4	1	1	2	1	3	3	26	33
	W	0	0	1	1	0	0	0	0	1	0	0	1	0	1	13	8
	E	0	0	0	0	0	0	1	0	0	0	1	0	0	0	6	2
Neoclassical II	R	1	2	2	2	2	3	3	4	1	1	1	1	2	2	26	29
	W	1	1	0	0	1	0	0	0	1	0	1	1	1	2	13	12
	E	0	0	1	0	0	0	0	0	0	0	0	0	0	0	3	2
Accelerator	R	1	2	1	1	3	3	3	3	2	1	0	0	2	3	25	27
	W	1	1	1	1	0	0	0	1	0	0	2	2	1	1	14	14
	E	0	1	0	0	0	0	1	0	0	0	0	0	0	0	5	3
Expected Profits	R	2	2	1	1	3	2	1	4	0	1	2	0	2	3	26	26
	W	0	1	1	1	0	1	2	0	2	0	0	2	1	1	13	15
	E	1	0	0	0	0	0	1	0	0	0	0	1	0	0	4	4
Liquidity Model	R	1	2	0	1	2	2	3	2	1	0	1	1	1	3	14	17
	W	0	1	2	1	1	1	0	2	1	1	1	1	2	1	25	24
	E	1	0	1	0	0	0	0	0	0	0	1	0	0	0	6	3
Naive Model	R	0	1	0	1	0	0	0	1	0	0	0	0	1	3	5	11
	W	2	2	2	1	3	3	3	3	2	1	2	2	2	1	34	30
	E	1	0	0	0	0	0	0	0	0	0	1	0	0	0	4	1

[1]These are abbreviations for the names of the firms which are listed in the same order as in Table 1.

[2]Peak   [4]Right direction   [6]Extra turning points in regression prediction
[3]Trough   [5]Wrong direction

To summarize: We have compared alternative theories of investment behavior with regard to their ability to explain corporate investment behavior. Although the relative performance of the alternative theories may be measured in a number of ways, all three measures of relative performance we have used—proportion of correct turning points, standard error of the regression, number of changes in desired capital entering the fitted distributed lag functions—produce the same ordering of alternative theories of investment behavior. For the post-war period this ranking is:

1. Neoclassical I.
2. Neoclassical II.
3. Expected Profits.
4. Accelerator.
5. Liquidity.

Our tests discriminate sharply among the Neoclassical theories and the Expected Profits and Accelerator theories and between these theories and the Liquidity theory. The discrimination between Neoclassical I and Neoclassical II theories, which differ in their treatment of capital gains realized on assets, is less sharp and deserves further examination.

6. CONCLUSION

The purpose of our study has been to compare five alternative theories of investment behavior: Neoclassical I, including capital gains on assets; Neoclassical II, excluding capital gains; Accelerator, based on output or capacity utilization; Expected Profits, based on the market value of the firm; and Liquidity or internal funds. The point of departure for our study is the flexible accelerator mechanism originated by Chenery and Koyck; we have generalized this mechanism in order to provide a wider range of possible time patterns for investment behavior. Due to the importance of correct specification of the lag structure underlying investment, we have determined the best distributed lag function for each alternative theory from the class of general Pascal distributed lag functions. To permit sharper discrimination among the alternative theories we have employed data for individual firms; we have selected the best lag distribution for each alternative theory for each of the firms included in our sample. Our results are free of biases that could result from misspecification of the lag structure or from inappropriate assumptions about the homogeneity of investment behavior across firms. To measure the relative performance of the alternative theories of investment behavior we have relied primarily on the criterion of minimum residual variance. This measure of performance has been supplemented by measures of the proportion of correct turning points and the number of changes in desired capital entering the fitted distributed lag functions. The three measures of relative performance produce essentially the same results for both post-war and combined pre-war and post-war data.

Our principal conclusion is that the neoclassical theory of investment behavior is superior to theories based on capacity utilization or profit expectations and that these theories are superior, in turn, to a theory based on internal funds available for investment. The latter part of our conclusion corroborates the previous results of Grunfeld and Kuh. Both of the versions of the neoclassical theory we have examined—including or excluding capital gains realized on assets from the cost of capital and the price of capital services— provide a better explanation of corporate investment behavior than any of the competing theories. The neoclassical theory including capital gains appears to provide a somewhat better explanation of post-war experience, which is most relevant for policy and prediction purposes. The neoclassical theory excluding capital gains provides a very slightly better explanation of combined pre-war and post-war data. Both theories are superior to the alternatives we have considered for both post-war and combined pre-war and post-war data.

Our conclusions bear on broader issues in the theory of the firm. Meyer and Kuh have suggested as a possible basis for the theory of investment behavior the assumption that business firms maximize utility defined more broadly than in the characterization of the objectives of the firm in the neoclassical theory of optimal capital accumulation:

> Partial recognition of institutional changes has led in recent years to shift the theory of the firm, and consequently of plant and equipment investment, from a profit maximization orientation to that of utility maximization. Primarily, this move represents a growing belief that profit maximization is too narrow to encompass the full scope of modern entrepreneurial motives, particularly once the previously assumed objective conditions are released from *ceteris paribus,* and the theory seeks to explain a much wider range of behavior response.[38]

Similar views on the theory of the firm have been expressed by Machlup [33], Simon [48], and many others. Simon argues that:

> . . . I should like to emphasize strongly that neither the classical theory of the firm nor any of the amendments to it or substitutes for it that have been proposed have had any substantial amount of empirical testing. If the classical theory appeals to us, it must be largely because it has a certain face validity . . . rather than because profit maximizing behavior has been observed.[39]

Simon ignores the entire econometric literature on cost and production functions, all of which is based on the neoclassical theory of the firm.[40] The evidence is so largely favorable to the theory that current empirical research emphasizes such technical questions as the appropriate form for the production function and the statistical specification for econometric models of production based on this theory. Simon's characterization of alternatives to the neoclassical theory of the firm is correct; this theory has not been subjected to substantial empirical testing. However, his characterization of the empirical evidence on the neoclassical theory is seriously deficient.

Our results strongly reinforce the evidence on the neoclassical theory of the firm from studies of cost and production functions. We conclude that the objections to the neoclassical theory of the firm as a basis for the theory of investment behavior by Meyer and Kuh are ill-founded. The appeal to a broader view of entrepreneurial objectives is not supported by evidence from econometric studies of cost and production functions or from studies of investment behavior. The neoclassical theory of the firm is far more powerful than the broader view suggested by Machlup, Meyer and

Kuh, and Simon in the sense that a much narrower range of conceivable behavior is consistent with the neoclassical theory. On the basis of our comparison of alternative theories of investment behavior we conclude that further research can fruitfully incorporate precisely the factors central to the neoclassical theory of the firm. Although these factors played some role in early studies of investment behavior, they were not properly evaluated due to imprecise formulation of the theory of demand for capital services and due to misspecification of the time structure of investment behavior. These deficiencies have now been overcome and a start has been made on both empirical and theoretical research that could lead to a satisfactory theory of corporate investment behavior.

Obviously, our theory of corporate investment can be improved by better empirical and theoretical analysis. A more sophisticated analysis of the effects of tax policy on corporate investment behavior can be made.[41] Alternative approximations to the cost of capital for individual corporations are possible.[42] All the variables that enter the neoclassical theory of investment behavior can be measured more accurately.[43] All of these further improvements will require time and effort. Our conclusions suggest that this work is likely to be fruitful and that the time and effort required will be justified by the results.

STATISTICAL APPENDIX

INTRODUCTION

The purpose of this statistical appendix is two-fold. First, the appendix discusses the methods of measurement of the various variables employed in the study and some of the problems encountered in the measurement process. Second, the appendix lists the sources of data employed.

METHODS AND PROBLEMS OF MEASUREMENT

A. Investment, Depreciation, and Capital Stock

Investment is dollars of gross investment in plant and equipment deflated by the investment goods deflator for manufacturing into 1954 dollars. To obtain benchmark figures for capital stock, net fixed assets for the years 1937 and 1961 as reported in the balance sheets of the firms listed in *Moody's Industrial Manual* [44] were used. These benchmark stock figures were deflated by the National Industrial Conference Board [4,6] fixed capital stock deflators for the particular industry in which the firm is a member. Given investment at constant prices and two benchmark capital stock figures, the remaining capital stock figures and replacement figures were computed using the following explicit model for replacement. It was assumed that replacement is a constant fraction of capital stock at the beginning of the period. Under this assumption the definition of capital stock, K_t, can be written:

$$K_t = (1-\delta)K_{t-1} + I_t,$$

where I_t is gross investment. This difference equation in capital stock has a solution:

$$K_t = (1-\delta)^t K_0 + (1-\delta)^{t-1} I_1 + (1-\delta)^{t-2} I_2 + \dots + I_t,$$

where K_0 and K_t are initial and terminal values of capital stock. An estimate of δ was obtained from this expression. This value of δ was used to compute capital stock for the other periods and compute replacement for all periods.

A number of difficulties are connected with this procedure. First, the deflator employed to deflate gross investment is based on the price of inputs to the equipment and construction industries rather than prices of the output of these industries. This leads to serious upward bias in the index since the measure neglects productivity increases in the inputs. Data are not available to remedy the problem. Second, the benchmark figures for net fixed assets were taken from the accounting records of the firms. These records are generally oriented toward minimizing the tax burden of the firm rather than calculating the "correct" measure for net fixed assets. However, investment data were not available earlier than 1934. Therefore, it was not possible to calculate capital stock by the perpetual inventory method with a depreciation rate based on the average length of life of the fixed assets.

B. Output, Liquidity, and Market Value of the Firm

The output variable was computed by adding the current value of sales to the change in the inventory stock. This variable was employed as the numerator of the neoclassical and the accelerator models. A more ideal course would have been to compute output as sales plus the change in finished goods inventory. This was not feasible since the breakdown of inventory into finished goods, goods in process, and raw materials was not available for all firms.

The output variable in the accelerator model was deflated by the wholesale price index of the industry of which the particular firm is a member. The denominator of the neoclassical models' desired capital stock will be discussed below.

The liquidity variable employed in this study was measured by profits after taxes plus depreciation less dividends paid. This is the variable employed by Kuh in his study. Other measures were tested on an experimental basis with only minor differences in the results. The liquidity measure was deflated by the investment goods deflator.

The market value of the firm variable which was employed in the expected profits model was measured as the market value of stocks outstanding and book value of debt including short-term liabilities at the beginning of the year. The market value of a particular stock was calculated by multiplying the number of shares outstanding at the beginning of the year by the average of the stock's price high and low for January and December. This two-month "average" of the price of the stock was taken to eliminate the influence of any short-term transitory factors in deriving the market value of the stock. Taking the book value of debt was necessitated by the fact that much of a corporation's debt is not publicly traded or only intermittently has a current market price.

C. User Cost and the Cost of Capital

For the capital gains version of the neoclassical model, Neoclassical I, price of capital services was defined:

$$c = q \left[\frac{1-uw}{1-u}d + \frac{1}{1-u}r - \frac{1}{1-u}\frac{\dot{q}}{q} \right].$$

To measure the price of investment goods, q, the investment deflator was employed; the rate of depreciation, d, was obtained from the computation of capital stock since under the replacement model assumed the rate of replacement equals the rate of depreciation; and the rate of capital loss,

$-\dfrac{\dot{q}}{q}$, was measured by the rate of change of the investment deflator. The income tax rate, u, was computed by taking the ratio of profits before taxes less profits after taxes to profits before taxes. The proportion of depreciation deductible for tax purposes, w, was taken as the ratio in current prices of depreciation deducted in the firm's accounts and the depreciation figure computed in the course of computing capital stock.

In the Neoclassical II model the capital gains term was set equal to zero. In that case, the expression for price of capital services becomes:

$$c = q \left[\frac{1-uw}{1-u}d + \frac{1}{1-u}r \right],$$

where all variables are measured the same as previously except for r, the cost of capital.

The cost of capital, r, for Neoclassical II is defined as:

$$r = \frac{PAT+CCA-qR}{VTA},$$

where PAT was measured by profits after taxes. Capital consumption allowances, CCA, were the amount of depreciation charged in the firm's income statement. Replacement cost, qR, was measured by the amount of replacement computed in the capital computation multiplied by the investment deflator. The value of total assets, VTA, was measured by the market value of all of the firm's securities at the beginning of the period.

For Neoclassical I the cost of capital, r, is:

$$r = \frac{PAT+CCA-q_1R+\dot{q}_1K_1+\dot{q}_2K_2+\dot{q}_3K_3}{VTA},$$

where K_1, K_2, and K_3 are depreciable, depletable, and inventory assets, respectively; and q_1, q_2, and q_3 are their corresponding price deflators. The wholesale price index for the particular industry in which the firm is a member was used for q_2 and q_3. For most of the firms in the sample, K_2, depletable assets were a very small proportion of total fixed assets and for all except one firm were not listed separately.

In these cases capital gains on the combined depreciable and depletable assets were measured by the rate of change in the investment deflator. For the one firm in which depletable assets were substantial and listed separately, International Paper, the rate of change of the appropriate wholesale price index was applied to the depletable assets to obtain a measure of capital gains from depletable assets.

For depletable and depreciable assets recorded capital gains on assets are essentially zero. However, for a large number of firms, inventory capital gains are included in recorded profits before taxes. In that case they do not have to be added to the profits after taxes figures. This is particularly true for firms pricing ending inventory on a FIFO (first-in, first-out) basis. Under the FIFO method of pricing of inventories, it is assumed that sales are made from the earliest acquisitions. Therefore, if a firm applies the FIFO method, ending inventory is priced at close to the ending period inventory prices and profits will include most of the capital gains or losses which accrued during the period. This is particularly true if inventory turns over a number of times during the year. Since any adjustment for capital gains or losses under FIFO inventory pricing would be minor these adjustments were not made on recorded profits for firms which employed this method. Also, since the adjustment to profits would be minor for firms which employed average-cost pricing of inventory, no adjustment was made for these cases either.

In contrast, if LIFO (last-in, first-out) inventory pricing is employed most of any inventory capital gains or losses will not enter recorded profits. Therefore, in these cases inventory capital gains or losses were added to profits when computing the cost of capital. Inventory capital gains or losses do not enter recorded profits when LIFO inventory pricing methods are employed because under LIFO pricing the stock remaining on hand at the close of the taxable year to the extent of the inventory on hand at the beginning of the year is priced at book value as of the beginning of the year. This means, if this practice is followed for a number of years, that the base stock which is carried over year after year will be priced at prices which prevailed a number of years prior. This procedure causes profits to be understated in periods of rising prices and vice versa.

Not many firms employ the LIFO method of inventory pricing. The Internal Revenue Code of 1939 allowed this method for the first time. A number of firms adopted it for part of their inventory. Others have adopted it partly or in whole since then. One problem with the data was the difficulty incurred in discovering exactly what method of inventory pricing the various firms employed and to what portion of the inventory it applied. For firms which used LIFO on a majority of their inventory stock, profits were adjusted for inventory capital gains. These firms were American Can, Swift, and Westinghouse Electric. For one other firm, Reynolds, profits were adjusted for inventory capital gains. Reynolds employed average cost pricing on their inventory, but the inventory consisted mostly of tobacco which must be held a year for curing purposes. To adjust for this, $(1-u) \triangle (qK_3)$ was added to the profits after taxes figure each year, where u is the rate of profits tax, q is the wholesale price index for tobacco products, and K_3 is Reynolds' stock of inventory.

SOURCES

The principal source for the data employed in this study is *Moody's Industrial Manual* [44]. Complete balance sheets and income statements plus supplemental data are published in Moody's each year. In most of the cases the data were checked with annual reports of the firms in question. Another major source was various issues of the *Commercial and Financial Chronicle* [3]. A list of the data underlying the study, together with their sources, follows.

1. Investment. Source: *Moody's Industrial Manual,* additions at cost item in property-account-analysis under balance sheet.
2. Replacement. Source: computed in the process of computing capital stock as described above.
3. Depreciation. Source: *Moody's Industrial Manual* from Supplementary Profit and Loss Data Schedule under the income statement.
4. Capital Stock. Source: computed as described in the above section. Benchmark figures from *Moody's Industrial Manual.*
5. Output. Source: computed by adding sales and change in inventory stock, both from *Moody's Industrial Manual.*
6. Profit after Taxes. Source: *Moody's Industrial Manual,* also called net income to surplus.
7. Dividends Paid. Source: *Moody's Industrial Manual.*
8. Market Price of Stock, high and low for December and January. Source: *Commercial and Financial Chronicle.*
9. Shares Outstanding. Source: Standard and Poor's *Standard Corporation Descriptions* [50].
10. Current Liabilities. Source: *Moody's Industrial Manual.*
11. Debt Outstanding. Source: *Moody's Industrial Manual.*
12. Profits before Taxes. Source: *Moody's Industrial Manual.*
13. Fixed Capital Stock Price Deflators. Source: D. Creamer [4-6].
14. Wholesale Price Indexes. Source: *Wholesale Prices and Price Indexes* [56].
15. Investment Goods Deflator. Structures and Equipment implicit price index was employed. Source: *U. S. Income and Output* [55] and *Business Statistics* [53].
16. Implicit Gross National Product Deflator. Source: *U. S. Income and Output* and *Business Statistics.*

NOTES

[1]See, for example, the results of Griliches and Wallace [16].
[2]This point has been emphasized by Kuh [30], especially Chapter 5, pp. 116-57.
[3]See Kuznets [31], Table 8, pp. 92-3; capital consumption has dominated gross capital formation for the economy as a whole since 1919.
[4]See Jorgenson [23], p. 254 and Jorgenson and Stephenson [25].
[5]See Meyer and Kuh [37], pp. 91-4.
[6]See Feller [13], pp. 286-93.
[7]Tinbergen [52], p. 34.
[8]The liquidity theory is discussed by Meyer and Kuh [37], especially Chapter 13, pp. 190-208; Anderson [1]; Meyer and Glauber [36]; and Kuh [30]. A theoretical analysis of the liquidity approach is presented by Duesenberry [7], especially Chapter 5.
[9]Kuh [30], Chapter 6, pp. 158-88.
[10]Kuh [30], p. 213.
[11]Grunfeld [17], p. 219. See also Eisner [8-10].
[12]See Tinbergen [52].
[13]See Klein [27, 28].
[14]See also: Jorgenson [22, 23] and Jorgenson and Stephenson [26].
[15]Kuh [30], p. 208; see also, pp. 12-22, and Eisner [9], p. 8.
[16]See Modigliani and Miller [39].

[17]Kuh [30], pp. 293-302.
[18]See Grunfeld [17].
[19]Koyck [29], pp. 74-110.
[20]See Mayer [35].
[21]Jorgenson and Stephenson [26], Table 2, pp. 21-2.
[22]Jorgenson [24], pp. 137-42.
[23]In the final form of a general Pascal distributed lag function, the function is written with a finite number of lags in both dependent and independent variables. For further details, see Jorgenson [24], p. 138.
[24]Jorgenson [24], p. 147.
[25]Griliches and Wallace [16], esp. p. 325.
[26]Kuh [30], p. 330.
[27]See Kuh [30], especially Chapter 5, pp. 116-57.
[28]For further details, consult the Statistical Appendix.
[29]Sales were used in places of output at the experimental stages of this study to check whether sales might be a better measure of changes in expected demand. The results were not materially different than those reported here.
[30]Kuh [30], pp. 63 and 208-9. In addition a number of ad hoc liquidity measures were employed at the experimental stages of this study with results not materially different from those reported here.
[31]Grunfeld [17], pp. 226-7.
[32]For further details, consult the Statistical Appendix.
[33]For further details, consult the Statistical Appendix.
[34]See Griliches [15] and Malinvaud [34].
[35]Grunfeld [17], Table 3, p. 219.
[36]Kuh [30], p. 213. See also, Eisner [8].
[37]Griliches and Wallace [16], p. 325.
[38]Meyer and Kuh [37], p. 9.
[39]Simon [48], p. 8.
[40]A recent survey of the literature by Walters [57] enumerates 345 references, almost all presenting results of econometric tests of the neoclassical theory which are overwhelmingly favorable to the theory.
[41]See, for example, Hall and Jorgenson [18, 19]; their analysis has not yet been extended to the level of the individual corporation.
[42]For example, it might be useful to include "growth opportunities" in the measurement of the cost of capital, as recently suggested by Modigliani and Miller [43].
[43]Further suggestions for better measurement are given in the Statistical Appendix.

REFERENCES

1. Anderson, W. H. L. *Corporate Finance and Fixed Investment*. Boston: Division of Research, Graduate School of Business Administration, Harvard University, 1964.
2. Chenery, H. B. "Overcapacity and the Acceleration Principle," *Econometrica*, 20 (January, 1952), 1-28.
3. *The Commercial and Financial Chronicle*. New York: William B. Dana Company, various daily issues.
4. Creamer, D. "Capital Expansion and Capacity in Postwar Manufacturing," *Studies in Business Economics*, No. 72, New York: National Industrial Conference Board, 1961.
5. ————, S. Dobrovolsky, and I. Borenstein. *Capital in Manufacturing and Mining: Its Formation and Financing*. Princeton: Princeton University Press, 1960.
6. ————. "Recent Changes in Manufacturing Capacity," *Studies in Business Economics*, No. 79, New York: National Industrial Conference Board, 1962.
7. Duesenberry, James S. *Business Cycles and Economic Growth*. New York: McGraw-Hill Book Co., Inc., 1958.
8. Eisner, R. "Capital Expenditures, Profits, and the Acceleration Principle," *Models of Income Determination*, NBER, Studies in Income and Wealth, Vol. 28, Princeton: Princeton University Press, 1964, 137-76.
9. ————. "A Distributed Lag Investment Function," *Econometrica*, 28 (January, 1960), 1-29.
10. ————. "Expectations, Plans, and Capital Expenditures: A Synthesis of Ex Post and Ex Ante Data," *Expectations, Uncertainty and Business Behavior*, M. J. Bowman (ed.), 1958, 165-188.

11. ————. "Investment: Fact and Fancy," *American Economic Review,* 53 (May, 1963), 237-46.
12. ————. "A Permanent Income Theory for Investment," *American Economic Review,* 57 (June, 1967), 363-90.
13. Feller, W. *An Introduction to Probability Theory and Its Applications,* Vol. I, 2nd edition, New York: Wiley, 1957.
14. *Fortune,* "Plant and Product Directory (The 500 Largest U. S. Industrial Corporations)," August, 1963.
15. Griliches, Z. "A Note on Serial Correlation Bias in Estimates of Distributed Lags," *Econometrica,* 29 (January, 1961), 65-73.
16. Z. Griliches and N. Wallace. "The Determinants of Investment Revisited," *International Economic Review,* 6 (September, 1965), 311-329.
17. Grunfeld, Y. "The Determinants of Corporate Investment," in A. C. Harberger (ed.) *The Demand for Durable Goods,* Chicago: University of Chicago, 1960, 211-66.
18. Hall, R. E. and D. W. Jorgenson, "Tax Policy and Investment Behavior," *American Economic Review,* 57 (June, 1967), 391-414.
19. ———— and ————. "The Role of Taxation in Stabilizing Private Investment," in V. P. Rock, (ed.), *Policy Makers and Model Builders,* New York: Gordon and Breach, 1969.
20. Hickman, B. G. "Capacity, Capacity Utilization, and the Acceleration Principle," in *Problems of Capital Formation,* NBER, Studies in Income and Wealth, Vol. 19, Princeton: Princeton University Press, 1957, 419-50.
21. ————. *Investment Demand and U.S. Economic Growth,* Washington: The Brookings Institution, 1965.
22. Jorgenson, D. W. "Anticipations and Investment Behavior," in J. S. Duesenberry, E. Kuh, G. Fromm, and L. R. Klein (eds.), *The Brookings Quarterly Econometric Model of the United States,* Chicago: Rand McNally, 1965, 35-92.
23. ————. "Capital Theory and Investment Behavior," *American Economic Review,* 53 (May, 1963), 247-59.
24. ————. "Rational Distributed Lag Functions," *Econometrica,* 34 (January, 1966), 135-49.
25. ———— and J. A. Stephenson. "Investment Behavior in U.S. Manufacturing, 1947-60," *Econometrica,* 35 (April, 1967), 169-220.
26. ———— and ————. "The Time Structure of Investment Behavior in U.S. Manufacturing, 1947-60," *Review of Economics and Statistics,* 49 (February, 1967), 16-27.
27. Klein, L. R. *Economic Fluctuations in the United States, 1929-1941,* Cowles Commission Monograph, New York: John Wiley and Sons, Inc., 1950.
28. ————. "Studies in Investment Behavior," National Bureau of Economic Research, *Conference on Business Cycles,* New York, 1951, 233-77.
29. Koyck, L. M. *Distributed Lags and Investment Analysis.* Amsterdam: North-Holland Publishing Co., 1954.
30. Kuh, E. *Capital Stock Growth: A Micro-Econometric Approach.* Amsterdam: North-Holland Publishing Co., 1963.
31. Kuznets, S. *Capital in the American Economy: Its Formation and Financing.* Princeton: Princeton University Press, 1961.
32. ————. "Relation between Capital Goods and Finished Products in the Business Cycle," in *Economic Essays in Honor of Wesley Clair Mitchell,* New York: Columbia University Press, 1934, 211-67.
33. Machlup, F. "Theories of the Firm: Marginalist, Behavioral, Managerial," *American Economic Review,* 57 (March, 1967), 1-33.
34. Malinvaud, E. "Estimation et Prevision dans les Models Economiques Autoregressifs," *Revue de l'Institut International de Statistique,* 29 (1961), 1-32.
35. Mayer, T. "Plant and Equipment Lead Times," *Journal of Business,* 33 (April, 1960), 127-32.
36. Meyer, J. R. and R. R. Glauber. *Investment Decisions, Economic Forecasting and Public Policy.* Boston: Division of Research, Graduate School of Business Administration, Harvard University, 1964.
37. ———— and E. Kuh. *The Investment Decision.* Cambridge: Harvard University Press, 1957.
38. Miller, M. and F. Modigliani. "Dividend Policy, Growth and the Valuation of Shares," *Journal of Business,* 34 (October, 1961), 411-33.
39. Modigliani, F. and M. Miller. "Corporate Income Taxes and the Cost of Capital: A Correction," *American Economic Review,* 53 (June, 1963), 433-43.
40. ———— and ————. "The Cost of Capital, Corporation Finance, and the Theory of Investment," *American Economic Review,* 48 (June, 1958), 261-97.
41. ———— and ————. "The Cost of Capital, Corporation Finance, and the Theory of Investment: Reply," *American Economic Review,* 49 (September, 1959), 655-69.

42. —————— and ——————. "The Cost of Capital, Corporation Finance, and the Theory of Investment: Reply," *American Economic Review*, 55 (June, 1965), 524-7.

43. —————— and ——————. "Some Estimates of the Cost of Capital to the Electric Utility Industry, 1954-57," *American Economic Review*, 56 (June, 1966), 333-91.

44. *Moody's Industrial Manual.* New York: Moody's Investors Service, various annual issues.

45. Nerlove, M. "Distributed Lags and Demand Analysis of Agricultural and Other Commodities," *USDA Agriculture Handbook No. 141*, Washington, D.C.: Superintendent of Documents, June, 1958.

46. Roos, C. F. "The Demand for Investment Goods," *American Economic Review*, 38 (May, 1948), 311-20.

47. —————— and V. S. Von Szeliski. "The Demand for Durable Goods," *Econometrica*, 11 (April, 1943), 97-122.

48. Simon, H. "New Developments in the Theory of the Firm," *American Economic Review*, 52 (May, 1962), 1-15.

49. Solow, R. M. "On a Family of Lag Distributions," *Econometrica*, 28 (April, 1960), 399-406.

50. *Standard Corporation Descriptions.* New York: Standard and Poor's Corporation, various annual issues.

51. Tinbergen, J. "Statistical Evidence on the Accelerator Principle," *Economica*, N. S., 5 (May, 1938), 164-76.

52. ——————. *Statistical Testing of the Business Cycle Theories, Vol 1: A Method and Its Application to Investment Activity,* Geneva: League of Nations, 1939.

53. U. S. Department of Commerce, Office of Business Economics. *Business Statistics: A Supplement to the Survey of Current Business,* various biennial issues.

54. ——————. *Survey of Current Business,* various monthly issues.

55. ——————. *U. S. Income and Output: A Supplement to the Survey of Current Business,* 1958.

56. U. S. Department of Labor, Bureau of Labor Statistics. *Wholesale Prices and Price Indexes,* various monthly issues.

57. Walters, A.A. "Production and Cost Functions: An Econometric Survey," *Econometrica.* 31 (April, 1963), 1-66.

ON THE COGNITIVE CONTENT OF ECONOMETRIC MODELS

Joseph F. Hanna
Michigan State University

ABSTRACT

An adequate understanding of the cognitive content of econometric analyses requires an explicit rendering of conceptual distinctions that are rarely noted in econometric practice.[1] The present paper is an attempt to improve our understanding of this cognitive content by clarifying the relationships among the four concepts of prediction, forecasting, explanation, and description. It appears that much of the confusion and controversy surrounding the evaluation of econometric models is due to economists failing to distinguish between a prediction and a forecast and between an explanation and a description.

Part I is devoted to the former distinction and Part II is devoted to the latter distinction. The intuitive rationale for the proposed definitions lies in notions from information theory. In brief, the explanatory (or predictive) power of a stochastic model is identified with information taken from (or transmitted by) the environment (e.g., the exogenous variables), while the descriptive power of a model reflects additional information taken from (or transmitted by) the data (i.e., the endogenous variables).

INTRODUCTION

At the beginning of his book *Econometric Models and Methods*, Carl Christ states the objectives of econometrics ". . . . to be the production of quantitative economic statements that either explain the behavior of variables that we have already seen, or forecast (i.e., predict) behavior that we have not yet seen, or both."[2] He goes on to point out that the terms "forecast" and "prediction" are being used interchangeably to refer to statements about behavior that has not yet been observed by the maker of the statements at the time the statements are made.

In a sense the present paper may be viewed as a lengthy footnote to this seemingly unproblematic statement of objectives. For I wish to argue that Christ has on the one hand collapsed an important distinction between a scientific *prediction* and a mere *forecast*, while on the other hand he has failed altogether to distinguish between an *explanation* and a *description*. The distinction between explanation and prediction has been much discussed in recent philosophic literature, but the equally important distinction between explanation and description has received very little attention. Similarly, the distinction between asserting that an event has occurred and explaining its occurrence is universally accepted, but the corresponding distinction between asserting that an event will occur (i.e., forecasting it) and predicting its occurrence is seldom recognized.

The principal objective of the present paper is to define or explicate these four concepts, thereby enabling one to say when a stochastic econometric model provides an explanation (rather than a mere description) or when it yields scientific predictions (rather than mere forecasts). The concept of transmitted information is the basis for distinguishing between the explanatory or predictive power of a model on the one hand and its descriptive power on the other hand. In brief, explanatory or predictive power is identified with information transmitted by empirical factors (e.g., values of exogenous variables) which can be determined prior to the data, while descriptive power is identified with total transmitted information, including information transmitted by the data (i.e., by endogenous variables). Thus, the difference between the descriptive power and the explanatory or predictive power of a theory can be attributed to information transmitted by the data itself.

It is noteworthy that despite the logical similarity of explanation and prediction (pointed to by Hempel and others), predictive inference seems to play a much more basic role than explanation in econometrics. This contrasts sharply with the situation in the physical sciences where (at least at the level of theory) explanation appears to be the more basic of the two concepts. There are several possible reasons for this inversion: e.g., the "local" nature of econometric models as contrasted with the more "global" physical theories, or the greater complexity of phenomena in economics. However, one significant factor contributing to the dominant role of predictive inference may be the difficult problem in econometrics of distinguishing "after the fact" between explanation and description. When we "fit" a linear regression model to past observations, for instance, is the resulting account explanatory or descriptive; does the linear model explain the data or simply describe it? The present analysis should be helpful in answering such questions.

Because of the pragmatic, if not logical, priority of prediction in econometrics the strategy followed in this paper is to focus on the concept of prediction, contrasting it with forecasting and description. The relationship between explanation and description will then follow as a corollary of this analysis.

ECONOMIC PREDICTION AND ECONOMIC FORECASTING

In everyday discourse any declarative statement about the future counts as a prediction and aside from the question of their success or failure "after the fact" there seem to be few generally accepted criteria for separating reasonable from unreasonable predictions. According to this usage the declarative statement, "Next year's Gross National Product (GNP) will exceed this year's GNP," is a *bona fide* prediction, even in the absence of any supporting evidence. Moreover, if I were to make this "prediction" today, its scope would not extend beyond next year. Indeed, if the GNP does rise next year then this specific prediction will have been verified for all time. However, this everyday use of the term "prediction" is much broader than its use in the context of science. I propose, therefore, to reserve the term "prediction" for the narrow scientific context and use the term "forecast" to cover the broader "ordinary language" context. In line with this proposal I will speak of future-tensed statements that are unsupported by evidence or acceptable argumentation as *forecasts*, while future-tensed statements embedded in a general scientific theory and supported by evidence I will call *predictions*.

However, the presence of supporting evidence is not the only feature that distinguishes predictions from forecasts. In fact, the most significant feature of scientific predictions is their generality or unlimited scope. Predictions, unlike forecasts, can never be conclusively verified because their scope extends over all future time. In order to clarify this point, it is helpful to analyze the structure of scientific prediction in greater detail.

Generally speaking, evidence presented in support of a scientific prediction consists of sentences of two sorts: namely, (i) descriptions of initial conditions and (ii) general laws of either deterministic or stochastic form. Thus, in this respect prediction seems to conform to Hempel's model of explanation.[3] If an economist predicts, for instance, that the value of a certain endogenous variable will increase as a function of changes in the values of relevant exogenous variables, he typically justifies his prediction in terms of at least vaguely articulated theoretical considerations, in addition to pointing to "initial conditions" represented by the observed values of the exogenous variables.

However, it might appear that the evidence included in the description of initial conditions would by itself provide adequate grounds for an acceptable scientific prediction. The following example illustrates this possibility. Consider a prediction of future aggregate consumption based upon a known change in aggregate income (resulting, say, from increased taxes). Loosely speaking, we may think of income as an independent or stimulus variable and of consumption as a dependent or response variable. An economist's prediction might take this form: if income during period t is y^* then consumption during period t will be c^*. Or more likely, the economist, recognizing the presence of stochastic disturbances, will phrase his prediction in terms of expected values or probabilities. Thus, his prediction might take the form:[4]

A. If aggregate income during period t is y^* then with probability p, aggregate consumption will be c^*; or in short, $Pr(c^*|y^*) = p$. Statement A appears to be a legitimate scientific prediction, involving initial conditions but, at least on the face of it, not involving any theoretical considerations. However, there are good grounds for arguing that A is itself a theoretical statement; at any rate, its interpretation involves theoretical considerations. Moreover, the theoretical content of A is not simply due to its being a probability statement: indeed, A would have theoretical content even if it expressed a uniform regularity between income and consumption.

Notice first of all that A *does not* refer to a specific concrete event; the significance of the prediction is that an aggregate income y*, *whenever it occurs during an appropriate period*, will give rise to aggregate consumption c* with probability p. Predictions in the empirical sciences characteristically refer to event types rather than to specific concrete events. It is precisely this feature which distinguishes predictions from mere forecasts. Thus in asserting statement A the economist is making a commitment which goes beyond any specific time period or any specific observation. Indeed, his commitment extends to all time periods during which the structure of the consumption sector of the economy remains constant. It may not be possible to determine, in practice, whether the structure of the economy has remained constant from one period to the next but, on the assumption that it has, all conditional predictions covering the first period remain in force during ensuing periods. In short, the scope of a scientific prediction is, in principle, never limited to a specific observation or event. Rather, the projection covers every recurrence of that event, regardless of the *accidental* circumstances (i.e., stochastic disturbances) under which it recurs. This highly significant feature of prediction is made explicit in the following *Condition of Predictive Consistency*:

CPC. If one predicts on the basis of evidence s that event r will occur with probability p, then one is committed to project r with probability p under any circumstances in which the evidence statement s is true.

In particular, the prediction that s and r are uniformly associated commits one to project r on *every* occurrence in which s is realized.

The gist of the condition of predictive consistency is that in science predictions never refer specifically to concrete events, but rather always refer to *events under a description*—hence to events which may repeat themselves. It follows, therefore, that predictions (unlike forecasts) can never be established (or disconfirmed) beyond question. The relevance of any particular observation, e.g., that aggregate income and consumption during period t_1 are y* and c*, respectively, is to a great extent a theoretical issue. This observation is relevant to prediction A if and only if the structure of the economy is the same during period t_1 as it was during period t. However, this latter issue is clearly not a straightforward matter of observation; in general, it involves highly theoretical considerations.

A further consequence of the above analysis is that the evidence upon which scientific predictions are based never consists simply of initial conditions. In the case of experimental sciences the additional theoretical content of predictions has to do with the conditions under which a specific experiment (say, as conducted by Jones in his laboratory) can be said to have been replicated (say, by Smith working in another laboratory). In the case of a quasi-experimental science such as macroeconomics, the additional theoretical content has to do with the conditions under which a specific economic structure can be said to have remained constant. Thus, in order to obtain a clearer view of the logic of economic prediction it is necessary to consider the concept of *structure* in greater detail.

According to Christ

> A *structure* is a set of autonomous relationships describing the complex of economic features that do not change during a given period. An equivalent definition, often used in econometrics, is this: a *structure* is a set of autonomous relationships sufficient to determine the numerical values of the endogenous variables, given the values of the exogenous variables.[5]

According to this conventional usage, a structure is a set of *formal* relationships among numerical variables (the products of measurement) rather than a set of empirical relationships among underlying empirical variables. However, following Suppes' distinction between formal and empirical relational systems it seems worthwhile to distinguish in the present context between formal (or theoretical) structures and empirical structures.[6] Let us turn first to the concept of empirical structure.

In general, economists recognize variables of three sorts: (i) *exogenous variables* which are, so to speak, "generated from outside" the economic sector under investigation and are in some sense directly under the economist's (or policy maker's) control, (ii) *endogenous* variables which are "generated from within" the economic sector under investigation and which are only indirectly under the economist's (or policy maker's) control, and (iii) a residue of variables (some recognized and some unrecognized) which may be subject to direct control, but which are viewed (at least within certain bounds) as accidental or noise features of the situation. For instance, the exogenous variable in the economic analysis considered above is aggregate income (which can be manipulated directly by wage and tax policies, etc.); the endogenous variable is aggregate consumption(which can only be influenced indirectly by policy decisions); and the residual environment consists of all the "accidental" features of the situation, including the state of other sectors of the economy that have not entered explicitly into the conditional prediction.

However, in actual practice the division of environmental factors into exogenous variables and residual variables is often not so straightforward. In fact, there is usually a class of variables on the borderline between these two categories: variables which may be treated explicitly as part of the empirical structure for some purposes, but treated as residual environment for other purposes. To some extent, these "background" variables serve to delimit the empirical structure, since in general any significant change in their values produces a new structure.[7]

Specific economic analyses are always formulated within the context of a theoretical framework which determines (at least vaguely) limiting or boundary conditions for the variables constituting the residual environment. In a sense, these boundary conditions define the limits of the empirical structure which the proffered economic analysis is intended to cover. The situation can be represented abstractly as follows. Let S be the set of possible values of the exogenous (stimulus) variables, let R be the set of possible values of the endogenous (response) variables, and let V be the set of possible values of the residual variables. There will often be several exogenous and endogenous variables, but since one can treat n distinct variables as a single variable whose values are ordered n-tuples, the above representation involves no essential loss of generality.

Now, a *specific empirical structure* e may be viewed as an ordered pair e = $<$s, v$>$, where s ε S and v ε V. A *generic empirical structure* E is a class of specific structures such that if $<$s, v$>$ and $<$s', v'$>$ belong to E, then $<$s, v'$>$ and $<$s', v$>$ belong to E. Let E be a generic structure, then the domain S_E of E constitutes the set of *initial conditions* for the generic structure, and the range V_E of E constitutes the set of *boundary conditions*.[8] A specific structure e is *an instance of* a generic structure E if e satisfies both the initial and boundary conditions of E, i.e., if e ε E.

For the most part boundary conditions are simply implicit in an economic analysis; it is recognized that when certain residual variables change in value the effect is to modify the economic structure, while the economic structure is relatively immune to changes in other residual variables. Boundary conditions become an explicit concern only when the economist is faced with anomalous observations (e.g., endogenous variables which do not behave as theory predicts they should) or when the limits of applicability of a formal model or theory are at issue. Moreover, doubts as to whether boundary conditions have been met by a specific empirical structure are often resolved in terms of vague, almost pretheoretic, intuitions regarding what is "going on" in the sector of the economy under analysis. For instance, an economic analysis involving a linear regression of consumption on income might be rejected because of a pronouncement during the prediction period of a future income tax rebate. The form and content of government pronouncements is a residual variable which under most conditions would not play a critical role in this economic analysis. However, some values of this residual variable are of sufficient significance to warrant the assertion that boundary conditions for the application of the regression model have been violated, or equivalently, that the economic structure of the consumption sector has changed. This generic empirical structure is conceived in a theoretical framework in which the factor of government pronouncements of future tax policy is judged to be relevant or related in a lawlike manner to consumption behavior. On the other hand, government pronouncements of a future increase in the defense budget or of an appointment to the Supreme Court would usually not constitute grounds for arguing that the structure of the economy has changed from some earlier period. These factors would more likely be viewed as "stochastic disturbances" of a fixed generic structure.

In other words, certain residual variables may appear in the light of general theoretical considerations to be related in a lawlike manner to the behavior of a sector of the economy being analyzed; other residual variables may appear to be only accidental or noise features of the given economic sector. The more relevant or lawlike a particular residual factor is thought to be, the more narrowly and exactly the generic empirical structure will circumscribe the boundary conditions associated with that factor. Those factors which are obviously and highly relevant (but are not explicitly treated as exogenous variables) may be thought of as determinants of the empirical structure and the economist will look to their behavior in deciding whether the structure has remained constant from one period to the next. Other factors are simply viewed as stochastic disturbances and only become a concern when predictions fail or seemingly anomalous behavior is observed.

The above considerations lead to a more exact and complete statement of the condition of predictive consistency presented earlier. In a sense, the revised condition CPC* specifies the cognitive content of economic predictions, thereby indicating the extent to which they involve a commitment which goes beyond that of mere economic forecasts.

CPC*. Let E be a generic empirical structure and E_S be the initial conditions of E (i.e., E_S is a set of values of the exogenous variables). Then to predict that with probability p, the initial condition E_S will bring about an effect E_R (where E_R is a subset of possible values of the endogenous variables) is to assert that in any infinite, random sequence of instances of E, the limiting relative frequency of event E_R is p.

The phrase "random sequence of instances" is to be interpreted as follows: $e_1,...,e_n,...$ is a random sequence of instances of E provided that the values v_i, $i = 1,2,...,n,...$ of the residual variables are a random sample subject to the constraints imposed by the boundary conditions; that is, if they are randomly sampled from V_E. Or stated somewhat differently, the sequence is random if the values of the endogenous variables can be viewed as the product of a "stochastic disturbance" acting on a fixed generic empirical structure.

With this revised condition of predictive consistency in mind, we turn now to the problem of defining measures of predictive and descriptive power of econometric models of generic empirical structures.

INFORMATION MEASURES FOR TESTING
STOCHASTIC MODELS

Predictive Power of Formal Structures

Formal models (usually stochastic in nature) represent a common source of predictions in economics. Such models, when applied to a generic empirical structure (e.g., the consumption sector of the economy) assign probabilities to the possible values of endogenous variables as a function of (i) initial conditions (i.e., observed values of exogenous variables) and (ii) certain model parameters whose values are either independently measured or else estimated from the data. It is customary to refer to a model with fixed parameter values as a structure; however, I will use the term "formal structure" to distinguish the set of autonomous formal relationships among numerical variables from the empirical relationships which hold among the underlying economic variables.

Thus, every value $\alpha = <\alpha_1,...,\alpha_k>$ in the parameter space p of a model determines a formal structure. Strictly speaking, models do not yield predictions; it is only when a formal structure has been specified by estimating parameters that a joint density function over the endogenous variables is determined.

Formally, a *model for a generic empirical structure* E is a function M whose domain is a class of ordered pairs, the first member of a pair ranging over the parameter space p and the second member ranging over the set S of initial conditions, and whose value for a fixed argument is a joint density function over the set R of possible values of the endogenous variables. A *formal structure*, M_α, $\alpha \; \varepsilon$ p, is a function of one argument obtained by fixing the parameter values. Let M_α, $\alpha \; \varepsilon$ p, be a formal structure for an empirical structure E, and $s \; \varepsilon$ S, $r \; \varepsilon$ R be observed values of the exogenous and endogenous variables, respectively, then $P_\alpha(r|s)$ is the probability (determined by the formal structure M_α) of r given s.[9] We say that the formal structure M is a *true representation* of a generic empirical structure E (with initial conditions s*) if all predictions of M regarding E are true. However, in view of CPC* this means that M is a true representation of E if $P_\alpha(r|s^*) = f_\infty(r|s^*)$ for every value $r \; \varepsilon$ R, where $f_\infty \; (r|s^*)$ is the limiting relative frequency of r in an infinite, random sequence of instances of E.

A formal structure determines a joint density function over endogenous variables as a function of exogenous variables and thereby generates statistical predictions. However, the correctness of these predictions cannot be assessed with complete reliability on the basis of any finite amount of data; ultimately, their correctness depends on the limiting frequencies of observed values of endogenous variables in certain infinite sequences of instances of the generic empirical structure. But since in practice we are forced to accept, revise, and reject stochastic models before all the data are in, it is essential to have some reliable means for tentatively assessing the predictive success or predictive power of formal structures on the basis of limited data.

The concept of information provides an intuitive measure of predictive power with several desirable formal properties. Any observation, e.g., the behavior of some sector of the economy during a given time period, may be viewed as containing a fixed amount of information, the quantity depending on the observer's background of knowledge and belief. For instance, in glancing out the window to see if snow has fallen during the night, I obtain an amount of information which generally depends on the actual state of affairs as well as upon my beliefs regarding the a priori likelihood of various meteorological events. If it is a June morning and the ground is covered with snow, the observation will be quite informative, because surprising; if it is a January morning with snow on the ground, the observation will convey less information. Thus, the information content of an observation depends on the unexpectedness of its outcome; I am informed by an observation just to the extent that its outcome is surprising when considered in the context of my other beliefs.

Following the classic work of Shanon, we adopt the logarithm of the likelihood as a numerical measure of information.[10] Specifically, let e be an empirical structure with initial conditions s and outcome r, and let $P_o(r|s)$ be the a priori (or pre-theoretic) probability that the observed value s of the exogenous variables will result in the value r of the endogenous variables, then the *a priori information content of e given outcome* r is

$$I_o = \log_k 1/P_o(r|s),$$

where k is the unit of information.

The a priori probability of a specific structure is determined in large part by vaguely articulated theoretical considerations. A particular outcome may appear improbable, and thus informative, simply on the basis of introspection or intuition, or possibly in view of previous behavior of the sector of the economy. Often, there will be no good reason to consider one outcome any more likely than another; in such cases the *principle of insufficient reason* suggests that all outcomes be assigned equal a priori probability.

The effect of an articulated theory (e.g., a stochastic model) is to alter the a priori probabilities of the possible values of endogenous variables. The revised probabilities determined by a formal theory will be referred to as a posteriori (or post-theoretic) probabilities. In altering the a priori likelihood of a given observation, a formal theory also alters its uncertainty or surprise value and thereby alters its information content. Specifically, if the a posteriori probability of the observed outcome *exceeds* its a priori probability, then the formal theory has accounted for some of the a priori information in the observation. On the other hand, if the a posteriori probability of the observed outcome is *less* than its a priori probability, then the formal theory is misinformative. Or using somewhat different terminology, we may say that if it increases the likelihood, a formal theory *transmits* information concerning the observation, while if it decreases the likelihood, it transmits misinformation.

These considerations lead to the following coefficient of predictive power. Let e be a specific empirical structure with initial conditions s and outcome r. Let I_o be the a priori information content of e given r and let $P_\alpha(r|s)$ be the a posteriori probability determined by the formal structure M_α. Then the *coefficient of predictive power of M_α relative to* e *and* r is

$$(1) \quad I_\alpha = I_o - \log_k 1/P_\alpha(r|s).$$

The measure I_α, or variants of it, has been introduced by several authors in connection with hypothesis testing and statistical inference and it can be given various interpretations. In the first place, I_α is the difference in the a priori and a posteriori information content of the observation associated with the empirical structure e; hence, it measures the information transmitted by the formal structure M_α concerning the outcome of e.[11] Viewing matters from a different perspective, Kullback has referred to a variant of I_α as the information in observation e for discriminating in favor of the a posteriori probability distribution determined by M_α as against the a priori probability distribution.[12] Finally, I_α can be algebraically transformed into the logarithm of the likelihood ratio, a measure which has a history in statistics dating back to the early work of Fisher.

Since I_α is to be a measure of predictive power, it is important that it be compatible with the Condition of Predictive Consistency (CPC*). This compatibility is insured by the following property of the measure.[13] Let E be a generic empirical structure. Then (i) within the class of formal structures for E, the true representation of E has the maximum expected predictive power over any infinite random sequence of instances of E; and (ii) every monotone function of the likelihood with property (i) is a log-linear transformation of I_α.

In effect, property (i) affirms that in the long run the true theory will have the largest coefficient of predictive power, and property (ii) asserts that the coefficient of predictive power is unique up to the choice of a unit of information k and the constant I_o.

It is convenient to adopt the inverse of the a priori likelihood as the unit of information. Thus we take $k = 1/P_o(r|s)$. As a result the coefficient of predictive power becomes:

$$(2) \quad I_\alpha = 1 - \log_k 1/P_\alpha(r|s).$$

The effect of this choice of unit is to normalize the measure: the coefficient of predictive power becomes the *percentage* of the a priori information which is accounted for by the formal structure. Thus, coefficients of predictive power can be meaningfully compared across empirical structures involving different amounts of a priori information.

Notice that with this choice of unit, the maximum value of predictive power is 1—associated with a posteriori probability 1. On the other hand, if the a posteriori probability is zero, the coefficient of predictive power is undefined. Hence, the measure cannot be applied if a formal structure assigns zero probability to the observed outcome of a specific empirical structure. Finally, if the a posteriori probability of an outcome equals its a priori probability, the coefficient of predictive power is zero, indicating that the formal structure transmits no information or misinformation.

To summarize the above discussion: predictions in economics (unlike economic forecasts) characteristically refer to generic rather than to specific empirical structures. In effect, predictions are open-ended—always subject, in principle, to disconfirmation—irrespective of whether they are deterministic or stochastic in form. Thus, on the one hand, no prediction is ever finally safe from disconfirmation, while, on the other hand, it is in principle always open to the theorist to reject any apparent disconfirmation of a prediction due to failure to meet boundary conditions.

A similar account holds for explanation. Explanations provide answers to "why questions," but the scope of such questions extends over generic empirical structures (i.e., to event types or events under a description); it is never limited just to specific observations (i.e., to concrete events). Though one might account for the past behavior of a given sector of the economy by means of a deductive or statistical explanation, the scope of the proffered explanation would never be limited to those past observations. In particular, failure of the explanation to account for the current behavior of the given sector of the economy would raise doubts, at the very least, about the adequacy of the "original" explanation.

Thus, by analogy with the condition of predictive consistency, to explain why (under appropriate boundary conditions) a given value s of the exogenous variables yields with relative frequency p a value r of the endogenous variables one produces a formal structure M_α such that $P_\alpha(r/s) = p$. This account makes it clear that the adequacy of any particular explanation in economics is again an open-ended question: explanations of uniform regularities, and even more so explanations of stochastic regularities, are unbounded in scope. However, the coefficient of predictive (or explanatory) power enables one to assess the adequacy of such explanations, as well as can be done, on the basis of limited and incomplete data.

Descriptive Power of Models

Although formal models are frequently used in econometrics to generate predictions and provide explanations of empirical phenomena, they undoubtedly function more extensively as descriptions. The purpose of this section is to clarify this distinction between the predictive or explanatory role of models, on the one hand, and their descriptive role, on the other hand.

Broadly speaking, to describe a phenomenon is to classify it or to place it appropriately in a hierarchy of concepts. For example, to describe an imprint in the sand as a human footprint or a set of data points as a straight line, is to place these phenomena in appropriate classes: the class of human footprints and the class of straight lines, respectively. Notice, however, that this aspect of description is not sufficient to distinguish it from explanation and prediction; for as Hempel and others have argued, to explain (or predict) a phenomenon is to bring it under appropriate covering laws, a procedure which at least implicitly involves classification. For example, in explaining a storm on the basis of atmospheric pressure, humidity, temperature, etc., a meteorologist *classifies* the situation as being in a specific way storm-producing. Thus, the distinction between explanation and description involves more than simply the presence or absence of classification.

From the present point of view, the nature of the substantiating evidence provides the basis for distinguishing between an explanatory (or predictive) and a descriptive account of some phenomenon: specifically, the distinction lies in the *source* of the evidence, whether from environmental factors or from the data, that is included in the account. The decision to classify or describe a particular imprint as a human footprint, for example, rests on a consideration of its physical properties: its size and shape, the texture of the sand, etc. In short, the description rests on information that could only be obtained by investigating the imprint. By contrast, explanations and predictions characteristically involve evidence (information) which is temporally prior and logically independent of the event to be explained. Thus, one *describes* the imprint as a human footprint on the basis of its physical properties, and from this description it follows (logically) that the imprint was made by some human (of an appropriate size and shape) moving (in an appropriate manner) on the beach.[14] One *explains* the imprint, on the other hand, as due to some human (of an appropriate size and shape) having moved (in an appropriate manner) on the beach, from which it follows (logically) that the imprint is a human footprint. The distinction depends, then, on the source of the evidence (information) contained in the account.

The linear regression model is typical of descriptive models in econometrics. To describe a set of data points as a straight line is to assert that there exist values of slope and intercept (these parameter values being estimated from the data) such that the resulting straight line fits the data points. Although the context is much less precise, a similar account can be given of the "human footprint" model: to describe an imprint as a human footprint is to assert (on the basis of the physical evidence at hand) that there exist "physical parameters" of the situation—such as someone's having moved at some recent time in an appropriate manner on the beach—in terms of which it is possible to give a satisfactory account of the imprint. Thus, the essential characteristic of description, as opposed to explanation or prediction, is that a substantial portion of the information required for the account is transmitted by the data, rather than by independent environmental factors.

We turn now from this intuitive characterization of description to the more specific context of stochastic econometric models, the goal being to define a formal measure, consistent with the above informal analysis, of the descriptive power of a model. Let E be a generic empirical structure, then a *model M is a true description* of E if there exists some parameter value $\hat{\alpha}\varepsilon p$ such that the formal structure $M\hat{\alpha}$ is a true representation of E. For example, the linear regression model provides a true description of aggregate consumption (as a function of aggregate income) if there exist values of slope (marginal propensity to consume) and intercept such that the resulting straight line is a true representation of the consumption sector of the economy. This notion of a true descriptive model motivates the following definition of descriptive power. Let e be an empirical structure with initial conditions s and outcome r, and let M be a model of e with parameter space p. Then, the *coefficient of descriptive power of model* M *relative to* e *and* r is

$$(3) \quad \hat{I}_M = \max_{\alpha\varepsilon p} I_{\hat{\alpha}},$$

where I_α is the coefficient of predictive power of the formal structure M_α relative to e and r.

Notice that the above measure is consistent with maximum likelihood estimation: the descriptive power of a model reflects the predictive power of the formal structure $M\hat{\alpha}$ associated with the maximum likelihood parameter estimate $\hat{\alpha}$. In effect, the best or "true" parameter value is inferred (by a process of inverse inference) from the data as that value which would make the observed value of the endogenous variables most probable. It is easily seen that the resulting coefficient of descriptive power meets the stipulation that a *true descriptive model of a generic empirical structure should have, in the long run, the maximum possible descriptive power.*

It should be pointed out that although the coefficient of descriptive power reflects information transmitted by the data, a large descriptive power does not necessarily imply an absence of predicative or explanatory power. Indeed, in some instances parameters may be virtually redundant—i.e., the likelihood function may be almost constant—in which case descriptive power and predictive (or explanatory) power would be essentially equivalent. Thus, even when parameters are estimated from the data, a model may have considerable predictive or explanatory power; the likelihood may reflect information transmitted by independent environmental factors (exogenous variables) in addition to reflecting information transmitted by the data (endogenous variables). This point is clarified in the next section.

Predictive Power of Models

Stochastic models are always embedded in a wider theoretical framework which gives them their substance. In many cases, general theoretical considerations enable one to place a priori constraints on the values of model parameters, thereby reducing the amount of information transmitted by the data in the estimation process. In effect, such constraints are a reflection of information (or possibly misinformation) transmitted by independent environmental factors, hence they influence predictive or explanatory power rather than descriptive power. Without loss of generality, we may think of this a priori information about the best or "true" value of a parameter as reflected in a probability distribution $g(\alpha)$ over the parameter space p. Specifically, for $\alpha^* \varepsilon p$, $g(\alpha^*)$ represents the a priori probability that α^* is the best or true value of parameter α.

Information incorporated in the a priori distribution may have several sources. In the first place, it is sometimes possible to identify parameters with environmental factors, e.g., with the values of important residual variables. Such identification is actually a form of measurement, and plays essentially the same role in the social sciences as measurements of coefficients of friction or viscosity might play in applications of the equations of motion in physics. As indicated above, general theoretical considerations may enable one to place constraints on the possible values of model parameters and thus represent a second source of a priori information regarding their true or best values. Finally, previously collected data provide a third source of a priori information about parameter values. In many instances, the econometrician's goal is to estimate model parameters from one set of data and then project the estimated values to new data. When this is possible, i.e., when parameters are sufficiently invariant across observation periods so that the empirical structure may be assumed constant, we may think of the original data as providing a measurement of the parameters, the result being reflected in a probability distribution over the parameter space.

When independent information concerning the best or true parameter values is unavailable, we may apply the *principle of insufficient reason* and consider all parameter values equally likely. This amounts to adopting the uniform probability distribution over the parameter space.

A *model* M together with an a priori probability distribution g determines a *formal structure* M_g according to the following expected likelihood equation:

$$(4) \quad P_g(r|s) = \int_{\alpha \varepsilon \rho} g(\alpha) \cdot P_\alpha(r|s) \cdot d\alpha,$$

where s and r represent, respectively, the initial conditions and outcome of some specific empirical structure e, and $P_\alpha(r|s)$ is the a posteriori probability of r determined by the formal structure M_α. Thus, the likelihood associated with M_g is the expected value of the likelihoods associated with the formal structures M_α, $\alpha \varepsilon p$, weighted in each instance by the a priori probability that α is the best or true parameter value. The resulting expected likelihood clearly reflects information transmitted by environmental factors rather than information transmitted by the data; for this reason it figures centrally in the following definition of a coefficient of predictive power for models.

Let e be a specific empirical structure with initial conditions s and outcome r, and let M be a model of e with parameter space *p*. Finally, let $g(\alpha)$ be an a priori probability distribution over *p*. Then, by analogy with Eq. 2, the *coefficient of predictive power of* M *relative to* e, r, *and* g is

$$(5) \quad \bar{I}_M = 1 - \log_k 1/P_g(r|s),$$

where $k = 1/P_0(r|s)$ is the unit of information and $P_g(r|s)$ is given by Eq. 4.

By virtue of the a priori distribution g, the coefficient $\bar{I}_M$ reflects information transmitted by exogenous variables, either from previous applications of the model or through theoretical restrictions on parameter values. Moreover, the coefficient of predictive power is independent of the estimation of parameters, so that it does not reflect information transmitted by the data. On the other hand, the coefficient of descriptive power (cf. Eq. 3) is a measure of the total information content of the model, reflecting information transmitted by the data as well as information transmitted by independent environmental factors. Hence, the difference

$$(6) \quad \Delta I_M = \hat{I}_M - \bar{I}_M,$$

which is always non-negative, is a measure of the information transmitted by (or taken from) the data. Since this information is transmitted, for the most part, through estimation of parameters, it is natural to think of ΔI_M as a measure of the power or *effect of model parameters*. In fact, this information measure appears to play much the same role as the notion of "degrees of freedom" in statistical hypothesis testing. One might suppose, for instance, that the information taken from the data in estimating parameters would correspond at least roughly with the number of free parameters estimated. Surprisingly, this is not the case.

This completes the formal development of the measures of predictive and descriptive power. These measures provide intuitively plausible distinctions among the notions of description, prediction, and explanation. In summary, we might say that a stochastic econometric model is *purely descriptive* if all information is transmitted by factors that are logically or semantically connected with the data (i.e., the observed values of endogenous variables); the model is *purely predictive* if all information is transmitted by logically and semantically independent factors and, moreover, there is no "direct" evidence for the data; and, finally, an account is *purely explanatory* if all information is transmitted by independent environmental, factors, but there exists independent evidence for the data (e.g., such evidence as eye-witness accounts, government statistics, or reports in the scientific literature). Finally, the present analysis also provides an important distinction between prediction and forecasting. These precise distinctions should increase our understanding of the cognitive content of stochastic econometric models.

NOTES

[1]The term "cognitive content" has been used by Karl Brunner to refer to the methodological status of quantitative economic propositions. The present paper is intended to further his work in formulating a more precise meaning for this term.

ON THE COGNITIVE CONTENT OF ECONOMETRIC MODELS 237

[2]Christ, C. *Econometric Models and Methods.* New York: Wiley, 1966, p. 4.

[3]Cf. Hempel, C. G. *Aspects of Sciencific Explanation, and Other Essays in the Philosophy of Science.* New York: The Free Press, 1965.

[4]In general, a stochastic prediction may take the form of an expected value of the endogenous variable or of a probability distribution over the possible values of the endogenous variable (cf. Christ, p. 28).

[5]Christ (1966), p. 21.

[6]Cf. Suppes, P., and J. Zinnes. "Basic Measurement Theory." In Luce, R. D., Bush, R. R., and Galanter, E. (Eds.) *Handbook of Mathematical Psychology*, Vol. 1. New York: Wiley (1963), 1-76.

[7]Christ (1966, p. 12) refers to such factors as parameters of the structure, but this terminology may lead to confusion with parameters of a formal model.

[8]The *domain* of a set of ordered pairs is the class of first members of the pairs and the *range* (or *converse domain*) is the class of second members of the pairs. The significance of the above definition of a generic structure is that the boundary conditions should not depend on which initial condition is present in any specific instance of the structure.

[9]Notice that r and s are the observed values of empirical variables, while the formal relationships which lead to the probability P_α (r|s) will typically involve a measurement (operational definition) of these variables.

[10]Cf. Shanon, C. E., and W. Weaver. *The Mathematical Theory of Communication.* Urbana, Illinois: University of Illinois Press, 1949.

[11]Cf. Hanna, J. F. "A New Approach to the Formulation and Testing of Learning Models," *Synthese* 16:344-80 (1966).

[12]Kullback, S. *Information Theory and Statistics.* New York: Wiley, 1959.

[13]For a proof of properties *i* and *ii* see Hanna (1966), p. 370.

[14]If the imprint were not made in some manner or another by a human foot, we might say that it was "like a human footprint" or that it was "an imitation of a human footprint," but we would not say that it *was* a human footprint.

ECONOMETRIC MODEL CONSTRUCTION AND PREDICTIVE TESTING*

Jon Cunnyngham
The Ohio State University

Econometricians like to think of themselves as scientists, and their methods as scientific. Students of the philosophy of science, on the other hand, have not had any notable success in relating the formal concepts of scientific method or the logic of scientific explanation and theory construction to either the method or the theory of econometrics. This, of course, does not necessarily imply that econometric theory and practice are nonscientific.

It does suggest, however, that there currently is relatively little professional interest in such methodological problems. This is quite understandable: the last decade has seen the creation of many new economic and econometric theories, and the construction of numerous associated quantitative models; it has witnessed the discovery and active use of new mathematical, statistical, and data-processing tools. In the scramble to absorb these new theories and tools, and apply them to current economic problems, the study of associated methodological problems frequently has been pushed aside. Perhaps this is as it should be.

But the lack of interest in methodological discourse, I fear,

*This essay represents a compression and clarification of the paper, "An Attempted Synthesis of the Theories of Econometric Construction and Predictive Testing," presented at the first OSU Conference on Econometrics on May 18-19, 1967. The comments of Robert L. Basmann, Karl Brunner, and Leonid Hurwicz have resulted in substantial improvements in this version. I am particularly indebted to the extended discussion and many helpful comments of Karl Brunner, whose continued interest and encouragement have been most appreciated.

goes beyond any implied priorities associated with the allocation of scarce research resources. It suffers most of all from a bad reputation. A prevalent attitude toward students of the philosophy of science appears to be patterned after the well-known cliché about university professors: "Those who can, do. Those who can't, write on methodology."

Although it may be of little consolation to current workers in the field, a similar attitude was prevalent toward mathematical economics not so very long ago. Until quite recently the works of mathematical economists were frequently defensive in tone and prefaced with extensive remarks concerning the importance and superiority of their methods. The hostility and misunderstanding they apparently perceived was very real; their work was generally considered to be insignificant, full of spurious profundity and rigor revolving around the manipulation of obscure symbolic languages and concepts. I cannot hope to live up to these high standards in this essay.

Instead, my hope is to develop an "inductive process" theory of econometric model construction and, in this fashion, focus on some of the problems involved in the predictive testing of economic theories and the construction of econometric models. Within the context of this inductive process theory I shall define several conditions that seem to be necessary for the predictive testing of economic theories.

THE INDUCTIVE PROCESS HYPOTHESIS

For illustrative purposes, consider a specific example borrowed from theoretical mechanics of a theory incorporating an inductive process hypothesis.[1] The theory asserts that the linear expansion of a metal rod as the temperature of the rod is increased may be accurately predicted by the following structural equation:

$$(1) \quad \Delta L = \alpha L_0 \Delta T,$$

where ΔL represents the linear expansion of a metal rod, L_0 represents the original length of the rod, ΔT represents the change in temperature, and α is called the coefficient of linear expansion. This is the complete specification of the invariant *structural form* of the theory. In a normal laboratory environment where nothing is expected to occur that would change the structure of the equation, the theory can be tested for its predictive accuracy at any time.

But consider for a moment a different kind of environment,

one where uncontrolled or uncontrollable changes can be expected to occur in the environment which will "cause" the structure of the equation to change. How can the theory be tested for its predictive accuracy in this kind of a situation? What additional information or specifications are required to test the theory if its structural form is not expected to be invariant over time, but instead, to change as the environment changes?

Clearly, what is required to test the theory in this situation is a precise specification of the environmental conditions under which the theory is presumed to hold. We cannot, after all, afford to reject the theory simply because it fails to predict accurately at all times. Even if the theory is correct as stated it will tend to produce inaccurate predictions whenever the structural form it specifies does not correspond to the form appropriate to the environment at that point in time. To insure that the theory is not falsely rejected, therefore, the specification of its structural form must be accompanied by additional specifications which serve to identify the environmental states for which it is defined. Only then will a user of the theory know when the theory is presumed to hold, and when a rejection of its structural form is also a rejection of the theory.

Before returning to the metal rods example, let us summarize the two conditions we have discussed so far which appear to be necessary for the predictive testing of economic theories. To be completely defined, scientific theories should specify two types of testable propositions. First, they should specify an invariant structural hypothesis, a hypothesis setting forth a structure of relationships representing a comprehensive explanation of some process, postulated as being "parameter invariant" under certain specific conditions. In the metal rods example the invariant structural hypothesis was symbolized by equation (1).

Secondly, they should specify an auxiliary hypothesis setting forth the relationship between this structural hypothesis and the specific conditions under which the structure is postulated as being parameter invariant. These specific conditions are typically referred to as either "states of nature" or "environmental states" or "initial conditions," depending on the substantive field of application. Let us elaborate on this second proposition a bit further. In the metal rods example the auxiliary hypothesis relates changes in the parameter of the structural relationship to a specific set of environmental states in the laboratory. It does this by specifying that *the constant of proportionality*, called the coefficient of linear expansion, *is different for different metals*.

In this essay an auxiliary hypothesis of this sort is called an "inductive process" hypothesis. As indicated above, its purpose is to complete the specification of a theory by defining the relationship between specific environmental states and the invariant structural hypothesis. The inductive process hypothesis in the metal rods example is defined by a list of metals (and other substances) with a constant of proportionality specified for each metal. The name of a specific metal in the list of metals can then be used to uniquely identify a specific inductive process for which the equation of linear expansion is expected to provide accurate predictions.

Once the specification of the inductive hypothesis is complete the testing and use of the structural hypothesis should be restricted to those situations where specific inductive processes are defined. In the metal rods example the equation of linear expansion (1) should be presumed true and operational only when it is verified that the coefficient of linear expansion α has been set to the value specified for the metal under observation.

Having introduced the concept of an inductive process, perhaps we should now explain more fully why we did. After all, economists and other social scientists have somehow managed to test and use theories up until now without introducing it. And it must be admitted that its application to the metal rods example doesn't exactly open up new research vistas in theoretical mechanics.

Let us begin our explanation with the proposition that the development of a theory, however naive it may be, always begins with the assumption that something remains *constant*. In applying this proposition to economic theories involving the construction of an econometric model, we have found it useful to break the model into two parts. First, we conceptually separate out from the rest of the model the kernel of the theory, putting in the first part those relationships which symbolize whatever the theory assumes will remain constant. This part constitutes what we have referred to as the *invariant structural form*. If the theory does not seem to contain at least one invariant structural hypothesis, then in this schema we must sharpen our pencil and try again, for until such an hypothesis has been identified the theory cannot be empirically validated or used. This is obviously a strong prescription, and may seem a bit presumptuous at first. However, we believe that it represents the essential core around which the concept of a "scientific" theory, as the term is generally understood, can be developed without diminished force in the social sciences.

Even when an invariant structural form has been identified, however, only two types of situations appear to exist in which an econometric model can be expected to produce accurate predictions.

The first occurs whenever the model is believed to be independent of all possible environmental states that could change its structure. Unfortunately, such beliefs are rarely justified in the social sciences, and unconditional models of this type are seldom confirmed. The second type of situation occurs whenever the econometric model is believed to be parameter invariant within a limited set of specific environmental conditions. We have conceptually broken the model into two parts to keep the specification of these limiting conditions separate and distinct from the structural hypothesis. In the second part, therefore, we put all the relationships which relate the parameters of the invariant structural form to specific (testable) environmental states. This part of the theory constitutes what we have referred to as the *inductive process hypothesis*. This, in brief, is the basic scientific rationale of the inductive process theory of econometric model construction.

The distinction between a theory and the initial or environmental states of its structural representation exists, of course, in all branches of science. However, in the physical sciences where controlled experiments are usually possible the specification of required initial or environmental conditions is often relegated to a much lower scientific status than the statement of the general physical theory, the determination of proper conditions being dependent on little more than good laboratory technique. In the social sciences the "historically conditioned" character of the stochastic processes makes the specification of environmental conditions in an inductive process hypothesis a somewhat more significant achievement.

To further clarify the concept of an inductive function, we shall turn once more to theoretical mechanics for an illustration of how the inductive process theory can be applied. Let us now consider one of the most renowned theories in theoretical mechanics, Newton's laws of motion for point-masses.[2] This theory states that the time-rate of change in the momentum of a point-mass can be accurately predicted by an invariant system of equations, called the "equations of motion":

$$(2) \quad m\frac{d^2x}{dt^2} = F_x \quad m\frac{d^2y}{dt^2} = F_y \quad m\frac{d^2z}{dt^2} = F_z$$

where m is the mass, t is time, and x, y, and z are spatial coordinates. However, this invariant physical system cannot produce accurate predictions until an auxiliary function, called the "force function," has been specified. The force function completes the specification of the laws of motion by defining the relationship between specific physical environments and the invariant equations of motion. For example, when analyzing the motion of a freely falling body near the surface of the earth, with the spatial coordinates oriented so that the z-axis is perpendicular to the earth's surface, the force function takes the specific form

$$(3) \quad F_x = 0 \qquad F_y = 0 \qquad F_z = mg$$

where g is a gravitational constant. In addition, the resulting second order linear differential equations have to be integrated to obtain a specific "mechanical state" of the system:

$$(4) \quad m\frac{dx}{dt} = mv_x = a_x \qquad m\frac{dy}{dt} = mv_y = a_y \qquad m\frac{dz}{dt} = mv_z = mgt + a_z$$

and upon further integration, we obtain

$$(5) \quad mx = a_x t + b_x \quad my = a_y t + b_y \quad mz = \tfrac{1}{2}mgt^2 + a_z t + b_z$$

where a_x, a_y, a_z and b_x, b_y, b_z are constants of integration called the "coordinates of state". The position and momentum of a point-mass for any one instant constitutes its "mechanical state," and the variables defining the mechanical state are called "state variables". Once a force function has been uniquely identified for the laws of motion, and the mechanical state of the physical system has been empirically determined at some arbitrary initial time, the mechanical state of the physical system at any time is completely and uniquely determined.

Although any attempt at breaking so elegant and compact a theory as Newton's laws of motion into component parts must remain somewhat arbitrary and capricious, we shall do so nevertheless for illustrative purposes. It should already be quite clear in this example that the "equations of motion" correspond to our invariant structural form, and the "force function" to our inductive process hypothesis, with equation (3) representing a specific inductive process. It probably is not quite so clear or unambiguous, however, how we should treat the specification of the specific "mechanical state" of the system and the associated "state variables": the use of the word "state" in their names would suggest that they also should be included as part of our inductive function hypothesis; it certainly would not be a violation of our schema to do so. However, we shall not include them in this way at first, for that would merely complicate the analysis without introducing anything new. Instead, we shall limit the application of the resultant model to the physical system of a single point-mass.

On this basis, we shall divide Newton's laws of motion into two parts and specify a corresponding econometric model capable, in principle, of estimating and predicting the mechanical state of a specific physical system. Let S be an invariant structural system representing the equations of motion:

$$(6) \quad \begin{aligned} x_1 &= \alpha_1 + \beta_{11}t + e_1 \\ x_2 &= \alpha_2 + \beta_{21}t + e_2 \\ x_3 &= \alpha_3 + \beta_{31}t + e_3 \end{aligned}$$

where e_1, e_2, and e_3 are inductive functions of E, an environmental state of S, and where

$$\begin{aligned} \alpha_1 &= b_x/m, & \beta_{11} &= a_x/m \\ \alpha_2 &= b_y/m, & \beta_{21} &= a_y/m \\ \alpha_3 &= b_z/m, & \beta_{31} &= a_z/m. \end{aligned}$$

If we let the inductive functions e_1, e_2, e_3 correspond to the specific force function described in equation (3) above, then E may be represented as

$$(7) \quad \begin{aligned} e_1(g) &= \beta_{12}t^2 \\ e_2(g) &= \beta_{22}t^2 \\ e_3(g) &= \beta_{32}t^2 \end{aligned}$$

where

$$\beta_{12} = 0 \qquad \beta_{22} = 0 \qquad \beta_{32} = \tfrac{1}{2}g.$$

Incorporating this specific environmental state E in the system S, we obtain an econometric model for estimating and predicting the motion of a specific point-mass freely falling near (but not too near) the earth's surface

$$(8) \quad \begin{aligned} x_1 &= \alpha_1 + \beta_{11}t + \beta_{12}t^2 + \varepsilon_1 \\ x_2 &= \alpha_2 + \beta_{21}t + \beta_{22}t^2 + \varepsilon_2 \\ x_3 &= \alpha_3 + \beta_{31}t + \beta_{32}t^2 + \varepsilon_3 \end{aligned}$$

where ε_1, ε_2, and ε_3 are error terms representing discrepancies in the system due to the traditional problems of measurement and specification. Note carefully that although we have used concepts such as mass, velocity, and gravitational attraction to construct this econometric model they do not appear anywhere in its final form. The resultant model is, in fact, very general: it is estimated by simply recording the location of the physical system at several points in time and computing the parameters of the system from these values.

We now return to the question of whether the "state variables" should also be incorporated in the inductive process hypothesis. The purpose of the hypothesis, we recall, is to provide a basis for the specific testing and use of a proffered theory. The essential ingredient which the inductive process hypothesis must supply, therefore, is a set of *basic statements* which are especially easy to test for validity. This objective has already been met in the example given above by the incorporation of a specific force function E in the equations of motion S. Given a time series of at least three observations on the location of a specific physical system, we may calculate values for all the parameters in the econometric model shown in (8) and then, with its state variables empirically estimated, we may employ the model for computing the mechanical state of the system at other times (not too far removed).

It is important to note, however, that there is no formal logical reason why an inductive process hypothesis should stop with any specific set of basic statements. Any set of basic statements always can be replaced by other basic statements with the help of some additional theory. For example, instead of identifying the mechanical state of a specific physical system by estimating the parameters of the econometric model shown above, we could use the more fundamental state variables of mass, position, velocity, and gravitational attraction to help identify its mechanical state. Let f_{10}, f_{11}, ..., f_{32} be inductive functions of F

$$
(9) \quad
\begin{aligned}
&f_{10}(x,m) = b_x/m && f_{11}(x,t) = v_x && f_{12}(g) = 0 \\
&f_{20}(y,m) = b_y/m && f_{21}(y,t) = v_y && f_{22}(g) = 0 \\
&f_{30}(z,m) = b_z/m && f_{31}(z,t) = v_z && f_{32}(g) = \tfrac{1}{2}g
\end{aligned}
$$

which, in conjunction with E,

$$
(10) \quad
\begin{aligned}
e_1(g) &= f_{12}(g)t^2 \\
e_2(g) &= f_{22}(g)t^2 \\
e_3(g) &= f_{32}(g)t^2
\end{aligned}
$$

constitutes an environmental state of the system S:

$$
(11) \quad
\begin{aligned}
x &= f_{10}(x,m) + f_{11}(x,t)t + f_{12}(g)t^2 \\
y &= f_{20}(y,m) + f_{21}(y,t)t + f_{22}(g)t^2 \\
z &= f_{30}(z,m) + f_{31}(z,t)t + f_{32}(g)t^2
\end{aligned}
$$

Insertion of the specific inductive functions (9) and (10) in the system (11)

$$
(12) \quad
\begin{aligned}
x &= b_x/m + v_x t \\
y &= b_y/m + v_y t \\
z &= b_z/m + v_z t + \tfrac{1}{2}gt^2
\end{aligned}
$$

clothes the specification of the physical system with the full analytic garb of its original form in equation (5) and allows the theory to be tested and used whenever the more fundamental state variables are known. More will be said later concerning this example and its extension.

Now, however, we return briefly to the metal rods example for further clarification of the concept of an inductive function. Let S now represent the simple invariant structural equation of linear expansion

$$(13) \quad \Delta L = f_i\, L_0\, \Delta T$$

where f_i is an inductive function of F, a structural state of S representing the coefficient of linear expansion for a specific metal i:

$$
(14) \quad
\begin{aligned}
f_1 &= \alpha_1 \\
f_2 &= \alpha_2 \\
&\;\cdot \\
&\;\cdot \\
&\;\cdot \\
f_i &= \alpha_i
\end{aligned}
$$

An interesting feature of this example is that, although the specification of a metal uniquely identifies a constant of proportionality for each specific inductive process, the example has provided no theory capable of defining an analytic specification of the inductive process in terms of more fundamental concepts. In this respect the metal rods example incorporates the simplest meaningful form of an inductive hypothesis. In this situation, where no algebraic formulation of the inductive process is available, the list of metals is used in the inductive hypothesis as "synthetic" parameters of an unexplained (but identified) set of inductive processes F.

The total absence of a theoretical basis for the observed magnitudes of the set of coefficients of linear expansion does admittedly leave us far from our desired goal of full understanding of the nature of the phenomena. However, it does not invalidate the inductive process hypothesis F. The hypothesis is not meaningless: it expresses a set of relationships between specific metals and their coefficients of linear expansion. Nor is the hypothesis useless in this case: its purpose is to provide a basis for the specific testing of the proffered theory, in the form of an invariant structural equation, that the linear expansion of metal rods is a function of the temperature of the metal rods. As before, the inductive process hypothesis supplies a set of basic statements allowing the chain of theory construction to terminate with statements which are especially easy to test and use.

If there were some additional theory, of course, the coefficients of linear expansion in the metal rods example could be explained in terms of a more fundamental inductive process hypothesis. If, for example, an analytic theory of the inductive process were to be specified in terms of more fundamental concepts, the coefficients of linear expansion would be replaced by other basic statements, such as arguments involving the molecular structure of the metal, so that the inductive process hypothesis could be stated in a specific equation form. A list of subsets of these basic statements, the molecular properties defining a variety of specific inductive processes within the defined set of inductive process, could then be properly described as "analytic" parameters of a specific inductive process. We shall have considerably more to say concerning the definition and use of "synthetic" and "analytic" parameters when we extend the analysis of inductive processes to include stochastic as well as deterministic theories.

The metal rods example illustrates another point which is worthy of emphasis. Even if a rich analytic inductive process hypothesis were available, which provided specific analytic parameters in terms of molecular properties, in most practical applications we would prefer to use the synthetic parameters—the list of metals—as the index set for the inductive process whenever it was easier to observe the type of metal being analyzed than to observe its molecular properties, just as we would use the equations of motion in their econometric form (8), rather than their analytic form (12), if this were more convenient.

Before proceeding further with the inductive process theory we should pause briefly to define more precisely several technical terms. Throughout this essay the term "process" is to be interpreted as an ongoing temporal ordering of events sharing a common description, frequently taking the form of a function whose values are variables. An "economic process," for example, is simply a series of economic events of some specific type. The use of the term "stochastic" is to be interpreted as a delimiter, indicating that the likelihood of a specific event occurring is represented by a probability distribution of the set of all possible events of that type. A "stochastic process" is a stochastic function of time whose values are stochastic variables. A "stochastic economic process," therefore, is a stochastic function of some specific type of economic events across time whose values are stochastic variables.

Whenever the term "inductive" is used it may be interpreted in the logical sense of a generalization obtained by extrapolation to all events of a set from an observed subset of those events. An "inductive process" is an ongoing temporal ordering of structural traits found to hold in an observed structural system; each empirical (i.e., nonlogical) constant or functional term in the process is associated, by means of an empirically defined estimation or specification procedure, with observable events which characterize specific states of the system.[3] An "inductive process hypothesis," therefore, consists of inductive generalizations based upon relations found to hold between structural traits and the events specified in the hypothesis.

A process is to be interpreted as being "parameter invariant" when the functional form of the process may be represented by a structural system over time whose parameters and form remain uniquely associated with a defined set of inductive functions, independent of the passage of time. In order to maintain consistency with current literature on stochastic process theory, the term "stationary" is reserved for the special case where the values of the inductive functions are fixed constants. An "invariant structural hypothesis" is a specific structural representation of a parameter invariant process. Finally, in this essay, a theory which combines the specification of an invariant structural hypothesis with a set of inductive processes within which the hypothesis is believed to be invariant is called an "inductive process theory."

STOCHASTIC INDUCTIVE PROCESSES

The inductive process theory has as its objective a unified framework for the testing and use of econometric models and their associated theories. If this objective is to be of any practical value, not only must a conception be developed which is methodologically sound but, in addition, it must be both operational and capable of encompassing—or, hopefully, extending—the state of the art of the applied economist. This is a tall order and much more than this essay aspires to achieve.

One essential requirement of such a theory which can easily be discussed here, however, is its extension to statistical explanations and stochastic processes. As a byproduct, we discover that the widespread concern and lamentation over the complete lack of *stationarity* in most economic time series may well be misplaced: our real concern should be focused on the possibility that we have been using econometric techniques backwards all this time. The inductive process theory provides a statistical explanation of why economic time series need not be expected to be stationary even when they are readily explained by economic theories corresponding to invariant structural systems. In it the logic of past economic practice is reversed: economic theory, riding on the back of an inductive function, puts to rout statistical theory as the principle determinant of the maintained structural hypothesis.

Before we turn to this, however, let us discuss briefly the concepts of analytic and synthetic parameter spaces and the development of a stochastic process interpreation of the inductive process theory. Our primary objective here is to develop an interpretation capable of providing a sharp empirical distinction between the invariant structural hypothesis and the inductive process hypothesis.

Consider first the well-known example of the class of *normal probability distributions*, specified by the formula

$$(15) \quad P(y_i) = \frac{1}{\sqrt{2\pi\sigma^2}}\, e^{-(y_i - \mu)^2 / 2\sigma^2}$$

and characterized in the parameter space by $N(\mu, \sigma^2)$. Since π and e are universal constants, the specification of magnitudes for the mean μ and the variance σ^2 in formula (15) is all that is required for the computation of the probability P associated with the value y_i. Using formula (15), therefore, we may analytically compute probabilities for all values of the stochastic variable $\{Y\}$. The magnitudes of any one pair of the parameters μ and σ^2 determines a point $\omega_j = (\mu_j, \sigma_j^2)$ in the parameter space $\Omega = N(\mu, \sigma^2)$.

In general, if a class of probability distributions depends on certain parameters ω, the domain of variation of the parameters is called the *parameter space* Ω and any particular set of parameters determines a point in that space. A parameter space Ω is said to be *analytic*, and the points ω_j *analytic parameters*, if the value or values assigned to each point are the parameters of a probability distribution function representing the probability measure of a stochastic variable $\{Y\}$. An analytic parameter space, therefore, may be defined whenever a class of probability distributions has been specified by means of an analytic formula, such as equation (15), so that all that remains undetermined is a set of parameters which characterize this class.

The points ω_j of the parameter space Ω need not be analytic however; all that is required is that the points provide a means of identifying a specific probability measure. Parzen[4] has recently introduced into statistical theory the conception of a *synthetic parameter space*, where a set of synthetic parameters determines each point in the space. The elements of the synthetic parameter space are conceived of as observable events capable of uniquely identifying specific probability distribution functions, but not able to complete the specification of an analytic formula in such a way that actual probabilities may be calculated. We may say, therefore, that if the points ω_j of the parameter space Ω are not the parameters of a probability distribution function then the parameter space Ω is said to be *synthetic* and the points ω_j are said to be *synthetic parameters*. This distinction between analytic and synthetic parameter spaces is very important in economics because many of the likelihood states encountered can only be characterized by synthetic parameters. With this simple yet powerful conception Parzen has set the stage for a major reevaluation of the role of statistical theory in econometrics.

Let us consider next an extension of the inductive process theory which incorporates a stochastic process interpretation embracing this conception of synthetic parameter spaces. We recall that the inductive process theory is built upon two propositions:

(1) Scientific theories should be capable of setting forth a structure of relationships representing a comprehensive explanation of some process, postulated as being parameter invariant under certain specified conditions, and

(2) They should specify an auxiliary hypothesis setting forth the relationship between the structural hypothesis and the specified conditions under which the structure is postulated as being parameter invariant.

Before an economic theory can specify an invariant structural hypothesis involving *stochastic economic processes*, however, it must also be able to specify the conditions under which the stochastic processes themselves are stationary. This is a very stringent requirement. Not only must the stochastic properties of the variables in the invariant structural form of an econometric model be identified and deductively explained in terms of its associated economic theory, but the stochastic properties so identified must be invariant—they must represent stationary distribution functions. Unfortunately, most observed economic processes are notoriously nonstationary.

Therefore, an additional pair of conditions appear necessary for the predictive testing and use of theories involving stochastic processes. To insure that structural hypotheses involving stochastic variables remain invariant with respect to the passage of time, scientific theories should specify two additional testable propositions concerning such variables:

(3) All stochastic variables which are part of a structure of

relationships representing a comprehensive explanation of some parameter invariant process should be postulated as having stationary distribution functions under certain specified conditions, and

(4) They should specify an auxiliary hypothesis setting forth the relationship between the stochastic variables and the specified conditions under which these variables are postulated as being stationary.

Individuals versed in the theory of econometric model estimation will immediately recognize the dual nature of this second pair of conditions with the first pair; what we choose to call "parameters" and what we call "variables" in the invariant structural system depends partly on our point of view as well as on the trade-off we select between past and current information. Two ways of conceptually viewing the inductive process of econometric model construction are apparent. One way is to deductively postulate an invariant structural system S with stationary variables Y, and then inductively search for a set of invariant parameters β and inductive processes E of the system S which incorporate a class of observable events O. Alternatively, we may deductively postulate an invariant structural system S with invariant parameters β, and then inductively search for a set of stationary variables Y and inductive processes E of the system S which also incorporate the observable events O. In practice, of course, our search for an invariant structural system can proceed iteratively from both viewpoints in an attempt to converge to a system S with both the invariant parameters β and the stationary stochastic variables Y conditional on a common set of inductive processes E incorporating the observable events O.

CLASSICAL ECONOMETRIC THEORY

Classical econometric theory and practice, however, does not proceed in this way. It can, with few exceptions, be treated as a special myopic view of the first conception. Consider for a moment the structure and "assumptions" of *multiple regression analysis*.[5] In matrix form the invariant structural system S is postulated as

$$(16) \quad \mathbf{Y} = \mathbf{X}\beta + \varepsilon$$

where $\mathbf{Y}$ is a stochastic "dependent" variable and the "independent" variables $\mathbf{X}$ are a fixed set of numbers, where β is a vector of invariant parameters, and where ε is a set of random errors which "obey" the assumptions that

$$(17) \qquad \begin{aligned} E(\varepsilon) &= 0 \\ E(\varepsilon\varepsilon') &= \sigma^2 \mathbf{I}. \end{aligned}$$

Thus, multiple regression analysis deductively postulates an invariant structural system S with stationary variables X, with the objective of *inductively estimating* a set of invariant parameters β. Let us consider this structural system term by term. The X variables are postulated as stationary in the structural theory—although in fact they hardly ever are—by the assumption that they are a fixed set of numbers and, therefore, are void *of any probability measure whatsoever*. Although inductive processes E are not formally incorporated in the system S, the need for them by applied economists has been widely recognized: they are often included informally as "dummy" variables representing a binary pair of structural states, or as "cross-product" terms which have the effect of modifying the structural coefficients of other variables in the system. Although the stochastic properties of the "dependent" variable Y are not specified explicitly, they always are implicitly specified by the linear combination of invariant parameters β, the fixed "independent" variables X, and the set of random errors ε; Y, therefore, is also postulated as stationary in the structural theory. But why does the theory of multiple regression analysis introduce a set of random errors ε into the invariant structural system S? And why does the theory state that they must "obey" the assumptions in (17) above.

Excellent answers to these questions are readily available when the objective is BLUE (Best Linear Unbiased Estimation). They are not so easy to come by when the objective is the predictive testing and use of econometric models. A basic conceptual difficulty in current econometric methodology for this latter purpose seems to lie in the treatment of the precision of economic measures. Economists tend to theorize in terms of exact functional relationships. For purposes of testing and use, however, the functional formulations are clearly inadequate since economic variables hardly ever map into functional forms in this sense. Therefore, a stochastic term ε is introduced which may take on positive or negative values, e.g.,

$$\mathbf{Y} = \mathbf{X}\beta + \varepsilon.$$

There are several very good reasons why measurement procedures must be specified with a stochastic term: ε is a proxy for all the specific economic measures which affect Y but are not considered significant in an economic theory; ε represents the unpredictable element of randomness in all economic measures; and ε encompasses all the errors in measuring economic concepts.

However, rather than treating the measurement process as consisting fundamentally of matching up points to a defined precision, and determining how far this property can be incorporated into the theory of econometrics without having to invoke arbitrary probability distribution functions, the approach more often has been to focus on the necessary statistical conditions which an *analytic parameter space* associated with the stochastic variable ε must possess for classical estimation procedures to produce valid *analytic* measures of the invariant structural parameters β.

It is important to note that the concept of measurement of points to a defined precision does not presuppose a special analytic theory of probability or a mathematical theory of errors. Precisely the reverse is true. The concept of a measuring interval provides a basis without which any statistical theory of errors would make very little sense.

Unfortunately, the subject of an extraordinary amount of econometric theory may be described as a class of detailed studies of the neuroses produced in the classical least-squares statistical measures when they are forced into the estimation of economic models incorporating measures which have few, if any, of the required statistical properties. In his classic book on the theory of econometric methods, Johnston candidly begins his discussion with the following remarks:

> In recent years a body of literature has developed which may appropriately be called the *theory of econometrics*. This body of literature stems directly from the single-equation linear model in that its basic preoccupation is with the assumptions of that model, with the applicability of these assumptions to the analysis of economic data, and with what, if anything, can be done if one or more of these assumptions is inappropriate.[6]

The requirement of consistency between the assumptions of the statistical theories and econometric model estimation procedures derived from them is well known and carefully incorporated in econometric theory; the result has been the widespread use of highly restrictive statistical assumptions for the derivation of precise econometric model estimators. In the process, however, the requirement of consistency between the postulated statistical assumptions and the actual stochastic variables defined in econometric model constructions has often been neglected.

Perhaps one reason why we have been able to proceed at all with the search for economic theories is that, in practice, most statistical measures are treated as synthetic rather than as analytic measures; least-squares procedures often provide useful synthetic statistics even when underlying statistical assumptions are not analytically known.

Let us now consider alternative approaches to classical econometric theory and practice. We begin by provisionally accepting as our maintained structural hypothesis an invariant structural system S which is consistent with the four testable propositions of the inductive process theory. This hypothesis can be accepted or rejected at any time on its ability to define an empirical model which maintains invariant parameters β and stationary variables Y throughout its domain of application as defined and conditioned by a set of inductive processes E of the system S. The central question remaining is how best to replace the requirements of classical econometric theory that:

a. ε be a set of analytically defined random errors, and
b. the "independent" variables X be a fixed set of numbers.

One approach to the first problem is to specify the synthetic parameterization of distribution functions by defining environmental states in the synthetic parameter space which map into one or more sets of *stationary distribution functions* of stochastic economic variables. It is understood that the elements of the distribution function parameter space are synthetic because they do not necessarily have the properties of parameters of an analytic formula capable of defining the probability elements of the distribution functions. In this fashion, the inductive function hypothesis can define a synthetic parameter space intended to hold specific predictive stochastic processes as stationary (in the "wide" observational sense of an invariant correlation function and mean value) as the purposes at hand require or the world of experience allows. Note that although a random error term may still be included in the model, and used when convenient for the solution of least squares or other estimators, it is not part of the specification for testing or use. For these purposes what is required is a *defined precision* of the measure of stationarity achieved by the predicted variables in the test statements.

In the inductive process conception past econometric practice is reversed: economic theory replaces statistical theory as the principle determinant of the maintained structural hypothesis. Analytically defined error terms are replaced with either analytic or synthetic inductive function statements. The specification of the maintained structural hypothesis becomes an integral part of the specific theory construction.

A similar approach can be taken to resolve the second problem. Stochastic economic theory can be conceived of as the analytic specification of the subset of observable environmental conditions of a stochastic economic process which are "critical"—in the sense that they would have to be held constant in the replication of the measurement process—for the observed results to be consistent with previously observed quantities. A fundamental meaning of "stationarity" is parameter invariance; the process remains in the same stationary condition or state as long as certain critical parameters do not change. Stochastic economic theory can be conceived of, therefore, as specifying the synthetic parameterization of probability distribution functions by the definition of observable elements E in the synthetic parameter space which are assumed to map into a class of *stationary distribution functions* of stochastic economic variables. Whether they do map in this way, both ex ante and ex post, is a matter subject to empirical confirmation.

The specification of a class of inductive hypotheses for the construction of a class of econometric models may be carried out by first specifying a measureable set of observable conditions E, with measure m, which is assumed to have a countable base and to satisfy the condition $m(E) < \infty$. A class of inductive hypotheses may then be described in terms of a set of inductive functions defined on the measurable set E.

Whenever specific analytic formulas have been specified for the inductive function hypothesis an *inductive process space* is defined. An *analytic structural parameter space* may then be defined on the class of econometric model constructions specified by the inductive process space. The specification of specific magnitudes $m(E)$ of inductive conditions analytically defines a specific set of parameter values in the structural parameter space. Therefore, the elements of both the *synthetic or analytic parameter space*, maping into the probability distribution space, and the elements of the *synthetic or analytic structural parameter space*, maping into the inductive process space, are drawn from the set of observable conditions E.

However, if current observable econometric practice is a reliable indicator of econometric intent, very few economic model builders are actually interested in the methodology of structural systems. The following section is included, therefore, to suggest that the inductive function approach is *practical*, that inductive function information filtering can also produce optimal econometric model constructions for applied econometric forecasting.

INDUCTIVE FUNCTION INFORMATION FILTERS

The use of finite-memory polynomial filters and predicators by communications and electronics engineers, in the application of statistical communications theory for the processing of information being transmitted, is now quite common. The problem may be viewed by economists as the problem of designing econometric model constructions which extract the "economic information" from stochastic economic variables which may also contain considerable "noise." In this context we define "noise" simply as all information we can't figure out what to do with. The basic idea is to try to design a model which provides a maximum reinforcement of a class of "properties" of the economic information—usually limited to statistical characteristics such as the parameters of its spectral decomposition—and a maximum rejection of the same class of properties of the noise.

Let us begin with the well-known function for information filtering of variable continuous processes

$$(18)\quad Y(t) = \int_{-\infty}^{\infty} W(\tau,t){\cdot}Z(t-\tau){\cdot}d\tau$$

where the weighting function $W(\tau,t)$ is a function of the response lag τ and of the calendar time t of an observed exogenous variable $Z(t-\tau)$. Note that functional dependence in this formulation of $W(\tau,t)$ on τ varies with the value of the calendar time, and vice versa.

The implication is that the weighting function $W(\tau,t)$ of the exogenous variable can be transformed to represent an underlying invariant information filter by conditioning it with respect to two external aspects of the stochastic process, the response lag and calendar time. These two aspects of the passage of time are to be treated as synthetic parameters of the weighting function $W(\tau,t)$ *unless an analytic proposition is introduced* which specifies the nature of the transformation required to make the underlying information filter invariant. Such an analytic proposition may be—but need not be—statistical in nature.

In many stochastic physical processes it is undoubtedly quite reasonable to employ the response lag of the mechanism and the passage of time (from the initiation of the process) as an index set representing an irreversible evolution of the underlying and un-observed (perhaps unknown) parameters of the physical process. The use of such a nonanalytic index set as the synthetic parameters of the stochastic process is justified for *engineering purposes* when-ever it is observed that resetting the process to a specific point in the synthetic parameter set also resets the observed weighting function $W(\tau,t)$ to a unique range. However, such a nonanalytic procedure can be successful as an engineering construction in only two situations: the procedure will prove successful either if the process has an invariant time evolution into which the time-based index set can synthetically map and when all of the critical environ-mental states are being controlled (or are defined) by the process itself, or when the critical environmental states are themselves constant functions.

In the social sciences, unfortunately, the use of calendar time as a synthetic index set representing changes in critical environ-mental states produces very little historical correspondence to the world of experience. The principal application of such an hypothesis has been, perhaps, the graphical use of the N.B.E.R. reference cycles of economic activity, where the calendar time is set to zero at the reference trough date. It also appears that the assumption of a stochastic economic process containing an invariant response lag mechanism only holds under rather special environmental condi-tions; hypotheses concerning the lag in response to monetary policy and the widespread use of the N.B.E.R. business cycle indicators are examples of the application in economic practice of the provi-sional assumption of an invariant response lag.

Since it is seldom reasonable in the social sciences to assume that either the socioeconomic process has an invariant time evolu-tion, or that the process either controls or defines the critical en-vironmental states, or that the environmental states are constant functions, we now turn to the explicit incorporation of inductive conditioning as part of the specification of stochastic information filters.

Consider next the introduction of a class of structural variables defined on a measurable set of environmental conditions $m(E)$ into the representation of variable continuous processes for information filtering

$$(19) \quad Y(t,X) = \int_{-\infty}^{\infty} W(\tau,X) \cdot Z(t-\tau) \cdot d\tau$$

In this formulation the stochastic economic variable $Y(t,X)$ is defined as representing a class of stochastic processes $\{Y\}_X$ in the distribution space whose distribution functions are labeled in the synthetic distribution parameter space by specific subsets of the class of structural variables X. Similarly, the weighting function $W(\tau,X)$ is defined as representing a class of invariant information filters in the inductive process space whose weighting functions are labeled in the synthetic process parameter space by the *same specific subsets* of the class of structural variables X.

The inductive filter may then be employed in several forms. The most obvious form is based on the additional stationarity assumption that the lag in response τ of the stochastic process is invariant once the process has been conditioned by a specific subset X representing a specific environmental state. This additional assumption of an invariant response lag is necessary for the interpretation $Y(t,X)$ as a class of stochastic processes $\{Y\}_X$.

The inductive filter need not assume the invariance of the lag in response τ of any member of the class of stochastic processes. Rather, it could incorporate alternative assumptions which define analytically, in the inductive process space, relationships between calendar time t, the lag in response τ and an additional subset of X representing, for example, a class of possible states of secular growth in the environment of the stochastic processes.

In either form, once the response lag has been defined on a linear metric space, we can represent the spectral transfer function of a variable continuous inductive process as the Fourier transform of the weighting function $W(\tau,X)$ with respect to the response lag τ, treating the subset of the class of structural variables X as a constant:

$$(20) \quad T(i\omega,X) = \int_{-\infty}^{\infty} W(\tau,X)e^{-i\omega\tau}d\tau,$$

and

$$(21) \quad \mathrm{Var}\{Y\}_X = \int_{0}^{\frac{1}{2}} T(i\omega,X)^2 P(\omega)d\omega,$$

where the variance of the stochastic variable $\{Y\}_X$ is also conditioned by a specific subset of the class of structural variables X, representing a specific environmental state.

Finally, consider the linear discrete analogue of the variable continuous inductive filter

$$(22) \quad Y(t,X) = \sum_{\tau=0}^{m} a(\tau,X) \cdot Z(t-\tau) - \sum_{\tau=1}^{n} b(\tau,X) \cdot Y(t-\tau,X)$$

where the process is represented as a linear combination of an inductive moving-average function of Z and an inductive autoregressive function of Y, both functions being conditioned by a subset of the class of structural variables X, representing a specific environmental state and synthetically labeling a specific parameter subset of the discrete process in the structural parameter space.

The representation of the spectral transfer function of the linear discrete inductive process, treating the subset of the class of structural variables X as a constant, is

$$(23) \quad T(i\omega,X) = \sum_{\tau=0}^{m} a(\tau,X) \left[e^{-i\omega\Delta t} \right]^{\tau} \Big/ \sum_{\tau=1}^{n} b(\tau,X) \left[e^{-i\omega\Delta t} \right]^{\tau}.$$

However, in this representation a rather nasty complication is revealed. The autoregressive function of the stochastic process requires a time series of $Y(t-\tau)$ *which is consistently derived from an environment held constant* in the state represented by a specific subset of the class of structural variables X. It would appear to be a formidable statistical task to synthetically label the class of parameter subsets in the structural parameter space representing a stochastic economic process undergoing shifts in its environmental state. In such a situation even applied econometric forecasters might be forced to turn to economic theory for an inductive function hypothesis in order to be able to specify a specific analytic formula for the inductive process space.

CONSTANT PROCESSES VERSUS CETERIS PARIBUS

We have been suggesting throughout this essay that economic theories should distinguish between two classes of testable propositions, invariant structural hypotheses and associated inductive process hypotheses relating the invariant structural hypotheses to specific observable events. It seems fitting, therefore, that we should close this essay with a presentation of the case of Constant Processes versus *ceteris paribus*.

Because of the complex nature of the interactions in a socio-economic system, economists have developed many language conventions for restricting their analyses of economic phenomena to a small subset of the interactions. Although it is conceptually possible to specify a general system where all factors affecting a given economic situation are jointly represented, virtually all testable economic theories involve a partial analysis with certain economic or environmental factors held constant. As Marshall said, unfortunately,

> (the economist) segregates those disturbing causes, whose wanderings happen to be inconvenient, for the time in a pound called Ceteris Paribus.[1]

Ever since, economists seem to have been wandering between statements of *ceteris paribus* intended to *hold parts of a structure of simultaneous equations constant* in order to undertake a partial analysis, and statements of *ceteris paribus* intended to *restrict the domain of application to that part of the structure which is constant.*

The importance of the difference between these two classes of statements for economic theorizing and econometric model construction is indicated by the fundamental difference in their analytic content. On the one hand, *ceteris paribus* statements implying only partial differentiation of the system of equations put forth as the desired structural hypothesis convey the understanding that *the specification of a structural parameter space is incomplete, with the stochastic economic process only partly developed,* independent of the specific economic or environmental states specified. Nor is any implication of the parameter invariance of the system contained in such statements. Predictive testing of econometric model and theory constructions under such conditions is quite impossible. Inaccurate results can always be explained away by irrefutable assertions that there was a change in some aspect of reality which the partial construction implicitly held constant. Similarly, it is always possible that correct predictions may be completely fortuitous, based only on shifts in some unspecified aspect of reality.

Ceteris paribus statements restricting the analysis to a subset of observable events, which hold the structural system constant, on the other hand, represent an entirely different analytic assertion. These statements assert that the *defined structural parameter space is invariant and that the stochastic economic processes are stationary* across all observations of any *specific subset of observable events.* The former statement is an admission of incapacity to completely specify an analytic hypothesis. The latter is a statement of an invariant economic theory.

Columbus, Ohio
April 21, 1970

NOTES

[1]I am indebted to Robert L. Basmann for introducing this clarifying example in the discussion of this paper at the first OSU Conference on Econometrics.

[2]The following example draws heavily on a discussion of Newton's laws by Ernest Nagel, *The Structure of Science* (New York: Harcourt, Brace & World, 1961), Chapter 10.

[3]The concept of an "inductive function," as implied in this definition, encompasses the mathematical concept of *definition by induction*. It has, as one of its extensions, the mathematical notion of a *general recursive function,* and may be interpreted in this sense. See S. C. Kleene, *Introduction to Metamathematics* (New York: Van Nostrand), 1952.

[4]Emmanuel Parzen, "Analysis and Synthesis of Linear Models for Time Series," Technical Report No. 4 (Department of Statistics, Stanford University), 1966.

[5]Although received econometric doctrine has many elaborations and extensions, each with its own set of problems and estimation procedures, the basic theory warmly embraces at its core a generalized version of multiple regression analysis, and can be summarized most easily in this form.

[6]J. Johnston, *Econometric Methods* (New York: McGraw-Hill, 1963), p. 145.

[7]Alfred Marshall, *Principles of Economics* (8th ed.), p. 366.

SUMMARY OF THE DISCUSSION

Jan Kmenta
Michigan State University

INTRODUCTION

The purpose of the conference was to examine the current state of econometrics in light of the early promise of a scientific counter-revolution against the casual empiricism common in economic literature. The timing and the occasion for the soul-searching appraisal was more or less inspired by the publication of the Brookings Model of the United States economy and the emergence of several other projects of large-scale model building. The proliferation of these models, made possible largely by the dramatic impact of computer technology on research, stirred up some doubts as to whether the speeding vehicle of "progress" is heading in the right direction. The authors of the key papers written for the conference took a very critical standpoint by charging that some of the common practices in econometrics represent, to a large extent, a violation of the basic principles of scientific method and that the early promise of econometrics has been frustrated. To use the words of one of the participants of the conference, econometrics has simply replaced "sloppy sentences by sloppy equations." Furthermore, the transgression of econometricians was alleged to be worse than that of the literary economists because of its misleading, pseudo-scientific veneer. Needless to say, not all of the participants shared this highly critical view of econometric practices. In fact, the discussion brought to light a variety of opinions, ranging from a mildly disturbed complacency to an outright condemnation. This diversity of opinions imparted a climate of lively dissension on the conference and fed the fire of the discussion throughout its duration.

It was said at another occasion that dissatisfaction or controversy itself is not enough to justify a conference, that the problems must be important. The preceding paragraph makes it quite clear that, providing the criticism raised has any real foundation, the issues *are* important. The question then arises of whether the criticisms raised are justified or not. The summary of the discussion that is presented on the following pages shows that, to say the very least, the critical comments of the papers are worthy of some consideration. But it must also be admitted that for some participants the issues discussed were lower on the list of priorities than other problems at present unresolved. This was expressed most clearly by one of the participants who, in the middle of the conference, stated that he expected an entirely different discussion; in his opinion, the really important issues are the fundamental statistical problems in connection with model building such as pretesting, pre-estimation, properties of dynamic solutions, and so on. Nevertheless, the conference was successful in achieving its purpose in the broad sense, namely producing dissatisfaction with received knowledge, articulating some unresolved problems, and suggesting new approaches.

There were three sessions at the conference, each session consisting of a brief summary of the scheduled papers followed by an extensive discussion of some aspects of the papers or related matters. The whole conference lasted for a day and half, and the transcript of the discussion from the tape recording took up 180 typewritten pages. In what follows we present a summary of the major points and issues raised by the participants. The summary is organized into five sections roughly corresponding to the main areas covered in the discussion. As could be expected in a venture of this kind, it is not feasible to summarize the contents of the discussion in neat and succinct conclusions. Rather, the aim of the summary is to capture the spirit of the exchange of views on the subject under discussion and to indicate some of the various positions taken by the participants.

ON CONSTRUCTION OF ECONOMETRIC MODELS

The discussion concerning the construction of econometric models covered a number of interesting issues. The main points raised in this connection centered around the question of invariance of the maintained hypothesis, the strategy of model formulation, the dilemma of choosing between a large and a small model, the conflict between hypothesis formulation and hypothesis testing, and the structural hypothesis of the Brookings Model. Throughout the discussion there was an implicit recognition of the difficulties involved. While in this respect there was general agreement, there was also a distinct lack of consensus in assessing the past and present achievements of econometric model builders. The latter became particularly apparent in the discussion of the large econometric models recently developed or presently under construction. Here the views ranged from a hopeful—although cautious—optimism to an outright condemnation. The result was a clear difference of opinion with respect to the direction of effort most desirable for the progress of econometrics and *ergo* economics.

The first focal point of the discussion was instigated by one of the central themes of Professor Cunnyngham's paper. According to Cunnyngham, economic theory embodied in an econometric model must specify an invariant structural hypothesis and define controlling environmental influences. The meaning of the term "invariance" was explained by Basmann with the help of the following two examples.

Example I. Let L = length of a metal rod, and t = temperature. Suppose $L = a + bt + ct^2$. Since the values of the parameters a, b, and c are different for different metals, there is invariance with respect to rods made from one and the same metal but not otherwise.

Example II. The prewar econometric model of the United States constructed by Klein referred to the prewar conditions and did not allow for the parameter shifts which occurred during the war and early postwar years. A use of this model for forecasting for the year 1946 and 1947 violates the requirement of hypothesis invariance.

Basmann's second example inspired the suggestion that the parameter shifts may have been due to, e.g., Government intervention in the economy, and that a lack of invariance may simply reflect an incomplete theoretical specification of the model. A more complete theory would incorporate *all* the relevant variables in the model. However, this may be difficult. In fact, Orcutt argued that it is virtually impossible; hypotheses are not and cannot be fully specified since we cannot enumerate all the factors that are to be held constant. All we can do is to find out by experience the circumstances under which the given hypothesis holds.

An alternative way of attempting to meet the requirement of hypothesis invariance is by specifying the realm of application.

This, as pointed out by Brunner, is what Papandreou termed the "social space" and should always be a part of the formulation of the hypothesis. With respect to Klein's prewar model of the United States, it should be explicitly confined to the period of no Government intervention. Basmann compared keeping Government intervention out of the realm of application to closing the door to outside influences in experiments. The trouble is that if the "social experimenter" obtains his results (such as rejecting a given null hypothesis) and *then* remembers that he had forgotten to "check whether the door was closed or open," he does not get his paper published if he admits it. Klein remarked that the outside influences which should be kept out of the model may not affect all the parameters involved. Thus, for example, price control may affect mainly the price determination equation but most other parameters remain unchanged.

The past attempts of econometricians to satisfy the requirement of hypothesis invariance, whether by including all supposedly relevant factors in the model or by specifying the presumed realm of application, have been less than completely successful. This is clearly due to deficiency of theoretical specification. Everybody agreed with that, but there was a division of opinion as to the causes of this deficiency. According to one view, the main cause is the failure of practicing econometricians to make full use of the existing economic theory. Brunner claimed that, while we all agree that a well-formulated theory is important, this agreement means very little in practice since it is rarely executed. Another view was that the cause is the deficiency of the economic theory itself. Kuh maintained that economic theory does not provide very much help in model construction; it certainly provides no information about the lag structure and the dynamics of the system in general. In this situation econometricians act like engineers: they have to use rules of thumb, they have to piece information together, and so on. According to Kuh it is a gross simplification to suppose that we are endowed with rich theory with vast ramifications which we simply "plug" into the model. While this may be the impression that one gets from the textbooks, in fact one soon finds out how meager the supply of theory really is. What is needed under these circumstances is a more pragmatic approach by recourse to observations. The relevant variables which are missing from the model can be found by testing (Kuh) while the general description of the domain of application can be defined by producing counterexamples, i.e., examples of cases for which the hypothesis does not hold (Nozick). Dhrymes further expressed the opinion that knowledge can no longer be acquired by deductive reasoning and that we should search our world to uncover hypotheses that could be generalized.

A strategic approach to the construction of econometric models was outlined by Zellner and is shown schematically in Figure 1. This approach found, by and large, general approval among the participants of the discussion. However, there was some concern about the possibility of not converging to "truth," although "truth" was never clearly defined. Zellner stated that he does not believe that one necessarily converges to *large* models. In commenting on the research strategy, Zellner pointed out the importance of establishing and understanding the dynamic properties of econometric models. Most econometric models recorded in the literature have not been studied thoroughly in this respect. Zellner emphasized that he feels very uneasy about using models for policy application until a lot of this kind of work has been done. Dhrymes' opinion was that the process of constructing models in a sequential fashion as outlined by Zellner should best be viewed as a process of generating rather than testing hypotheses about the world. This, according to Dhrymes, is the spirit in which much of the research in econometrics has to be taken. Zellner added that one should use new data to test the previously generated hypotheses.

The chart on research strategy presented by Zellner is an open-ended one, thus implying that the construction of econometric models is a sequential process which could be carried on indefinitely. This brought up the discussion on the "convergence to truth" to which an allusion has been made above. In this context a major point of dispute centered around the question concerning the approximate size of an econometric model. Klein proclaimed that the size of a model is not relevant except for the fact that large models give more detailed information. For example, only a relatively large macroeconomic model would contain an equation explaining the demand for refrigerators. This advantage of large models was also mentioned by Kuh who pointed out that a large model such as the Brookings Model gives information about the interindustry structure of the economy which would not have been possible had the model been substantially cut in size. Further, Kuh stated, we often have very weak prior beliefs at the macro-level but relatively good prior knowledge at the micro-level so that large disaggregated models are likely to be more useful. Also, a promising way of finding an answer to the question of the most appropriate size of a model may be by starting with a large model and then examining how aggregation affects its dynamic properties. If one considered only small, highly aggregated models, one would not be

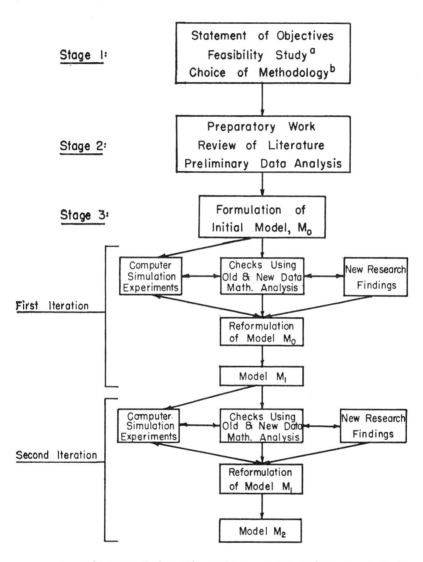

a. It is assumed that this study shows the projects to be feasible.

b. It is assumed that a "modeling" approach is selected.

FIGURE 1 Schematic of Research Strategy

able to answer this question. According to Kuh it is the results of the work on large models against which the appropriateness of the small models can be judged.

The appropriateness of the large models was strongly questioned by Brunner. The rationale for a large-scale model appears to be the belief that there exists a true "super-model" in the Platonic realm. It is this super-model which the large-model builders are presumably trying to approximate. This means that the more one disaggregates, the better approximation one gets. Put in this way, the belief appears to represent an implicit denial of the relevance of empirical science. An objection to small models on the grounds of the so-called aggregation problem implies that the relevant permanencies occur only on the micro-level. While this may be the case, the alternate idea—that there are permanencies on the macro-level—deserves exploring. Another objection to large models such as the Brookings Model was voiced by Ames who questioned these models on the grounds of comprehension. A "consumer" of economic models wants to know what they say and how they work. The Brookings Model appears to fail on these grounds. Ames added, however, that size alone does not necessarily prevent intelligibility: one can easily understand an input-output model no matter how large it is. Chow sympathized with Ames but thought that this was a moot point; if the builders of large-scale models believe that the world is complicated, they cannot give a simple description of it.

The research strategy of Figure 1 with its implied sequential process of search also stimulated a discussion about the distinction between hypothesis formulation and hypothesis testing. This was one of the main issues discussed in Brunner's paper. Zellner stated that—because of all the problems with prior information, pretesting, and pre-estimation—the estimators in the published version of a model will not have the properties which are claimed, nor will the probability levels associated with significance tests be completely accurate. Brunner criticized the fact that we do not know what the various standard errors mean and yet we put an interpretation on them which they simply cannot bear. Klein agreed with the criticism and conceded that it applies to the Brookings Model as well. However, he did not consider it desirable to take a very purist view. At the present stage of our knowledge the correct interpretation of the standard errors is one of the unanswered questions of econometrics. Dhrymes' position was that the sequential process enables one to formulate hypotheses rather than test them. The discussion then led to the problem of continuous reestimation of a model; a report on this discussion is presented in a separate section below.

Concerning the structural hypothesis of the Brookings Model, the main criticism was expressed by Basmann who contended that the hypothesis is incomplete so that empirical testing is impossible. In particular, there are too many variables in the model and too few observations; hence the system can be fitted in an infinite number of ways. This means that there exists no determinate degree of confirmation. The builders of the Brookings Model dealt with this problem by eliminating some of the predeterminate variables, which implies an imposition of certain restrictions on the structural parameters. However, the elimination of the variables was done by the computer and is unknown to the builders of the Brookings Model. Therefore we do not know how to appraise the numerical values of the estimators and test statistics. Basmann pointed out that if the number of observations is smaller than the total number of lagged endogenous and exogenous variables, as in the case of the Brookings Model, then we must reduce the number of functionally independent unknown structural parameters in the system. In other words, we have to have a sharper maintained hypothesis. This sharpness can be achieved by specifying further hypothetical restrictions on the structural parameters by resorting to economic theory. Instead of this, the builders of the Brookings Model have chosen to adopt purely computational devices for combining predetermined variables.

Klein, in his reply to Basmann's criticism, stated that one should consider all other work in connection with the Brookings Model, not only what is presented in the book.[1] In constructing the model the builders of the Brookings Model have conducted precisely the kind of experiments that were outlined schematically by Zellner. In dealing with the degrees-of-freedom problem emphasized by Basmann, the model builder has a choice of either reducing the number of parameters by means of hypothetical restrictions or to reduce the data on the predetermined variables. The builders of the Brookings Model preferred data reduction to parameter reduction because they did not have the prior information necessary for the latter. The reduction of data can be achieved by using the block-recursive layout of Franklin Fisher[2] or by applying the principal components method.[3] In using the former method one has to specify the instrumental variables used, and this has been done in connection with the Brookings model. The principal components method achieves data reduction in a mechanical manner; it is intended to use this method when the whole

Brookings Model is reestimated. Hypothetical restrictions of economic theory and institutions should be used in any case and its use should not depend on sample size. Basmann commented that using the method of instrumental variables developed by Fisher is equivalent to imposing certain functional dependencies on the parameters. One would get the same results by first imposing functional dependencies on the parameters and then requiring the estimation procedure to maintain them.

In defense of the Brookings Model, Sutch asserted that the reason for building it was largely pragmatic, namely that economists felt uneasy about making policy suggestions. In a question addressed to Basmann, Sutch asked what should have been done instead. Basmann replied that for all the attention that policy makers pay to economic models there is no need to feel uneasy about any suggestions. This, Basmann said, he learned from his experience in a large private corporation. If one produced a great big model and made a forecast confirming the wisdom of undertaking the project which the policy makers wanted to start, they would be very happy, praise the model, and tell others about the bright young man they had on the staff. If, on the other hand, the forecast did not support such a policy, they would pat the model-builder on the head, tell him to keep up the good work, and that would be the last he would hear about it. As for the Brookings Model, Basmann continued, perhaps the real purpose of it is to assist the varied needs of policy makers in their effort to get people to carry out certain things for them. In that case it would be unfair to evaluate it almost solely as a contribution to economic science.

The discussion about the theoretical foundations of the Brookings Model brought out sharply the difference in views concerning the main area of deficiency and, therefore, the most urgent need for improvement of our knowledge with respect to econometric model building. On one side there was the view that the most urgent problems to be solved are those of a purely statistical nature and those of establishing and understanding the dynamic properties of models, while on the other side the major deficiency was thought to be that of insufficient exploitation and incomplete formulation of theory. This controversy was to some extent carried over to the discussion on reestimation which we present in the next section.

ON CONTINUOUS REESTIMATION OF MODELS

Brunner in his paper and in his comments on the Brookings Model during the conference questioned the common practice of continuous reestimation of the structural parameters of the model. Such a revision of the estimates is presumably necessary because of the perennial evolution of the economy which continually modifies the existing economic interrelations. Brunner suggested two possible interpretations of such a contention. One interpretation is that it is impossible to construct empirical theories and that all that one can do is to provide a quantitative description of history. This implies that there is no stable underlying population distribution which generates the observations on the endogenous variables of the economic system. The alternative interpretation is that for some reason our theory is incomplete in that it omits explanation of the presumed changes of the structural parameters. In either case, if the contention is true, the model does not satisfy the requirement of representing an invariant structural hypothesis. The consequence of this would be that the meaning of the computed standard errors and test statistics is obscure and, therefore, difficult to assess.

In his letter to the conference Ando stated that he sees no objection to the continuous reestimation of the structural parameters if one operates within the Bayesian framework. Continuous reestimation then simply leads to a continuous revision of the posterior distribution. In reply Brunner pointed out that if the theory is to have any empirical content, something has to be specified about the stochastic properties of the parameters. Dhrymes asserted that continuous reestimation may simply mean taking into account additional observations as they become available and, therefore, obtaining more efficient estimates. This is desirable whether one approaches the estimation problem from the Bayesian point of view or not. New empirical evidence should not be neglected. Brunner replied that he did not object to utilizing new empirical evidence as it becomes available but that he objected to the implied change in perspective.

An alternative justification of the need for continuous reestimation was further offered by Dhrymes. Suppose that our linear models are, in fact, approximations of nonlinear relations and that observations refer only to a certain portion of the conceivable sample space. Then reestimation may simply amount to changing the linear approximations in response to having a larger (or different) portion of the sample space. But if this is the case, retorted Brunner, then we have no grounds for assessing our theory since we always have an escape hatch open. Whatever we do, we always have a specification error because of the fact that we are using linear relations instead of nonlinear ones. The presence of the specification error can be used as an explanation any time the data do not appear to be consistent with the model. Sutch added that, given the present computer technology, there is no excuse for not estimating nonlinear relations if they are postulated by prior considerations.

As a point of clarification, Hurwicz suggested that there exist three potential sources of variability of the estimates of the regression coefficients which ought to be distinguished. First, there is the variability due to the fact that new observations provide new information about the population coefficients but the population coefficients themselves remain constant. Secondly, the population coefficients may vary over time. For instance, the coefficients may be, in fact, random variables as in the model examined by Rubin.[4] Finally, the variation of the estimates may be due to a specification error such as using linear relations to approximate nonlinear structures as suggested by Dhrymes. In the first case there is no objection to reestimation; on the contrary, reestimation is desirable because it reduces the variance of the estimates The second case is the one which drew Brunner's criticism. If the coefficients are, in fact, different at different points of observation, the existence and the characteristics of the change ought to be specified as a part of the maintained hypothesis. Hurwicz agreed with the criticism but pointed out that the one simple specification of change which is likely to be used in practice, namely specifying no change of the parameters for the first n-years and postulating a change in the (n+1)-st year, appears to be very implausible. Concerning the third potential source of variability of estimates, Hurwicz expressed the hope that the nature of the misspecification, such as the nonlinearity of the relation, would be revealed by outlying observations. In this case additional observations would be used for the purpose of revealing nonlinearities rather than providing more information about linear relations.

Kuh pointed out that Daniel Suits at the University of Michigan changes his model of the United States economy every year as more information becomes available. In Kuh's opinion this practice may lead to improved forecasting but there can be no testing of hypotheses under these circumstances. The practice of continuous reestimation in this case is presumably rationalized by the belief that with more observations we learn more about the specification errors of the existing model. The specification errors are typically those of omitting relevant variables and possibly including some irrelevant ones. The new observations are then, in fact, used for the purpose of revising the maintained hypothesis. Thus the procedure of reestimation is, in this case, one of a search for hypotheses rather than one of evaluation, and leads to formulation rather than testing of models. Of course, if the resulting models are always expected to be short-lived and not to be exposed to systematic testing, then the theoretical propositions contained therein have no empirical content.

ON MEASUREMENT PROCEDURES AND THE MEANING OF NUMBERS

One of the major points of Brunner's paper was the argument in favor of the use of a rigorous language in all attempts at clarification of logical issues in connection with the formulation and tests of economic hypotheses.[5] In particular, Brunner claimed that there is a need for awareness of the semantic background of the mathematical equations representing theoretical relations. This is necessary so that we can justify numerical operations and statistical procedures that we use in the process of formulation and assessment of the theories involved. For example, a variable characterized by observations which cannot be measured but only ranked cannot be subjected to simple operations such as addition or multiplication. Brunner cited two examples from recent literature of violating this basic principle. Basmann made this point one of the two major criticisms of the Brookings Model. According to Basmann, the authors of the Brookings Model paid insufficient attention to the fact that observations on the endogenous and exogenous variables are supposed to represent magnitudes of economic quantities. Because of this, Basmann asserted that the quantitative foundations of the hypothesis represented by the Brookings Model are seriously defective. For example, one variable used in the Brookings Model is the "inclination to buy cars." Observations on this variable are represented by values of an "attitudinal index" and thus can be replaced by any order-preserving transformation, each transformation being associated with different standard errors and different R^2's. An interpretation of these statistics is then impossible. This, Basmann stated, is the result of the disregard of the basic principle that if we use numbers, we must provide justification for using them.

Replying to Basmann's criticism, Klein stated that the attitudinal index brings in *some* information, and that it has proved itself well in forecasting. Hurwicz pointed out that the situation with respect to the attitudinal index is analogous to that of a utility index in standard economic theory. The fact that there is no justification for a utility index as a quantity is no argument for not using it or for not experimenting with it. It is perfectly possible to give an orderable number an operational meaning, and this is precisely what the modern utility theory has done. Perhaps we ought to develop a new regression theory that would enable us to deal with orderable explanatory variables in a meaningful way. In fact, the constructive aspect of Basmann's criticism is that it encourages us to do so.

In his contribution to the discussion, Brunner pointed out that whenever we engage in numerical or statistical operations, we assert that certain empirical relations exist and can be assessed. With the mass of numbers which we use, the assertion that they represent quantities is very plausible and we are quite willing to accept it. With respect to some numbers, on the other hand, there are grounds for doubting. In Brunner's opinion it is very useful to alert ourselves that this kind of problem exists so that we are careful and properly interpret what we are doing. Hurwicz's point about the use of a utility index is very relevant in this context: when we are properly aware of the problem, the awareness challenges our ingenuity to find appropriate hypotheses which permit replacement of an orderable aspect by a measurable one.

The question of the appropriateness of using an attitudinal index stimulated considerable discussion. A specific frame of reference was proposed by Meltzer who posed the following question. Suppose we have a relation

$$C_t = a + bA_t$$

where C_t is a quantity but A_t is an attitudinal index. Suppose further that this hypothesis is better confirmed than any other alternative. Is it correct, then, to reject this relationship and to ignore the predictions rendered by it? Basmann replied that all that the "high degree of confirmation of the hypothesis" would indicate is that A_t and C_t both measure the same quantity, whatever it is. In response to Hurwicz's query Basmann further clarified this to mean that A_t and C_t may be interpreted as measuring the same property. Another question raised concerned the interpretation of the case of a perfect correlation between C_t and A_t (or C_t and A_{t-1}). Basmann stated that by supposing that there is a perfect correlation, one in fact already assumes that both variables involved are quantities.

The insistence on a high degree of rigor with respect to measurement procedures and the form of language in general was questioned by a number of participants in the discussion. Nozick wanted to know why econometricians should insist on using regimented language if physicists and other scientists generally do not. Morgenbesser thought that Basmann was committed to an extreme version of operationalism which would not be satisfied in most physical sciences. Hurwicz pointed out that in physics there are possibly a great many things which, strictly speaking, have no real counterpart and which nevertheless are very useful devices for relating a variety of observable phenomena. Orcutt made a lengthy statement which, in a way, was the summary of a moderate position on the subject. In Orcutt's opinion economists should worry about measurement problems, and Basmann's criticism that the builders of the Brookings Model have not really worried whether their variables are reasonably applied is quite relevant. However, our concern over this matter should not be carried to an extreme. In terms of Meltzer's example, even if we do not know what A_t is, as long as it is a good predictor of C_t it is useful and should not be neglected. The question whether A_t is or is not a quantity is not irrelevant, but our concern over it should not stop us from using the predictions. While precise language is important, it is not as important as other problems. The crucial criterion is usefulness, not the form of language. Orcutt then concluded by claiming that the slow progress of our work in econometrics has been caused mainly by the lack of testing power which, in turn, has been due to not having enough observations. This, according to Orcutt, is a more crucial problem than that of measurement procedures. Parzen added that an indicator may be useful even if we do not know what it measures. As an example, Parzen stated the case of the concept of probability. If anybody wants to know what probability is he is, in Parzen's view, a fool. One should work with probability and gradually come along to say what the term means in one's particular context, otherwise the paradoxes involved will only confuse him.

The moderate position of Orcutt and others did not raise any major opposition. Brunner stressed that he does not advocate the use of regimented language as a matter of course, but only on occasions to serve as a "magnifying glass." Basmann responded to Orcutt's remarks by agreeing that we should not cut out working until we solve the problem how quantities are measured. However, he did believe that this problem ought to be given attention and should have been considered in connection with the decisions about priorities in allocating limited funds for the purpose of improving economic science. The discussion of the subject of measurement procedures was rounded off by some comments on the existence of real counterparts of GNP and its components.

ON INTERDEPENDENT AND RECURSIVE SYSTEMS

L'Esperance in summarizing his paper for the conference described the main differences in the interdependent system and the recursive system approaches to econometric model building. The arguments for viewing either system as a valid conceptual representation of the economic mechanism were briefly reviewed and the alleged superiority of recursive over interdependent systems was being disputed. In the process L'Esperance emphasized the crucial role played by the concept of causality in the dispute. The discussion was commenced by Hurwicz who pointed out that there are situations in which we not only cannot know what is the cause of a certain event, but even may not want to know. To support this contention, Hurwicz quoted the following example attributed to Bertrand Russell and extensively discussed by Braithwaite. It concerns two factories, one in London and one in Edinburgh. At noon at each factory, the whistle announcing lunch is heard and five minutes later the workers at each factory file out. The question then is how do we know that the workers in London do not leave the factory because of the whistle in Edinburgh. If one could somehow disconnect one of the whistles, then one could find out. But if the world, or one's assumption about the world, is such that it is in principle impossible to disconnect any of the two whistles, then we would never know which is the cause of which. Furthermore, by one's view of the world in this case one would also rule out any possible situation in which one would want to know—since any time one whistle works, the other works too. So perhaps we should be less ambitious about insisting that we always must be able to get a full causal picture.

The meaning of causality was further considered by Basmann who thought that it is important to distingush between a causal relation—in the ontological sense—in the real world and the particular mathematical function chosen to represent it. In Basmann's opinion the Wold-Strotz approach to the problem of conceptualizing causality is based on the confusion of mathematical symbols with allegedly existing relations among things. To illustrate the difference Basmann gave the following example: Suppose we have a mathematical relation

$$y = f(x) .$$

Here, our saying that varying x will "cause" y to change makes no sense. However, suppose we have two objects, A and B, such that whenever we move A then B also moves but whenever we move B nothing happens to A. In this case it is meaningful to speak of causality.

Basmann's point was picked up by Orcutt who contended that causality is a little like a word in search of a meaning. However, the meaning is not important; what is important, at least for the purpose of policy, is to know what to do to make something happen. This may be difficult to find because the data that we observe may not have been generated in a way so as to show this. Orcutt further remarked that this point was made a few years ago by Phillips, who pointed out that policy makers are a part of the system and are, in fact, responding to it. But when it comes to policy recommendations, the policy maker wants to know how the world will be different if he does—quite independently—this or that. Hurwicz commented that to discover the existence and direction of causality ultimately necessitates some "disconnecting" of components as in the example about factory whistles. Brunner thought that such "disconnecting" could be achieved by devising appropriate experiments, i.e., data situations.

Another complication in the effort to discover causality was seen in the possibility of observational equivalence of recursive and simultaneous equation models. Zellner mentioned, in the way of a historical note, that when he saw Wold in 1958 he suggested to him that the structural coefficient matrix could be made triangular by an appropriate transformation. Wold did not agree and claimed that this would upset the conditional expectations. Zellner said that while it was not clear to him just what implications this would have, it occurred to him that it might concern the parameterization of the system. The elaboration of this point is as follows:[6] If we have an interdependent model, say M_I, with its parameters, say θ_I, and prior information about θ_I, it will not be true in general that a pure causal chain model, M_{pcc} with parameters θ_{pcc}, derived mathematically from M_I, will be observationally equivalent, given that separate prior information about θ_{pcc} is introduced. To make this point specific, consider the following simple model:

$$y_{1t} = \gamma y_{2t} + u_{1t}$$

(1)

$$y_{2t} = \beta x_t + u_{2t}$$

where y_{1t} and y_{2t} are endogenous variables, x_t is an exogenous variable, and u_{1t} and u_{2t} are *correlated* disturbance terms. With this nonzero correlation, the system is not a pure causal chain model (pcc). Suppose that an investigator has reason to believe that $\gamma < 0$.

Now transform the system in (1) to make it a pcc model as follows:

$$y_{1t} + cy_{2t} = \gamma y_{2t} + c\beta x_t + u_{1t} + cu_{2t}$$

(2)

$$y_{2t} = \beta x_t + u_{2t}$$

where c is such that $E(u_{1t} + cu_{2t})u_{2t} = 0$. Write (2) as

$$y_{1t} = \gamma^* y_{2t} + \beta^* x_t + u^*_{1t}$$

(3)

$$y_{2t} = \beta x_t + u_{2t}$$

where $\gamma^* = \gamma - c$, $\beta^* = c\beta$, and $u^*_{1t} = u_{1t} + cu_{2t}$.
If a person using (3) introduces the prior information $\gamma^* < 0$, this is of course not the same as $\gamma < 0$, and thus (3) with $\gamma^* < 0$ is not observationally equivalent to (1) with $\gamma < 0$.

As another example consider the well-known Haavelmo model:

$$c_t = \alpha y_t + \beta + u_t$$

(1)   with $0 < \alpha < 1$

$$y_t = c_t + z_t$$

and the model

(2) $y_t = \gamma_0 + \gamma_1 z_t + v_t$ with $-\infty < \gamma_1 < \infty$.

Now the equation in (2) can be derived mathematically from those in (1); however, taking account of the prior information, the models are not observationally equivalent. The reduced form equation for y_t from (1) is $y_t = \dfrac{\beta}{1-\alpha} + \dfrac{1}{1-\alpha} z_t + \dfrac{u_t}{1-\alpha}$ and the prior information about α implies that the multiplier, $m = \dfrac{1}{1-\alpha}$ satisfies

$1 < m < \infty$, a "Keynesian" view, while γ_1 satisfies $-\infty < \gamma_1 < \infty$, perhaps the view of a "Quantity Theorist." Thus (1) and (2) are not observationally equivalent in a very fundamental sense. For example, if you regress y_t on z_t and come up with a negative multiplier estimate, this is consistent with (2) but not with (1).

The discussion on the causal and interdependent systems was terminated without bringing to light any obvious points of major disagreement among the participants. Rather, the general feeling on the subject seemed to be one of minor bewilderment combined with lassitude.

ON EVALUATION OF ALTERNATIVE MODELS

The main thrust of Brunner's paper was directed at the failure of econometrics to provide well-defined criteria for assessing alternative models. Brunner observed that we have by now more than twenty large-scale econometric models of the United States economy but that we have attempted no evaluation of their comparative cognitive status. As yet we have developed no mechanism that would enable us to compare alternative models and to select the one with the greatest explanatory power. The discussion of this criticism was started by Zellner who stated that, in fact, attempts have been made to provide operational methods to deal with this problem. In a recently published paper, Box and Hill[7] compare alternative models in the context of experimental situation. The authors show how to start with given prior probabilities associated with alternative models, and how to use data to revise the prior probabilities to get posterior probabilities. While the exposition is confined to single-equation models, the technique can be generalized to be applicable to more complex models. Another attempt deals with the problem of misspecification as a result of treating an endogenous variable as an exogenous one, or vice versa. The particular case examined involves two simple Keynesian models studied by Haavelmo,[8] one with purely exogenous investment and one with investment being partly exogenous and partly dependent on income. By determining the posterior distribution of the coefficient attached to income in the investment equation, one has an effective discriminatory device for choosing between the two models.[9] This suggests that whenever we are able to construct a generalized model, we can make inferences about the specialized model (or models) using conditional posterior probability density functions.

The possibility of associating probabilities with alternative models was questioned by Orcutt who pointed out that there may be problems of comparability in the sense that competing hypotheses may be applicable over different, though overlapping, domains. For instance, in physics, hypotheses may continue to compete for a hundred years simply because they say useful things about different areas of experience. Orcutt's point was interpreted by Meltzer as follows: Suppose we have two hypotheses H_1 and H_2 such that

$$H_1 \text{ implies } X_1 \text{ and } X_2,$$

$$H_2 \text{ implies } X_2 \text{ and } X_3.$$

Unless we develop a general hypothesis, H_1 and H_2 may be rivals for a long time. The comment sparked off a discussion about the possibility of formulating a general hypothesis which would subsume rival hypotheses as special cases. Chow thought that instances in which this can be done are rare and that Zellner's example about Haavelmo's models is very special. Hurwicz, on the other hand, saw no difficulties in making a model general enough to subsume alternative hypotheses. Parzen drew attention to a paper by Cox[10] dealing with a general functional form which includes specific forms such as the linear model as special cases. Brunner was sceptical about the possibility of formulating a common maintained hypothesis that would subsume rival theories and at the same time would be useful for testing. Ames saw some difficulties with respect to attaching prior probabilities to alternative hypotheses within the context of simultaneous equations. Jorgensen also pointed out that the problem of assessing alternative models is open to an approach other than Bayesian, namely the multiple comparison procedure.[11]

The conventional methods of assessing competing models by their "forecasting record" and similar criteria were criticized by Brunner on the grounds that they typically rely on personal judgements. Brunner claimed that there are no generally accepted criteria that would allow us to evaluate alternative theories. A forecasting record is not enough to do this unless the differences are substantial.[12] Brunner's comment prompted a shift of the discussion to the question of observational evidence. The importance of this was emphasized by Kuh who put the blame for our inability to appraise competing models on the weak discriminatory power of data. According to Kuh, considerably more attention ought to be paid to data than has been done so far. Kuh's remark brought a lively response—a response which clearly indicated a sharp difference of opinion. Orcutt agreed with Kuh by seeing the main reason for the slow progress of our work in econometrics in the lack of testing power which would be increased if we had more observations. Similarly, Zellner was of the opinion that "good and plentiful data will help more than anything else." On the other hand, Ginsberg thought that it is not so much the data but the theory that is not discriminating. Brunner also thought that the fault lies largely with the nondiscriminatory power of theories. No matter how much data we have, if we specify practically nothing about the theory, we cannot test very much.

The problem of evaluating competing models was brought into a sharp focus by the discussion of the FRB-MIT Model currently being constructed by Modigliani, Ando, and others. The first question raised at the outset of the discussion concerned the reason for constructing another large-scale model of the United States economy in the wake of the recently completed Brookings Model. The question became particularly pertinent in the light of Klein's statement concerning the plan of future work on the Brookings Model. The plan includes

    (i) reestimating the whole system on the basis of new and updated data,
    (ii) using improved methods of estimation,
    (iii) enlarging the monetary sector, and
    (iv) building a bigger input-output sector.

Sutch, in his statement on the FRB-MIT Model, emphasized that the main purpose of the model is to answer questions about how much the monetary policy works in the United States economy. According to Sutch, the questions being asked are such that they cannot be answered by anyone else's model. The reasons why the Brookings Model is not considered satisfactory in this respect are:

    (i) The financial sector of the Brookings Model is not designed well enough for the purpose of answering the questions that arose in connection with the well-known Friedman-Meiselman and Ando-Modigliani controversy. The deficiency lies not only in omitting some of the influences thought to be relevant, but also in insufficient emphasis on the lag structure.
    (ii) The Brookings Model contains details that are unnecessary; therefore, working with the model would be cumbersome.
    (iii) The economic hypotheses of what the Brookings Model represents do not fit the prior beliefs of Modigliani.

Sutch concluded by asserting that the question as to which of two models is a better one cannot be asked, when—as in the case of the Brookings and the FRB-MIT Models—the models have been built for different purposes. When two models have been built for the same purpose, one might use several criteria such as the fit of the estimated relations (within as well as outside the sample period), but a very important criterion is whether one does or does not like the implications of the model. We do not have, or cannot pretend to have, any formal criteria for testing one model against another.

The reasons for constructing the FRB-MIT Model given by Sutch were not found altogether convincing by some of the discussants. Brunner did not see any substantial difference in purpose since the Brookings Model was presumably also constructed for the purpose of monetary and fiscal policy. Ames contended that since both models are supposed to describe the working of the United States economy, it should be possible to determine how they differ, and why. Nozick also thought that a comparison should be possible; if one model is more detailed in some sectors and less detailed in other sectors, the less detailed parts of one model could be viewed as approximations of the corresponding more detailed parts of the other model. Sutch had doubts about the possibility of making a meaningful comparison between the two models because the FRB-MIT Model is "quite different" from the Brookings Model. Sargent mentioned some of these differences, such as the more extensive use of distributed lag relations, of nonlinear specifications, and of more appropriate methods of estimation. Hurwicz, in reply to Nozick, pointed out that the differences between the two models which make a comparison difficult are those of prior specification rather than those of detail.

Meltzer's interpretation of the situation was that Modigliani has apparently different prior information and beliefs than Klein. These prior beliefs of Modigliani are to be exposed to the constraints imposed by the set of observations that are available to him, and in this sense he will be forced to make some compromises. The question then is how can one find out if Modigliani's beliefs are more correct than Klein's. Alternatively it is possible, Meltzer thought, that neither Modigliani nor Klein wants to find out. Samuelson presumably said that there is absolutely no set of observations that would change his view of the world. This seems to be an intellectually more satisfying position than presenting one's prior information by reestimating equations through a computer. If we do the latter, Meltzer asserted, then we are back in the camp of literary economists for whom the econometric revolution was originally intended. There does not seem to be very much difference between being a literary economist and having the prior beliefs in one's head or being an econometrician and having the prior beliefs written down in the form of four hundred equations. Meltzer concluded by claiming that Klein's and Modigliani's models represent largely, if not completely, a denial of the scientific procedure of evaluation.

Kuh saw the importance of Meltzer's criticism in bringing up the conflict between hypothesis formulation and hypothesis testing. If one keeps on fitting observations until one comes upon a relationship which one likes, one is obviously not testing a hypothesis. On the whole, econometricians fit curves rather than test hypotheses. This is a perfectly valid scientific procedure, providing that the qualitative properties of the resulting models are properly examined and the search is not confused with testing. Cunnyngham saw a problem with this in the context of policy recommendations. If the Brookings and the FRB-MIT Models are just two different engineering constructions, the policy makers would not know which one of them to follow. Meltzer, in reply to Kuh, stated that he was not advocating throwing away prior information, that he only objected to an improper use of it. A researcher cannot get a scientific statement out of a hypothesis if he rejects it just because it does not satisfy his prior beliefs. If this is what he does, then he is not estimating equations but only putting down what he believes.

The question of the role of prior information in econometric research was considered at some length by Hurwicz. The following points were made. First, prior information need not always be effective, as in the case when the prior information about α is that $\alpha \leq 0.90$ and the estimate of α is 0.75. Secondly, consider the case of the researcher who keeps on looking for variables to be included in the regression equation until he finds a combination of variables that gives $R^2 = 0.9$ or more. This simply means that a part of the researcher's prior beliefs is that the population coefficient of determination is greater than or equal to 0.9. This prior belief is imposed as a constraint on estimation. Thirdly, if among the 3,000 variables which are stored in the MIT file there is not one that is really relevant for the relationship under investigation but one finds one which fits well for the twenty or so years for which observations are stored, the irrelevance of this variable will show up in the long run by making the forecasts wrong. The discussion was concluded by Alchian who declared that if economics is to make any progress, different prior beliefs have to converge.

NOTES

[1]J. S. Dusenberry, G. Fromm, L. R. Klein, and E. Kuh, *The Brookings Quarterly Econometric Model of the United States*, Chicago: Rand McNally, 1965.

[2]"Dynamic Structure and Estimation in Economy-Wide Econometric Models," in *The Brookings Quarterly Econometric Model of the United States, op. cit.*, pp. 589-636.

[3]See T. Klock and L. B. M. Mennes, "Simultaneous Equations Estimation Based on Principal Components of Predetermined Variables," *Econometrica* 28 (January, 1960), pp. 45-61.

[4]H. Rubin, "Note on Random Coefficients," in T. C. Koopmans (ed.), *Statistical Inference in Dynamic Economic Models,* New York: John Wiley, 1950.

[5]A reference in support and elaboration of this point was made to Ernest Nagel, "Assumptions in Economic Theory," *American Economic Review* 53, *Papers and Proceedings* (May, 1963), 211-219, and to T. C. Koopmans, *Three Essays on the State of Economic Science,* New York: McGraw-Hill, 1957.

[6]The following two paragraphs are reproduced from a letter written shortly after the conference and circulated among some participants of the conference.

[7]G. E. P. Box and W. J. Hill, "Discrimination Among Mechanistic Models," *Technometrics* 9 (February, 1967), 57-72.

[8]T. Haavelmo, "Methods of Measuring the Marginal Propensity to Consume," *Journal of the American Statistical Association* 42 (March, 1947), 105-122.

[9]See V. K. Chetty, "Bayesian Analysis of Simultaneous Equation Econometric Models," doctoral dissertation, University of Wisconsin, Madison, 1966.

[10]D. R. Cox, "Tests of Separate Families of Hypotheses," in *Proceedings of the Fourth Berkeley Symposium on Probability and Statistics,* University of California Press, 1961, Vol. I, 105-124.

[11]See, e.g., Henry Scheffe, *The Analysis of Variance,* New York: John Wiley, 1959.

[12]Parzen suggested that comparisons should be made not only by one-step predictions but also by predictions arbitrarily far in advance.